# Noam Chomsky
# RADICAL PRIORITIES

### EDITED BY C. P. OTERO | EXPANDED THIRD EDITION

## PRESS
EDINBURGH • LONDON • OAKLAND

**RADICAL PRIORITIES**
by Noam Chomsky
Expanded Third Edition

ISBN 1-902593-69-3

Copyright 1981, 1984 and 2003 by Noam Chomsky.

Editor's Introduction and Notes Copyright 1981, 1984 and 2003 by
Carlos-Peregrín Otero.

| | |
|---|---|
| AK Press | AK Press U.K. |
| 674-A 23rd Street | PO Box 12766 |
| Oakland, CA 94612-1163 | Edinburgh, EH8 9YE |
| USA | Scotland |
| (510) 208-1700 | (0131) 555-5165 |
| www.akpress.org | www.akuk.com |
| akpress@akpress.org | ak@akedin.demon.uk |

The addresses above would be delighted to provide you with the latest complete AK catalog, featuring several thousand books, pamphlets, zines, audio
products, video products and stylish apparel published and distributed by AK
Press. Alternatively, visit our websites for the complete catalog, latest news and
updates, events and secure ordering.

Library of Congress Cataloging-in-Publication data
A catalog record for this title is available from the Library of Congress

Printed in Canada

Cover design by John Yates
Copy-editing by Seamus Thompson
Cover photograph by Victor J. Blue
Original artwork by Chris Wright

# Table of Contents

## PART II

## U.S.A.: Myth, Reality, Acracy

# PART III

# Editor's Preliminary Note to the Third Edition

A substantial novelty of this third edition are the four last selections, all four fairly recent and of unusual significance, which make up a full-fledged Part III, this is especially true of the very last one, which may be read as a sort of Chomsky's counterpart both to Rousseau's remarkable "discourse" on inequality (1755), "in many ways a revolutionary tract," and to the 1848 call to international solidarity and action in the most famous of manifestos, as working people not far from Boston, without the benefit of socialist writings or the help of foreign radicals, were doing what they could to resist the degrading "new spirit of the age" still being drilled into everyone's head today ("gain wealth, forgetting all but self"). Also new are the references throughout to more recent publications, particularly those by Chomsky, and some additions and slight revisions, mostly stylistic, in the Introduction and the Editor's Notes.

The main purpose of the collection continues to be "to provide relatively easy access to Chomsky's libertarian philosophy and political analysis," as stated at the very beginning of the preliminary note to the first edition, written in March, 1981. Also applicable is the "unremitting personal feeling" behind the project from the start, explained in more detail there: "The feeling that a major handicap of the libertarian left is the faulty transmission of libertarian culture, a rich fund still largely untapped," this being particularly true of Chomsky's exceptionally rich contribution to it, "(arguably) the highest point in the libertarian socialist tradition."

Those remarks are, if anything, even more apt today, after almost a quarter of a century more of Chomsky's unremitting activism, including a good number of his countless writings, among them approximately 85 books, adding up to thousands of pages, many of which saw the light after 1981. (Some of the major ones in this context can be found in the "List of Abbreviations" and in the notes of selection 29.) Still, the picture presented in the first edition requires no face lifting: the insightful vision and the framework of analysis was there from the very beginning, and it continues to be as fresh, insightful and unique as on day one.

Thus the Chomsky who "was treated like a Hollywood celebrity" almost a year ago in Porto Alegre, Brazil, in February 2002 (see the Editor's Notes to selection 30), who had just become the author of a "bestseller" (*9-11*)—his first—, is still very much the Chomsky of the early 1980s (when the first two editions of this book appeared), who in turn continued to be the Chomsky of the 1960s (the depth of his conviction and of his personal integrity seems to be as remote as it is humanly possible from the "God that failed" affliction that crippled so many in his generation).

What has changed dramatically in the intervening years is the depth and range of his reach, now more transparently world-wide. (Ten years ago he was the most cited living person and the eighth most cited overall between 1980 and 1992 in the Arts and Humanities Citation Index, and one of the most cited individuals published in the past twenty years in two other citation indices.) Over thirty years of dedicated work of a very particular kind, intensely pursued, cannot fail to leave its imprint on a not inconsiderable number of the most humane humans. The writings are just a part of his hard to match and so far unmatched effort, which seems to intensify every year. "It is as if he were trying to keep pace with the increasing urgency of the situation, brought about by a quick succession of very disturbing events" (last but certainly not least current ones), as suggested in the preliminary note to the second edition. To quote his very last sentence in this third edition: "It is hard to overestimate what is at stake."

The immediate spark behind the original goal of the book was to provide an antidote to the perceived "decline of activism in the 1970s," an activism that to some appeared to be languishing, as if the 1970s had not been the period of both the feminist movement and the ecological movement. No one could have anticipated at the time that that activism was soon to lead to a new kind of mass demonstration (anticipatory rather than counteractive), first exemplified on May 3, 1981, in Washington, D.C., and by meaningful solidarity of the people of the United States with the people of Latin America the very moment a glimpse was detected of what was to become the Reaganite onslaught (now in its second cycle under the very same terror-bounded protagonists). It was certainly a movement without historical precedent: never before had the citizens of an imperial superpower sided with its victims, promptly and courageously trying to protect and defend them as much as they were able to (regrettably, not nearly enough).

It is not easy to ascertain to what extent, if any, the first two editions of this book have contributed to bringing about some of the forward-looking and potentially decisive developments of the last twenty some years. They do seem to have contributed to a more accurate image of Chomsky both as a deeply original creative inquirer of unusually broad range and as a highly dedicated activist, a dedication even more rare among major scientists and philosophers: key quotes from the Introduction have been repeated again and again in all sorts of printed sources, from book covers to typical leaflets distributed at his talks. Be that as it may, what matters most now is what is yet to come, which will hopefully be encouraging.

Carlos-Peregrín Otero
January 23, 2003

## Editor's Preliminary Note to the Second Edition

In the few extra pages available for this edition, it is not possible to give a representative sample of the extensive social and political writings published by the author in the 1980s (just two of his major political books add up to about one thousand densely printed pages, while his total published output for the first third of the decade is probably close to two thousand); it is as if he were trying to keep pace with the increasing urgency of the situation, brought about by a quick succession of very disturbing events. The few additional pages included might at least give some idea of his most recent work. The references provided should make it possible for the reader eager to go beyond these limits to move on to his other publications.

As Chomsky points out in a recent interview (*Open Road*, Spring 1984), "the alleged decline of activism in the seventies was partly mythical. This was, after all, the period of the rise of the feminist and ecological movements, and much else. In fact, there remained from the sixties a proliferation of activist groups of many sorts, doing valuable work, generally locally oriented, and many new people joined or began afresh. As the State gradually returned to its natural stance of militancy, subversion and aggression after its partial failures in Vietnam, and as the economic crisis deepened, this activism quickly emerged to the public view." His own activism might serve as an exemplary case. His "political courage and uncompromising commitment to reason" (as Joshua Cohen and Joel Rogers write in their admirable *On Democracy: Toward A Transformation of American Society*, New York: Penguin, 1983) significantly inspired some of the best thought and action of recent vintage, and no doubt will continue to be a major source of inspiration.

It is hoped that this book might be of help to the activists of the 1980s.

Carlos-Peregrín Otero
Los Angeles, June 14, 1984

## Editor's Preliminary Note to the First Edition

The main purpose of this collection is to provide relatively easy access to Chomsky's libertarian philosophy and political analysis. There is no piece that is not fairly brief and straightforward, and a good number of them are extremely concise—little more than "abstracts" of longer papers. The reader who wants to look carefully at the evidence can always refer to the massively documented full-length studies. Thus the collection might be viewed as a sort of anthology of some of Chomsky's major themes presented in sharp outline. But it is also the only source for some pieces that appear here for the first time in English (Selections 1 and 6), and it makes readily available others that are widely scattered and often very difficult to obtain. Part I is assembled here for the first time; Part II was first published in Spanish translation by the present editor under the same title (*USA: Mito, Realidad, Acracia*, Barcelona: Editorial Ariel, 1978).

The editor was led to give his time to this project by an unremitting personal feeling: The feeling that a major handicap of the libertarian left is the faulty transmission of libertarian culture, a rich fund still largely untapped. In particular, Chomsky's work, which is (arguably) the highest point in the libertarian socialist tradition, doesn't seem to have received the attention it deserves (see, for example, *Reinventing Anarchy*, one of the most suggestive recent publications on the topic); worse still, it is often ignored or distorted, both in America and in Europe. One can even hear some anarchists with an untapped potential willingness for activism and a wealth of future accomplishments in store proclaim that Chomsky is not "really" an anarchist. The "Introduction to Chomsky's Social Theory" is an attempt to put at the disposal of anyone interested, when possible in Chomsky's own words, some of the basic information that is necessary for a well-founded judgment. I hope this is enough justification for its length. On the other hand, it can always be passed over. It is important, however, that the reader keep in mind that Chomsky's theory involves no less than four crucial choices: (1) A conception of human nature that sees creativity (rather than acquisitiveness) as the most fundamental human need (call this conception "libertarianism" to distinguish it from acquisitive "liberalism"); (2) Socialism (vs. capitalism); (3) Egalitarianism (vs. elitism); (4) Self-management (vs. any sort of atavism).

The editor tried hard to be objective, but he doesn't claim to be impartial. It is only fair then to say a word about his convictions. For reasons that cannot be given in just a few lines, he is particularly impressed both by the evolution of ideas that link Marx and Bakunin with Chomsky and by the achievements of the social revolution initiated in the summer of 1936 in Spain, immediately after Franco's military coup against the government of the Republic—both seen with a critical eye, yet with the eye of an art lover looking for what is enduring. And he is convinced that the development of a broad based movement guided by the

4

leading ideas of libertarian socialism and the best libertarian action (call it "anar-cho-syndicalism," "social anarchism" or something else) would be the best, per-haps the only possible way to arrive safely at the year 2000 without doing irreparable damage to the ecosystem.

The editor is deeply indebted to Noam Chomsky in numerous ways. He is also thankful to Dimitri Roussopoulos for the interest he showed in the project from the first moment, and to Judith Strozer for the (long) hours she donated during the last sprint.

The abbreviations listed below for the titles of Chomsky's books are the ones used in the notes. They appear in alphabetical order. Where there is no explicit mention of a publisher, it should be understood that the book was pub-lished by Pantheon in New York.

Carlos-Peregrín Otero
Los Angeles, March 13, 1981

## List of Abbreviations:

**APNM** — *American Power and the New Mandarins: Historical and Political Essays.* New York: Pantheon, 1969. New edition includes foreword by Howard Zinn. New York: The New Press, 2002.

**AWA** — *At War with Asia.* New York: Pantheon,1970. Oakland: AK Press, 2004.

**CD&E** — *Chomsky on Democracy and Education.* Ed. C. P. Otero. New York and London: RoutledgeFalmer, 2003.

**ChR** — *The Chomsky Reader.* Ed. James Peck. New York: Pantheon, 1987.

**CL** — *Cartesian Linguistics: A Chapter in the History of Rationalist Thought.* New York: Harper & Row, 1966.

**CT** — *The Culture of Terrorism.* Boston: South End Press, 1988.

**DD** — *Deterring Democracy.* London: Verso, 1991. Updated, second edition, Boston: Hill and Wang, 1992.

**EP** — *Ecrits Politiques 1977–1983.* Peyrehorade (France): Acratie, 1984.

**FRS** — *For Reasons of State.* New York: Pantheon,1973. New York: New Press, 2003.

**FT** — *Fateful Triangle: The United States, Israel and the Palestinians.* Boston: South End Press, 1983. Updated edition, Boston: South End Press,1999.

**HR** — *"Human Rights" and American Foreign Policy.* Chapter 2 reprinted here in *Radical Priorities* as chapter 12. Nottingham, England: Spokesman Books (Bertrand Russell House), 1978.

**IS** — *Intellectuals and the State.* Included in **TCW**, pp 60–85.

**KL** — *Knowledge of Language: Its Nature, Origin, and Use.* New York: Praeger, 1986.

**L&M** — *Language and Mind.* New York: Harcourt, 1969. Enlarged edition. New York: Harcourt, 1972.

**L&P** — *Language and Politics.* Ed. C. P. Otero. Oakland: AK Press, 2004.

**L&R** — *Language and Responsibility.* Paris: Flammarion, 1977. (Conversations avec Mitsou Ronat) New York: Pantheon, 1979. Included as Part I of *On Language: Chomsky's Classic Works Language and Responsibility and Reflections on Language in One Volume.* New York: New Press, 1998.

**NGDL** — *A New Generation Draws the Line: Kosovo, East Timor and the Standards of the West.* London and New York: Verso, 2000.

**NHSL** — *New Horizons in the Study of Language and Mind.* Cambridge: Cambridge University Press, 2002.

**NI** — *Necessary Illusions: Thought Control in Democratic Societies.* Boston: South End Press, 1989.

**NMH** — *The New Military Humanism: Lessons from Kosovo.* Monroe, Maine: Common Courage Press, 1999.

**P&E** — *Pirates & Emperors: International Terrorism in the Real World.* New York: Claremont Research and Publications, 1986. (Reprints: Brattleboro, VT: Amana Books, 1986, and (with a fourth chapter) Montréal: Black Rose Books, 1987. New edition [expanded from 3 to 7 chapters plus an Introduction], *Pirates &*

*Emperors, Old and New: International Terrorism in the Real World.* Cambridge: South End Press, 2003.

**P&P** — *Powers and Prospects: Reflections on Human Nature and the Social Order.* Boston: South End Press, 1996.

**PE** — (with Edward S. Herman). *The Political Economy of Human Rights.* Boston: South End Press, 1979. (2 volumes).

**PKF** — *Problems of Knowledge and Freedom: The Russell Lectures.* New York: Pantheon, 1971. New York: New Press, 2003.

**PME** — *Peace in the Middle East? Reflections on Justice and Nationhood.* New York: Pantheon, 1974. Included in *Middle East Illusions.* Lanham, Maryland: Rowman and Littlefield, 2003.

**POP** — *Profits Over People: Neoliberalism and Global Order.* Introduction by Robert W. McChesney. New York: Seven Stories Press, 1999.

**RI** — *Réponses Inédites à mes Détracteurs Parisiens.* Paris: Spartacus, 1984.

**RL** — *Reflections on Language.* New York: Knopf, 1976. Reprinted as Part II of *On Language: Chomsky's Classic Works Language and Responsibility and Reflections on Language in One Volume.* New York: New Press, 1998.

**RR** — *Rules and Representations.* New York: Columbia University Press, 1980.

**RS** — *Rogue States: The Rule of Force in World Affairs.* Cambridge: South End Press, 2000.

**TCW** — *Towards a New Cold War: Essays on the Current Crisis and How We Got There.* Includes the first chapter of **HR**. New York: Pantheon, 1982. New York: New Press, 2003.

**TT** — *Turning the Tide: U.S. Intervention in Central America and the Struggle for Peace.* Boston: South End Press, 1985. Enlarged edition with a sixth chapter, *Turning the Tide: The U.S. and Latin America.* Montréal: Black Rose Books, 1987.

**WOON** — *World Orders Old and New.* New York: Columbia University Press, 1994. Expanded edition, New York: Columbia University Press, 1996.

**Y501** — *Year 501: The Conquest Continues.* Boston: South End Press, 1993.

# Introduction to Chomsky's Social Theory*

One of the most celebrated Spanish bullfighters was once asked to rank himself. Without the slightest hesitation, he answered that he was obviously number one and that there was no number two. As a possible number three he suggested the name of his no less famous rival.

When one reads in the *New York Times Book Review* that "judged in terms of the power, range, novelty and influence of his thought, Noam Chomsky is arguably the most important intellectual alive,"[1] it is hard not to wonder who could be a plausible candidate for third place.

This is not the occasion to discuss his work in linguistics and philosophy[2], but a brief comment on the immediate impact of his first political writings does seem in order as a point of departure. Back in 1970, at the peak of active opposition to the Indochina War, when colleges and universities were closed down in protest against the invasion of Cambodia and demonstrations of concerned Americans swept the country, Chomsky was unquestionably number one (with 38 "votes") in the scale of "intellectuals most influential on the discussion of the Vietnam issue within the intellectual community, as perceived by peers," according to a careful, if curious, study by a Columbia University Sociologist.[3] Number two and number three went to Hans Morgenthau (with 25 "votes") and John Kenneth Galbraith (with 19 "votes"), respectively. However, Morgenthau and Galbraith, like others who scored below them, opposed American interventionism on unprincipled grounds, not on the grounds that aggression is wrong even if it is both American and relatively bloodless, costless and successful. Neither of the two was prepared to challenge the divine right of the United States to intervene by force in the internal affairs of other countries (be it Vietnam or Cambodia, Cuba, the Dominican Republic or El Salvador). On this, Chomsky was alone, or virtually alone, among the "American intellectual elite," in 1970, and things don't seem to have changed for the better since then.[4]

## An independent mind with awesome powers

What is of special significance about Chomsky's stand, besides its plain decency and its hard-to-match brilliance, is his willingness to apply to foreign and domestic policy discussions the intellectual standards taken for granted in more scrupulous and far more profound disciplines. The case that he has built against the policies of the U.S. Government is overwhelming. It is also, to my knowledge, the best argued by far. This is not surprising. Referring to Chomsky's most recent contribution to the philosophy of mind, which he suggests could be retitled "Chomsky Against the Philosophers," a distinguished reviewer has written that "it is like watching the grand master play, blindfolded, 36 simultaneous chess matches against the local worthies."[5] As the reader of *American Power and the New Mandarins* or some of his subsequent books is most likely aware, arguing against the Kissingers and Brzezinskis of our day, or any other State apologist past or present, is somewhat less difficult than debating a philosopher of considerable logical sophistication.[6]

It is also far more urgent and far more decisive for survival. The sooner we are clear about what is at stake, the better. But it will take some doing. Under the crippling effects of insidious indoctrination, unaided common sense might not always be able to see clearly through the sophistry. The power of State propaganda, even in a relatively open society, can hardly be overestimated. In fact, as Chomsky makes clear, the totalitarian system of thought control is far less effective than the democratic one, since the overt official doctrine parroted by the intellectuals at the service of the State is readily identifiable as pure propaganda, and this helps to free the mind. In contrast to the totalitarian system, the democratic system seeks to determine and limit the entire spectrum of thought by leaving the fundamental assumptions unexpressed. They are presupposed, but not asserted. The situation is, therefore, considerably more complex under capitalist democracy:

> The press and the intellectuals are held to be fiercely independent, hypercritical, antagonistic to the 'establishment,' in an adversary relation to the state... The more vigorous the debate, the better the system of propaganda is served, since the tacit unspoken assumptions are more forcefully implanted. An independent mind must seek to separate itself from official doctrine—and from the criticism advanced by its alleged opponents. Not just from the assertions of the propaganda system, but from its tacit presuppositions as well, as expressed by critic and defender. This is a far more difficult task. Any expert in indoctrination will confirm, no doubt, that it is far more effective to constrain all possible thought within a framework of tacit assumptions than to try to impose a particular explicit belief with a bludgeon. It may be that some of the most spectacular achievements of the American propaganda system, where all of this has been elevated to a high art, are attributable to the method of feigned dissent practiced by the responsible intelligentsia.[7]

It is hard to think of a person better qualified than Chomsky to lend a helping hand in this difficult task, though many other people can make a contribution here, in one way or another. The vast majority of our contemporaries do not have the time to do all alone what it takes to extricate oneself and to help others extricate themselves from the maze of ideological deception and official mythology, and the victim of a lifetime of indoctrination, conformism and moral blindness might, understandably, lack even the inclination. Yet if large numbers of people are not engaged in the struggle for peace and justice soon, the hopes for a nonelitistic transformation of society in time to ensure survival are not bright. The engineering of the world's annihilation goes hand in hand with the engineering of the world's consent. It follows that any contribution to widespread demystification is a step forward.

## A pariah of the "free press"

The force of this observation has not escaped those who benefit the most from "brainwashing under freedom" or from less subtle forms of indoctrination. A particularly revealing illustration is provided by the contrasting reactions to two recent extensive studies on the media. One of them, *The Political Economy of Human Rights* (a title reminiscent of *The Political Economy of American Foreign Policy*, an unusually frank study published over twenty years ago—see Selection 19), gives substantial evidence in support of the thesis that the media systematically distort the truth to excuse or even justify the nature and consequences of U.S. Government policies and to prepare the public for more of the same, often including direct or indirect interventionism, the Free World's version of Attila's scourge of our time. For readers who have learned about the world only from the "free press," the study is an eye opener, providing "indispensable tools to understand present political reality and to interpret future developments," that is, tools that help us "to scrutinize more critically the current coverage of Afghanistan, Iran, El Salvador, and Zimbabwe."[8] These are all things that are presumably welcome in a true democracy. Yet despite the authors' impeccable and rather impressive credentials (Chomsky is Institute Professor at M.I.T., an honor usually reserved for Nobel Laureates, and Edward Herman is Professor of Finance in the prestigious Wharton School, University of Pennsylvania), the two volume, massively documented work "has yet to be reviewed in any major newspaper in the United States or Canada," so it "has ended up illustrating much of what the authors have to say about the control of ideas in America." Herman is surely right on target when he says that he is "much more impressed with (their) theory as a result of the handling of the book."[9] The opening sentence of a two-page review commissioned by the Boston *Globe* (which, naturally enough, neglected to publish it) makes exactly the same point: "This is an important book which, if its thesis is correct, will not get the attention it deserves."

Conversely, the other study (Peter Braestrup's *Big Story*) received far more attention than it actually deserves; it was extravagantly praised in the very media it feigns to criticize as "conscientious" and "painstakingly thorough," and it was hailed as nothing less than "one of the major pieces of investigative reporting and first-rate scholarship of the past quarter century," giving "endless attention to accuracy," even though (because?) its author indulges in "massive fabrication of evidence and gross distortion of the documentary record, including even substantial misrepresentation of material presented in the accompanying volume of documents."[10] It is only fair to add, however, that it has one virtue the mind managers cannot help liking: It attempts to buttress the myth that the press is "fiercely independent, hypercritical, antagonistic to the 'establishment'," and that its relation to the State is that of an adversary.

At this point it is natural to ask: How much genuine freedom of expression can the Free Press accommodate? Not very much, it would appear, in the absence of even the bare beginnings of a mass-based movement capable of guaranteeing a measure of evenhandedness. Thus, at the peak of active opposition to the Indochina War, Chomsky's writings, which were widely read, "covered interminable pages in the *New York Review of Books*" (as a New Mandarin, unhappy with the situation, put it at the time), and he even had token access to the mainstream media. Today, although in some ways the media are more open, unable to escape the transformation brought about by the spirit of the 1960s, even his letters to the editor responding to innuendo or direct attack fail to find an obscure corner in the Free Press. How low has a culture to fall before it can make a pariah out of its "most important intellectual alive" (arguably)?

It is not hard to surmise. Not only is it becoming more difficult to bring the truth into the open and to demystify the misinformation that might secure popular support for much that is evil (as I write, the Reagan Administration announces the release of "nearly 200 pages of documents" about the struggle in El Salvador, in preparation for a "response"), but objections are being raised even to the defense of the most elementary principles and of the most elementary and long recognized human rights, as if the Enlightenment were still to come. Two samples might be enough to give an idea of some attitudes which, unfortunately, are not uncommon these days. The first one is the closing paragraph of a letter Chomsky wrote to the editor of the *NY Times* on December 8, 1980, commenting on an editorial published that very day (see Selection 5):

> The fact is plain that the Indonesian aggression [against East Timor] and its grim consequences are in significant measure the direct responsibility of the United States. Furthermore, for almost four years, the U.S. media were virtually silent apart from occasional reports echoing State Department fabrications. Is it really accurate, then, to say that it is Indonesia that is 'shamed' by these events, and that the U.S. role is only something less than 'glorious'? It is important to address this question honestly, not only to understand our actual international role, but also to change it; and not only with respect to Timor, where the brutality continues while the U.S. continues to obstruct UN efforts to terminate Indonesian aggression and the man who takes prime responsibility for the obstruction [Senator Moynihan in his UN memoirs] joins in condemning the United Nations for failing to uphold peace and justice.

The second sample is related to the "Faurisson affair." It is most of what was published in *The New Republic*, Feb. 14, 1981, of a letter Chomsky wrote on January 5. After explaining that the editor, Martin Peretz, had not permitted the publication of an earlier response to a false allegation by Peretz, "an interesting revelation of journalistic standards" (this part of the letter was censored by *The New Republic*)," Chomsky goes on to say:

> Now Peretz claims that 'on the question... as to whether or not six million Jews were murdered, Noam Chomsky apparently is an agnostic.' My views on the holocaust are easily accessible: e.g., in my book *Peace in the Middle East?* (1974), where I wrote that 'the Zionist case relies on the aspirations of a people who suffered two millennia of exile and savage persecution culminating in the most fantastic outburst of collective insanity in human history,...' (p. 57); repeatedly, elsewhere. But facts are not Peretz's business. What Peretz is distorting for his current purposes is my support for the right of Robert Faurisson to express his sharply contrary views, irrespective of the character or quality of his views. Peretz apparently prefers the Zhdanov doctrine, that ideas that are 'objectively harmful' should be suppressed. Or perhaps, once again, he is simply revealing his commitment to elementary honesty.[12]

Given the usual limitations of space in *The New Republic*, perhaps, Chomsky couldn't go on to make a basic point he makes in his response to Dr Jacob Gewirtz (of the Board of Deputies of British Jews), whose "support for Israel" Chomsky regards as "support for policies that will lead to its destruction" (letter to the *Guardian*, Feb. 2, 1981):

> The views I hold were called 'Zionism' in the past within the Zionist movement, and still are by many today. What Gewirtz calls my 'hostility to Israel' is hostility to particular policies of Israel. I am unaware of any 'present predicament' [Gewirtz's reference to Chomsky's defense of Faurisson's rights and the reaction to it.— CPO]. I continue to maintain, as in the past, that the right of free expression (including academic freedom) should be defended—in this case, for views that are almost universally reviled. I have defended this principle in far more controversial cases than the present one; for example, at the height of the Vietnam war, with regard to people I believe to be authentic war criminals, or scientists who claim that Blacks are genetically inferior in a country where their history is hardly pleasant and where such views may well contribute to virulent racism, which persists. Whatever one may think of Faurisson, no one accuses him of being the architect of major war crimes, nor does he claim that Jews are genetically inferior, nor does he receive a tiny fraction of the support afforded in these more controversial cases—in which, I might add, my advocacy of principles I continue to hold valid elicited not a peep of protest... The kernel of truth in Gewirtz's statement is that I strongly oppose discriminatory, repressive and aggressive policies of Israel, not 'although' I am 'of Jewish origin' as he

puts it, but in part because I am Jewish, and have been deeply concerned with these issues since childhood. I would also have no difficulty in tracing my current positions to basic elements of the Jewish
and even Zionist tradition, as perhaps Dr. Gewirtz is aware.

Since the new Zhdanovists seem to be prepared to push cultural development back, apparently to pre-Voltarian levels, they have to distort or at least
ignore the record of the libertarian left. Especially revealing is the fact that their
mindless assault on the feared left is coupled with "the 'discovery' of Gulag and
of the deeply authoritarian character of Leninist state socialism and its various
offshoots, all familiar for many decades, both in gory detail and in general character and historical background, to the libertarian left, but now invoked by new
enthusiasts as part of a post facto justification for imperial aggression."[13]

## Contagious ideas

Could it possibly be that the defenders of the *status quo* and democracy (in
that order) are actually terrified by the prospect that the best evidence and argument the libertarian left has to offer might reach large numbers of people and
win their hearts and minds? Maybe Marcuse had a point, after all. I remember
him telling a crowd at UCLA, in the late '60s, that the control of ABC, CBS and
NBC for a single month would suffice to turn the country around. Apparently
for some people the claim is not all that extravagant, since they appear to fear the
consequences of far less than a month, a week, a day, or even of an hour of
unmystified television. If only their potential antagonists would take note!

What is it that makes Chomsky's writings especially frightening for those
that have nothing to lose but their power and wealth? Why is he so carefully kept
away from the general public, as a potential transmitter of a still not well-known
condition? Why is he the one to pick on, even for Nixon and his acolytes, who
placed him on an enemies list that had very little room for people outside the
mainstream, let alone libertarian socialists? Is it because of the content of
Chomsky's writings, because of his stature or because of his honesty and dedication?

My guess is that what makes Chomsky's writings potentially far more subversive than those of any author I can think of is a combination of elements,
including those mentioned. But I suspect that their potential impact would not
be greatly reduced if they were circulated anonymously. Still, I wouldn't like to
underestimate the part played by his intellectual stature and by his epoch-making contribution to the cognitive sciences and philosophy. After all, we are not
used to seeing a really outstanding figure in the history of thought, with so much
to risk, committing a large part of his seemingly inexhaustible energies to relentlessly combating present evils at home and defending the rights of the poor and
the oppressed everywhere. However, Einstein's intellectual stature loomed no less
large, and, to my knowledge, no watchdog of the State lost any sleep worrying
about the contagious effects of his political writings, including his "Why
Socialism?" (1949), perhaps the best known of them. It is unlikely that this lack

of interest was entirely due to the fact that Einstein's efforts were incomparably less intense than Chomsky's are. As for Chomsky's dedication and honesty, it is true that in his case the 1970s didn't reveal anything not known from the very beginning about the depth of his conviction and his personal integrity, but honesty and dedication are not the sort of things that catch the eye of the unscrupulous. So we are left with the content of his unusually cogent and well-informed writings, which no doubt gain tremendously in force and significance because of the moral conviction they convey and the honesty and wisdom they reflect. Who would deny that?

To develop a comprehensive knowledge of Chomsky's major political essays requires a sustained effort, not only because of their volume, but also because of the unusual amount of documentation he adduces. If one gets lost among the trees, it is not easy to see the outline of the forest. One of the purposes of the present collection is to allow the reader to by-pass the documentation, which is readily available in the full-length essays and the book-length discussions. There is no piece here that is not fairly short and straightforward, while many are extremely concise—little more than "abstracts" of a single topic. Thus the collection might be viewed as a sort of anthology of some of Chomsky's major themes presented in sharp outline. The reader interested in a fuller account can always refer to the writings in which the evidence is given.

Another difficulty is that a close analysis of the contemporary political reality such as that provided by Chomsky (in sharp contrast with a great deal of writing that is often taken to be in his political tradition) doesn't always allow explicit reference to general principles, let alone a systematic presentation of the framework that underlies it. When the reader attempts to supply what is left implicit or implied, he is often misled by conventional assumptions that are at odds with his fundamental principles. It might therefore be helpful to have, as a point of reference, a systematic sketch of Chomsky's framework of assumptions and its historical background. This is what I would like to offer in the following pages.[14]

## Vision and analysis

In Chomsky's view, an intellectual who takes his responsibility seriously is confronted with two tasks, which are closely related. "One is to imagine a future society that conforms to the exigencies of human nature, as best we understand them; the other, to analyze the nature of power and oppression in our present societies."[15] The first one involves little risk, even under the yoke of a totalitarian state. One can always get together with one's friends to discuss the possible forms of one's preferred Utopia, say, "anarchocommunism," to the end of time, pretty sure that those in power are likely to leave the nonactivist alone. They couldn't care less. In fact, they have reasons to be quite happy. Quietistic daydreaming is just as welcome by those in power as plain apathy. In contrast, to offer an analysis of the nature of power and oppression in our present societies in a way that is sufficiently revealing to suggest effective action before the millennium and to act upon it is not likely to be without consequences. A small sample of such an analysis might help to see the difference more clearly:

> By the 1970s, the world system based on U.S. hegemony and leadership of the crusade against independent development, while it had achieved many successes, was in disarray. There are many reasons, among them the end of the era of cheap and abundant energy, the rise of a number of centers of competing industrial capitalism, and the enormous costs of the Vietnam failure. The response, at the global level, has been what is called 'trilateralism,' though one should bear in mind Henry Kissinger's important footnote to trilateral doctrine as perceived by U.S. elites: Other powers have regional responsibilities, which they are to fulfill within the overall framework of order managed by the United States. At the domestic level, the response to the crisis is to be a kind of 'Brazilianization' of the home countries. There is a striking parallel between the Trilateral theory as to how to overcome the political and ideological crisis at home and the liberal counter-revolutionary ideology developed earlier for application in the Third World. The American political scientist Ithiel Pool explained over a decade ago that in such countries as Vietnam, the Congo, and the Dominican Republic, order depends on restoring 'passivity and defeatism' among 'newly mobilized strata.' This is exactly what is proposed now by Trilateral theorists for the industrial societies themselves. It is necessary to return the population to apathy, passivity and defeatism if democracy is to survive. It is necessary to destroy hope, idealism, solidarity, and concern for the poor and oppressed, to replace these dangerous feelings by self-centered egoism, a pervasive cynicism that holds that all change is for the worse, so that one should simply accept the state capitalist order with its inherent inequities and oppression as the best that can be achieved. In fact, a great international propaganda campaign is underway to convince people—particularly young people—that this not only is what they *should* feel but that it is what they *do* feel, and that if somehow they do not adopt this set of values then they are strange relics of a terrible era that has fortunately passed away. This process of imposing passivity and defeatism is, of course, to be accompanied by other features of the Brazilian model: Restricting real income and social benefits for the working classes, demoralization of unions and other popular organizations, and so on. At the ideological level, the process is already well advanced.[16]

Is Chomsky's analysis successful? Very much so, I believe. The reason for it is not hard to find. He simply follows the principles that have been used with so much success in the natural sciences, that is to say, the only known principles of rational inquiry. Under normal circumstances, following the only serious path known would be nothing to rave about, but in a highly indoctrinated society it stands out as something truly exceptional. The reason is that the "logic" the specialists use in their writings is quite different. Here is what they usually do: A general principle is proposed, say, "the United States follows the Wilsonian principle of self-determination" or "the United States follows the Carterian principle of respect for human rights" (which, we are told, replaced the earlier one—see Selection 12). "Then specific examples are surveyed. We discover that where the principles could be applied, they were not applied; where they could not be applied, they were advocated (and their advocacy demonstrates that we are not aggressive and imperialistic)." An apologist of the State can still conclude that "it is ironic that the general thesis fails when tested" and that the general principle has not been disconfirmed.[17]

This avenue is not open to a genuine rational inquirer, however. Having only recourse to ordinary logic, a serious inquirer is led to conclude instead that it is not true that the United States is committed to the principle of respect for human rights. A scientist cannot even place the word "true" or "truth" in quotes, as Kissinger and other practitioners of their peculiar modality of non-ordinary logic do, because a serious inquirer cannot feel the contempt that those non-ordinary logicians feel for this concept, which for them has been preempted by the concept "utility." They will readily admit that there is no "truth" in an outright lie; the relevant question for them, however, is whether there is any "utility."

As is to be expected, Chomsky's approach leads to some interesting anticipations and predictions, which goes a long way towards justifying the belief that he is not a "specialist" or "expert" in the field. We didn't have to wait for his talk on Mar. 22, 1979, at the University of Paris VIII (Vincennes) to know about the "process of imposing passivity and defeatism" (see quote above); its substance can be found already in his justly admired essay "Objectivity and Liberal Scholarship," parts of which were delivered as a lecture at New York University in March 1968. The following lines were written shortly afterwards, that is, more than a decade before the publication of Bertram Gross's *Friendly Fascism: The New Face of Power in America* (1980):

> Anger, outrage, confessions of overwhelming guilt may be good therapy; they can also become a barrier to effective action, which can always be made to seem incommensurable with the enormity of the crime. Nothing is easier than to adopt a new form of self-indulgence, no less debilitating that the old apathy. The danger is substantial. It is hardly a novel insight that confessions of guilt can be institutionalized as a technique for evading what must be done. It is even possible to achieve a feeling of satisfaction by contemplating one's evil nature. No less insidious is the cry for 'revolution,' at a time when not even the germs of new institutions exist, let alone the moral and political consciousness that could lead to a basic modification of

social life. If there will be a 'revolution' in America today, it will no doubt be a move towards some variety of fascism. We must guard against the kind of revolutionary rhetoric that would have had Karl Marx burn down the British Museum because it was merely part of a repressive society. It would be criminal to overlook the serious flaws and inadequacies in our institutions, or to fail to utilize the substantial degree of freedom that most of us enjoy, within the framework of these flawed institutions, to modify them or even replace them by a better social order. One who pays some attention to history will not be surprised if those who cry most loudly that we must smash and destroy are later found among the administrators of some new system of repression.[18]

Perhaps it is not very surprising to discover that these words failed to attract as much attention as a remark in his preceding paragraph, which was repeatedly quoted at the time it appeared: "to me it seems that what is needed is a kind of denazification." At this point it should be kept in mind that no one urged that "those responsible for the massacre of the people of Vietnam, their forced evacuation from their homes, and the destruction of their country be jailed or executed, or even that 'denazification' procedures of the sort instituted against 13 million Germans in the United States Zone be applied to the American population." And yet everyone who is committed to law and order would agree with the U.S. prosecutor at Nuremberg that "if certain acts and violations of treaties are crimes, they are crimes whether the United States does them or whether Germany does them," because a law-and-order citizen would not be "prepared to lay down a rule of criminal conduct against others which we would not be willing to have invoked against us."[19] Should we then call to account, for the foreseeable consequences of their acts, those responsible for Hiroshima and Nagasaki, for B-52 "carpet bombing," and (last but not least) for the "successes" of Orwellian "pacification" and "urbanization"?

For some, that would be senseless—after all, those responsible for those actions fulfilled their duties scrupulously. What some people think is urgently needed is to call to account those who advocated obedience to "the supreme law of the land," people so pragmatically blind as to be incapable of seeing the "utility" of horrendous crimes of war.[20] Needless to say, if and when these dangerous "radicals" (read: people respectful of the supreme law of the land) are "called to account for the historical consequences of [their] previous political stands, Noam Chomsky would inevitably be one of the first to be called upon to testify." Why? Presumably, because "for ten years between 1965 and 1975 Noam Chomsky's political writings were treated with enormous respect in the United States" ("his political writings were published in many of the most widely read intellectual publications of this country"), because "the sources of Chomsky's prestige [are] obvious" ("he is the most important theoretical linguist of modern times—a man referred to by many as a genius in his field... a man of enormous intelligence"), and, last but not least, because "since 1965 Chomsky has demonstrated a seem-ingly boundless political energy."[21] The fact that he had nothing to contribute to the program of "pacification" and "urbanization" should also count, at least before a tribunal of Harvard experts. After all, 1984 is just around the corner.

Another way in which Chomsky departs radically from the expert in legiti-mation is in not being afraid to ask the forbidden (which often happen to be the relevant) questions:

> If we hope to understand anything about the foreign policy of any state, it is a good idea to begin by investigating the domestic social structure: Who sets foreign policy? What interests do these people represent? What is the domestic source of their power? It is a reason-able surmise that the policy that evolves will reflect the special inter-ests of those who design it. An honest study of history will reveal that this natural expectation is quite generally fulfilled. The evidence is overwhelming, in my opinion, that the United States is no exception to the general rule—a thesis which is often characterized as a 'radical critique,' in a curious intellectual move... Some attention to the his-torical record, as well as common sense, leads to a second reasonable expectation: In every society, there will emerge a caste of propagan-dists who labor to disguise the obvious, to conceal the actual work-ings of power, and to spin a web of mythical goals and purposes, utterly benign, that allegedly guide national policy. A typical thesis of the propaganda system is that 'the nation' is an agent in internation-al affairs, not special groups within it, and that 'the nation' is guided by certain ideals and principles, all of them noble... A subsidiary the-sis is that the nation is not an active agent, but rather responds to threats posed to its security, or to order and stability, by awesome evil forces.[22]

## Two major themes

In the State capitalist societies of the Western World, objective power is based ultimately on control of capital, not on party membership or expertise (contrary to the illusions of some "post-industrial" experts). Since World War II there has been an accelerated tendency towards economic concentration and cen-tralization of decision-making in the executive (which are closely related), with a vast increase in overseas investment, marketing and resource extraction. In Chomsky's view, these developments have greatly increased the stake of the mas-ters of the corporate economy in foreign affairs, who as privileged segments of Western industrial society benefit disproportionately from their substantial con-trol over global resources, human and material, and are not ready to give up their privileges. This is why they cannot view with indifference the economic trans-formation of less developed countries in ways which threaten their control. "It is the recognition of this threat that has inspired American counterrevolutionary intervention in the Third World, though the specter of Russian or Chinese aggression in Western Europe, Asia, the Middle East, Africa and Latin America has been dangled before the public as a more acceptable threat."[23] In a non-totalitarian state without direct coercion, interventionism must be preceded by appropriate indoctrination, in particular indoctrination of the young. This, Chomsky argues, is the function of the intelligentsia.

From this perspective it is easy to see why Chomsky's political writings are basically concerned with two major themes, which are of course intimately related: One is the role that the intellectuals have often tended to adopt in the modern period with regard to State power; the other is the contribution of the American intelligentsia to the reconstruction of imperial ideology and to restoring State dogma against all odds in order to induce passivity and obedience in the "silent majority." Here is his main thesis:

> Contrary to widespread belief and self-serving doctrine produced by the intelligentsia themselves, the fact is that, by and large, intellectuals have tended to be submissive and obedient to one or another state—generally their own, though naturally episodes of apologetics for foreign states tend to receive more attention, conformity to domestic power being tacitly assumed as the norm.[24]

This is of course the very same thesis we find in the best writings of Bakunin, about a century ago. It was Bakunin who "coined the phrase 'new class' in reference to those who were coming to control technical knowledge. In a series of analyses and predictions that may be among the most remarkable within the social sciences, Bakunin warned that the 'new class' will attempt to convert their access to knowledge into power over economic and social life. They will try to create 'the reign of scientific intelligence, the most aristocratic, despotic, arrogant, and elitist of all regimes. There will be a new class, a new hierarchy of real and counterfeit scientists and scholars, and the world will be divided into a minority ruling in the name of knowledge, and an immense ignorant majority, And then, woe unto the mass of ignorant ones'."[25]

But for all his historical foresight and his eloquent exaltations of human freedom, Bakunin didn't succeed in putting his amazingly penetrating insights on a solid intellectual foundation. What is worse, he (and many of his followers after him) unwittingly adopted an epistemological position that offers no basis for his stand—essentially the position that led Skinner to proclaim that we are "beyond freedom and dignity."[26] In contrast, Chomsky has contributed far more than anyone else to a theory of the human mind that, if it can be developed into a science, might lead to a plausible justification for the sort of society Bakunin seemed to have in mind. And he is certainly better equipped to defend Bakunin's ideas against the "new class" than Bakunin was. There is nothing nineteenth-century like or even preChomskyan in what Chomsky takes from Bakunin.

This brings us to the historical background of Chomsky's ideas. An excellent point of departure is his book *Cartesian Linguistics* (one of the ten "most notable" nonfiction books of the 1960s, according to *Time*, Dec. 26, 1969: p. 56). We could begin by saying that his social theory is Bakuninian in exactly the sense in which his grammatical theory is Cartesian—with a crucial difference, however: He has not deepened our understanding of social systems and their evolution to the extent he has deepened our understanding of language systems and their evolution. It is in this sense that his remark about his not being an anarchist thinker, but just a "derivative fellow traveler," must be understood, I believe (see Section 21). Still, his anarchism is no less ahead of Bakunin's anarchism than his rationalism is ahead of Descartes' rationalism.

It will be helpful to keep in mind that when he considers earlier stages of thought and speculation, Chomsky's approach is not that of a historian of philosophy or science (see, e.g., François Jacob's *The Logic of Life*). That is, he doesn't attempt "to reconstruct in an exhaustive manner what people thought at the time, but rather to bring to light certain important insights of the period that have been neglected, and often seriously distorted, in later scholarship, and to show how at that time certain persons had already discerned important things, perhaps without being fully aware of it," things "relating to questions of contemporary significance," "anticipations of later developments." He himself has repeatedly offered this analogy:

> I am not proceeding in the manner of an art historian so much as in that of an art lover, a person who looks for what has value to him in the seventeenth century, for example, that value deriving in large measure from the contemporary perspective with which he approaches these objects. Both types of approach are legitimate. I think it is possible to turn toward earlier stages of scientific knowledge, and by virtue of what we know today, to shed light on the significant contributions of the period in a way in which the most creative geniuses could not, because of the limitations of their time. This was the nature of my interest in Descartes, for example, and in the philosophical tradition that he influenced, and also Humboldt, who would not have considered himself a Cartesian. I was interested in his effort to make sense of the concept of free creativity based on a system of internalized rules, an idea that has certain roots in Cartesian thought, I believe.[27]

This aspect of his work has not been sufficiently appreciated but the fact is that one can learn more about, say, Rousseau, in one of Chomsky's footnotes than in a whole chapter of Bertrand Russell's *History of Western Philosophy*, to say nothing of Bakunin's or Rocker's view of the author of the *Discourse on the Origins and Foundations of Inequality Among Men* (Rousseau's second "discourse"), published two centuries almost to the day before Chomsky finished his monumental first book, *The Logical Structure of Linguistic Theory* (1955).[28]

Perhaps this can be better appreciated from a different angle: There is a recent book of essays, "by possibly the most brilliant and engaging intellect of our time, [which] illuminate dazzlingly both the Russian mind and the role of ideas in history" (in the opinion of Arthur Schlesinger, Jr.). Compare the essay entitled "Herzen and Bakunin on Individual Liberty" with what Chomsky has written or not written about Bakunin and Herzen.[29] Why are the two reactions and their implications so diametrically different? One answer could be: Because they are separated by the Chomskyan revolution. This answer could almost be sufficient to understand why one would look in vain for what can be learned from some passing remarks by Chomsky about Vico (and, indirectly, about authors deeply influenced by Vico, such as Marx) in the best monographic studies on Vico, including one "by possibly the most brilliant and engaging intellect of our time."[30] In the case of Bakunin and Herzen, far more seems to be involved, but this is not the place to dwell on the topic. The reader should keep in mind, however, Cervantes's admonition: He wanted to be praised not as much for what he had written as for what he had left unwritten. It doesn't seem entirely accidental that Godwin's name is conspicuously absent from Chomsky's writings, or that he is far more attracted by Bakunin's work than by Kropotkin's (see Selection 21), in sharp contrast with many contemporary anarchists. The close attention he has given to some of Rousseau's writings is no accident either, as we are about to see.

## The nature of human nature

I have been trying to show why Chomsky is especially interested in cultural evolution, particularly in cultural advance, not in the mere reconstruction of the past. As is well known, cultural evolution is possible on this planet only in the case of humans. Human life changes radically and in some periods quite rapidly, and although it is extremely varied, it doesn't result in diversity within the human species (a Papuan child raised in New York will become a New Yorker, to use Chomsky's example). The genetic differences that some find are, in his view, superficial and trivial. On the other hand, apes and monkeys are extremely conservative, far more so than the most conservative humans: They all live as they lived millions of years ago. According to some biologists, no baboon will ever give a thought to the possibility of phasing out the rigid hierarchical structure typical of baboonic society.

What makes cultural evolution possible? The answer seems obvious enough: Human nature. However, many seem sceptical about the possibility of developing a concept of "human nature" as a well-defined biological concept, independent of social and historical conditions. Chomsky doesn't share this scepticism. For him, the nature of *homo loquens* (the only known creature with "the gift of tongues") is not a product of history; it exists independently of history, immutable except for biological changes in the species. It is true that the biological notion "human nature" is not yet within the range of science, but it is equally undeniable that "in specific domains such as the study of language, we can begin to formulate a significant concept of 'human nature', in its intellectual and cognitive aspects," if, with Chomsky, we "would not hesitate to consider the faculty of language as part of human nature."[31]

Curiously enough, it is precisely the obvious reality of cultural evolution that led many to deny the not less obvious reality of human nature. Rousseau was not one of them. In fact, he had something really new to say on the matter:

> Rousseau diverges from the Cartesian tradition in several respects. He defines the 'specific characteristic of the human species' as man's 'faculty of self-perfection,' which, 'with the aid of circumstances, successively develops all the others, and resides among us as much in the species as in the individual.' The faculty of self-perfection and of perfection of the human species through cultural transmission is not, to my knowledge, discussed in any similar terms by the Cartesians. However, I think that Rousseau's remarks might be interpreted as a development of the Cartesian tradition in an unexplored direction, rather than as a denial and rejection of it. There is no inconsistency in the notion that the restrictive attributes of mind underlie a historically evolving human nature that develops within the limits that they set; or that these attributes of mind provide the possibility for self-perfection; or that, by providing the consciousness of freedom, these essential attributes of human nature give man the opportunity to create social conditions and social forms to maximize the possibilities for freedom, diversity, and individual self-realization. To use an arithmetical analogy, the integers do not fail to be an infinite set merely because they do not exhaust the rational numbers. Analogously, it is no denial of man's capacity for infinite 'self-perfection' to hold that there are intrinsic properties of mind that constrain his development. I would like to argue that in a sense the opposite is true, that without a system of formal constraints there are no creative acts; specifically, in the absence of intrinsic and restrictive properties of mind, there can be only 'shaping of behavior' but no creative acts of self-perfection. Furthermore, Rousseau's concern for the evolutionary character of self-perfection brings us back, from another point of view, to a concern for human language, which would appear to be a prerequisite for such evolution of society and culture, for Rousseau's perfection of the species, beyond the most rudimentary forms.[32]

Here we come to the core of Chomsky's conception of humankind (human nature and human society). From this perspective it is easy to understand why for him, as for Rudolf Rocker, anarchism is not "a fixed, self-enclosed social system but rather a definite trend in the historic development of mankind, which, in contrast with the intellectual guardianship of all clerical and governmental institutions, strives for the free unhindered unfolding of all the individual and social forces in life;" why "even freedom is only a relative, not an absolute concept, since it tends constantly to become broader and to affect wider circles in more manifold ways;" why, in one word, many anarchists pay no attention to those commentators that "dismiss anarchism as utopian, formless, primitive, or otherwise incompatible with the realities of a complex society," and continue to insist that beyond the best conceived Utopia there is always Utopia.[33]

## Libertarianism vs. "liberalism"

It would of course be absurd to conclude from this that anything goes. Our vision of a future society should conform with the exigencies of human nature, as best we understand them, and many people would agree that the essence of human nature is "freedom." But, what is "freedom"? For many libertarians, among them Rocker, "freedom is not an abstract philosophical (or legal) concept, but the vital concrete possibility for every human being to bring to full development all the powers, capacities, and talents with which nature has endowed him, and turn them to social account." This is precisely the root of the libertarian opposition to the State. A libertarian will readily admit that the innate powers, capacities and talents of every individual without an identical twin are different from those of any other individual, and will see in the differences the basis for a genuinely human society (see n. 72): "a vision of hell is a society of interchangeable parts" (Chomsky). But s/he will argue that every individual feels the need for creative work (manual or mental), for free creation without the arbitrary limiting effect of coercive institutions, and that for the majority of people this need cannot be fully satisfied while the elements of repression and coercion that exist in our society as a historical residue are not overcome.

From now on I will reserve the term "libertarian" for this conception, the conception of "classical liberalism" in Chomsky's terms, which should not be confused with what is generally referred to as "liberalism" in the American press of our day. The two conceptions may be characterized with quotes from Wilhelm von Humboldt's *The Limits of State Action* (1792) and from Adam Smith's *An Inquiry Into the Nature and Causes of the Wealth of Nations* (1776), respectively.

For Humboldt, the true end of a human being is "the highest and most harmonious development of his powers to a complete and consistent whole" (ch. II). Such a development presupposes two conditions, "intimately connected": first of all, an absolutely indispensable one: freedom; then, a variety of situations, no less essential.

This view of the uniqueness of human nature is quite different from the one described by Smith. When he considers "The Expenses of the Sovereign or Commonwealth" (Book V, Ch. I), and in particular "The Expense of the Institutions for the Education of Youth," he points out that in the "progress" of the "division of labour," "the employment of the far greater part of those who live by labor, that is, of the great body of people, comes to be confined to a few very simple operations, frequently one or two" (Chaplin might have gotten the idea for his film *Modern Times* reading this passage). Then he goes on to say:

> The man whose whole life is spent in performing a few simple
> operations, of which the effects are perhaps always the same, or very

nearly the same, has no occasion to exert his understanding or to exercise his invention in finding out expedients for removing difficulties which never occur. He naturally loses, therefore, the habit of such exertion, and generally becomes as stupid and ignorant as it is possible for a human creature to become... Of the great and extensive interests of his country he is altogether incapable of judging, and unless very particular pains have been taken to render him otherwise, he is equally incapable of defending his country in war... His dexterity at his own particular trade seems, in this manner, to be acquired at the expense of his intellectual, social, and martial virtues. But in every improved and civilized society this is the state into which the laboring poor, that is, the great body of the people, must necessarily fall, unless government takes some pains to prevent it.

It is otherwise in the barbarous societies, as they are commonly called,... In such societies the varied occupations of every man oblige every man to exert his capacity, and to invent expedients for removing difficulties which are continually occurring. Invention is kept alive, and the mind is not suffered to fall into that drowsy stupidity which, in a civilized society, seems to benumb the understanding of almost all the inferior ranks of people. In those barbarous societies, as they are called, every man... is in some measure a statesman, and can form a tolerable judgment concerning the interest of the society...

I hope I haven't quoted more from Smith than the reader was prepared to tolerate. The terms "civilized," "civilization" were fairly new at the time.[34] Needless to say, the libertarian conception of civilization is radically different. This of course does not mean that the libertarian society has to retain features of the "barbarous" societies of the past, as if one who chooses the boat were not able to choose the rudder. The division of labor described by Smith is not the only social alternative, and it is rejected by every true "libertarian." (I will return to this question in another connection.) A general critique of the implicit assumptions, from a strictly economic point of view, can be found in Karl Polanyi's *The Great Transformation: The Political and Economic Origins of Our Time*, first published in 1944.[35]

The most fundamental condition that the libertarian vision places on any future society is not the condition of freedom "to truck, barter, and exchange one thing for another," making a profit in the process, but the condition of freedom for self-realization. Thus the first genuine choice we have to confront is the choice between "free creativity" and "free enterprise." For a libertarian, a decent society should maximize the possibilities for "free creativity" to be realized; a "free enterprise" system of the familiar variety has very little to do with anything we know about nature or natural law, and even less with Marx's "realm of freedom." It can only live in symbiosis with that archaic structure called the State, which is why the libertarian is an adversary of State power. (See n. 42).

## Socialism vs. capitalism

This brings us to the second crucial choice. As Rocker argued, the classical libertarian ideals were wrecked on the realities of capitalist economic forms. Here is the explanation Chomsky gave a few years ago in a television interview broadcast by the BBC in 1978:

> The world Humboldt was considering—partially an imaginary world—was a post-feudal but pre-capitalist world. It was a world in which there was (at least in theory) no great divergence among individuals as to the kind of power they had or the wealth they commanded, but a tremendous disparity between individuals on the one hand and the State on the other... He was not thinking of an era in which a corporation would be regarded as a legal individual, or in which such enormous disparities in control over resources and production would distinguish individuals... While opposition to State power in an era of such divergence of private power still conforms to Humboldt's conclusions, it doesn't do so for his reasons. His reasons now lead to a range of different conclusions, namely that we must dissolve the authoritarian control over production and resources which leads to such disparity among individuals, and thus drastically limits human freedom. One might draw a direct line between classical liberalism and a kind of libertarian socialism—which I think can be regarded as adapting the basic reasoning of classical liberalism to our very different social era.[36]

If the first choice had to do with State power, the second has to do with the power of capital. A consistent libertarian "must oppose private ownership of the means of production and the wage slavery which is a component of this system, as incompatible with the principle that labor must be freely undertaken and under the control of the producer. As Marx put it, socialists look forward to a society in which labor will 'become not only a means of life, but also the highest want in life,' an impossibility when the worker is driven by external authority or need rather than inner impulse: 'no form of wage-labor, even though one may be less obnoxious than another, can do away with the misery of wage-labor itself.' A consistent [libertarian] must oppose not only alienated labor but also the stupefying specialization of labor that takes place when the means for developing production 'mutilate the worker into a fragment of a human being, degrade him to become a mere appurtenance of the machine, make his work such a torment that its essential meaning is destroyed'."[37] A consistent libertarian, then, should be a socialist, "libertarian" socialism being the polar opposite of "liberal" capitalism (in the senses stipulated above).

A truly human society should meet then this minimal condition: It should be a form of libertarian socialism. As is well known, this ideal was common to Bakunin and Marx. Contrary to what some people think, Marx's Utopia was not different from Bakunin's—or from Chomsky's, for whom the basic ideas of libertarian socialism "deserve close attention as the most serious expression, in [his] view, of a concept of a just and decent society that incorporates serious and critical principles while attending to significant social and historical facts."[38]

## Acracy vs. autocracy

But for a reformer or a revolutionary to have a vision of a future society that conforms to the exigencies of human nature, as best we understand them, and to understand the nature of power and oppression in our present societies, is not enough. A reformer or revolutionary needs a strategy to bring the existing society closer to the one s/he envisions, and must be committed to do what s/he can to bring about a more just society. It is at this point that we are confronted with a third crucial choice: That between a popular cultural transformation of society and an elitistic political revolution.

For some self-styled socialists, the main task of a reformist or revolutionary movement is to gain State power. They conceive of the revolution as an essentially political change, its main purpose being the transfer of State power to the leaders who are to exercise it in the name of the "proletariat." The exercise of State power gained this way, like the exercise of State power gained without having the "proletariat" in mind, has often enough resulted in an extended "Gulag." Thus the differences between Stalinism and Nazism are rather subtle from the point of view of their victims. There is nothing subtle, however, about the repeated attempts to reduce the whole range of Marxist positions to the worst features of Leninism and its various offshoots. No rational person would deny that Gulag is not entirely unrelated to the deeply elitistic character of Leninism or Fascism anymore than they would deny that Hiroshima, Nagasaki and the merciless bombing of Indochina are not entirely unrelated to the deeply elitistic character of "liberalism"—or that the "auto da fe" of an earlier age is not entirely unrelated to the deeply authoritarian character of a nonmarginal tradition of the Catholic Church. It is true that there are other sides to "liberalism" and Catholicism, as can be surmised from a recent American book.[39]

One cannot emphasize too much, then, that a libertarian socialist sees the challenge of social change differently than an authoritarian socialist. In a libertarian organization there is no place for elitism, and violence is acceptable only when it has been justified, "perhaps by an argument that it is necessary to remedy injustice." From this socialist perspective, a revolution is not a sudden, cataclysmic event that takes place overnight, but rather an uninterrupted cultural and social transformation directed toward libertarian goals, a sort of erosion wearing away archaic ideas and fossilized forms of authority and oppression that survive from an earlier era. For a socialist of a libertarian persuasion, a social struggle "can only be justified if it is supported by an argument—even if it is an indirect argument based on questions of fact and value that are not well understood—which purports to show that the consequences of this struggle will be beneficial for human beings and will bring about a more decent society." Put another way: the class struggle "can only be justified by an argument that it will bring an end to class oppression, and do so in a way that accords with fundamental human rights."[40]

Another automatic consequence of a non-elitistic approach is that the "relevant choice" in the organization of production is between self-management and autocratic control (whether by State or private capital). For a libertarian socialist, there is little difference between a "liberal" (i.e. neoliberal) and a totalitarian organization of production. There is a book by an American businessman that tries to show that "free enterprise" is "the opium of the American people."[41] If we are ready to admit that, the term "free enterprise," as it is generally used, simply designates "a system of autocratic governance of the economy in which neither the community nor the work force has any role—a system that we would call 'fascist' if translated to the political sphere,"[42] it becomes obvious that the term has a much wider application (as is well known, Lenin was a great enthusiast of Taylorism). And, again, we can see that the real choice is not between totalitarianism and liberalism, but between elitism (liberal or totalitarian) and true egalitarianism. In this respect, it is significant that Marx saw the revolutionary more as a "frustrated producer" than a "dissatisfied consumer."[43]

## Anarcho-syndicalism vs. atavism

Marx's work is also a good point of reference for the fourth and last crucial choice I would like to consider. I cannot think of a better way to introduce the topic than Chomsky's answer to a question posed to him by Mitsou Ronat:

> Contemporary Marxist philosophy has been linked in large part to Leninist doctrine, at least until recently. European Marxism after World War I developed unfortunate tendencies, in my opinion: the tendencies associated with Bolshevism, which has always seemed to me an authoritarian and reactionary current. The latter became dominant within the European Marxist tradition after the Russian Revolution. But much more to my taste, at least, are quite different tendencies, for example, that range of opinion that extends roughly from Rosa Luxemburg and the Dutch Marxist Anton Pannekoek and Paul Mattick to the anarcho-syndicalist Rudolf Rocker and others.
>
> These thinkers have not contributed to philosophy in the sense of our discussion; but they have much to say about society, about social change, and the fundamental problems of human life. Though not about problems of the sort that we have been discussing, for example.
>
> Marxism itself has become too often a sort of church, a theology. Of course, I'm generalizing far too much. Work of value has been done by those who consider themselves Marxists. But up to a certain point this criticism is justified, I'm afraid. In any case, I do not believe that Marxist philosophy, of whatever tendency, has made a substantial contribution to the kind of questions we have been discussing.
>
> For the rest, what I know has not impressed me greatly and has not encouraged me to seek to know more.[44]

This should not surprise those who remember the remark in his first political essay about "non-Bolshevik Marxism, as represented, for example, by such figures as Luxemburg, Pannekoek, Korsch, Arthur Rosenberg, and many others"—if they also remember his preference for looking at the past much as an art lover does, that is, looking for what has value from the perspective of the present. Nor should they be surprised to discover that he looks the same way at Marx's work. One who finds much to admire in Descartes's work or in Kant's work, but doesn't fail to reject, say, the "mechanical philosophy" or the assumption that "innate ideas" are accessible to introspection, is bound to find much in Marx which doesn't square with what we now know or are beginning to understand, even if he finds much of undiminished value (e.g., Marx's critique of capitalism or his analysis of ideology as a mask for class interest). On the other hand, he is unlikely to be misled by the fact that the timetable that Marx envisioned was in error.

As I have already pointed out, there is no essential difference between Marx's Utopia and the Utopia of libertarian socialism. Particularly significant is the fact that the ideas of the young Marx were as far from empiricist doctrine (at least in spirit) as those of other socialists of his time, something which cannot be said about many of his twentieth-century followers. This of course doesn't mean that anyone trying to understand the empiricism/rationalism controversy today should try to find the answer to this or other philosophical questions in Marx's writings.[45] He excelled mainly as a theoretician of capitalism, and as such he was greatly admired by Bakunin and other revolutionaries who disagreed with him on an important point, namely, the issue of conquest versus destruction of State power. Many still think that his analysis of capitalism has been essentially confirmed by the way the capitalist system has actually evolved, in particular by the increasing tendency towards economic concentration and centralization of decision-making we are witnessing. A good case could be made that Marx's analysis has been, in fact, adopted by the capitalist planners, and much of the evidence would come from major official documents such as the Peace-War Studies of the Council of Foreign Relations and the Pentagon Papers.[46] (See Selection 12.)

If we use the term "syndicalist" to designate those socialists who believe that Marx's analysis of capitalism is on target, the fourth choice is between "socialist syndicalism" and other forms of socialism.[47] Historically speaking, the two most representative conceptions of what I'm calling "socialist syndicalism" are anarchosyndicalism (as described by Rudolf Rocker) and council communism (as conceived, for example, by the left-wing Marxist Anton Pannekoek). Either modality includes a strategy that carries us out of the realm of pure philosophy into the realm of action. As has been repeatedly pointed out by Chomsky, the movements inspired by these two "socialist syndicalist" conceptions of social change tend to converge, while often showing clear differences in emphasis and approach. Chomsky's anarchism, which is very closely related to Bakunin's and Rocker's, appears to be the most developed conception of anarchism to date, and the deepest and best founded, intellectually speaking.

Summing up this part of the discussion, we can say that this up-to-date conception of anarchism involves the following four choices, which can be seen as successive steps both logically and historically:

*Vision:*
  **1.** (Libertarian) self-realization (vs. neoliberal acquisitiveness)
  **2.** (Socialist) common appropriation of capital (vs. private expropriation)
*Strategy:*
  **3.** (Popular) cultural transformation (vs. elitist political revolution)
  **4.** (Industrial) syndicalism (vs. any atavistic alternative)

It should be emphasized that a consistent "syndicalist" (in the sense stipulated) agrees with Marx and Bakunin that alienated labor and the stupefying specialization of labor is not an inevitable concomitant of technological development and industrialization, but rather a feature of specific capitalist relations of production. As Chomsky has written, quoting from Marx's *Capital*, "the society of the future must be concerned to 'replace the detail-worker of today... reduced to a mere fragment of a man, by the fully developed individual, fit for a variety of labors... to whom the different social functions... are but so many modes of giving free scope to his natural powers.' The prerequisite is the abolition of [private] capital and wage labor as social categories... The reduction of man to an appurtenance of the machine, a specialized tool of production, might in principle be overcome, rather than enhanced, with the proper development and use of technology, but not under the conditions of autocratic control of production by those who make man an instrument to serve their ends, overlooking his individual purposes, in Humboldt's phrase."

We come now to a key point, not fully appreciated by some contemporary avowed anarchists:

> Anarcho-syndicalists sought, even under capitalism, to create 'free associations of free producers' that would engage in militant struggle and prepare to take over the organization of production on a democratic basis. These associations would serve as 'a practical school of anarchism'...
>
> In his attack on the right of private or bureaucratic control over the means of production, the anarchist takes his stand with those who struggle to bring about 'the third and last emancipatory phase of history,' the first having made serfs out of slaves, the second having made wage earners out of serfs, and the third which abolishes the proletariat in a final act of liberation that places control over the economy in the hands of free and voluntary associations of producers.[48]

Why do anarcho-syndicalists insist so much on self-management (Selection 22)? Why do they reject so emphatically what they see as the twin options of a social democratic conquest and exercise of State power or "stultifying parliamentarianism" of the liberal democratic sort? Because, as Rocker put it,

...only the producers themselves are fitted for this task, since they are the only value-creating element of society out of which a new future can arise. Theirs must be the task of freeing labor from all the fetters which economic exploitation has fastened on it, of freeing society from all the institutions and procedure of political power, and of opening the way to an alliance of free groups of men and women based on co-operative labor and a planned administration of things in the interest of the community. To prepare the toiling masses in city and country for this great goal and to bind them together as a militant force is the objective of modern anarcho-syndicalism, and in this its whole purpose is exhausted.

To which Chomsky adds:

As a socialist, Rocker would take for granted 'that the serious, final, complete liberation of the workers is possible only upon one condition: that of the appropriation of capital, that is, of raw material and all the tools of labor, including land, by the whole body of workers.' As an anarcho-syndicalist, he insists, further, that the workers' organizations create 'not only the ideas, but also the facts of the future itself' in the prerevolutionary period, that they embody in themselves the structure of the future society—and he looks forward to a social revolution that will dismantle the state apparatus as well as expropriate the expropriators. 'What we put in place of the government is industrial organization'.[49]

A few pages later Chomsky comes back to the same idea from a different perspective:

What is far more important [than the ideas which lead libertarian socialists to oppose state socialism and the resulting bureaucratic despotism] is that these ideas have been realized in spontaneous revolutionary action, for example in Germany and Italy after World War I and in Spain (not only in the agricultural countryside, but also in industrial Barcelona) in 1936...

The phrase 'spontaneous revolutionary action', can be misleading. The anarcho-syndicalists, at least, took very seriously Bakunin's remark that the workers' organizations must create 'not only the ideas but also the facts of the future itself' in the prerevolutionary period. The accomplishments of the popular revolution in Spain, in particular, were based on the patient work of many years of organization and education, one component of a long tradition of commitment and militancy... And workers' organizations existed with the structure, the experience, and the understanding to undertake the task of social reconstruction when, with Franco's coup, the turmoil of early 1936 exploded into social revolution. (See Selection 21 and 19.)

## Spontaneous growth vs. bureaucratic fiat

A committed anarchosyndicalist is not satisfied with being a good arm-chair revolutionary—one who has made every effort to understand the contemporary world in the light of what is best in the libertarian socialist tradition, drawing from the achievements of the past lessons that will enrich the culture of liberation (not a small thing). Anarchosyndicalists are prepared to take their stand with those who wish not only to understand the world, but also to change it. They are perfectly aware of the power of non-violent resistance and direct action (recently demonstrated once more, in an unexpected and striking way, in Poland). They are also more than willing to participate anonymously in the spontaneous actions of popular forces that are capable of creating new social forms in the course of the struggle for complete liberation, fully conscious that social creation enhances and promotes the very intellectual creation that inspired it. And, needless to say, they agree with Murray Bookchin that "direct action not only means the occupation of a nuclear power plant site but the less dramatic, often prosaic and tedious forms of self-management that involve patience, commitment to democratic procedures, lengthy discourse, and a decent respect for the opinions of others within the same community." After all, a liberation movement that structures itself "in the form of the very society it seeks to create" must foster "embryonic growth, cell by cell as it were, as distinguished from bureaucratic growth by fiat and inorganic accretion." As Bookchin continues:

> "At a time when consociation is faced with the deadly prospect of dissociation, Anarchism opposes social form to political form, individual empowerment through direct action to political powerlessness through bureaucratic representation. Thus Anarchism is not only the practice of citizenship within a new public sphere, but the self-administration of the revolutionary movement itself. The very process of building an Anarchist movement from below is viewed as the process of consociation, self-activity and self-management that must ultimately yield that revolutionary self that can act upon, change and manage an authentic society."

After this interesting paraphrase of traditional anarchosyndicalist ideas, Bookchin goes on to emphasize that "the most advanced Anarchist theories, today, do not involve a mystical return to a 'natural man,' a crude antistatism, a denial of the need for organization, a vision of direct action as violence and terrorism, a mindless rejection of sophisticated theory, an opaqueness to what is living in the work of all Socialist theories"—all points that need to be emphasized again and again. And he concludes with this "very important consideration," no less timely:

> Anarchism has raised almost alone those ecological issues, feminist issues, community issues, problems of self-empowerment, forms of decentralization, and concepts of self-administration that are now at

the foreground of the famous 'social question.' And it has raised these issues from within its very substance as a theory and practice directed against hierarchy and domination...[50]

The thrust against hierarchy and domination in the home, the school and the community has its roots of course in the libertarian thought of the Enlightenment. If a person is fundamentally a free, creative, searching, self-perfecting being, and freedom of thought and enlightenment are not only for the elite or for one sex in preference to the other, it follows that, as Humboldt wrote, echoing Rousseau, there is something degrading to human nature in the idea of refusing any person the right to be a person. In Proudhon's words: "No long discussion is necessary to demonstrate that the power of denying a man his thought, his will, his personality, is a power of life and death, and that to make a man a slave is to assassinate him"—an outrageous statement if meant to exclude women. As Humboldt emphasized, "all moral culture springs solely and immediately from the inner life of the soul, and can only be stimulated in human nature, and never produced by external and artificial contrivances."

From this we must conclude, as Chomsky does, that education "must provide the opportunities for self-fulfillment; it can at best provide a rich and challenging environment for the individual to explore, in his own way."

> Even a language—he goes on to say—cannot, strictly speaking, be taught, but only 'awakened in the mind: one can only provide the thread along which it will develop of itself.' I think that Humboldt would have found congenial much of Dewey's thinking about education. And that he might also have appreciated the recent revolutionary extension of such ideas, for example, by the radical Catholics of Latin America who are concerned with the 'awakening of consciousness,' referring to 'the transformation of the passive exploited lower classes into conscious and critical masters of their own destinies' much in the manner of Third World revolutionaries elsewhere. He would, I am sure, have approved of their criticism of schools that are 'more preoccupied with the transmission of knowledge than with the creation, among other values, of a critical spirit. From the social point of view, the educational systems are oriented to maintaining the existing social and economic structures instead of transforming them.' But Humboldt's concern for spontaneity goes well beyond educational practice in the narrow sense. It touches also the question of labor and exploitation.

To Humboldt, as to William Morris many years later, "it seems that all peasants and craftsmen might be elevated into artists."[51]

However, the libertarians of the Enlightenment did not foresee that the liberal propensity "to truck, barter, and exchange one thing for another" in order to make a "profit" would soon lead to a predatory capitalist economy that, unchecked, would bring about the total destruction of the environment, as Karl

Polanyi emphatically argued (see n. 35). Unfortunately the ecological thrust of libertarianism, eventually triggered by the workings of the profit-driven market-economy, began to develop only recently—hopefully in time to prevent the worst.[52] The ecological movement is then nothing more than a development of the libertarian tradition in a direction imposed by the disastrous results of the long hegemony of profit-making and its "exploitation" of nature.

To sum up and complete the discussion of anarcho-syndicalism: There are still revolutionaries so much under the dead weight of the XIX century that they tend to see the history of libertarian thought and action as a mere changing reflection of the changing social context, and, naturally enough (under their assumption), they are ready to forget yesterday's insights in today's context. Chomsky is not one of them. He appears to be totally free of every vestige of XIX century historicism; what's more, one of his major achievements is to have made it easier for everyone to overcome every vestige of historicism, which is ultimately rooted in Medieval scholasticism.[53]

This is one of the reasons he tries to look at the past, not as an antiquarian, but as an art lover. When he proceeded to extract from the history of libertarian thought a living, evolving, uninterrupted tradition, he discovered that the best it has to offer to people living today is to be found in the crucible of anarchosyndicalism—if one of course looks at the history of anarcho-syndicalism with the eyes of an art lover. In fact, he is persuaded that, for the reasons he gives, a broad-based, up-to-date form of anarcho-syndicalism in which feminists and ecologists feel completely at home is just the right one for a genuine movement for radical or revolutionary change in advanced industrial societies such as the United States and Canada.

Not surprisingly, he does not agree with those who think that the solution to the problems of the factories or the schools is virtually to eliminate them. The reason is obvious. On the libertarian conception of life, the creative impulse is to have maximum utilization, and the automated factory and the well-planned school should be able to free the adults from stupefying chores and to provide the proper environment for children who are developing their physical and mental powers.[54]

Perhaps it is worth adding here that Chomsky, like many other revolutionaries, in particular Peter Kropotkin, believes that it is overwork, not work, that "is repulsive to human nature": "Overwork for supplying the few with luxury—not work for the well-being of all." Far from being repulsive to human nature, work "is a physiological necessity, a necessity of spending accumulated bodily energy, a necessity which is health and life itself."[55] The Dadaist demand of "universal unemployment" must be interpreted in this light.

## Creativeness vs. receptiveness

Chomsky's anarcho-syndicalism is, I believe, one of the crucial factors that make his work far more threatening for those in control of the First World economy and everything else than the work of any other libertarian socialist activist on record. It is easy to see that he has done more than anyone else to undermine the deceptive intellectual foundation on which the present economic structure rests. What's more, the motivation to accomplish just that was there from the very beginning. From the time he was a graduate student, if not before, he was motivated to investigate the intellectual basis of the dominant ideology. By then the propensity "to truck, barter, and exchange one thing for another" with profit as the main goal had already brought us innumerable and horrifying perversions, including Hiroshima and Nagasaki ("the second being, so it appears, history's most abominable experiment," one certainly not dwarfed by Dachau and Auschwitz). As he writes in the very first page of his first political essay, "The responsibility of intellectuals" (a key to his thought and action), referring to a series of articles he had read as an undergraduate:

> To what extent were the German or Japanese people responsible for the atrocities committed by their governments? To what extent are the British or American people responsible for the vicious terror bombings of civilians, perfected as a technique of warfare by the Western democracies and reaching their culmination in Hiroshima and Nagasaki, surely among the most unspeakable crimes in history? To an undergraduate in 1945–1946—to anyone whose political and moral consciousness had been formed by the horrors of the 1930s, by the war in Ethiopia, the Russian purge, the 'China incident,' the Spanish Civil War, the Nazi atrocities, the Western reaction to these events and, in part, complicity in them—these questions had particular significance and poignancy.[56]

However, not everyone whose political and moral consciousness was formed by those horrors was willing or equipped to search for the root of all that evil as Chomsky was. And it didn't take him long to focus on a natural bedfellow of economic liberalism, namely, the empiricist (non-nativist), including behaviourist, doctrine of human behaviour—in part for political reasons, as he himself declared in a very revealing interview:

> These theories were then very much in fashion, and they even aroused a certain degree of euphoria, I think it is fair to say. In the intellectual milieu of Cambridge there was a great impact of the remarkable technological developments associated with World War II. Computers, electronics, acoustics, mathematical theory of communication, cybernetics, all the technological approaches to human behaviour enjoyed an extraordinary vogue. The human sciences were being reconstructed on the basis of these concepts. It was all connected. As a student at Harvard in the early 1950s all of this had a great effect on me. Some people, myself included, were rather concerned about these developments, in part for political reasons, at least as far as my personal motivations were concerned… because this whole complex of ideas seemed linked to potentially quite dangerous

political currents: manipulative, and connected with behaviourist concepts of human nature... But of course these motivations were irrelevant to showing that all this was wrong, as I thought it was. I believed that these theories could not really offer what they promised. As soon as they were analyzed carefully, they unraveled, though not without leaving substantive and important contributions.[57]

As soon as they were analyzed carefully by Chomsky, that is, the empiricist theories unraveled. Now the controversy is no longer centered on whether or not the human mind is a "blank tablet" at birth—more precisely, whether the structures of the human mind are genetically determined, i.e. "innate"—, since it is generally admitted that they are, but on the specificity of those structures. Relying primarily on his investigation of the faculty of language, the best known part of the human mind and human nature, Chomsky has forcefully argued that they are very specific and that the mind is a creative power.[58] The importance of this conclusion for libertarian socialism becomes clear in this often quoted passage from one of his major essays, "Language and Freedom," to my mind the highest point to date in the history of libertarian socialist thought:

> I have discussed these traditional ideas at some length, not out of antiquarian interest, but because I think that they are valuable and essentially correct, and that they project a course we can follow with profit. Social action must be animated by a vision of a future society, and by explicit judgments of value concerning the character of this future society...
>
> Predatory capitalism is not a fit system for the mid-twentieth century. It is incapable of meeting human needs that can be expressed only in collective terms, and its concept of competitive man who seeks only to maximize wealth and power, who subjects himself to market relationships, to exploitation and external authority, is anti-human and intolerable in the deepest sense... Modern science and technology can relieve men of the necessity for specialized, imbecile labor. They may, in principle, provide the basis for a rational social order based on free association and democratic control, if we have the will to create it.
>
> A vision of a future social order is in turn based on a concept of human nature. If in fact man is an indefinitely malleable, completely plastic being, with no innate structures of mind and no intrinsic needs of a cultural or social character, then he is a fit subject for the 'shaping of behaviour' by the state authority, the corporate manager, the technocrat, or the central committee. Those with some confidence in the human species will hope this is not so and will try to determine the intrinsic human characteristics that provide the framework for intellectual development, the growth of moral consciousness, cultural achievement, and participation in a free community. In

a partly analogous way, a classical tradition spoke of artistic genius acting within and in some ways challenging a framework of rule. Here we touch on matters that are little understood. It seems to me that we must break away, sharply and radically, from much of modern social and behavioural science if we are to move towards a deeper understanding of these matters.[59]

## Generative grammar and libertarian values

Chomsky goes on to say that here too the libertarian tradition has a contribution to offer, namely, the work on language, in particular Humboldt's. "Humbolt was, on the one hand, one of the most profound theorists of general linguistics, and on the other, an early and forceful advocate of libertarian values." Is there any relation between his linguistics and his libertarianism? Though he does not "explicitly relate his ideas about language to his libertarian social thought, there is quite clearly a common ground from which they develop, a concept of human nature that inspires each."[60] For this reason, "Humboldt's conception of language must be considered against the background provided by his writings on social and political theory and the concept of human nature that underlies them." He has been described by Rudolf Rocker as "the most prominent representative in Germany" of the doctrine of natural rights and of the opposition to the authoritarian state. "His denunciation of excessive state power [and of any sort of dogmatic faith] is based on his advocacy of the fundamental human right to develop a personal individuality through meaningful creative work and unconstrained thought." For him "the urge for self-realization is man's basic human need (as distinct from his merely animal needs)… But state control is incompatible with this human need." "There is something utterly degrading to humanity in the very thought that some human being's right to be human could be abrogated," he writes. It is clear, then, Chomsky goes on to conclude, that "Humboldt's emphasis on the spontaneous and creative aspects of language use derives from a much more general concept of 'human nature,' a concept which he did not originate but which he developed and elaborated in original and important ways."[61]

It is no less clear that those remarks about Humboldt are at least just as applicable to Chomsky. There is a long way, however, from the Humboldtian concept "form of language" to the deepest and most developed form of the theory of human language (generative grammar).[62] If it is true that "a good case can be made in support of the empirical claim that such a system can be acquired, under the given conditions of time and access, only by a mind that is endowed with certain specific properties that we can now tentatively describe in some detail," this is due mainly to Chomsky's work. Furthermore, the study of language inspired in his work provides a model for other cognitive sciences, since it suggests that "other aspects of human psychology and culture might, in principle, be studied in a similar way":

Conceivably, we might in this way develop a social science based on empirically well-founded propositions concerning human nature. Just as we study the range of humanly attainable languages, with some success, we might also try to study the forms of artistic expression or, for that matter, scientific knowledge that humans can conceive, and perhaps even the range of ethical systems and social structures in which humans can live and function, given their intrinsic capacities and needs. Perhaps one might go on to project a concept of social organization that would—under given conditions of material and spiritual culture—best encourage and accommodate the fundamental human need—if such it is—for spontaneous initiative, creative work, solidarity, pursuit of social justice.[63]

The polar opposite is not hard to fathom:

In the same way we can imagine a society in which no one could survive as a social being because it does not correspond to biologically determined perceptions and human social needs. For historical reasons, existing societies might have such properties, leading to various forms of pathology.[64]

We might conceivably develop a true social science in the future, but it is not around the corner. For the time being, "scientific socialism" or "scientific anarchism" are expressions which do not refer to anything we know or can come to know. Contrary to some XIX century speculations that are rather naive, all known varieties of socialism are utopian, although not all of them have to be chimerical also.[65] None seems to have more in its favor than libertarian socialism. Being free of dogma, it is not incompatible with anything known or with anything true scientists might discover. In particular, it appears to be the one "advanced and given substance as we discover the rich system of invariant structures and principles that underlie the most ordinary and humblest of human accomplishments," that is, the creative use of language.[66] This is of some importance. Anyone concerned with human distinctiveness and potential is led to a consideration of the properties of language. Even behaviourist psychologists recognize that only through a successful analysis of language can we hope to come to terms with human behaviour, or if you prefer, with conduct (we don't speak of the "conduct" of an animal or a falling stone).[67]

If the first necessary step towards a truly scientific psychology is a theory of language, it is of some interest to know that we already have the beginnings of such a theory. Since the epoch-making breakthrough, brought about only a quarter of a century ago [ca. 1950], "we can at least begin to speculate coherently about the acquisition of certain systems of knowledge and belief on the basis of experience and genetic endowment, and can outline the general nature of some device that might duplicate aspects of this achievement."[68] Nothing comparable has been achieved so far in any other branch of psychology. Thus the theory of language might offer an entering wedge, or perhaps a model, for an investigation of the mind that would provide the grounding for a much broader theory of human nature—perhaps broad enough to include a true "social science" and truly scientific theories of ethics and aesthetics.

At the moment this is little more than wishful thinking, which is why Chomsky is extremely careful not to relate his view of anarcho-syndicalism too closely to the scientific work on generative grammar, recognizing, however, that "there are very loose and tenuous relations that one can find." How does he see these relations? Here is the most recent statement on the matter I am aware of:

> I believe that the study of human cognitive structures and human intellectual achievements reveals a high degree of genetically deter-mined innate structure that lies at the basis of the creative aspect of human intellectual achievement, which is easily perceived in every aspect of normal intellectual development, most strikingly, most eas-ily, perhaps, in the acquisition and free use of the system of language, which permit the free expression of thought over an unbounded range.
>
> Similarly, I think—we can here only speculate because so little is known—that related aspects of human nature lie at the core of the continuing human search for freedom from authoritarian rule, from external restriction, from repressive structures, what might be called an instinct for freedom. It is conceivable that such an instinct for free-dom exists and is deeply rooted in human nature and is related some-how, in ways that we don't know, to the elements that we can already discover in studying some aspects of human nature, such as human cognitive achievements. However, again I would want to be extreme-ly cautious in drawing any connections between these two areas. We certainly can't draw any clear, explicit connections between them, only some general hints.[69]

As he had written ten years earlier, "for the moment, an honest scientist will admit at once that we understand virtually nothing, at the level of scientific inquiry, with regard to human freedom and dignity;" "we cannot, at present, turn to science for insight into these matters. To pretend otherwise is pure fraud."[70] But science does have something to say about the basic similarity and equality among human beings, and it is not exactly what some people would like to hear:

> It seems to me a matter of fact, as far as current science perceives it, that there are basic and fundamental elements of human nature in its cognitive aspects which are uniform across the species. The areas that are best understood, in particular such matters as language— here we find, as far as we can tell, a very rich innate endowment which seems to be shared across the species. If there are variations, they are so slight, at least by current measures, that we can barely detect them. This is not to say that there are no individual differences,

only that they are extremely slight and marginal as compared with the major principles and structural elements that simply are definitive of human nature in these domains. That much seems to be true.[71]

The fact that there is no known scientific basis for racism should not blind us to the point of denying the obvious or deploring what we should welcome. "Experience seems to support the belief that people do vary in their intellectual capacities and their specialization":

> Human talents vary considerably, within a fixed framework that is characteristic of the species and that permits ample scope for creative work, including the creative work of appreciating the achievements of others. This should be a matter for delight rather than a condition to be abhorred... My pleasure in life is enhanced by the fact that others can do many things that I cannot, and I see no reason to want to deny these people the opportunity to cultivate their talents, consistent with general social needs. Difficult questions of practice are sure to arise in any functioning social group, but I see no problem of principle.[72]

## Theory and action

We may or may not "like to believe that the intensive study of one aspect of human psychology—human language—may contribute to a humanistic science that will serve, as well, as an instrument for social action," but for those committed to social justice or survival, action cannot await a firmly established social science. No human tradition can count on a more solid intellectual fund than that of libertarian socialism—or on a fund which has been tapped proportionately less. Scholarly or State Department Newspeak propagated by the media is not the only obstacle libertarian socialism has to contend with, but other difficulties would not loom that large once apathy and defeatism are overcome. For a rational person the effectiveness of any attempt to present a vision of a future society depends on the coherence of the argument, and no argument known to me is more coherent than the libertarian socialist one for people in touch with the simple virtues—people who are honest and truthful, responsible and concerned. There is much that is wrong with the world today, but there are also encouraging signs. A crucial one is that the renewed impulse the Indochina War gave to self-analysis and the search for alternatives is still alive:

> There is a growing realization that it is an illusion to believe that all will be well if only today's liberal [or illiberal] hero can be placed in the White House, and a growing awareness that isolated, competing, individuals can rarely confront repressive institutions alone. At best, a few may be tolerated as intellectual gadflies... In a fragmented, competitive society, individuals can neither discover their true interests nor act to defend them, as they cannot do so when prevented from free association by totalitarian controls.[73]

It is a fair guess that recognition of these facts will no doubt contribute to bring people together in various forms of resistance, in addition to fostering new attempts at community organizing, confirming Chomsky's earliest projections, as well as more recent ones. It seems only fitting to close this outline of his social theory with a timely quote from his latest political essay, written just a few weeks ago (on Feb. 4, 1981, to be exact), which is unlikely to lose its validity any time soon:

> Political, intellectual and business 'elites' are intent on learning the lessons of the Vietnam war, and the same should be true for people who are appalled by their commitment to murder and oppression in the service of their needs and wants. The spontaneous and largely leaderless mass peace movement in the United States, which so frightened those in power, had its impact, but it was far too slow to develop. The time to stop the Vietnam war was in 1960-1, when plans were being laid for the direct U.S. attack on South Vietnam that began shortly after as it became clear that the regime installed by the United States would be unable to control the population with the resources of violence and repression that had been provided. Correspondingly, the time to stop the coming Central American war is now. And the opportunity is there. While the propaganda system is continually announcing the shift to the right and conservative takeover, the fact is that popular opposition to U.S. aggression is far higher now than it was at a comparable stage of the Vietnam intervention…
>
> [The author of a revealing article published in the Winter 1980-81 issue of the journal *Foreign Affairs* of the Council of Foreign Relations under the title "The Purposes of American Power"] draws back from directly advocating the more 'appealing' program of resurgent America (the more drastic) on grounds of an estimate of costs, including the costs of an aroused public opinion, a factor that can be influenced, as in the past. His outline of this program, and the many others like it, should not be dismissed as outlandish or absurd, but rather taken as a warning to be heeded, before it is too late.[74]

Carlos-Peregrín Otero

# Notes

* I am indebted to Kaky McTigue for a long and very thoughtful letter on my underlying theme, and for a careful reading of the following pages and the changes it led to.

1. Paul Robinson, review of Chomsky's *Language and Responsibility*, in *New York Times Book Review*, 25 Feb. 1979, pp. 3 & 37 (see also Linda McQuaig's review of Chomsky & Edward S. Herman, *The Political*

*Economy of Human Rights*, in *Maclean's*, 19 Aug. 1980, p. 37). "Reading Chomsky on Linguistics—he writes—, one repeatedly has the impression of attending to one of the more powerful thinkers who ever lived." He believes that "the most important matters to take note of are his uninflected rationalism and his awesome dialectical skill" (see n. 5 below), and goes on to suggest that Chomsky is sort of modern Tacitus. See. below, in particular the pages including nn. 16–18.

2. As a point of departure, the interested reader may refer to Justin Leiber, *Noam Chomsky: A Philosophic Overview*, New York: St. Martin's Press, 1975; John Lyons, *Noam Chomsky*, 3rd ed., Fontana, 1991. Other overviews of his work are R. Salkie, *The Chomsky Update: Linguistics and Politics* London: Unwin Hyman 1990; M.C. Haley & R. L. Lundsford, *Noam Chomsky*. New York: Twayne, 1994; P. Wilkin, *Noam Chomsky: on Power, Knowledge and Human Nature* London: Macmillan; New York: St. Martin's Press,1997; J. McGilvray, *Chomsky: Language, Mind, Politics,* Cambridge, U.K.: Polity Press, 1999; N. Smith, *Chomsky: Ideas and Ideals.* Cambridge, U.K.: Cambridge University Press, 1999; C. P. Otero, *Chomsky for Everyone* and *Chomsky's Revolution: Cognitivism and Anarchism,* (Oxford: Blackwell), (forthcoming). There is also a *Chomsky for Beginners.* D. Cogswell. New York: Writers and Readers Publishing, Inc./London: Writers and Readers, 1996 and, in the same vein, *Introducing Chomsky.* by J. Maher & J. Groves New York: Totem Books, 1997. R. Barsky's *Noam Chomsky: a Life of Dissent,* (Cambridge, MA: MIT Press, 1997), includes very interesting biographical information.

   For a wide range of comments on a variety of aspects of Chomsky's work, see *Noam Chomsky: Critical Assessments*, ed. C. P. Otero. London: Routledge, 1994. (A 4-volume, 8-tome collection of articles on Chomsky's linguistics,philosophy, and anthropology and on the impact of his work's on contemporary thought), and references there, in particular those in the introduction to each of the 4 volumes.

3. Charles Kadushin, *The American Intellectual Elite*. Boston and Toronto: Little, Brown and Co. 1974, p. 188. See. *Time* magazine, 9 May 1969, pp, 48–49.

4. See Chomsky, **IS**, in particular p. 24; **TCW**, p. 76. (For the abbreviations of the titles of Chomsky's books, see the Editor's Preliminary Note.)

5. Ian Hacking. review of Chomsky's *Rules and Representations*, in *New York Review of Books* (23 Oct. 1990), 47–50. Professor Hacking (who was at the time chair of the Department of Philosophy at Stanford University) adds that Chomsky "almost always wins," but he does not identify the instance or instances of a draw or worse that he might have in mind. See. *The Behavioral and Brain Sciences* 3 (1980), pp. 1–61. See now Rudolf P. Botha, *Challenging Chomsky: the Generative Garden Game*. Oxford: Basil Blackwell, 1989; also, C. P. Otero, "Language, Meaning and Interpretation: Chomsky Against the Philosophers," to appear in *Semantics: Critical Concepts*. ed. J. Gutiérrez-Rexach, London: Routledge, 2003.

6. Interestingly, the full version of Chomsky's review of Kissinger's *White House Years*, completed in January 1980 (included in **TCW** as ch. 6.), never found a place in an English periodical. A shortened version was published in *Inquiry* (Apr., 1980) under the title "Deception as a Way of Life" (an original strip on the cover to go along with the review was given the title "Whitewash Years"). I return to the question of the logical prowess of the typical State apologist in the passage that includes n. 17.

7. **IS**, pp. 31–32; **TCW**, pp. 80–81. See now **NI**, motivated by the concern that "citizens of a democratic societies should undertake a course in intellectual self-defense to protect themselves from manipulation and control, and to lay the basis for meaningful democracy" (p. viii), which he has repeatedly expressed since at least June 1966 (see **CD&E**, ch. 16).

8. Eloise Trosan & Michael Yates. "Brainwashing Under Freedom," *Monthly Review* Jan. 1981, p. 51. Trosan and Yates continue: "the authors make a powerful case against the media by analyzing almost exclusively the *best* and *most liberal* establishment newspapers and magazines. Imagine how much more 'brainwashing under freedom' they would have uncovered had they studied radio and television news and small-town media. We live in a town where most people never read the *NY Times*. Instead they read a newspaper which does not allot adequate space even to local labor disputes, let alone the transgressions of the Shah, and which does not feature a single liberal columnist." (see the n. to Selection 6.) See also George Scialabba, "The Free World Gulag," *The Village Voice* 18–24 Jun. 1980, p. 35.

9. The quotes are from the review by Linda McQuaig (see n. 1). As she points out, an earlier version was suppressed by the Warner communications and entertainment conglomerate, the parent firm of its American publisher (see the "Prefatory note" to volume I of **PE**). Fortunately, "Three small publishing houses—one in London, one in Boston and Black Rose in Montréal—then persuaded Chomsky and Herman to expand the draft into a larger work, which they did."

10. Chomsky, Introduction (written in June 1980) to a collection of his political writings in Japanese. Braestrup claims to demonstrate that the U.S. media contributed to the defeat of U.S. arms in Vietnam by biased and distorted reporting of the Tet offensive. For a contrary view and a justification of the statement quoted, see Chomsky's review of Braestrup's book in *Race and Class* 20 (1978). See now **NI**, p. 5ff.

11. Here is (between brackets) the part censored by the liberal editors:

"In TNR, Jan. 3, Martin Peretz complains that 'You don't write about Noarn Chomsky unless you are eager to get into a long correspondence or willing to be a bad correspondent' [referring to his comments on my alleged 'apologetics on behalf of the Honorable Pol Pot.' The facts are worth noting.
In TNR, Feb. 17 1979, Peretz wrote about these alleged 'apologetics,' basing himself not on anything I had written but on gossip he had picked up in Paris. I wrote a letter in response. In June, I inquired about the failure to publish my letter. Peretz informed me apologetically that it had been 'lost' but would of course be published at once. Several months later I inquired again and was informed by Peretz that he would not permit my letter to be published, an interesting revelation of journalistic standards. This is the 'long correspondence' to which he refers.] Now Peretz claims…"
To show his true colors even better, Martin Peretz attached a "reply" to the mutilated letter dealing, thoroughly dishonestly, "with the question of Chomsky's honesty"—a reply in the tradition of Zhdanov (characterized in n. 12). See Chomsky, "The Faurisson Affair: His Right to Say It," *The Nation*, 28 Feb. 1981, pp. 231–234, **EP**, **RI**, and **CD&E**, ch. 6, pp. 120–124 and 419.

12. It shouldn't hurt to add here that Andrey Zhdanov (1896–1948), party secretary of the Central Committee in control of ideology and a close associate of Stalin, was the initiator and first promoter of Zhdanovism, a cultural policy introduced in the Soviet Union in the period 1946–48 ('the Zhdanov time' or *Zhdanovshchina*), sometimes associated more readily with Orwell's *1984*, which brought heavy pressure to bear on prominent writers who were deemed not to be following Party doctrine. See Selection 26.
13. Chomsky, Introduction to **HR**. For a libertarian and much earlier denunciation of Gulag, see Gregory P. Maximoff, *The Guillotine at Work : Twenty Years of Terror in Russia (Data and Documents)*, in two volumes. First published in Chicago in 1940 by the Alexander Berkman Fund, reissued in 1979 by Cienfuegos Press (Over the Water, Sanday, Orkney, KW17 2BL, Great Britain) with an Introduction by Bill Nowlin and a note on Maximoff by his disciple Sam Dolgoff. See also n. 8 of my Introduction to **L&P**.
14. I will draw freely from a paper on Chomsky's social theory I presented at the First International Symposium on Anarchism, which took place at Lewis and Clark College, Portland, Oregon, Feb. 17–24, 1980. I am indebted to the organizers of the Symposium and to many of the participants for their reactions and comments.
15. Chomsky, **L&R**, p. 80.
16. Chomsky, "Restoring the faith," *Black Rose* 4 (Winter 1979), pp. 23–24. The dire consequences of apathy are stressed again and again in Chomsky's work, from the very beginning, e.g. Introduction and page before Epilogue in **AP**, chapter 2 of **PKF** (in particular, p. 93).
17. Chomsky, **HR**, p. 35.
18. Chomsky, Introduction to **AP**, pp. 17–18.
19. Quoted by Chomsky in **AWA**, p. 305: see also p. 311. Cf. **FRS**, especially chapter 3.
20. See *Crimes of War*, ed. by Richard A. Falk, Gabriel Kolko & Robert Jay Lifton, New York: Random House, 1971, in particular "Pacification in Vietnam" by David Welsh and the section "Machines Against People" of Kolko's "War crimes and the nature of the Vietnam war."
21. Stephen Morris, "Chomsky on U.S. Foreign Policy," *Harvard International Review* 3.4 (1981), p. 3. On the program of "forced-draft urbanization and modernization" proposed by Samuel Huntington ("The Bases of Accommodation", *Foreign Affairs*, July 1968) to "produce a massive migration from countryside to city" by the "direct application of mechanical and conventional power" (Newspeak for "mass murder and physical destruction of a defenseless rural society"), see **AP** (in particular p. 13, p. 42ff.), **AWA**, **PKF**, **FRS**, and many other writings by Chomsky. See Selections 2 and 12.
22. **HR**, pp. 1–2. See Selection 1.
23. **IS**, p. 37. See also **AP**, in particular p. 350; **AWA**, especially chapter 1; and **FRS**, especially chapters 1–2. Cf. Selection 10.
24. Introduction to Japanese collection (see n. 10 above).
25. **IS**, p. 4. For an excellent selection of Bakunin's writings ("by far the best available in English," in Chomsky's opinion), see *Bakunin on Anarchism*, edited by Sam Dolgoff. Revised edition. (Montréal: Black Rose Books, 1980). A monumental edition of Bakunin's complete works in French and Russian, with Introductions and copious notes by Arthur Lehning, an extremely dedicated and knowledgeable student and disciple of Bakunin, is now in the process of being published for the Amsterdam International Institute of Social History, and is being reprinted in volumes of smaller size by Editions Champ Libre, Paris. Seven volumes have been published to date (of the projected fifteen), each exceeding 350 pages.
26. See "Psychology and Ideology," reprinted as chapter 7 of **FRS**.
27. **L&R**, pp. 77–78. See the confrontation of Chomsky's and Foucault's ideas in "Human Nature: Justice vs. Power," printed edited version of a Dutch television broadcast included in *Reflexive Water: The Basic Concerns of Mankind*. ed. by Fons Elders, Ontario. Canada: J.M. Dent & Sons, 1974. pp. 133–197, and

C. P. Otero, "Chomsky v. Foucault: Pursue Justice or Grab Power?," in Chomsky's *The Masters of Mankind*, ed. Mark Pavlick (to appear).

28. See **CL**, n. 51; **FRS**, ch. 9, n. 15. It is worth noting that Chomsky's first book was published (still not complete) only twenty years later (in 1975).

29. Isaiah Berlin, *Russian Thinkers*, New York: Penguin Books, 1979, pp. 82–113. Se Paul Avrich, *The Russian Anarchists*. Princeton University Press, 1967.

30. **RR**, p. 9 (see also p. 242). See Isaiah Berlin, *Vico and Herder: Two Studies in the History of Ideas*. London: The Hogarth Press, 1976. Berlin points out that "Vico was a conservative, not to say reactionary, intellectually as well as personally close to the Jesuits" and that "the whole of Vico's doctrine… has a conservative tendency" (p. 122). It is then of particular interest to notice, as Chomsky does, that Vico is among those who observed that "there is no liberty when people are 'drowned… in a sea of usury' and must 'pay off their debts by work and toil' " (Chomsky, "[Equality:] Language development, human intelligence, and social organization," in *Equality and Social Policy*. ed. by Walter Feinberg, University of Illinois Press, 1978, pp. 163–188, reprinted in **ChR**, pp. 183–202, and in **CD&E** as ch. 6, henceforth "Equality," with page references to **CD&E**). Vico's observation can be read as an anticipation of the idea that "capitalist economic relations perpetuated a form of bondage which, as early as 1767, Simon Linguet had declared to be even worse than slavery" (**FRS**, ch. 9, p. 400). Cf. the references of n. 37 below.

11. **L&R**, p. 77. See also **L&R**, p. 95; **RL**, ch. 3 (in particular the last pages); and n. 59ff. below.

32. **FRS**, ch. 9, pp. 395–396 (for more on Rousseau, see ch. 9, nn. 15 and 19; cf. p. 374). See also note 59 below.

33. These quotes and the following one are from Chomsky's "Notes on Anarchism," reprinted as ch. 8 of **FRS** (pp. 370–371). As he has pointed out, "Marx would not have disagreed" with Rocker's conception of freedom, "and the basic conceptions can be traced back to earlier libertarian thought" ("Equality," p. 108). Some of the roots of these conceptions are discussed in "Language and Freedom," reprinted as ch. 9 of **FRS**. I will return to the basic points of agreement of "such socialists as Marx, Bakunin, Rocker, and others of the [authentic] left" ("Equality", p. 108–109). See n. 38ff., and n. to Selection 9.

34. See Emile Benveniste, *Problèmes de Linguistique Générale*. Paris: Gallimard, 1966, last paper in the collection.

35. Reprinted by Beacon Press in 1957. See also *Primitive, Archaic and Modern Economies: Essays of Karl Polanyi*, ed. by George Dalton, reprinted by Beacon Press in 1971, in particular Dalton's Introduction. See chapt. 4 ("Linguistics versus Liberalism") of Geoffrey Sampson's *Liberty and Language*. Oxford University Press, 1979, reviewed by James D. McCawley in *Language* 56 (1980), 639–647, and earlier in *Inquiry* (10 Sept 1979, pp. 22–24), and, far more perceptively, by D. Lightfoot in *Journal of Linguistics* 17 (1981), pp. 160–173. See n. 36.

36. *Men of Ideas. Face to Face with Fifteen of the World's Foremost Philosophers*. by Brian Magee, New York: The Viking Press, 1978, pp. 222–223, a paraphrase of a passage in Chomsky's "Language and Freedom" (**FRS**, p. 400), which is itself a paraphrase of a passage in his "Notes on Anarchism" (**FRS**, pp, 375–376). Needless to say, the so-called "new libertarians" of our own day fail to adapt the basic reasoning of the classical liberals, here called libertarians, of the XVIII century to our very different social era. See Chris Hables Gray, "The new libertarians," *Black Rose* 3 (1979), pp. 29–39.

37. **FRS**, ch. 8, pp. 376–377 (the internal quotes are from Marx). See also "Equality," p. 109–10.

38. "Equality," p. 108; see also **FRS**, ch. 8, pp. 381 and 383–384, and below, including the text corresponding to note 44. See Paul Thomas, *Karl Marx and the Anarchists*. London, Boston and Henley: Routledge & Kegan Paul, 1980; C. P. Otero, "De Marx y Bakunin a Chomsky," *Cuadernos de Ruedo Ibérico* 55–57 (1977), pp. 107–125.

39. Penny Lernoux, *Cry of the People*. Garden City, N.Y.: Doubleday, 1980. See the references of n. 51 below.

40. **L&R**, p. 80, and the interview conducted by Fons Elders (see n. 27 above). On the legitimacy of violence, see "On resistance" and its supplement in **AP**, and the panel discussion in *Dissent, Power, and Confrontation*, edited by Alexander Klein, (New York: McGraw-Hill, 1971), pp. 95–133. (The panelists were Hannah Arendt, Noam Chomsky, Robert Lowell, and Conor Cruise O'Brien, and the discussants Mitchell Goodman, Susan Sontag and Robert Paul Wolff; the discussion took place in New York on December 15, 1967, that is, just a few days after "On Resistance" appeared in *The New York Review of Books*.)

41. Victor Lebow, *"Free Enterprise:" The Opium of the American People*, (New York: Oriole Books, 1972).

42. This characterization is given by Chomsky in an interview conducted by Mitsou Ronat in March 1977 which was to appear in *Nouvel Observateur*. It was first published (more than ten years later) in **L&P** as I8 (I9 in the second edition).

43. See **FRS**, ch. 8, n. 18. See the references of n. 38 above.

44. **L&R**, p. 74. These remarks bring to mind a comment by an anarcho-syndicalist of long standing (and a dear friend) to the effect that the trouble with anarchism today is that it doesn't have a philosopher with the stature of those of the so-called Frankfurt School. See the references of note 2 above, in particular the first one.

45. See n. 31 above.

46. See Laurence H. Shoup & William Minter, *Imperial Brain Trust: The Council of Foreign Relations and U.S. Foreign Policy*, (New York: Monthly Review Press, 1977), and **FRS**, chs. 1 and 2.

47. There are conceptions of anarchism which apparently reject "syndicalism" (in the sense stipulated). Cf John P. Clark, "What is Anarchism?" in *Anarchism*, ed. J. Roland Pennock & John W. Chapman, New York: New York University Press, 1978 (*Nomos* XIX), pp. 3–28, in particular p. 23. Clark's sense of obsolescence seems to have been affected by the mirage of the twenty years following World War II (see the reference of **FRS**, ch. 8, n. 27); ironically enough, his position is reminiscent of that of the Spanish physician Isaac Puente, murdered by Franco partisans in August 1936 (see the outline of the principles of "comunismo libertario" Sam Dolgoff gives in the collection edited by him under the title *The Anarchist Collectives: Worker Self-management in the Spanish Revolution 1936–39*). Montréal: Black Rose Books, 1974. In any case, Clark's approach to the history of anarchism differs radically from Chomsky's (see the quote corresponding to n. 27 above). Still, his paper is, to my mind, one of the most valuable among those included in volume XIX of *Nomos* (yearbook of the American Society for Political and Legal Philosophy). See the references of n. 48–50 below and *Reinventing Anarchy* ed. by Howard J. Ehrlich et. al. Oakland: AK Press, 1996, especially Part 3.

48. **FRS**, ch. 8, pp. 377–378 (see also pp. 372 and 376, and ch. 9, pp. 403–404). The internal quote "a practical school of anarchism" is from Fernand Pelloutier's "L'anarchisme et les Syndicats Ouvriers" (1895), reprinted in D. Guérin's excellent historical anthology *Ni Dieu, Ni Maitre* (in English *No Gods No Masters*. Oakland: AK Press,1998, 2 vols.); the expression "third and last emancipatory phase" is from Buber's *Paths in Utopia* (see note 65 below). See the references of n. 37 above and the last two quotes of n. 30.

49. **FRS**, ch. 8, pp. 371–372.

50. "Anarchism: Past and present," *Comment* I.6 (1980), especially pp. 2 and 9–10, a corrected version of a lecture given at UCLA on May 29, 1980. Bookchin concedes that the emphasis of anarcho-syndicalists "on an ethical socialism, on direct action, on control from below, and their apolitical stance may serve to keep them afloat" (p. 6). See C. P. Otero, "Acracia o Anacronismo," *Cuadernos de Ruedo Ibérico* 58–60 (1977), pp. 123–155, and *Reinventing Anarchy* (n. 47 above).

    It seems worth noting that Bookchin's contrast between "embryonic growth" and "inorganic accretion" is reminiscent of the emphasis of the Romantics, in particular the great libertarian Wilhelm von Humboldt, on "organic form." See **CL**, ch. 1, especially p. 22ff.; also, C. P. Otero, Introduction to **CD&E**, p. 15ff.

51. **FRS**, ch. 9, pp. 398–399, see also ch. 6.

52. See *Carbon Dioxide and Climate: A Scientific Assessment*, Washington, D.C.: National Academy of Sciences, 1979 (a report of an ad hoc study group completed in July 1979, which apparently is far more optimistic than more recent unpublished estimates), and, for a survey of the literature, indicating an increase in concern during the years 1975–1978, Gregg Marland & Ralph M. Rotty, "Carbon dioxide and climate," *Review of Geophysics and Space Physics* 17.7 Oct. (1979), pp. 1813–1824; see now *The Impact of Carbon Dioxide and other Greenhouse Gases on Forest Ecosystems*, ed. David F. Karnosky et al., Oxon [England]; New York: CABI Pub. in association with the International Union of Forestry Research Organizations, 2001 (Report no. 3 of the IUFRO Task Force on Environmental Change) and Martyn Turner & Brian O'Connell, *The Whole World's Watching: Decarbonizing the Economy and Saving the World*, Chichester, West Sussex, England; New York: John Wiley, 2001, among many other publications. See the reference to Polanyi (see n. 35 above) in **FRS**, ch. 9. p. 400.

    As to the likelihood of nuclear war before the end of the century, see, in addition to the Mar. 1981 issue of *The Bulletin of the Atomic Scientists*, the "Notes from the editors," *Monthly Review* 32.9 (1981), the article by E.P. Thompson in *The Nation* 24 Jan. 1981, and *Nuclear Armaments: An interview, with Dr. Daniel Ellsberg*, The Conservation Press (Box 201, 2526 Shattuck Av, Berkeley, CA 94704), among many other recent references, in particular Ellsberg's *Papers on the War*. New York: Simon and Schuster, 1972, and his recent *Secrets: A Memoir of Vietnam and the Pentagon Papers*. New York: Viking, 2002.

53. See C. P. Otero, "Human Nature: From Medieval Scholasticism to Chomskyan Rationalism." 1980 UCLA ms., published, under the title "[Contribution to the round table on] the conception of human nature in Chomsky," in *Quaderni di Semantica* [an international journal of theoretical and applied semantics published in Bologna, Italy] 2 (1981), 241–247. Reprinted in *Noam Chomsky: Critical Assesments*, III.

54. See Chomsky, "Toward a humanistic conception of education," in *Work. Technology, and Education: Dissenting Essays in the Intellectual Foundations of American Education*, ed. by Walter Feinberg & Henry Rosemont, Jr., Champaign: University of Illinois Press, 1975, pp. 204–220, especially p. 213; David Corson, "Chomsky on Education," *The Australian Journal of Education* 24.2 (1980), pp. 164–185. See now **CD&E**, where Chomsky's essay is reprinted together with other writings by him on education and democracy.

55. Quoted in **PKF**, p. 55, from a quote by Bertrand Russell from Kropotkin's "Anarchist Communism." See **FRS**, ch. 7, especially pp. 346 and 352.

56. **AP**, pp. 323–324; see also "The Revolutionary Pacifism of A.J. Muste," in particular pp. 163–169, beginning with the passage: "There is no particular merit in being more reasonable than a lunatic; correspondingly, almost any policy is more rational than one that accepts repeated risk of nuclear war, hence a near guarantee of nuclear war in the long run—a 'long run' that is unlikely to be very long, given the risks that policy makers are willing to accept…"

57. **L&R**, p. 128; see also **L&M**, ch. 1. For a critique of behaviourism, see **FRS**, ch. 7; also ch. 3 of Leiber's book (n. 2 above). See n. 59 below.

58. See *Language and Learning: The Debate Between Jean Piaget and Noam Chomsky*, ed. by Massimo Piattelli-Palmarini,(Cambridge: Harvard University Press,1980), and **RR**. See also n. 53 above.

59. **FRS**, ch. 9, 403–404.

60. Ibid., p. 397.

61. **CL**, pp. 24–26; see also the interview "Linguistics and Politics," *New Left Review* 57 (1969), pp. 21–34 (reprinted in **L&P** as I4), and **L&R**, p. 3ff. Cf. Leiber, ch. 3, and Lyons, Appendix 2 (see n. 2 above).

62. See Chomsky, *Lectures on Government and Binding: The Pisa Lectures*, Dordrecht, Holland: Foris Publications, 1981, (revised ed., 1982; 7th reprint, 1993), completed in December 1980; *Knowledge of Language: Its Nature, Origin, and Use*. New York: Praeger, 1986; *The Minimalist Program*. Cambridge, MA: The MIT Press, 1995; and, especially, his latest technical paper, "Beyond Explanatory Adequacy," *MIT Occasional Papers in Linguistics, no. 20*, Cambridge: MIT Working Papers in Linguistics, MIT Department of Linguistic and Philosophy, 2001.

63. **FRS**, 9, p. 405.

64. **L&R**, p. 70. Here is the latest example of a manifestation of social pathology to come to my attention: Although "more children are murdered by their parents in the United States than in Japan," "homicides of children aged 4 or younger in the United States constitute a mere 4.3 percent of the total; in Japan, such homicides account for more than 25 percent of a much smaller total." "Scholars cite a weakening of the family as society's main pillar and the stress women suffer as a result of the continuing limitations placed on their role in Japanese society" (*Los Angeles Times*, Mar. 8, 1981, Part I–A, pp. 1–2). Chomsky has denounced many others, no less criminal. A single paragraph may serve as illustration: "Over 90 percent of the population lived under conditions of increasing misery, for many, comparable to Central Africa. In rural areas with ample fertile land—in the hands of landowners protected by the security forces and devoted to agroexport in the approved manner—medical researchers describe a "new species," pygmies, with 40 percent the brain size of humans, the result of protracted starvation. Cities compete for world championships in child slavery and murder of street children by security forces. University of Sao Paulo Professor of Theology Father Barruel informed the UN that "75 percent of the corpses [of murdered children] reveal internal mutilation and the majority have their eyes removed," allegedly for an international organ transplant racket. The luckier ones survive, sniffing glue to relieve hunger. The litany of horrors is endless." (**WOON**, ch. 2, p. 137.)

65. See Martin Buber, *Paths in Utopia*, Boston: Beacon Press, 1958, (completed in the spring of 1945, and first published in English in 1949).

66. **PKF**, p. 51.

67. It might be to read too much into a terminological innovation, but the preference for "behaviour" over "conduct" seems revealing (see 1. **L&M**, ch. 3). Recall that John Dewey's *Human Nature and Conduct* appeared in 1922.

68. **FRS**, ch. 7, p. 363.

69. Chomsky, interview conducted by Hanna Reime in Pisa, Italy, on Jun. 7, 1979, included in **L&P** as I39 (I13 in the second edition). (I am indebted to Jan Koster for having sent me a typed copy). See also **FRS**, ch. 7, p. 361. see **CL**, especially p. 14. See now Noam Chomsky: *Critical Assessments* (n. 2 above).

70. **FRS**, ch. 7, p. 363, see also ch. 9, p. 406.

71. Chomsky, Pisa Interview (see note 69). As Harry Bracken has argued, "racism is easily and readily stateable if one thinks of the person in accordance with empiricist teaching" (see **RL**, ch. 3, p. 130; also, **L&R**, p. 92).

72. "Equality", p. 116.

73. Introduction to **AP**, p. 18.
74. "Resurgent America," *Socialist Review* (included in **TCW**). On the Council on Foreign Relations, see Shoup & Minter (note 46 above) and Shoup, *The Carter Presidency and Beyond: Power and Politics in the 1980s*. Foreword by Richard A. Falk, Palo Alto: Ramparts Press, 1980. See Selection 12. (The first important expression of "popular opposition to U.S. aggression" by Americans in the 80s was clearly manifested on May 3, particularly in Washington. D.C.. as reported in *Win*, Jun. 15, 1981, pp. 16-21.)

# Part I:

## In Defense of the Third World

## Editor's Notes to Chapter 1

Written on Jan. 28, 1977 for *Partisan Review*. Unpublished.

The concern with terminology, in particular when special usage is part of an effort to delude the public, is pervasive in Chomsky's political writings since "The Responsibility of Intellectuals" (e.g., "There is much to be learned from a careful study of the terms in which this distinction is drawn," **APNM**, p. 333 (for the abbreviations, see the Editor's Preliminary Note); "The crucial words are...," **APNM**, p. 343). His observations on "Pentagonese" (**FRS**, ch. 1, p. 78) are of course reminiscent of Orwell's characterization of Newspeak, except that Chomsky is much better equipped for the job (see his comments on the "conceptual framework" for counter insurgency, in particular on the concept of "aggression," e.g., **APNM**, p. 59, **FRS**, 1.6; see now his **NHSL**). On the mentality behind the terminology of the social sciences, see, e.g., **APNM**, p. 41 ff.

For Chomsky, this sort of conceptual analysis (for a more sophisticated example, see "Equality" ("Introduction to Chomsky's Social Theory," n. 30)) has little to do with the study of the structure of language. But for other linguists, it does, and it is somewhat ironical that some of them deplore Chomsky's lack of interest in the matters they are concerned with (usually because they consider only Chomsky's "professional" writings).

About "the idea that foreign policy is derived in the manner of physics is sheer myth," see Selection 12.

# 1. On the "National Interest"

The concept "national interest" has been so debased by propagandists that it is probably best abandoned. Nevertheless, it is conceivable that it might be rehabilitated as a useful term for the analysis of international affairs in a world of nation-states. In such a world, it might on occasion be the case that in the welter of individual, class, and other group interests, some concerns might be identified that are largely shared by citizens of a particular nation-state. The interest in not being overrun by foreign force, for example. In practice, the "nation" will be divided even on this elemental issue; no occupying army has lacked collaborators to perform its filthy work. Still, at the level of vagueness and generality characteristic of the terminology of social and political analysis, one might resurrect a reasonable notion of "national interest" along these lines.

But the exercise is academic, even deceptive. Within the nation-state, the "national interest" will be articulated by those who control the central economic and political institutions. There is no reason to suppose that the "national interest," so articulated, will have any relation to such common interests as might be generally shared within a society.

It is often held that rejection of "national interest" in favor of "class interest" is a radical stance, but that is incorrect. It is common enough outside of radical circles, though the point is often presented in a somewhat different way and remains implicit. Consider, for example, the work of Hans Morgenthau, who has written extensively and often perceptively on the national interest, perhaps more so than any other American political analyst. In the most recent presentation of his views (*New Republic*, 22 Jan. 1977), he states that the "national interest underlying a rational foreign policy" is not defined by the whim of a man or the partisanship of party but imposes itself as an objective datum upon all men applying their rational faculties to the conduct of foreign policy." He then cites as illustrations such commitments as support for South Korea, containment of China, and upholding of the Monroe Doctrine. He further observes that "the concentrations of private power which have actually governed America since the Civil War have withstood all attempts to control, let alone dissolve them... (and)... have preserved their hold upon the levers of political decision." True, no doubt. Under such circumstances, do we expect the "national interest" as actually articulated and pursued to be simply the outcome of the application of rational faculties to objective data, or to be an expression of specific class interests? Obviously the latter, and a serious investigation of the cases Morgenthau cites, which is beyond the scope of these remarks, will demonstrate that the expectation is amply fulfilled. The real interests of Americans were in no way advanced by the crushing of popular forces in South Korea in the late 1940s and the imposition of a series of dictatorial regimes, to cite just one of his examples. But it can be argued that the interests of the "concentrations of private power" in the United States that effectively dominate the world capitalist system were advanced by this pursuit of the "national interest." The same holds quite generally. The idea that foreign policy is derived in the manner of physics is sheer myth.

Or, consider a recent analysis by Walter Dean Burnham in *Trialogue* (Fall, 1976), the journal of the Trilateral Commission. He notes that the "basic functions" of the state are "the promotion externally and internally of the basic interests of the dominant mode of production and the need to maintain social harmony." Radicals would not disagree, in essence, though they would observe that the formulation is highly misleading. In the first place, these "basic functions" of the state are not a matter of metaphysical necessity but arise from specific causes. Furthermore, the "dominant mode of production" does not have interests; rather, those individuals or groups who participate in it have interests, often conflicting ones. And since those who own and manage this system are also in effective control of the state apparatus—a fact that should be sufficiently obvious to those familiar with the Trilateral Commission, which dominates the new Administration in a most remarkable way—the "basic interests" pursued will be theirs. There are no grounds in history or logic to suppose that these interests will coincide to any significant extent with interests of those who participate in the dominant mode of production by renting themselves to its owners and managers.

Concepts such as "socialism" and "democracy" have been no less debased in contemporary political discourse. To libertarian socialists, at least, socialism and freedom are inseparable. There is no socialism worthy of the name under a party dictatorship. And democracy is an empty pretense to the extent that production, finance and commerce—and along with them, the political processes of the society as well—are under the control of "concentrations of private power." The "national interest" as articulated by those who dominate the state-capitalist or state-socialist societies will be their special interests. Under these circumstances, talk of "national interest" can only contribute to mystification and oppression.

If libertarian socialist forces develop on any significant scale, they will be compelled, at the outset at least, to adapt themselves to the system of nation-states, and will undertake to dissolve these systems of class dominance from within while working in solidarity with others across national lines to reconstruct international society as well. Short of this, authoritarian states, whether they call themselves "socialist" or "democratic" (or both) will act to perpetuate the particular interests of those who are in a position to organize the resources and productive institutions of the society. It is futile to ask whether the United States or the Soviet Union, or for that matter lesser powers, might undertake a commitment to general interests of their own populations or others on any significant scale. In the interest of preserving order ("social harmony"), it may be necessary to pursue such policies in any society—feudal, fascist, state socialist, democratic capitalist, or whatever. And by sheer historical accident, policies undertaken in the interest of ruling groups may on occasion have such effects. But power will work for its own purposes, whatever the rhetoric employed to disguise or legitimate it.

## Editor's Notes to Chapter 2

This "preview" of **PE** was written on February 11, 1977, and it was published in the RESIST Newsletter no. 112, Feb. 28. (See the Editor's Notes to Selections 5, 9 and 11.)

As some of his books indicate, Chomsky became "a figure of national attention" through his participation in RESIST and through his brilliant criticism of American life, so it seems appropriate to point out here that RESIST is unique among the organizations of the 1960s in that it is still going, now as an independent and non-sectarian socialist fund-raising organization that funnels money to groups which concentrate on anti-racist, feminist and pro working-class organizing (its current address is 259 Elm Street, Suite 201, Somerville, MA 02144, www.resistinc.org, (617) 623-5110).

When it was founded, in 1967, RESIST focused on issues of imperialism abroad and repression at home. The first "Call to Resist Illegitimate Authority" (see the *New York Review of Books* (henceforth *NYR*), Oct. 12, 1967), signed by thousands, figured prominently in the conspiracy trial of the Boston Five (see N. Chomsky, P. Lauter & F. Howe, "Reflections on a Political Trial," *NYR* 9: ( 22 Aug. 1968): pp. 23–30, reprinted, followed by a comment by Arlene Siegel published in the RESIST Newsletter of Aug. 7, 1969, in N. Chomsky et al., *Trials of the Resistance*, A *NYR* Book, 1970, pp. 74–105). The second one, "A New Call to Resist Illegitimate Authority" (Sept. 1969), was reprinted in *The Movement Toward a New America: The Beginnings of a Long Revolution: (A collage). A what? 1. A comprehension 2. A compendium 3. A handbook 4. A guide 5. A history 6. A revolution kit 7. A work in progress. Assembled by Mitchell Goodman, a charter member of the Great Conspiracy, in behalf of The Movement.* Philadelphia: Pilgrim Press / New York, Alfred A. Knopf: 1970, pp. 468–469. (Mitchell Goodman was one of the Boston Five.)

Over the years, RESIST's political views have evolved. The latest "New Call to Resist Illegitimate Authority," dated Aug. 1976, which can be obtained from the address given above, assumes that "now the major thrust of resistance to illegitimate authority must be *to build toward socialism* in the United States because the essential source of illegitimate authority in the United States today is capitalism." Recognizing that "any fundamental change in the society entails radical alteration of the economic system," it also expresses the conviction that such a radical change "will not come about—nor will racism, sexism, and national chauvinism be eliminated—*without building a culture of equity and solidarity.*" See **CD&E**, pp. 431–432.

# 2. Vietnam Protest And The Media

On December 29, 1976, the International League for Human Rights called a news conference to release to the American press a protest against violations of human rights in Vietnam signed by many former peace movement activists. The statement had been the subject of much controversy. Some of this private dialogue has since surfaced. The issues are multiple and serious. I would like to explore a few of them, in part from a somewhat personal point of view. I did not sign the statement myself, but I do not agree with much of the criticism that has been directed against the signers and regard the matter, or, at least certain facets of it, as rather ambiguous. Among the questions that arise are the following:

1. Was the statement accurate; that is, are there violations of human rights in Vietnam of the sort alleged?

2. Assuming so, does this repression merit public protest, given its character and the circumstances?

3. Assuming so, should such a protest be initiated by Americans, even Americans who were active in opposing the war, and released in the United States, presented to the general public through the American mass media, with their record and their commitments?

4. What is the significance of the way in which the press dealt with the statement, and more generally, what is the significance of the protest and the manner of its release, taken as a political act?

These questions involve factual, political, and moral judgments. I will briefly consider the questions just raised, in turn.

## The present situation in Vietnam

First, what is the present situation in Vietnam? Evidence is slim but not entirely lacking. Before turning to it, I would like to emphasize some facts that the press predictably ignored. South Vietnam was virtually destroyed by American force in an attack of unprecedented savagery that was later extended to the rest of Indochina with comparable ferocity. Furthermore, the U.S. has now retreated to the traditional fall-back position when some region of the world extricates itself from the U.S.-dominated world system: namely, the most severe policies are being pursued, short of actual war, to reduce the prospects for those "ideological successes" that have always so concerned American global planners and that underlie the rational forms of the "domino theory." That is, the U.S. has acted in such a way as to maximize the difficulties of social and economic reconstruction in the society that it has systematically demolished and to increase the likelihood that harsh measures will be instituted, in the hope that the new society will not provide a model for oppressed people in Thailand, Malaysia, Indonesia, and other regions that remain within the U.S.-dominated system.

These are realities that cannot be ignored when a political act regarding Vietnam is undertaken in the United States.

Consider now the present situation in Vietnam. There have been fairly detailed reports by non-communist observers who have visited the country. The most extensive appear in the recent book by Jean and Simonne Lacouture, who visited Vietnam in the spring of 1976 (*Vietnam: Voyage à Travers une Victoire*, Seuil, Paris: 1976). They describe a society being reconstructed from the ravages of the American war. The southern part of the country is undergoing what they call "Nor(th)-malization," an inevitable consequence of the American victory in South Vietnam that destroyed the popular forces there. They observe that the Vietnamese revolutionaries "are probably the first victors of a civil war (embittered, aggravated by two foreign interventions) who have not launched any operation of massive reprisals." Quite different, they comment, from Paris or Rome in 1944. They visited "re-education camps" and commented—"with prudence"—on what they have seen and heard. Among those subject to "re-education" are "100,000 drug addicts left behind by the American Expeditionary Corps (drugs, including opium, were rarely used in Vietnam until 1960, except by foreigners)" and unknown numbers of other social victims of the American war (prostitutes—they give the figure of 500,000, petty criminals, etc.). "The Vietnamese resistance," they point out, "more honorable than their French comrades of 1944, have not shaved the heads of the victims." The re-education camps "are evidently not Gulag" (in contrast, the *NY Times* headlined a statement on the camps by a former USAID worker "Vietnam's 'Gulag Archipelago'"). Neither are they finishing schools. "Evidently, it is not terror, but it is also not quite clemency."

Apart from the re-education camps, they point out that there are surely people who courageously opposed the Diem and Thieu regimes and who will find no place in the new society. They discuss one poignant case.

The protest statement released in New York cites Father Tran Huu Thanh as someone who "opposed the Thieu government" and is now a political prisoner. Oppose the government he did, because it was not conducting the war with sufficient success. Prior to such opposition, he had been an active participant in the American initiated programs of repression. He was an instructor of anti-Communism for Saigon military officers and director of an anti-Communist psychological warfare programme. A group he headed condemned Thieu over a clandestine radio station in Saigon in 1974; a genuine third force activist, Father Chan Tin, suspected a CIA hand. Thanh's group refrained from calling for implementation of the Paris Agreements and put forth their programme: the

Communists "have to accept to come and live with us as a minority" (*NY T,* 31 Oct., 1974)—the standard U.S. government position at the time, and a position with consequences that will be easily understood by anyone familiar with the nature of the regimes imposed by American force since 1954. There are no doubt standards under which someone with his record should not be sent to a re-education camp, but they are rather elevated.

A certain historical perspective is useful. Even if we put aside the massive atrocities committed by the resistance and others in liberated Europe under American occupation in 1944, consider American policy towards defeated Germany. U.S. High Commissioner Lucius Clay, in his report of 31 December 1950, stated that denazification procedures in the American zone alone involved 13.5 million people, "of whom three and two-thirds million were found chargeable, and of these some 800,000 were made subject to penalty for their party affiliations or actions," all of this "apart from the punishment of war criminals." Applying the standards by which the Vietnamese are condemned for their treatment of Tran Huu Thanh, the American denazification programme was an intolerable outrage, not to speak of the fate of collaborators at the hands of those who had suffered directly from Nazi terror.

### The Vietnamese analogue to "denazification"

Consider the second point: does the repression merit public protest at this time and under the existing circumstances. Two issues must be distinguished: (1) the Vietnamese analogue of "denazification"; (2) the character of the new society. The second question is a most important one, but it is not at issue here. If one objects to the course being taken in reconstructing Vietnamese society, the proper medium of protest is not a press conference and a public statement, just as we do not call a press conference to present a statement denouncing the U.S. or Germany or Japan for their commitment to state capitalism, wage-slavery, denial of the right of worker's control in industry, and so on. Matters of the highest importance, no doubt, but not relevant in this context. What is at stake is (1), allegations concerning the abuse of human rights on the part of the ruling authorities, in the narrow sense of the term that the International League for Human Rights takes as its province.

Let us assume that credible information is produced indicating that there are severe human rights violations in Vietnam of the sort alleged: thousands of political prisoners, and so on. Then protest is warranted. But some serious questions arise about the proper mode, given the historical record and existing circumstances. Included here are some elementary questions of simple good taste. Speaking personally, I would agree to sign an appropriately worded protest against human rights violations in Vietnam if it were released, say, in Sweden, or were presented to the public through some medium that emerged with a shred of honor from the catastrophes of the past years. But as for a protest presented to the public through the American mass media, that is quite another matter. The American press, despite current pretense, supported the war through its worst atrocities, lying and concealing crucial information in the service of the state. There were exceptions; in particular there were a few honest correspondents. But as a general statement, this is fair enough. To cite only one of innumerable examples, eyewitness reports by noncommunist observers on the savage bombing of defenseless Northern Laos were knowingly concealed by the national press for a long period, as were many other horrors. Furthermore, the background of the war in the imperial planning of the 1940s and 1950s has always been concealed, despite ample documentation. The origins and nature of the war were grossly distorted throughout and still are, a fact that I and others have documented in considerable detail and that need not be reviewed here.

To put the matter in what seems to me a proper perspective, imagine the following analogy. Suppose that World War II had ended in a stalemate after the liberation of France (from the Nazi point of view, the conquest of peaceful France by Anglo-American aggressors). Suppose that Germany had remained a world-dominant power despite this setback, internally unchanged. Suppose now that a group of German anti-Nazi resisters decided to protest the atrocities against collaborators in France—which, I repeat, vastly exceeded anything credibly charged to the Vietnamese. Should they have chosen to release such a protest through the German press, under these circumstances? How would we have reacted to such a political act, even if the protest statement were precisely accurate in detail? The analogy is a good deal more apt than many Americans believe, particularly those whose perceptions of recent history have been derived through the American mass media or academic scholarship, with their fundamental commitment to state power and its exercise and to the sources of that power in American society.

## The protest and the American press

There never was much doubt that the protest would be presented to the public through the American press. It is striking that European non-communist leftists, at least in my contacts with them, seem quite generally to regard this performance as indecent if not obscene. Americans tend to have a different perception. In my opinion—for some, at least, the reason may lie in the remarkable submissiveness of American intellectuals to the state propaganda apparatus and its doctrines.

What about the fourth point, the treatment of the protest by the press and the nature of the protest as a political act. Here the facts are clear for everyone to see. The coverage was extensive—a bit ironic, when one recalls the efforts to bring information about the war to the press for many years. Quite predictably, the press passed in silence over the fact that the protest called for "massive reparations for the destruction" caused by American violence or its reference to the horrors suffered beneath America's bombers," though the *NY Times* did observe that some protesters "felt that United States involvement in the war had been unjust." The press reported that others refused to sign the protest "because of its criticism of Hanoi, the sponsors said." This is false, in some cases at least, as the sponsors know very well but have yet to state publicly.

I will omit any discussion of what the protesters are alleged to have said at the press conference. But one participant, Congressman Edward Koch, has explained his views in a letter to the *Times* (Jan. 28, 1977). He says that he opposed the war "from a conviction that the United States should not become embroiled in a civil war between two repressive regimes." This remarkable version of history must have aroused cackles of amusement in the propaganda bureaus and editorial offices. It conforms precisely to the fabrications of the state propaganda apparatus but is a little difficult to reconcile with the historical record. This shows that the U.S. first supported the French, then imposed on South Vietnam a regime of murder and oppression, then engaged directly in military action against what were always recognized to be the mass popular forces in South Vietnam, and then extended the war beyond—well before there was any direct North Vietnamese military engagement in support of the Southern resistance to American force, as the Pentagon Papers and other sources make very clear.

The primary victims of American violence were always the people of South Vietnam. They were the ones subjected to pacification and "population control," the Phoenix programme and destructive ground sweeps, defoliation and ecocide, pounding by bombs and artillery in free fire zones, and the rest of the familiar story. The war was extended to the North in an effort to compel the North Vietnamese to put pressure on the Southern resistance to desist at a time when American intelligence knew of no direct participation by North Vietnamese military units. The savage attack on Laos and Cambodia had nothing to do with "a civil war between two repressive regimes." Furthermore, even if Koch's fanciful account were correct, consider the tacit assumption. Suppose that the regime imposed by American force had been benign, and had been engaged in a civil war against a repressive opponent. Then, Koch seems to be saying, U.S. military intervention would have been legitimate. This is a most intriguing interpretation of our legal commitments under the UN Charter for example. But we need not pursue these fantasies, Koch's rendition of history serves as a remarkable tribute to the effectiveness of the state propaganda apparatus.

Koch goes on to say that he sees no "real difference between the tiger cages of South Vietnam and the 'education camps' of the Vietnam of today." Again, a most amazing comment, if we rely on the evidence now available. I will simply cite again Jean Lacouture, on whom the initiators of the protest statement rely as "a trusted source of news":

> There were other pictures too: those of the penal colony of Poulo-Condore, created by the French, perfected by the Americans with their terrible 'tiger cages.' Tens of thousands of men and women rotted away there. Only one prisoner in four survived.

Congressman Koch is telling us that he sees no real difference between these penal colonies created and perfected by foreign force and what he has reported about the "education camps" of today. By similar logic, some German dissident in 1944 might have said that he sees no "real difference" between the punishment of collaborators in France and the Holocaust.

Koch adds finally that for him "there is only a single standard." That is true enough: it is the standard of subservience to the state and its propaganda. Even the most extreme advocate of American "intervention" will delight in Koch's interesting rendition of history.

## Propaganda fabrications

The editorial comment in the press is no less remarkable. Consider the *Christian Science Monitor*, which not long ago was featuring commentary by its leading pundit on the relative advantages of bombing trucks and bombing dams. The latter, he observed, is so much more satisfying to the pilots as "the water can be seen to pour through the breach and drown out huge areas of farm land, and tillages, in its path." Bombing dams "will flood villages, drown people, destroy crops." But perhaps it is still not worthwhile because "there is no evidence that this causing of pain to civilians in North Vietnam (sic)" will bring Hanoi to the negotiating table (Joseph Harsch, Sept. 5, 1967). Today, with the hypocritical moralism that is its hallmark, the *Monitor* discusses the lessons that have "been all too belatedly learned by activists from the movement against American involvement." Hanoi's rejection of the protest "can only confirm the aggressive authoritarianism which Americans got into the war to resist. "Typically, the *Monitor* makes its characteristic contribution to reinforcing the propaganda fabrications of the state it serves, with regard to the origins of the war and the motives of those who opposed it. As if the character of the North Vietnamese regime had anything to do with opposition to the American attack against the rural population of South Vietnam and later the rest of Indochina!

The *Monitor* editorial then has the unmitigated gall to proclaim that now "the U.S. and other nations have to evaluate Vietnam's potentiality as a responsible world citizen." After the events of the past years, the United States must evaluate Vietnam as a responsible world citizen," helped in this assessment by the *Monitor*, which has so clearly revealed its moral stand and appreciation of historical events, as the quoted comments demonstrate. One can only watch open-mouthed in astonishment. I will refrain from pursuing the analogy to Nazi Germany, cited earlier.

## The protest as a political act

These responses are not untypical. They reveal clearly the significance of the release of the protest to the American press, understood as a political act. Any such public statement is, of course, a political act, to be evaluated in terms of its likely consequences. The intention of the signers was, no doubt, to help victims of repression. The clearest and most significant consequence of the mode of protest they have chosen, which could easily have been foreseen and is now entirely obvious, is somewhat different. This political act contributes to the efforts on the part of the state propaganda apparatus—I include here the mass media—to reconstruct the history of the American involvement in Vietnam to fit the image of American benevolence, occasionally misguided; that is, to help lay the basis in public opinion for new episodes of this sort in the future.

There is absolutely no reason for anti-war activists to remain silent in the face of credible evidence regarding human rights violations in Vietnam, or more deeply, with regard to the society being constructed in Vietnam—though I stress again that this crucial question is not what is at issue here. But history suggests a certain degree of caution. Many of us, myself included, have criticized the North Vietnamese sharply in the past for alleged atrocities that were later revealed to be fabrications of American and Saigon intelligence. The land reform of the early 1950s is a striking example. It is equally striking that long after the propaganda fabrications had been exposed by Gareth Porter, and conceded by the former head of the Central Psychological War Service in Saigon, nevertheless these fabrications are solemnly repeated as fact. This is not the only example, as people who have followed the events closely are well aware.

By all means, we should continue to apply the single standard of judgment so grossly violated by the press, by academic scholarship, by Congressman Koch, and quite generally by those who are sometimes called "the American intellectual elite." But this commitment should not translate itself into service to the institutions of state propaganda. I believe that this is what has happened in the present case. Those who initiated the appeal now have an excellent opportunity to set the matter right. They have a public platform that is generally denied to those who oppose the atrocities of the state. I see no reason why they should not use it.

## Editor's Notes to Chapter 3

Written on May 21, 1975, it was published in *Seven Days* June 2: p. 13.

For an expanded version, see the Epilogue to "The United States in Indochina," completed on June 1, 1975, and published under the title "U.S. Involvement in Vietnam," in *Bridge (An Asian American Perspective)* 4.1 (1975): pp. 4–21. It includes this paragraph: "Here we see again the Nazi-style mentality—I use the term advisedly—that has characterized much of the reaction to the American war in Indochina among the liberal intelligentsia. They understand nothing; they have learned nothing." After referring to the fact that Kissinger "advocated bombing the Cambodian main land with B-52's" during the Mayaguez crisis ("thankfully, he was overruled by others who felt that carrier-based bombers would be punishment enough"), the author closes with these words: "From 'Mad Jack' in 1845 to 'Mad Henry' in 1975; that is the story of the United States in Indochina." (John Percival, known as 'Mad Jack', was the commander of a ship of the U.S. Navy whose sailors disembarked at Danang and proceeded to terrorize the local population, firing on an unresisting crowd and killing several dozen people before Mad Jack withdrew in failure.) See Christopher Hitchens, *The Trial of Henry Kissinger*. London: Verso, 2001.

See now **TCW**, ch. 4.

# 3. Cambodia: No Holds Barred

On May 17th, the U.S. Coast Guard boarded the Polish trawler *Kalmar* and forced it to shore in San Francisco. The ship was allegedly fishing two miles within the twelve-mile limit established by the U.S. The crew was confined to the ship under armed guard for six days, until a fine of $350,000 was paid and the ship released.

Five days before the seizure of the *Kalmar*, the merchant ship *Mayaguez* was intercepted by a Cambodian patrol boat within three miles of a Cambodian island, according to Cambodia (seven miles, according to the ship's captain). Shortly after midnight Washington time on May 14th, U.S. planes sank three Cambodian gunboats. At 7:07 p.m., the Cambodian radio announced that the ship would be released. A few minutes later, U.S. Marines attacked Tang Island and boarded the deserted ship nearby. At 10:45, a boat approached the U.S. destroyer *Wilson* with the crew of the *Mayaguez* aboard. Shortly after, U.S. planes attacked the mainland. A second strike against civilian targets near Sihanoukville took place 36 minutes after Ford was notified that the *Mayaguez* crew was safe.

## Many Similar Incidents

The *Kalmar* incident was barely noted in the press. There have been many like it. In one week in January, Ecuador reportedly seized seven American tuna boats, some up to 100 miles at sea, imposing heavy fines which were paid by the United States. President Ford stated in a May 19th interview that the U.S. was aware that the same Cambodian gunboats had intercepted a Panamanian and a South Korean ship a few days earlier and then released the ships and crews unharmed. But, he added, "You couldn't help but feel that the potential treatment of an American crew would be quite different..."

Evidently, the *Kalmar* and *Mayaguez* incidents are not comparable. Cambodia has just emerged from a brutal war, for which the U.S. bears direct responsibility. For twenty years, Cambodia has been the victim of U.S. subversion, harassment, and direct aggression. It has been subjected to devastating American air attacks, at first "secret," thanks to the self-censorship of the media.

Cambodia has announced that hostile U.S. actions continue, including espionage flights, "subversive, sabotage, and destructive activities," and penetration of coastal waters by U.S. spy ships "engaged in espionage activities there almost daily." Thai and Cambodian nationals have been landed, Cambodia alleges, to contact espionage agents, and have confessed to being in the employ

**63**

of the CIA. There can be no doubt that Cambodia has ample reason, based on history and perhaps current actions, to be wary of U.S. subversion and intervention.

## Humiliating Discussion

According to Kissinger, the U.S. decided to use military force to avoid "a humiliating discussion." He did not add that under international law and the UN Charter the U.S. is legally obliged to limit itself to such means as "humiliating discussion" if it perceives a threat to peace and security. Therefore the U.S. informed the UN that its actions were an exercise of the inherent right of self-defense against armed attack, though it is absurd to describe the Cambodian action as an "armed attack" against the U.S., in the sense of the UN Charter.

Despite official denials, the U.S. military actions were clearly punitive in intent. The *Washington Post* reports that U.S. sources privately conceded "that they were gratified to see the Khmer Rouge government hit hard." Cambodia had to be punished for its insolence in withstanding the armed might of the U.S.

The domestic response indicates that the illegal resort to violence—if it succeeds—will continue to enjoy liberal support, Senator Kennedy stated that "the President's firm and successful action gave an undeniable and needed lift to the nation's spirit, and he deserves our genuine support."

That everyone's spirits were lifted by still another blow at Cambodia, after years of U.S. terror and savagery, may be doubted. Still, this reaction, from the Senator most closely concerned with the human impact of the American war, is important and revealing. Senator Mansfield explained that Ford's political triumph weakens anti-imperialist forces in Congress. Indeed, on May 20, the House voted overwhelmingly against reducing American troops overseas.

There have been a few honorable voices of protest. Anthony Lewis, in the *NY Times*, observed that "for all the bluster and righteous talk of principle, it is impossible to imagine the United States behaving that way toward anyone other than a weak, ruined country of little yellow people who have frustrated us." We need only add that the world was put on notice—as if notice were needed— that the U.S. will tolerate no reproach for its sadistic war against Cambodia (or the rest of Indochina), and, more generally, that the world's most violent power intends to persist in the illegal use of force for global management, confident that success will bring support within the political mainstream.

**Editor's Notes to Chapter 4**

Written on June 26, 1978, in answer to the questions posed by *Dissent*, it was published in this journal ("devoted to radical ideas and the values of socialism and democracy") in the Fall issue (pp. 386–389), together with answers by Hans J. Morgenthau and Michael Walzer. See **PE**, 11, ch. 6, n. 7.

I haven't seen the original of the letter to the *NY Times*, so I don't know whether it was published in full (*NYT*, 8 Dec., 1978, p. A28).

# 4. The Cynical Farce About Cambodia

"Do the recent events in Cambodia warrant a reconsideration of our opposition to the Vietnam war ?" Consider the factual and moral premises that allow this question to be seriously raised.

Let us assume the accuracy of the condemnations of the Khmer Rouge (noting, however, that the susceptibility of intellectuals to fabricated atrocity stories has been no less notorious since World War I than their apologetics for some favored state, and that scepticism is aroused in this case by the many documented falsehoods). On this assumption, should we reconsider opposition to the Vietnam war?

One who raises this question must be assuming (1) that the U.S. war was intended to avert Khmer Rouge barbarity, or might have had this likely effect; and (2) that the U.S. has the right to exercise force and violence to avert potential crimes.

Assumption (1) is ludicrous in the light of the factual record. Cambodia was an island of relative tranquillity prior to the American invasion of 1970, though it had repeatedly been attacked by American and U.S.-backed forces from 1957 on. There was limited local insurgency, aroused by government repression, even by the late 1960s. As Vietnamese were driven to a narrow border strip by the savage American military operations of early 1967, direct U.S. attacks on Cambodia escalated. By May 1967 the Pentagon was concerned that Cambodia was "becoming more and more important as a supply base-now of food and medicines, perhaps ammunition later," an obvious consequence of U.S. operations in Vietnam and Laos. In March 1969, shortly after the "secret" bombings began, Sihanouk vainly called upon the Western press to publicize his government's protest over the "criminal attacks" on Khmer peasants. The 1970 invasion helped organize the Khmer Rouge rebellion as thousands of peasants rallied to the resistance under the impact of the vicious bombing and ground attacks of the U.S. military and the Vietnamese forces it organized. Charles Meyer, who had long been close to ruling circles in Cambodia, warned then that "it is difficult to imagine the intensity of the hatred (of the peasants) for those who destroyed their villages and their possessions" (*Derrière le Sourire Khmer*). This was well before the murderous American bombings of the 1970s, which surely inflamed peasant hatred and desire for revenge.

Those who failed to devote their energies to ending the American war in Indochina bear a double burden of guilt: for the atrocities committed under

American initiative, and for the legacy of starvation, disease, hatred and revenge that was a direct and predicted consequence of the attack on rural Cambodia. Similar remarks apply in the case of Vietnam and Laos.

Assumption (2) has not been defended explicitly. One can easily see why. If the U.S. is entitled to launch a major war to avert potential barbarism, then *a fortiori* it is entitled to invade countries where state violence currently proceeds, say, much of Latin America which turned into a horror chamber in one of the recent successes of U.S. foreign policy. Surely the absurdities of this position are obvious.

Furthermore, one may ask why the U.S. should be uniquely privileged to serve as global judge and executioner. By virtue of its historic role in defense of freedom and human rights within its own sphere of influence, perhaps? Again, discussion is superfluous.

One who advocates the resort to force must present an overwhelmingly powerful argument. There is ample reason to adopt as a guiding principle the restriction on use of force, now codified in law, to self-defense against armed attack. In fact, the official claim always was that the U.S. was defending South Vietnam from "aggression from the North." Internal documents were more honest. Immediately after the Geneva accords of 1954, the U.S. undertook to help its clients "to defeat local Communist subversion or rebellion not constituting armed attack," with potential "use of U.S. military forces either locally or against the external source of such subversion or rebellion"—all as determined unilaterally by the U.S. It was the secret plan that was pursued; the official defense is no less ludicrous an assumption.

The U.S. at once installed a client regime in South Vietnam that abrogated the terms of the Geneva settlement and initiated a program of repression and massacre. When resistance ensued, the U.S. turned to direct military action by 1962 and an outright invasion of South Vietnam in 1965. Government analysts never doubted that the South Vietnamese enemy was the only mass-based political force, while the regimes the U.S. imposed as a basis for its intervention had negligible support. The peace treaty signed but immediately undermined by the U.S. in January 1973 was virtually a paraphrase, in essentials, of the programme of the South Vietnamese forces that the U.S. was dedicated to destroy.

By the time the first North Vietnamese battalion was detected in the South—more than two months after the initiation of the systematic bombing of the North and the far more extensive bombing of the South—more than 150,000 South Vietnamese had been killed "under the crushing weight of American Armour, napalm, jet bombers and, finally, vomiting gasses." This is the judgment of Bernard Fall, a committed hawk, who turned against the war because he feared that "Vietnam as a cultural and historic entity... is threatened with extinction" as "the countryside literally dies under the blows of the... (American)... military machine." The U.S. won its filthy war in South Vietnam, decimating the local forces that resisted American violence and the peasant society in which they were rooted, thus guaranteeing North Vietnamese dominance of the wreckage and leaving ample opportunity for the hypocrites who now bewail this consequence of the American war that they supported.

Now we are asked whether opposition to the U.S. attack on rural South Vietnam, later all Indochina, was legitimate, in the light of postwar suffering and atrocities that are in large measure a result of this aggression. With comparable logic, Germans might have asked whether opposition to Nazi aggression should be reconsidered after the massacre of tens of thousands in France under American civil-military rule.

We are sometimes told that "the story is more complex." That is true; the real world is more complex than our descriptions, a fact that may be exploited by the cynical or deluded. They can dismiss as a guide to attitude and action the salient features of this real but too complex world.

Like most colonial wars, the U.S. war in Indochina was in part a civil conflict, though in scale and savagery the U.S. intervention has had few historical parallels. Such wars are generally brutal, and the domestic losers often suffer grievously. Those who devoted themselves to ending American aggression and who now work to reverse the inhuman policy of refusing reparations or even aid to its victims have a moral right to condemn repressive acts of the regimes that have arisen from the ruins. Comparably, anti-Nazi resisters had the moral right to condemn the atrocities committed after liberation. Others may well be accurate in their condemnation, but it reeks to high heaven.

The American media have been deluged with denunciations of postwar Indochina, while more favorable accounts, however credible, receive little notice; and murderous repression within the American sphere—in Timor or Uruguay, for example—is consistently ignored. That should not surprise us. As had been predicted, a major effort is underway to reconstruct the interventionist ideology that eroded as popular opposition to the Vietnam war developed. History must be rewritten and principle revised to conform to the needs of a power that will be called upon to lead the industrial capitalist world in the "North-South" conflict. We read that we must overcome our "Vietnam hang-up" and be willing to use force to defend our interests, often disguised in cynical humanitarian rhetoric. Or we are informed that revolutionary regimes are capable of great brutality, as has been obvious for centuries, and that "we" should rise to the defense of peoples, not states; reasonable enough (and no less familiar) if the term "we" refers to individuals, though it is easily transmuted to refer to state power in a new version of colonialist doctrine.

One who protests barbarism or repression must consider the probable human consequences of his acts. That is why, for example, Amnesty International urges that one write *politely* to the most miserable tyrant. Unless the goal of protest is self-aggrandizement or service to one's state, finite energies will be distributed in accordance with a likely impact. A Russian who condemns American behaviour in Vietnam or Chile may speak the truth, but we do not admire his courage or moral integrity. Similar considerations apply here. The central responsibility for Americans is to try to modify policies that we can influ-

ence; primarily, those of the American government and its client regimes, or elsewhere, when there is a likelihood that protest can contribute to the relief of
human misery.

Returning to the specific questions of this symposium: events in postwar
Indochina amply reinforce the moral imperative of protest and resistance against
the American war. Principled opponents of that war should now devote themselves with no less energy to attempting to heal its wounds and help its victims—
those in exile, those who are oppressed, and those who are struggling to construct
a viable society from the ruins left by American terror. If honest inquiry reveals
terror and repression, protest is legitimate. One who undertakes it must ask how
his acts may help those who suffer, bearing in mind also the domestic consequences and the fate of future victims of the interventionist ideologies now being
reconstructed. One will of course win acclaim in the West by joining the chorus
of protest focussed on those who have escaped the Western orbit, but for ugly
reasons. It is easy to avoid these considerations, but an honest person with true
human concern will not lightly do so. Individuals may differ in their assessment
of these complex issues, but they deserve more careful attention than they often
receive. We cannot escape the world in which we live, inconvenient though that
fact may be.

## POSTSCRIPT: Letter to the New York Times

To the Editor:

In the Editorial Notebook of November 20, Walter Goodman refers to my
response in the magazine *Dissent* to the question "Do the recent events in
Cambodia warrant a reconsideration of our opposition to the Vietnam war?" He
avoided the contents of this response, which explored the factual and moral
premises that allow people like Goodman to take the question seriously. But his
misrepresentations nicely illustrate one of the points that I was making.

Goodman states that this response "recalls" elements of the peace movement
that marched "for a Communist victory." No such view is expressed or even hint-
ed at, as Goodman knows, just as he is no doubt aware of my published work on
Marxist-Leninist ideology and practice. Hence his resort to insinuation rather
than direct allegation.

To support his claim, Goodman states that I compare American actions in
Southeast Asia... with the Nazis' behaviour in World War II." I accused the U.S.
of setting up crematoriums, perhaps? How such a comparison would "recall"
support for a Communist victory he does not explain, but the question is academic. The actual "comparison" that Goodman distorts for his purposes is this:
Commenting on the question whether opposition to the Vietnam war should be
reconsidered "in the light of postwar suffering and atrocities that are in large
measure a result of (American) aggression," I wrote: "With comparable logic,
Germans might have asked whether opposition to Nazi aggression should be
reconsidered after the massacre of tens of thousands in France under American

civil-military rule." It requires quite an imagination to interpret the actual "comparison" as "marching for a Communist victory."

Goodman then continues as follows: "In regard to the charges against the Khmer Rouge, however, he notes 'that the susceptibility of intellectuals to fabricated atrocity stories has been no less notorious since World War I than their apologetics for some favored state, and that scepticism is aroused in this case by the many documented falsehoods.'" Here is the context that Goodman omits. I wrote: "Let us assume the accuracy of the condemnations of the Khmer Rouge (noting, however, that the susceptibility... )." Only the parenthesized comment, which is quite accurate, survives in his rendition.

Note that even such selective quotation offers no basis for Goodman's claims. Documentation of the susceptibility of intellectuals to fabricated stories of "Hun atrocities" in World War I does not "recall" support for the Kaiser. Documentation of the many falsehoods that have appeared with regard to Cambodia does not entail or "recall" support for its present regime, though it does give some insight into Western propaganda. Only someone engaged in apologetics for his favored state in just the manner I described in the response will be so irrational as to interpret opposition to its depredations and documentation of the falsehoods that appear in its media as support for its enemies and victims.

Goodman's misrepresentations are of little consequence in themselves, but they are a small contribution to a propaganda effort of much greater significance. The U.S. pounded Indochina to rubble. The population was driven into urban concentrations and the economies ruined. The U.S. refuses reparations, meaningful aid or trade and even tries to impede aid from other sources. As people in Indochina die from starvation and disease and the governments resort to draconian measures, U.S. propagandists gleefully blame the suffering of Indochina on Communist iniquity.

No one familiar with modern history will be surprised to discover that people who object to this cynical farce, as I did in my response, will be subjected to distortion and abuse.

Noam Chomsky
Cambridge, Mass., November 22, 1978

## Editor's Notes to Chapter 5

Published in the RESIST Newsletter 128 (Jan.–Feb. 1979), this article was edited from one prepared by Liberation News Service from the "Statement Delivered to the Fourth Committee of the U.N. General Assembly," which Chomsky prepared in November 1978. In another form, it appeared in *Inquiry* (19 Feb.: pp. 9–15) under the title "East Timor: The Press Cover-up." See **PE**, 1.3.4.4.

Chomsky delivered a second statement on East Timor to the same committee in October 1979.

See now **TCW**, ch. 13. In a recent letter (December, 2001), he wrote:

"As someone who has been deeply involved with the issue of self-determination for East Timor since before Indonesia invaded, I can attest to the tremendous—and maybe even decisive—difference that ETAN's wonderful work has made. Since 1991, ETAN has effectively advocated for human rights for East Timor and accountability of the U.S. government. ETAN channeled our voices of opposition to U.S. policies blocking East Timorese self-determination, and in so doing became a powerful force for change…

East Timor held its first democratic election last August 30, the second anniversary of its historic independence referendum. The election for a Constituent Assembly, which recently finished writing the country's constitution, was peaceful and fair. Over 90 percent of voters turned out, dramatically demonstrating their strong desire to actively participate in building the country for which they have sacrificed so much…

During the 24-year-long Indonesian military occupation, more than 200,000 people—one-third of the population—were killed. Following East Timor's vote for independence in 1999, the Indonesian military destroyed the country in retaliation. In one month, this massive military operation murdered some 2,000 people, raped hundreds of women and girls, displaced three-quarters of the population, and demolished 75 percent of the country's infrastructure. In early 2000, a UN commission called for an international tribunal to try war crimes and crimes against humanity committed in East Timor, stating a tribunal is 'fundamental for the future social and political stability of East Timor'—but the country has yet to see justice. With increased international pressure, high-ranking Indonesian military and government personnel responsible can finally be tried.

These two important issues have been priorities for ETAN over the last year. They are but two reasons why our voices and our continued support of ETAN's work are essential."

# 5. The Hidden War In East Timor

*The following statement was read by Noam Chomsky before the General Assembly's Colonialism Committee at the United Nations on December 1st. He shows how the U.S. sustained Indonesia's three-year war effort against the former Portuguese colony of East Timor. Despite ample evidence of Indonesian atrocities against the Timorese people—with U.S. complicity—Chomsky shows how the U. S. media has consistently censored news reports which conflict with U.S. interests in Southeast Asia.*

My primary concern is not Southeast Asia but rather the Western industrial societies, particularly my own country, the United States: its foreign policy, the domestic matrix in which this policy arises and the ways it is interpreted in journalism and scholarship. In this context I have become much concerned over the years with the impact of American policy on Southeast Asia and other regions. I have strenuously opposed certain basic elements of this policy, and believe that it is often seriously misrepresented at home, a matter of considerable significance, since such misrepresentation facilitates the pursuit of dangerous and harmful programs without the constraints that an informed public opinion might and sometimes does impose.

On December 7, 1975, Indonesian military forces invaded East Timor, capturing the capital city of Dili, the first major step in a war of aggression that has repeatedly been condemned by the United Nations but that still continues without respite. The United States surely knew of the impending invasion, which had been widely forecast in the international press, was expected by Australia and took place immediately after the departure of President Gerald Ford and Henry Kissinger from a visit to Jakarta, where Kissinger had pointedly told newsmen that "the United States understands Indonesia's position on the question" of Timor.

Although Indonesia has effectively sealed off East Timor from the outside world, refusing entry even to the International Red Cross, nevertheless reports have filtered through indicating that there have been massive atrocities, with estimates by neutral or even pro-Indonesian observers of 50,000–100,000 slaughtered, roughly 10 percent of the population. The evidence compares very well in credibility with what is available concerning other areas of world closed to direct investigation where atrocities have been alleged. Yet, the American press—indeed, the Western press quite generally—has evaded the issue or has, with rare exceptions, adhered closely to the position of Indonesia and the U.S. government, a position that was succinctly expressed by Congressperson J. Herbert

Burke, ranking minority member of the House Subcommittee on Asian and Pacific Affairs, when he wrote that "it is in all our interests to bury the Timor issue quickly and completely."

## U.S. government and press conceal massacres

At every crucial point, the U.S. government, with the press trailing loyally in its wake, has denied or concealed the atrocities committed by its Indonesian ally and has taken the position that whatever minor improper actions may have occurred in the past, it is now a matter of history and no useful purpose is served by questioning Indonesian control of East Timor. The effect has been that the United States and its allies have been able to take part in massacres and repression in East Timor by providing Indonesia with the material support it requires to carry on its continuing war of aggression. This ideological support enables it to do so virtually in secret. Again, I want to stress the significance of press complicity in these atrocities, unknown to a public that might be sufficiently aroused by the facts so as to prevent the governments of the industrial democracies from making their decisive contribution to what Shepard Forman, an anthropologist who worked in Timor, described in Congressional Hearings as "annihilation of simple people." I want to stress as well that this is not ancient history. Only a few weeks ago *Canberra Times* reported that a group of Australians who entered Dili Harbor in a disabled yacht saw "frigates, patrol boats, barges crammed with Indonesian soldiers, and heard many aircraft and helicopters," heard explosions in the distance, and "were left without doubts that Dili was still a war zone." The Indonesian effort to suppress the independence movement of East Timor continues, with the support of the industrial democracies. The whole affair has great import well beyond Timor.

According to the recent UNESCO declaration on news organizations, the mass media throughout the world "contributes effectively to promoting human rights, in particular by giving expression to oppressed peoples who struggle against colonialism, neo-colonialism, foreign occupation and all forms of racial discrimination and oppression and who are unable to make their voices heard within their own territories." The example of East Timor is one of the many that show how far that vision is from reality. The submissiveness of the media has left the general public unaware of the massacres in East Timor and of the direct complicity of the United States and its allies in them. Thus, far from giving expression to oppressed peoples, the mass media in the rich and developed countries participate effectively in continuing oppression and major violations of human rights.

## FRETILIN wins victory

East Timor had never been included within the colonial or post-colonial boundaries of Indonesia and, as Forman points out, "Indo-Japanese and Islamic influences barely can be noted." After World War II, he observed, mountain people "have proclaimed repeatedly their right of self-determination" and eagerly welcomed the steps toward independence which followed the 1974 Portugal revolution. As soon as Portugal announced that independence would be granted to the colonies, the tiny elite of Timor formed several political parties, of which the most important were the UDT and FRETILIN. The UN study *Decolonization* reports that though UDT was initially regarded as the most influential party, "its lack of positive policies, its associations with the 'ancien regime,' together with its initial reluctance to support the ultimate goal of full independence led many of the party's original followers to swing their support to FRETILIN which by early 1975 was generally considered to have become the largest party in the Territory." In August 1975 the UDT staged a coup, probably with Indonesian complicity, setting off a bloody civil war that ended a few weeks later in a complete victory for FRETILIN. The UN study estimated the numbers killed at 2,000–3,000... After reports of later Indonesian atrocities began to surface, the U.S. tried to claim that many of those killed were victims of the civil war.

## U.S. news management

The handling of the reports by the first foreign visitors after the brief civil war gives a revealing insight into the pattern of news management that has since prevailed in the United States. On September 4, the *NY Times* published an account by Gerald Stone, who was described as "the first reporter allowed there since the fighting began." The *Times* story was actually revised and excerpted from a longer report on September 2 carried by the *London Times*. The modifications are instructive.

Stone attempted to verify reports of large-scale destruction and atrocities, attributed primarily to FRETILIN by Indonesian propaganda and news coverage based in it, then and since. His major conclusion was that the reports of destruction were vastly exaggerated and that "many of the stories fed to the public in the past two weeks were not simply exaggerations; they were the product of a purposeful campaign to plant lies." He implicated the Portuguese, Indonesian and Australian governments in this propaganda campaign.

In reviewing Stone's report for an American audience, the *NY Times* deleted his statement that there had been "much distortion and exaggeration" of the destruction and it eliminated entirely his major conclusion about the purposeful lies of Indonesian and Western propaganda. What the *NY Times* did retain was Stone's description of terrible conditions in FRETILIN hospitals (the Portuguese had withdrawn the only doctor) and maltreatment of prisoners by FRETILIN. The sole subheading in the article reads: "evidence of beating." The process of creating the required history advanced yet another step in the *Newsweek* account of the edited excerpts that appeared in the *NY Times*. According to *Newsweek,* Stone had reported "devastation," "bloodshed" and FRETILIN atrocities, and his "dispatch supported the stories of many of the 4,000 refugees who have already fled Timor."

Note carefully the transition. A journalist visits the scene of reported devastation and atrocities which, he reports, were "filtered through the eyes of frightened and exhausted evacuees" or produced by Portuguese, Indonesian and Australian officials, all of whom "had reason to distrust... (the) national independence movement with a moderate reformist program..." He concludes that the reports are vastly exaggerated, in fact, in large measure propaganda fabrications. After editing by the *NY Times* that eliminates his major conclusion and modifies others, *Newsweek* concludes that he found that the reports were true. Thus the reading public is reinforced in the belief that what *Newsweek* calls "the Marxist FRETILIN party" is bent on atrocities and that liberation movements are to be viewed with horror. And the stage is set for general acquiescence when U.S.-backed Indonesian military forces invade to "restore order." This pattern of news management persists with rare exceptions.

## U.S. military involvement expands

The U.S. government claims to have suspended military assistance to Indonesia from December 1975 to June 1976. Military aid during this period actually was above what the State Department had originally proposed to Congress, and has increased since. Furthermore, at least four new offers were made during this period, in express contradiction to Congressional testimony by representatives of the State Department and the Pentagon. These included supplies and parts for OV-10 Broncos which are, according to Cornell University Professor Benedict Anderson, "specially designed for counter-insurgency operations against adversaries without effective anti-aircraft weapons, and wholly useless for defending Indonesia against a foreign enemy." The professor added that this policy has continued under the Carter Administration.

In Congressional testimony, the Deputy Legal Advisor of the State Department, George Aldrich, conceded that the Indonesians—were armed roughly 90 percent with our equipment." He also contended that "...we really did not know very much. Maybe we did not want to know very much, but I gather that for a time we did not know." U.S. "aid suspension" was secret—so secret that the Indonesian government was never informed of it.

One purpose for the continuing flow of U.S. arms, testified David T. Kenney, Country Officer for Indonesia in the State Department before Congress, is "to keep that area (Timor) peaceful." Another State Department representative at hearings just last February, conceded that the conflict persists but notes "a certain change in the situation" in that a large number of people have moved from areas where they could be "protected by the Indonesian government"—or to translate into plain English: have fled the merciless attack supplied and concealed by the U.S. government.

Nine months after "integration," in March 1977, David Kenney testified that about 200,000 of the 650,000 people of East Timor "would be considered in areas under Indonesian administration"—an assessment that contrasts strikingly with the government claim that the war was essentially over in early 1976 and that Timor has effectively become a part of Indonesia." Their "decision" was expressed in the fraudulent "People's Council," implemented in July 1976 by

Indonesia with U.S. support. Of course, there were still the two-thirds of the population who had not as yet been able to express their "decision" because they were not under Indonesian administration—or as the State Department explained, because they are as yet "protected" by Indonesia.

## Chronicle of Indonesian atrocities

The Indonesian attempt to conquer East Timor has been a story of mounting atrocities attested by refugee reports, church officials and letters smuggled out of the country. Virtually all independent observers estimate the numbers slaughtered are in the range of 50,000 to 100,000. Foreign Minister of Indonesia, Adam Malik, estimated the number killed as "50,000 people or perhaps 80.000," according to the Australian *Age*. But, he added, "what does this mean if compared with 600,000 people who want to join Indonesia." The U.S. media's response to Malik's admission was silence. And it has remained silent in light of pro-Indonesia, anti-FRETILIN church officials from Indonesia who found that 500,000 people were not under Indonesian military control in late 1976 and that local priests estimated the numbers killed at 100,000. The Indonesian church officials describe a town of 5,000 that originally welcomed the Indonesian troops, only for some 4,000 to escape a year later to join FRETILIN in the mountains.

On the rare occasions when the press has deigned to refer to this "indiscriminate killing on a scale unprecedented in post-World War II history," it has followed the U.S. government in pretending that the killings took place largely during the civil war. On February 15, 1976, the *NY Times* devoted all of 150 words to a report that "about 60,000 people have been killed since the outbreak of civil war in Portuguese Timor last August, according to the deputy chairman of the territory's provisional government"—that is, the government installed by the Indonesian army. The *Times* report went on to say that FRETILIN had been fighting "forces favoring union with Indonesia." Recall that in the civil war, perhaps 2,000 to 3,000 were killed, a fact that was not reported in the *Times*. Thus, the remainder of the estimated 60,000 were victims of the U.S.-backed Indonesian invasion. As for the forces "favoring union with Indonesia," these had been defeated in September and played no significant part in the subsequent fighting. These forces did not, in fact, favor such union for the most part, certainly not prior to their defeat in September 1975 and probably not thereafter, if we discount the effects of Indonesian coercion.

James Dunn presented evidence of Indonesian atrocities in Congressional hearings in March 1977, based on his interviews with Timorese refugees in Portugal. His testimony was reported, but the story quickly died. The U.S. press, which is assiduous in seeking out refugee reports alleging atrocities in countries that have escaped U.S. domination, has yet to interview these refugees; nor have they appeared before Congress, though Dunn reported that the refugees were eager to testify.

The pro-Indonesian bias appeared in a September 27, 1978 Reuters dispatch from Dili. The reporter discusses "the bitter civil war that preceded the merging of East Timor into Indonesia:" "After the Portuguese colonial rulers departed in December 1975, pro-Indonesian forces, later aided by regular Indonesian troops, defeated left-wing FRETILIN independence guerrillas in an eight-month civil war." Note than this report is false in every crucial particular, though it accords very well with the needs of Indonesian and U.S. propaganda. The Portuguese left just before the end of the civil war in September 1975, and the merging of East Timor into Indonesia, not recognized in most of the world, came ten months later, not after a "civil war" but after an Indonesian invasion that even the State Department concedes had conquered only a third of the population in nine months... after 15 months of bitter warfare.

We have here two paired examples of comparable allegations concerning major violations of human rights. For westerners concerned with human rights, the case of East Timor is, obviously, of vastly greater significance. Whatever the situation may be in Cambodia, it is beyond the reach of Western human rights activists. But the case of East Timor is radically different. Even a show of displeasure by the great power that provided 90 percent of the arms for the Indonesian invasion and that continues to provide Indonesia with material and diplomatic support would be likely to have significant effects. And the same is true of the other powers that are working to bury the issue as quickly and completely as possible as they seek to join in the bloodshed by supplying arms themselves. For Westerners who speak of human rights out of genuine moral concern, then, it is quite obvious that the case of East Timor should be the focus of far greater attention than alleged atrocities in Cambodia.

### First hand reports

Few reports by Western journalists counter Indonesian propaganda. One UPI dispatch from Singapore, however, reports than "30,000 Indonesian troops are still roaming East Timor slaying men, women and children." The report is based on the account of a French photo-journalist Denis Reichle of *Paris Match*, who was deported from Timor after a six-year visit to a mountain retreat of FRETILIN in East Timor. He gives "a safe estimate" of 70,000–75,000 East Timorese killed by the Indonesians in 18 months of combat. The Indonesians, he reports, do not seek combat with FRETILIN forces but "were 'systematically wiping out' the populations of villages known or suspected to be FRETILIN supporters and destroying FRETILIN supply lines and sources." He said, "Catholic missionaries, led by the Bishop of Atambua (in Indonesian Timor), were the only voices in Timor trying to stop the 'systematic killing-off of East Timorese.' " The Bishop, he said, "had been trying to get an interview with Indonesia's President Suharto for two and a half months, but his requests had so far been ignored," and he reported that a "German priest had been driven insane by the constant killings in his area." This eyewitness report by a Western journalist did not reach the U.S. media.

## Press adheres to state department line

The press, once again, adheres strictly to the State Department version of events. *NY Times* reporter Henry Kamm reported that "the diminishing of supplies of the FRETILIN guerrillas appears to have caused them to lose much of their hold over the significant part of the population of about 600,000 whom they have forced to live in regions under their control." How does Kamm know that the population has been "forced to live" under FRETILIN "control"? How are the "scattered FRETILIN groups," who barely exist according to the Indonesian propaganda ministry and the *NY Times*, able to exert control over the population? These questions do not arise. It is a matter of doctrine, not fact, that FRETILIN must have "forced" the population to live under their control, and that they are now fleeing to areas where they can be "protected by the Indonesians." It is hardly imaginable that the distinguished correspondent of the *NY Times*—who had just won the Pulitzer Prize for his reporting of the suffering of refugees from Communism in Southeast Asia when this dispatch appeared—would report the observation by Denis Reichle after his visit to East Timor: FRETILIN forces "are simply East Timorese who would rather die fighting than submit to what they consider to be Indonesian slavery."

The Times Pulitzer prize-winning specialist on victims of Communism does not provide the source for his insight into the minds of the refugees fleeing from the regions where they have been "forced to live" by the "scattered FRETILIN groups." Perhaps it was General Ali Murtopo, who explained that Indonesian military control was based on "anti-foreign feelings among Timorese." Westerners have often been baffled by what they call the "xenophobia" of Asian peasants and tribesmen, a phenomenon not yet explained by modern anthropology, which seems to arise among groups that are subjected to saturation bombing, forced population removal and other modes of "protection" designed by their foreign benefactors.

## Human rights report: No mention of Timor

In the March 1977 Human Rights Report, covering the period of the Indonesia-launched attack, there is no mention whatsoever of Timor. The omission is rectified in the 1978 Report, which deals with allegations of genocide in Timor as follows: "Questions have been raised concerning atrocities by Indonesian troops in East Timor in 1975 and 1976 prior to the incorporation of East Timor into Indonesia. The Indonesian Government withdrew and disciplined offending units guilty of individual excesses, but most of the human losses in East Timor appear to have occurred prior to Indonesia's final intervention."

The final statement is a disgraceful falsehood. No less disgraceful is the refusal even to concede that questions have been raised concerning atrocities after July 1976, let alone to consider the substantial evidence supporting the allegations that there have been massive atrocities and that the U.S. government is participating in them, and that with the complicity of the press, it is concerned to bury the issue quickly and as completely as possible.

## Comparison with press coverage of Cambodia

I will conclude these remarks by offering a comparison which, I believe, gives some insight into the ways in which the mass media in the West "contribute effectively to promoting human rights," in the words of the UNESCO declaration. Western press reports cite another country—Cambodia—where major atrocities have been alleged in exactly the same time frame as East Timor. The harshest critics claim that perhaps 100,000 people have been slaughtered since Apr. 1975. Comparing East Timor with Cambodia, we see that the time frame of alleged atrocities is the same, the numbers allegedly slaughtered are roughly comparable in absolute terms, and five to ten times as high in East Timor relative to population. I have reviewed both cases in considerable detail and my own conclusion is that the sources in the East Timor are more credible than those that have received massive international publicity in the case of Cambodia, though there are of course fewer sources in the case of East Timor, since the West prefers silence and apologetics.

It is instructive, therefore, to compare the Western reaction to these two cases of reported atrocities. In the case of Cambodia, stories of atrocities and repression have not only been eagerly seized upon by the Western media and offered massive international publicity, but also embellished by substantial fabrication. In the case of Timor, in dramatic contrast, the media have shown no interest in discovering or exposing what may have happened; quite the contrary. Apart from Australia, there has been near total silence. On the rare occasions when the press deals with Timor it generally presents as fact the latest handout of the Indonesian propaganda agencies or the State Department, or else reports the iniquity of the resistance, which is forcing people to live under its control.

The difference in international reaction is revealing. Specifically, it reveals how empty and hypocritical is much of the "human rights" glamour in the West. It teaches us something about the meaning of the sudden concern for "human rights" that has moved to center stage just at the moment when the luster of classical colonialist and interventionist ideologies had dimmed.

The nations of the world and honest journalists in free countries need not adhere to these practices and doctrines. They can demand that the International Red Cross, UN observers and independent journalists be admitted to East Timor, and that the flow of arms to Indonesia be halted, so that the invaders will be forced to cease their savage attacks and the right of the people of the Territory to self-determination may finally be exercised.

**Editor's Notes to Chapter 6**

Written on November 16, 1979, at the request of *Los Angeles Times*, which neglected to publish it. (It did publish, on November 29, an article by Richard Falk with the title "U.N. Could Set up Tribunal to Try Shah, Other Tyrants.")

A Spanish translation appeared in an anarchist journal published in Barcelona (*Ideas* July–Aug.: 1980), under the title "Iran: Aceleración de las Peores Tendencias de la Política Exterior de USA." An English translation of this Spanish version was published in London in mid 1981 (*Black Flag* 6:6).

The English original, misidentified as "a letter to the *Los Angeles Times*," was included in *RIPEH: Review of Iranian Political Economy and History* 3.2 (Fall 1979): pp. 148–153, under the title "Emotions Manipulated, Perceptions Shaped." (I am indebted to Richard Swedberg for this reference,)

# 6. The Iranian-American Conflict

The developing conflict between Iran and the United States is likely to have drastic consequences. It is therefore important to make a serious effort to understand the issues and to react intelligently to them. When human lives are at stake, emotions naturally run high, even more so when the "national honor" is allegedly threatened. We would do well to recall earlier incidents when popular hysteria was inflamed. Recall, for example, the alleged North Vietnamese attack on U.S. destroyers in Tonkin Gulf in August 1964, which was exploited by the government to arouse popular support for its massive attack on Vietnam. Only years later did we learn that even if the attack took place, it was probably a reaction to U.S. military actions that were concealed by the U.S. government. The general willingness to accept official propaganda and to join in the chauvinist hysteria had dire consequences that I need not discuss. History affords many similar examples.

The media have served the public poorly on the Iranian upheaval. Media coverage provides little basis for understanding why Iran is consumed with hatred for the Shah and for the U.S. Government. The Shah was overthrown by a mass popular movement that engaged virtually all sectors of Iranian society, suffering some 20,000 deaths as it confronted and overcame one of the world's most powerful armies. The Shah was portrayed by the media as a liberal reformer who somehow failed to communicate his noble intentions to his benighted people. But his Iranian victims saw him, more accurately, as one of the bloodiest tyrants of modern history, with "a history of torture which is beyond belief," as Amnesty international observed, adding that "no country in the world has a worse record in human rights than Iran."

The Shah's "modernization" program benefited the wealthy, the state bureaucracy and foreign investors, while bringing misery to much of the population in a potentially rich society that was plundered by the Shah and his foreign friends. The United States which had installed him in power in a CIA-backed coup, trained and advised his murderous secret police and flooded the country with armaments and technical assistance to buttress his brutal and corrupt rule. While proclaiming that human rights is "the Soul of our foreign policy," President Carter lauded the Shah for his benevolence and spoke of "the respect, admiration and love which your people give to you," while continuing to supply him with the means to repress the popular uprising that sought to free Iran from the clutches of this tyrant. When the historical background is excluded, Iranians may appear to be acting in an irrational and inexplicable manner. But the picture is radically different when we attend to the facts.

In a careful study of the media, Professor William Dorman of the California State University at Sacramento found that "Americans were urgently and persistently informed that Iranian unrest was wholly the result of religious fanaticism and leftist trouble-making... we could find no mainstream news medium that viewed events in Iran from even a slightly different perspective." It was only at the very end, when U.S. government policy began to waver as it was recognized that the U.S.-backed regime could not be saved. that the media slightly modified the pattern of silence and distortion. Current events continue to be portrayed without serious consideration of the crucial historical facts.

There are three issues that arise in the current conflict. The first is the Iranian demand for the return of the Shah's plunder, amounting to billions of dollars. The second is the demand for extradition. The third is the issue of the hostages. Let us consider them in turn.

As for the first, Iran surely has a strong case. On the matter of extradition, surely the United States accepts the principle. The U.S. government is now attempting to extradite Chileans charged with complicity in the Letelier-Moffit assassinations in Washington, and the U.S. and other Western powers have frequently extradited individuals charged—sometimes on flimsy evidence—with crimes that do not begin to compare with those of the Shah. It is therefore difficult to perceive any moral basis in Western practice for the refusal to consider extradition in this case, particularly, when we recall U.S. government complicity in the Shah's crimes. One might argue that proper procedures have not been followed, but then the rational response would be to urge that these procedures be undertaken, not to dismiss the demand as unacceptable or absurd.

What of the matter of hostages? By humanitarian standards, the taking of hostages is to be condemned. But when we consider the standards of Western practice, the matter is more complex. The U.S. consistently objects to the taking of hostages—in small groups. But with equal consistency it supports the practice of holding whole nations as hostage under the severe threat—indeed, the reality —of starvation and death on a huge scale. In Laos, missionaries report that hundreds of thousands of people face starvation in an impoverished country where the agricultural system was destroyed by U.S. violence. But the U.S. refuses more than a trickle of aid, holding the population hostage to induce policy changes. In Vietnam too the economy was virtually destroyed by the U.S., which refuses reparations, aid, trade or even normalization of relations while the population starves, and has even succeeded in driving Vietnam to an alliance with the Soviet Union which it probably did not want. In June 1977 the Senate voted to instruct U.S. representatives to block aid by international institutions to Vietnam, and to reduce U.S. contributions by a corresponding amount if such aid was granted over U.S. objections. Only a few weeks ago, Congress voted to cut its contribution to the World Bank by $20 million, precisely the U.S. share of funding for the Bank's only development programme in Vietnam. Furthermore, Bank director Robert McNamara has agreed to cancel all loans to Vietnam on the cynical grounds that projects there would not be beneficial to the population. The postwar U.S. policy of imposing suffering and death in societies ruined by U.S. violence is intended to achieve the aims thwarted by successful resistance. These examples of holding a nation hostage, causing massive death and suffering, are particularly grotesque because of the direct U.S. responsibility for much of the current travail of Indochina. The examples, however, are far from unique.

Another striking example is the case of East Timor, invaded by Indonesia in 1975 and since subjected to incredible destruction and massacre, backed at every step by the U.S. which provides the required armaments and diplomatic support while the media have concealed the slaughter. It is unfortunate, but easily demonstrated, that the media tend to ignore atrocities for which their own state bears responsibility. The Indonesian Foreign Minister recently conceded that the situation in East Timor may be even worse than Biafra or Cambodia, and the few independent observers permitted entry by Indonesia tend to agree. The same Indonesian official, a year ago, stated that Indonesia would accept aid for East Timor but only if donor countries acknowledged Indonesia's sovereignty. For almost four years, even the International Red Cross was excluded by the Indonesian invaders. In short, the population has been held hostage, while tens of thousands die, in an effort to gain international recognition of the results of Indonesian aggression. The U.S. continues to back Indonesia in these monstrous policies, as it has from the start.

To summarize, the United States indignantly opposes the weapons of the weak, such as the taking of small numbers of hostages. But it uses and silently approves the much more dread weapons of the strong, such as the holding of whole nations hostage while causing—not merely threatening—enormous suffering and death. This should not surprise us. The United States is not alone in these practices, nor are its media unique in concealing such crucial facts of modern history. But consideration of actual historical practice reveals that the show of moralistic outrage is the sheerest cynicism.

These remarks are too brief to portray the real character of the current situation in Iran and elsewhere. But they suggest directions that Americans might wish to pursue as they consider how we should respond to the events now taking place. Whatever their outcome, there will be substantial efforts to develop support for policies of intervention and subversion that have caused immense suffering in the past decades. American citizens should consider carefully how their emotions are being manipulated and their perception of history shaped. The consequences may be extremely serious for us as for many others in an increasingly troubled world.

## Editor's Notes to Chapter 7

Written on June 12, 1978 for the Baltimore *Sun,* which published it a few days later. See **PME**, ch. 5, and **FT**, in particular 2.2.3. See also **TCW**, chs. 1 and 2.

An important sub-theme of this and the following Selection was later developed in "Some Observations on the U.S.-Israel 'Special Relationship'" (Aug. 6, 1982), a shortened version of which appeared in *The Progressive*, Dec. 1982, pp. 22–28, under the title "America and Israel: The End of the Affair? Even After the Strain of Lebanon, the 'Special Relationship' Endures." It was the difficulty of finding a place for the full paper that led to the idea of expanding it so that it could be published independently as a small volume. The final result was **FT**. For a recent and specially revealing addition, see "Chomsky's *Fateful Triangle*; An Exchange," *The New York Review of Books* (16 Aug. 1984): pp. 49–51, reprinted in *Noam Chomsky: Critical Assessments*, ed. C. P. Otero, London: Routledge, 1994, vol. III, pp. 373–400. See now *Middle East Illusions*. New York: Rowman and Littlefield, 2003.

# 7. Israel And The American Intelligentsia

Last April a group of 37 prominent American Jews announced their support for an Israeli "peace group" that had urged greater flexibility in negotiations with Egypt. *The NY Times* accorded their statement front-page coverage, with an editorial applauding it as "path-breaking" and a "major event." This quite typical reaction is more significant than the statement itself, as we see when we consider it against the background of the Israeli and international debate over the troubled Middle East.

For the past decade, U.S. policy has fallen between two bounds: the Rogers Plan, which called for a peace settlement on the pre-June 1967 borders with insubstantial modifications, and what should properly be called "the Kissinger Plan," never explicitly enunciated, which amounted to massive military, economic and diplomatic support for Israel's own policy of development and integration of substantial parts of the territories occupied in 1967.

The Rogers Plan was shelved after the Jordanian crisis of 1970, when Israeli power blocked Syrian moves seen in Washington as a threat to the oil-producing regions of the Arabian peninsula. A radical Arab nationalist or Russian-backed threat to this region, with its central role within the U.S.-dominated global system, will not be tolerated by the United States. Israel's contribution in 1970 had a powerful impact in Washington, solidifying the "special relationship" and leading to a substantial increase in U.S. aid to Israel.

The "special relationship" rests in large measure on the perceived role of Israel as a guardian of American interests in the region. One might dismiss Israeli protestations to this effect as selfserving, but a close look at the record shows that they have plausibility, though the facts are naturally suppressed in domestic propaganda in favor of alleged "moral commitments."

The Kissinger Plan, which led directly to the October 1973 war, was slightly modified in the wake of the surprising Arab successes, but continues to guide U.S. government policy in practice. Israel receives close to half of total foreign military aid. Rhetoric aside, the U.S. continues to give substantial material support for the Israeli policies of development in the occupied territories, scheduled to expand once again in the coming year. The U.S. has also refused to join the growing international consensus in favor of a settlement that would recognize and safeguard Palestinian as well as Jewish national rights.

Sadat's diplomacy has been predicated on two assumptions: that a comprehensive peace settlement along the lines of the Rogers Plan is possible, and that the U.S. holds the cards. In February 1971 he offered such a proposal, welcomed by Israel as a genuine peace offer but rejected on grounds that Israel would not return to the 1967 borders. In January 1976 the Arab "confrontation states" backed a similar proposal in the UN Security Council. It was vetoed by the United States. Sadat's dramatic moves last November were little different in substance, though he did succeed finally in overcoming the refusal of the American media to recognize what had long been obvious.

In this context, we can return to the "Path-breaking" statement. It was critical of the Carter Administration for applying pressure to Israel. Thus the signers set themselves apart from the small group of Israeli doves who have called for a settlement recognizing both Jewish and Palestinian national rights and who repeatedly urge that the U.S. cease its direct intervention thwarting such a settlement and use its influence instead to advance it.

The "peace group" to which the message was addressed has put forth no specific programme. The major political opposition within Israel scarcely differs from the governing Likud coalition on these issues. Former Prime Minister Golda Meir, for example, recently denounced Begin for making too many concessions to Sadat. Though the statement of the 37 also expresses no clear position, it falls within the mainstream of Israeli politics in its lack of concern for the fate of the former inhabitants of Palestine, now living in exile or under military occupation or as second-class citizens in Israel, and in its criticism of Carter for his slight gestures in their direction, which come nowhere near a recognition of their national rights.

The statement was remarkable in some respects. The signers described themselves as "lifelong friends of Israel, nothing can destroy that friendship or the efforts on Israel's behalf that follow naturally from it." They pledged themselves "to work on Israel's behalf," adding that they "shall never rest in fulfilling our pledge." Replace "Israel" with the name of any other state and the response to such pronouncements would be one of astonishment. Rarely has a group of intellectuals pledged their commitment to any state—let alone a foreign state—in such terms. Why then are such expressions, combined with a criticism of Carter for deviating ever so slightly from the Israeli stand, regarded as a "major event," a courageous expression of "independence of judgment," as the *Times* describes it?

These events give some insight into the attitudes that have prevailed among American intellectuals, not only Jewish, since Israel's overwhelming military victory of 1967. Prior to that dramatic conquest, the situation was rather different. Like U.S. government policy, "support for Israel" on the part of many American intellectuals corresponds fairly closely to perceived Israeli power, a fact that deserves some thought.

One might argue, as the *Times* does, that the source of the "special relationship" is a moral concern. That is very dubious. The Palestinians have suffered the fate that Israeli Jews rightly fear, but somehow that fact arouses no moral anguish and does not influence policy. Would the reaction have been the same, in Mach. 1978, if a quarter of a million Jews had been driven from their homes by an overwhelming Arab military assault? Nor can these attitudes be explained on grounds of fear for Israel's security. On the contrary, "support for Israel" rose dramatically when Israel's regional power appeared to be overwhelming and in fact increasing, as was commonly believed in the 1967–73 period.

I believe that the primary sources for the unprecedented articulate support for Israel lie elsewhere. Individuals have their own reasons, but the phenomenon is so general as to motivate a search for underlying causes. These are, I believe, largely domestic. In the late 1960s the comfortable world of the intelligentsia, a privileged sector of American society, was threatened from every direction. The Indochinese revolutionaries were refusing to submit to American violence; contrary to current illusions, American intellectuals tended to support the American war in Vietnam, turning against it, as business circles did, primarily on "pragmatic" grounds—it was unlikely to succeed at reasonable cost. At home, popular movements were developing out of the control of their "natural leaders." Ethnic minorities were demanding their rights. Students were pressing for a relaxation of ideological controls in the universities and an end to their subservience to state power. The smashing Israeli victory was in a way symbolic: an advanced technological society administered a crushing defeat to the forces of darkness threatening privilege and power at home and throughout the world. A case can be made that this was one major factor in generating the remarkable attitudes towards Israel that developed in this period among the American intelligentsia, attitudes that are reflected in the media and that generally correspond, as noted, to the internal calculations of the U.S. government, based on geopolitical, economic and strategic considerations.

The U.S. opposition to a comprehensive settlement that accommodates Palestinian rights alongside of those of Israeli Jews may serve short-term interests. But moral considerations aside, it bears the seeds of disaster. It is most unfortunate that the prevailing political culture in the United States still makes it so difficult to discuss these issues, as they are constantly and openly discussed elsewhere in the world, Israel included.

## Editor's Notes to Chapter 8

Introduction, dated January 1, 1980, to Livia Rokach's *Israel's Sacred Terrorism*: A study based on Moshe Sharett's *Personal Diary* and other documents. (Belmont, MA: Association of Arab-American University Graduates, Inc., 1980) pp. xi–xiii. (For further information on AAUG, write to: P.O. Box 456, Turnpike Station, Shrewsbury, MA 01545.) The reference to footnotes 42, 43 is to Rokach's monograph. See **PME**. See also Chomsky, "Bellow's Israel." *New York Arts Journal* 2.1 (1977): pp. 29–32 (reprinted in *Gazelle Review of Literature on the Middle East* 2 (1977): pp. 24–32, and later included in **TCW**), and "An Exchange on Israel: Chomsky on Schoenbrun, "*New York Arts Journal* 6 (Sept.–Nov. 1977): pp. 11 & 13–16.

Michael Klare's "Prussians" "include representatives of both parties (Ronald Reagan and Barry Goldwater from the Republicans, Henry Jackson and John Stennis from the Democrats), ex-military officers (Maxwell Taylor, Elmo Zumwalt), old-line union officials (George Meany, Lane Kirkland of the AFL-CIO International Division), and a fair sprinkling of cold-war intellectuals with impeccable 'Yankee' credentials (Paul Nitze and Eugene Rostow). This faction seeks to restore American military superiority at any cost, and it places U.S. national interests ahead of intra-capitalist harmony... (the Prussians) have never become reconciled to the easing of racial, sexual, and class barriers following the uprisings of the 60s... The Prussian camp also includes some U.S.-based industrialists whose profits are threatened by the flood of cheap imports produced by the multinational corporations in low-wage areas abroad... Traditionally the Prussians have been represented by the military and aerospace associations... but recently they launched the Committee on the Present Danger to attract a broader following. The Committee's founders include such stalwarts as Taylor, Kirkland, and Rostow, as well as pro-Israeli intellectuals like Saul Bellow and Norman Podhoretz, who believe that a hawkish U.S. defense posture best serves Israel's security interests... The Traders are most concerned about the fragility of the world economy and the danger of conflict within the capitalist camp. They are also worried about the growing disaffection of industrial workers in the advanced countries and unemployed slumdwellers in the Third World... at the nuclear level, the Traders speak of 'controlling' the arms race through an accelerated series of SALT talks, while the Prussians seek to enhance the 'thinkability' of nuclear war by introducing new 'limited-war' scenarios." "The most distinguished voice of [the Traders] is, of course, David Rockefeller's Trilateral Commission," but they enjoy "the support of numerous trade and business organizations" (M. Klare, "The Traders and the Prussians." *Seven Days*, Mar. 26, 1977: pp. 32–33; see now M. Klare, "Beyond the Vietnam Syndrome: Renewed U.S. Interventionism in the Third World." *Radical America* 15 (1981): pp. 153–159.) See **AWA**, chapter 1.

See now **TCW**, in particular the Introduction and ch. 8.

# 8. Outside Of Israeli "Official History"

History, particularly recent history, is characteristically presented to the general public within the framework of a doctrinal system based on certain fundamental dogmas. In the case of the totalitarian societies, the point is too obvious to require comment. The situation is more intriguing in societies that lack the cruder forms of repression and ideological control. The United States, for example, is surely one of the least repressive societies of past or present history with respect to freedom of inquiry and expression. Yet only rarely will an analysis of crucial historical events reach a wide audience unless it conforms to certain doctrines of the faith.

"The United States always starts out with good intentions." With this ritual incantation, a liberal critic of American interventionism enters the area of permissible debate, of thinkable thoughts (in this case, William Pfaff, "Penalty of Interventionism," *International Herald Tribune*, Feb. 1979). To accept the dogma, a person who is unable to tolerate more than a limited degree of internal contradiction must studiously avoid the documentary record, which is ample in a free society—for example, the record of high-level planning exhibited in the Pentagon Papers, particularly the record of the early years of U.S. involvement in the 1940s and early 1950s when the basic outlines of strategy were developed and formulated. Within the scholarly professions and the media the intelligentsia can generally be counted on to close ranks; they will refuse to submit to critical analysis the doctrines of the faith, prune the historical and documentary record so as to insulate these doctrines from examination, and proceed to present a version of history that is safely free from institutional critique or analysis. Occasional departures from orthodoxy are of little moment as long as they are confined to narrow circles that can be ignored, or dismissed as "irresponsible" or "naive" or "failing to comprehend the complexities of history," or otherwise identified with familiar code-words as beyond the pale.

Though relations between Israel and the United States have not been devoid of conflict, still there is no doubt that there has been, as is often said, a "special relationship." This is obvious at the material level, as measured by flow of capital and armaments, or as measured by diplomatic support, or by joint operations, as when Israel acted to defend crucial U.S. interests in the Middle East at the time of the 1970 crisis involving Jordan, Syria and the Palestinians. The special relationship appears at the ideological level as well. Again with rare exceptions, one must adopt certain doctrines of the faith to enter the arena of debate, at least before any substantial segment of the public.

The basic doctrine is that Israel has been a hapless victim—of terrorism, of military attack, of implacable and irrational hatred. It is not uncommon for well-informed American political analysts to write that Israel has been attacked four times by its neighbors, including even 1956. Israel is sometimes chided for its response to terrorist attack, a reaction that is deemed wrong though understandable. The belief that Israel may have had a substantial role in initiating and perpetuating violence and conflict is expressed only far from the mainstream, as a general rule. In discussing the backgrounds of the 1956 war, Nadav Safran of Harvard University, in a work that is fairer than most, explains that Nasser "seemed bent on mobilizing Egypt's military resources and leading the Arab countries in an assault on Israel." The Israeli raid in Gaza in February 1955 was "retaliation" for the hanging of Israeli saboteurs in Egypt—it was only six years later, Safran claims, that it became known that they were indeed Israeli agents. The immediate background for the conflict is described in terms of fedayeen terror raids and Israeli retaliation. The terror organized by Egyptian intelligence "contributed significantly to Israel's decision to go to war in 1956 and was the principal reason for its refusal to evacuate the Gaza Strip" (*The Embattled Ally*, Harvard University Press, 1978).

To maintain such doctrines as these, or the analysis of alleged fact that conform to them, it is necessary scrupulously to avoid crucial documentation. Safran, in his 600-page study, makes no use of major sources such as the diaries that Livia Rokach reviews here, relevant parts of which had been made public in 1974, or the captured Egyptian documents published in Israel in 1975, or other sources that undermine these analyses (see n. 42, 43). Much the same is true of the mainstream scholarly literature and journalism fairly generally.

Moshe Sharett's diary, to which Livia Rokach's monograph is devoted, is undoubtedly a major documentary source. It remains outside of "official history"—that version of history that reaches more than a tiny audience of people unsatisfied by conventional doctrine. It is only reasonable to predict that this will remain true in the United States as long as the "special relationship" persists. If, on the other hand, Israel had been, say, an ally of the Soviet Union, then Sharett's revelations would quickly become common knowledge, just as no one would speak of the Egyptian attack on Israel in 1956.

In studying the process of policy formation in any state, it is common to find a rough division between relatively hard-line positions that urge the use of force and violence to attain state ends, and "softer" approaches that advocate diplomatic or commercial methods to attain the same objectives—a distinction between "the Prussians" and "the traders," to borrow terms that Michael Klare has suggested in his work on U.S. foreign policy. The goals are basically the same; the measures advocated differ, at least to a degree, a fact that may ultimately bear on the nature of the ends pursued. Sharett was an advocate of the "soft" approach. His defeat in internal Israeli politics reflected the ascendancy of the positions of Ben-Gurion, Dayan and others who were not reluctant to use force to attain their goals. His diaries give a very revealing picture of the developing conflict, as he perceived it, and offer an illuminating insight into the early history of the state of Israel, with ramifications that reach to the present, and beyond. Livia Rokach has performed a valuable service in making this material readily available, for the first time, to those who are interested in discovering the real world that lies behind "official history."

## Editor's Notes to Chapter 9

Reprinted from the NAM Newspaper (Sept. 1975), slightly revised, in the RESIST Newsletter 96 (Sept. 30). See Editor's Notes to the previous Selection, and Selection 24.

A few months later Chomsky used the expression "the authentic left" again, adding the following footnote: "Evidently there is a value judgment here, for which I do not apologize." The context was this: "In a socialist society, as envisioned by the authentic left, a central purpose will be that the necessary requirements of every member of society be satisfied. We may assume that these necessary requirements will be historically conditioned in part and will develop along with the expansion and enrichment of material and intellectual culture. But 'equality of condition' is no desideratum, as we approach Marx's 'realm of freedom' individuals will differ in their aspirations, their abilities, and their personal goals" ("Equality," see Introduction, n. 30).

See **TCW**, chs. 9–12, and **FT**.

# 9. On The Middle East

The recent flurry of reports about nuclear weapons in the Middle East, and in general the extraordinary and still rising level of armaments, has appeared only to underline the urgency of the U.S. government's efforts to bring about a separation of forces agreement in the Sinai. The next war, should it come, would probably achieve new levels of brutality. It is unlikely that Israel's cities would again be spared, and the devastation of Arab civilian targets is likely to go well beyond the destructive attacks of the past. And, given the international stakes, a regional conflict might well explode into a general conflagration.

Therefore it would seem that Kissinger's efforts to turn aside the threat of immediate conflict are to be welcomed, as they may buy time to heal the wounds that remain. But a closer analysis suggests something quite different.

To be sure, for the tenure of the agreement Israel's southern front will be neutralized and the threat of another "October War" significantly alleviated. Such an agreement serves the short-run interests of Egypt and Israel, as well as of the U.S. But what are its likely consequences in the long run?

With the reduction of the military threat, Israel will be free to pursue the policies to which the major political forces are committed. There are three sources of evidence concerning these policies: statements of political spokesmen, actual programs in operation or projected, and the historical record. Evidence from these sources converges. Israel will continue its development projects in the occupied territories, leading to integration and eventual annexation. The political leadership has repeatedly insisted that under any longterm agreement, Israel will retain the Gaza Strip, adjoining areas of Northeastern Sinai, Sharm el-Sheik (Israeli "Ophira") and an access to it, most of the Golan Heights, a considerably expanded Jerusalem, parts of the West Bank (Judea and Samaria), including a region along the Jordan River that will be Israel's effective border with the Arab world to the east. Since 1967, substantial resources have been devoted to development projects in these areas, and despite the severe economic crisis, these projects have been accelerated. Under conditions of relaxation of the military threat, there is every reason to believe that these efforts will continue.

In the region west of Gaza, thousands of Arab peasants have been expelled to clear the area for Jewish settlement, and plans for a deep water port (Yamit) are in progress in a region that is universally regarded outside of Israel as Egyptian territory.

These programs ensure that there will be no lasting peace between Egypt and Israel. Civilian settlement and industrial development in the Golan Heights guarantees that there will be no peace between Syria and Israel. Comparable projects in the West Bank and the environs of Jerusalem spell the end of any hopes for even a quasi-independent Palestinian nationalism, and thus guarantee that terrorism will intensify, since all alternatives will have been blocked. Correspondingly, the harsh Israeli repression in the West Bank and Israel's military operations in Lebanon will continue, further embittering relations.

Israel hopes that the "facts" built in this way will eventually be accepted by the Arab states, or at least that the Arab world will be powerless to alter them. The political leadership seems to believe that "responsible" Arab political forces will accept some kind of home rule under Israeli military control in areas of the West Bank that are not directly integrated or annexed, perhaps under Jordanian civil administration; that Egypt will abandon Northeastern Sinai and "Ophira" and return to its pressing internal problems; that Syria will fume in impotent silence; and that Israeli force will be able to restrict the Palestinian threat to tolerable limits. After the "seven lean years," the Israeli political leadership argues, alternative energy sources will undermine Arab economic pressures. Thus, Israel can regain the position of military security and regional hegemony that it enjoyed, so it was thought, after the overwhelming military victory of 1967.

But the real world is likely to evolve along quite a different course. There is little reason to expect that the effectiveness of "Arab blackmail" on the industrial societies will diminish. For the U.S., the problem is not primarily dependence on Arab oil, but rather the danger that its industrial rivals might get privileged access to the vast energy resources of the Arab world. For the present, business and financial circles in the U.S. are not displeased with the course of events. The U.S. currently has a favorable trade balance with the Arab world, and the U.S.-based energy corporations retain their positions of international dominance.

As a large portion of Arab oil income has returned to the U.S. in purchases and investments, while Europe had depended for a much greater proportion of her energy needs on Middle Eastern oil, the major effect of Arab "oil politics" so far has been to compel European and Japanese capitalism to subsidize U.S. economic recovery. It is for such reasons that one hears little from business circles about military intervention in the Persian Gulf. Rather, these notions are the province of liberal ideologists for the most part, for reasons that deserve an independent discussion. Investment prospects in the region are promising. There are also excellent prospects for sale of military equipment, an area where the U.S. has a major competitive advantage in foreign trade. Europe and Japan have no realistic alternative to reliance on Middle Eastern oil in the foreseeable future, and will continue to maintain as much of a role as the U.S. permits them in the developing economies of the region.

The major oil-producing states will be able to mount significant pressures, if they so choose. Whether they do or not, they will continue to increase their military capacity, encouraged by the international arms producers, with the U.S.

far in the lead. Israel does not have to match them gun for gun, and can rely on its own rapidly expanding armaments industry. But to maintain some sort of military balance, Israel's economic resources will have to be devoted to the purchase of rapidly obsolescing advanced military technology and materiel, a crushing burden.

Immigration to Israel has dropped significantly, while emigration, particularly of the educated and increasingly native born, has increased to record heights, a further drain on scarce resources. Investment and gifts have fallen off, an important matter for a state so dependent on funds from abroad. Terrorism will never be eliminated, and may increasingly involve segments of the repressed Arab minority, particularly as the level of education rises with the concomitant frustrations that are inevitable in a state founded on the principle of discrimination.

Whatever the private hopes of the leadership of the Arab states, frustrated Palestinian nationalism will serve as a rallying cry and a source of internal conflict. Nor will the "confrontation states" relinquish the territories that Israel intends to absorb. Conflict will simmer and occasionally erupt. Sooner or later there will be a war. Even short of war, conditions within Israel and the surrounding states will be difficult if not intolerable, as they devote their limited resources to preparation for war.

There is little point in setting forth more precise "scenarios." It is difficult to construct one of any plausibility that does not lead to bitterness and eventual disaster. It is conceivable that the situation will stabilize with Israel in control of the bulk of the occupied territories, but no person with a sense of reality will place much confidence in such possibilities. This would require the destruction of Palestinian nationalism, a result tolerable only to a racist mentality.

I have been describing the likely consequences of the recent Kissinger negotiations. Had they failed the timetable would simply have been accelerated. For this reason the concern over their outcome was largely misplaced, and the lively debate over who was to blame an irrelevant exercise. A rational person will, rather, ask a different question: is there another framework?

In fact, a realistic alternative to the politics of suicide and destruction does exist. It requires that we focus on the underlying conflict between Israeli Jews and Palestinian Arabs, who claim national rights in the same territory, rather than the military conflict between Israel and Egypt (and secondarily Israel and Syria). Israel's only hope for decent survival lies in a political accommodation. This fact, not to speak of elementary considerations of justice and humanity, demands that Palestinian national rights be satisfied in some manner.

Prior to the October war, various possibilities existed. Now there remains only one. Israel must return to (essentially) its pre-June 1967 borders. A Palestinian state, which will of course be organized by the PLO, will then be established in the West Bank and the Gaza Strip. The other occupied areas must be returned to Egypt and Syria, with some form of demilitarization, international supervision (on both sides of the border, as distinct from the pre-1967 period, when observers were permitted only on the Arab side), and efforts to reduce the level of armaments in the entire region. Jerusalem might become an open city, perhaps joint capital of both states.

Such a solution is in the interest of the superpowers, a fact that is recognized with some trepidation in Israel. Prior to the October 1973 war, such proposals were hopelessly unrealistic. Israeli power, backed by the United States, seemed unchallengeable. Now the situation has dramatically changed and a settlement along these lines is entirely feasible.

Since 1971, Egypt has repeatedly indicated its willingness to accept a settlement along these lines, and the Arab oil producers would probably welcome such an outcome. The Palestinians have no alternative apart from national suicide, At the moment, Israeli opposition is the primary barrier to a political settlement along these lines. The grounds put forth are "security," but the argument is extremely weak, as has been convincingly argued by critics within Israel, including several outstanding military analysts. Israel's long term security can only rest on accommodation with its neighbors and a reduction of the factors that drive them toward military conflict to regain lost lands or (in the case of the Palestinians) to find some basis for their national existence.

Of course, such a settlement carries no "guarantee" of security for Israel— or for the surrounding Arab states, including the Palestinian state, which also have a severe "security problem" in the face of Israeli military might, a fact often ignored in the U.S. In the real world, there are no "iron clad guarantees" of security. Those who call for them are either remarkably thoughtless or are disguising other motives.

For Israel, the optimal solution would be to achieve such a settlement by its own initiatives. Under present circumstances, this is unlikely. It is for this reason that much of the Israeli left privately hopes that American imperial power will compel Israel to move toward a political accommodation. If American pressure mounts, Israel will face two options: to yield, or to undertake a preemptive military strike in the hope that an Arab oil boycott or Russian moves (after suitable provocation) will compel the U.S. to intervene to preserve its hegemony in the region, thus restoring the situation of 1967–1973. If Israel's leadership senses that they would receive substantial support in the United States, they might pursue this desperate and possibly suicidal course.

Some Israeli analysts argue that the next war—which they are sure is coming—will enable Israel to demolish Arab military forces. To cite an extreme case, General Aharon Davidi, now a lecturer at Tel Aviv University, writes in a mass circulation journal that Israel should not only destroy the Arab armies but should also—destroy the economic, transport, social and leadership infrastructure specifically, hitting "the Arab intelligentsia" in Egypt, "the strata that go from Sadat to the high school graduates." He argues that "the Egyptian fellah does not hate us so much," so that destruction of the educated strata may provide some respite. Elsewhere, he has explained that "the most simple and humane" solution to the Palestinian problem is "a transfer of all Palestinians from their present places to the Arab countries," a proposal which will, perhaps, seem quite natural to those American liberals who have commented favorably on "population transfer" as a solution to Israel's dilemmas. In the past, genocidal threats from some Arab sources received wide publicity in the West, but the prevailing double standard requires that Davidi's be dismissed in silence,

After a recent tour in the United States General Mattityahu Peled, a leading Israeli Arabist at the Hebrew University who served on the General Staff during the 1967 war, wrote in the Israeli journal *New Outlook* that the "state of near hysteria" among the American Jewish community and their "blindly chauvinistic and narrow minded" support for the most reactionary policies within Israel poses "the danger of prodding Israel once more toward a posture of calloused intransigence." He concluded that "the established Jewish leadership in America does not really support Israel as a free democratic nation, but is completely mobilized in the service of a certain particular school of political thinking in Israel," namely, the most expansionist and intransigent elements.

He might have added that the same is true of major currents of American left-liberalism, with their vulgar apologetics for Israeli "exclusivism" (the current euphemism for the discriminatory policies that are the foundation of the Jewish state, not unlike its Muslim neighbors), their contempt for Palestinian rights, and their support for Israeli expansionism under the guise of a plea for "security" and "defensible borders." Among such groups, and not only the American Jewish community, "the idea that Arab hostility is immutable is raised to the level of a dogma of faith rather than considered as a political reality susceptible of change, and the occupied territories are regarded as a strategic asset to Israel though events prove that they are fast becoming an unbearable liability" (Peled). The deplorable behaviour of these groups contributed to the outbreak of the 1973 war, a near-disaster for the state of Israel. If they maintain their grip on substantial segments of American opinion, they will help pave the way for further disaster, along with their natural though relatively insignificant partners, those segments of the American left that urge the Palestinians on to suicide while denying Jewish national rights.

An imposed imperial settlement that leaves a Jewish state and an Arab state west of the Jordan, each based on the principle of discrimination and suppression of the minority that remains within their territories (Arabs and Jews, respectively), is hardly a welcome prospect. Unfortunately, under present circumstances, it is difficult to envisage a more favorable outcome. If such a settlement is reached, perhaps there will arise opportunities for slow evolution away from "exclusivism" and ultimately toward the kind of binational accommodation that is the only sane policy for either national group.

For the authentic left, at least, it will be essential to work to overcome the discriminatory framework of Israel and, no doubt, its Palestinian counterpart, and to construct alliances that cross national lines. to work for radical social change in the two national societies in the hope that barriers can be overcome in a joint struggle for democracy and socialism. It is conceivable that the American left might play a positive role in such developments, but only if current illusions are overcome and there is a willingness, now all too rare, to face up honestly to some of the realities that are obscured in the apologetics and diatribes that often pass for political commentary.

**Editor's Notes to Chapter 10**

Review of *North-South: A Program for Survival. The Report of the Independent Commission on International Development Issues under the Chairmanship of Willy Brandt*, London: Pan Books Ltd., 1980. It was written in March 1980 for the *Near East Business,* and it appeared in the issue 5.4 (May 31) pp. 26–29. It was reprinted in *Philosophy and Social Action* 7.2 (Apr.–June 1981): pp. 27–32. See now **Y501**, esp. 2.1.

# 10. The "North-South" Conflict

The Independent Commission on International Development Issues, founded in September 1977 under the chairmanship of Willy Brandt, took as its task "to study the grave global issues arising from the economic and social disparities of the world community and to suggest ways of promoting adequate solutions to the problems involved in development and in attacking absolute poverty." The report under review was issued in December 1979. The participants were from the OECD [Organization for Economic Cooperation and Development] and Third World countries, virtually all with past or present roles in government. In the words of the chairman, the report "discusses North-South relations as the great social challenge of our time," warning that the "two decades ahead of us may be fateful for mankind" and seeking "to demonstrate that the mortal dangers threatening our children and grandchildren can be averted; and that we have a chance—whether we are living in the North or South, East or West—if we are determined to do so, to shape the world's future in peace and welfare, in solidarity and dignity." Recommendations are sketched dealing with a wide range of problems. The recommendations, as the report notes, are far from radical; most have been put forth by international commissions in the past, apart from a few suggestions for new international coordination and advisory structures. Apart from such matters as agrarian reform in the South, the question of social change within the states of the international system is not considered, and it is assumed that the structure of the international system itself will undergo no significant modification, despite some scattered references to restructuring of an unspecified sort.

## A gloomy prospect for the human race

The most powerful argument in support of the recommendations is the gloomy prospect for the human race if present trends persist: mass starvation, ecological catastrophe, waste of scarce resources in increasing military production, the likelihood of war as conflict over diminishing resources mounts, the slowdown in economic growth, the tragic coincidence of unused productive capacities among the wealthy and impoverishment and misery on a vast scale. These problems would no doubt be alleviated if the recommendations offered were followed. Thus, "largescale transfer of resources" from the wealthy to the most impoverished countries should contribute to reducing the likelihood of mass starvation or other concomitants of poverty, such as the virtual enslavement of tens of millions of children in Latin America, India, Thailand and elsewhere reported in a recent study of the London-based AntiSlavery society. As the commission reports, the rich countries of the North, with rare exceptions, have demonstrated little interest in such transfers. OECD countries averaged 0.35 percent of GNP for official development assistance in 1978 (in comparison, the Soviet-bloc countries provided aid at the estimated level of 0.04 percent of GNP, and the OPEC countries have contributed nearly 3 percent of their GNP, with Saudi Arabia, Kuwait, and the Gulf states providing between 6 and 15 percent of GNP in past years and 4–5 percent in 1978). In dramatic contrast, the sale of arms has been growing at the rate of $5 billion a year and is estimated at $25 billion in 1979, with every indication that the trends will continue (*Business Week,* 24 Mar. 1980). According to Brandt, "The annual military bill is now approaching 450 billion U.S. dollars, while official development aid accounts for less than 5 per cent of this figure." And the trends are plainly in the wrong direction.

### Institutional causes

The Commission rightly deplores these tendencies, and urges that they be reversed. It does not, however, ask why they persist. In general, the report does not probe very deeply into existing institutional structures, state or private, or into the actual structure of power in the international system or within particular societies. The report notes that "The most basic of all needs is the right to participate in change and to share in the outcome." Brave words, but they say very little in the absence of any effort to spell out just what they mean. Do they mean, for example, that coercive state structures and private ownership of resources and means of production should be abolished, so that people may achieve "the most basic of all needs?" It is hardly likely that the commissioners had this in mind. They limit themselves to urging a "new outlook" and to declaiming that "A new international economic order will need men and women with a new mentality and wider outlook to make it work, and a process of development in which their full capacities flourish." The problems of international society might indeed be manageable if their root cause was the failure of individuals to develop the proper outlook and mentality. If the causes are institutional, however, the problems are somewhat more severe and programs of a completely different kind are necessary to avert disaster. The report notes that the main proposals for change have made little headway," particularly when "structural change" in North-South relations is at issue. Their reluctance to carry out a structural and institutional critique leaves these failures as a mystery, explained perhaps by failure to adopt the right outlook. But it is difficult to rest much confidence in such an analysis, or to expect that matters might change now that new recommendations, not very different from those that have been on the table for many years, have been put forth by an international commission, however well-meaning.

## The competition for scarce resources

The commission argues that mutual interests dictate the need for large-scale transfer of resources from North to South. The North has come to depend on the South for its markets. Aid can therefore be regarded as a device for export-promotion, given "the coexistence of the great needs in the South and the under-used capacity in the North." But governments have generally regarded aid in just this way, not only in North-South relations. The commission is therefore hardly recommending a "new outlook" in this regard. Nor does the report indicate why this conception of "mutual interests" should motivate significantly different policies in the future.

The report urges, reasonably and humanely, that the North should contribute to the kind of industrial and agricultural growth in the impoverished countries that would actually benefit their populations. At the same time it points out that "It is certain that the pace and pattern of economic expansion which has characterized the last century cannot be extended indefinitely," and that "one of the biggest difficulties ahead could be the competition for scarce exhaustible resources, especially in the field of energy, if economic growth among the rich countries were to continue at the intensity of use (and rate of expansion of use) of these resources exhibited in the past." In the light of these observations, why should we expect those who have real power in the wealthy societies to permit, let alone encourage, development in the South that would increase the demand for scarce resources and limit their own access to and control over them? These questions are not raised. They are also not answered by appeal to mutual interests.

## The reasons for arms sales

One can surely not quarrel with the pleas of the commission to halt the escalating arms race and to replace arms transfers to the Third World by transfer of resources that can be used for productive development. The commission holds that "The major powers sell weapons mainly to suit their own foreign policy or to maintain regional balances, rather than to benefit their economies." One might argue—correctly in my view—that there is no small degree of mystification in this formulation, as would become clear if such phrases as "to suit their foreign policy" and "to maintain regional balances" were decoded in terms of the real interests that determine foreign policy. The report itself notes that "With the recession in the arms industry in the early 1970s—following the end of the Vietnam war—and the emergence of new profitable markets, particularly in the Middle East, the drive to sell weapons to the Third World was intensified, often aimed at stimulating new demand irrespective of real defense needs." This observation tends to undermine their analysis of the reasons for arms sales. The analysis would have profited by a closer look at some of the major transfers of armaments—say, to the Shah of Iran under the Nixon Doctrine, or from the USSR to Ethiopia (for defense against Eritrea?).

The report argues that resort to arms sales to stimulate the economies of the Western powers is an error, citing analyses that suggest that "investment in arms production creates fewer jobs than in other industries and public services." But it does not ask why this "error" persists. To do so would lead into territory that the report avoids: the actual structure of power within the societies of the North. Abstracting away from existing political and economic institutions, one can argue that state intervention in the economy may stimulate production as well by investment in public services or useful production as by production of waste (armaments). But this abstraction eliminates crucial factors that determine policy. The military-bureaucratic elite that governs the USSR can maintain and extend its power by military production, whereas this power might erode if resources were directed to desperately needed consumer goods. In the capitalist societies, the state—which is hardly independent of private power—will tend to act in such a way as to reinforce powerful private interests, not to compete with them, and will also tend to resort to chauvinistic appeals to justify a higher tax burden rather than try to organize or support popular forces that seek to undermine authoritarian structures such as the structures of the private corporate system. An appeal to "error" or failure of perception is not a convincing explanation for deep-seated and persistent tendencies such as these. Rather, it is necessary to undertake the kind of institutional analysis that the report skirts.

## Agribusiness and undernutrition

The same is true with regard to the recommendations concerning agriculture. The report observes that "The rich of the world could also help to increase food supplies if they used less fertilizer for non-food purposes, and also if they ate less meat." Elsewhere, they take note of the fact that "Transnational corporations, in particular, were often developing cash crops for export at the expense of local food availability, and were contributing to the problems of global food supplies." The report urges that transnational corporations follow more humane policies in the Third World. But there are reasons for the fact that in Costa Rica and Guatemala, beef is produced for export while the price of milk puts it out of reach of most families, or the fact that the Del Monte corporation exports 90 percent of its Philippine production while "the average Filipino has an even more inadequate calorie intake than the average Bangladeshi and serious protein-calorie undernutrition affects an estimated half of all Filipino children under four— one of the highest rates in the world" (F.M. Lapp and J. Collins, *Food First*). The reasons seem, in fact, rather obvious. As long as the underlying causes remain unchanged, there is every reason to expect that the policies that the commission deplores will persist. By refusing to examine these causes, the commission simply consigns its recommendations to irrelevance.

Given its composition, it is no wonder that the commission avoids penetrating analysis of the causes for the policies that it rightly finds so shocking, and keeps largely to moral appeals directed to institutions that regard them as totally irrelevant to decision-making. The report is very careful to avoid giving offense to the powerful, state or private. It notes that since World War II some ten million people have been killed in the Third World in wars using non-nuclear weapons. "In some of these wars," it adds, "such as in Korea and Indochina, the major powers were actively engaged." This seems a rather delicate reference to the actual cause of massacre and destruction, or its agents, in these cases. Who was it who bombed the dikes in North Korea in an effort to bring about massive starvation, or who destroyed the agricultural systems of Indochina while killing vast numbers of people and driving much of the rural population to urban slums by force and violence? The report notes the miserly record of the USSR in aiding the Third World, but the chairman informs the reader that he has "been assured by Soviet leaders and those of East European countries that they view mankind's common problems with great seriousness"—very touching, given the historical record.

## Comparison with the Nazis

Only in one instance is diplomatic caution abandoned. Chairman Brandt writes: "Speaking perhaps undiplomatically: since the death camps in Europe and the Hiroshima bomb, mankind has never been so humiliated as in Indochina recently, and especially in Cambodia." The context is a discussion of "one of the most tragic consequences of current conflicts and tensions: millions of refugees whose lives have been uprooted and often desperately impoverished." The policies of the leadership of devastated Vietnam which contributed to the tragedy of the "boat people" merits comparison with the Nazis, but American actions in Indochina did not "humiliate mankind" to this degree. Similarly, the policies of the Vietnamese leadership are Nazi-like, but not those of the Indonesian military, who presided over the massacre of hundreds of thousands of people, mostly landless peasants, in 1965–6, and who, since 1975, have been engaged in a huge massacre in East Timor in the course of their aggression (backed at every step by the West), while reducing the territory to a situation that, relief officials finally admitted after almost four years of horror, compare to what is observed on the Thai-Cambodian border. One of the commissioners is Adam Malik, Minister of Foreign Affairs of Indonesia from 1966–77, and others are representatives of governments that have provided the military and diplomatic support for this atrocity, which does not compare in brutality, according to Chairman Brandt, to the policies of the Hanoi government during the same period. The high moral tone of the report is perhaps less impressive than it might be.

## Self-interest and policy decisions

In his introduction, Willy Brandt comments that "Morally it makes no difference whether a human being is killed in war or is condemned to starve to death because of the indifference of others." His observation is pertinent and the sentiment is laudable, but it does not reach as far as it might. Indifference is not the primary cause of starvation and misery, though it is a contributing factor.

Policy decisions are taken within a structure of institutions, and as long as these are not subjected to analysis, understanding will be limited, responsibility will not be properly attributed, and recommendations for change will have little effect on practice.

One might argue, in defense of the report, that it is only realistic to assume the relatively stable character of state and private power and the institutional structures in which it is exercised, and to appeal for more humane policies within this framework, emphasizing the self-interest of the powerful in such policies. Perhaps a case can be made for this view, but we should be careful to avoid succumbing to or contributing to illusions about what can be achieved in these terms. I find it difficult to persuade myself that by adopting these assumptions, one can look forward with any optimism to solutions or even significant amelioration of the grave and menacing problems that are eloquently reviewed in the commission's report. Perhaps its major contribution might be to focus attention on these problems, and to provoke a far more searching inquiry that sets aside the limitations that were tacitly adopted by the commission in its deliberations.

### Editor's Notes to Chapter 11

Written on March 2 1980, it appeared in the RESIST Newsletter 132 (June 1980).

A Spanish translation appeared in an anarchist journal published in Madrid (*Adarga* no. 1, Junio 1980).

For a more recent and far more explicit variation on the same theme, see *Radical America* 15 (1981): pp. 141–151, a transcript of a talk given by Chomsky in May 1980.

He gave another talk on the topic at the Polytechnic of Central London on June 9, 1981, an edited and shortened transcript of which appeared as "The Cold War" in *The Guardian* (Manchester-London), June 15, p. 7, and in *Guardian Weekly,* June 21; it was later reprinted as an editorial in *Monthly Review* 33.6 (1981): pp. 1–10, under the title "The Cold War and the Super-powers."

A much expanded version, prepared in June 1980 for a Japanese collection of his writings (see "Introduction to Chomsky's social theory," n. 10), appears in **TCW**. See also ch. 8 (p. 56 n. 74 above) and Introduction in **TCW**.

# 11. The New Cold War

After the hostage crisis erupted in Iran, the *NY Times* printed a front-page article by Hedrick Smith headlined "Iran is Helping the U.S. to Shed Fear of Intervening Abroad" (2 Dec. 1979). Smith reported "an important shift of attitudes" in Washington—that, many believe, will have a significant long-term impact on the willingness of the United States to project its power in the third world and to develop greater military capabilities for protecting its interests there." "We are moving away from our post-Vietnam reticence," one policy maker said. Democratic national chairman John White stated that "We may have reached a turning point in our attitude toward ourselves, and that is a feeling that we have a right to protect legitimate American interests anywhere in the world." Senator Frank Church indicated support for military intervention in the Middle East "if our interests were threatened." The "lesson of Vietnam" is that we must be "more selective" in the use of military power, with a more careful calculation of the costs to us, as we consider intervention "in such troubled regions of potential American influence as the Middle East and the Caribbean"—consider what must be intended if our influence in these regions is regarded as only "potential."

## The protection of "our interests"

It is intriguing to speculate on what the reaction would be here if Kremlin political spokesmen were to express themselves in comparable terms, adopting a comparable conception of the scope of their "legitimate interests anywhere in the world" which afford them the right of military intervention. Or if some other power were to claim the right of military intervention in the United States if our agricultural resources were denied them.

In January 1978, Secretary of Defense Harold Brown ordered the Pentagon to plan for a rapid deployment force of 100,000 men backed by air and naval units for possible intervention in the Persian Gulf region or elsewhere, renewing plans that had been blocked by a Congress hobbled by "post-Vietnam reticence" —for example, by the conservative Senator Richard Russell who warned that "if it is easy for us to go anywhere and do anything, we will always be going somewhere and doing something," with consequences that were dramatically evident at the time. The taking of hostages in Iran was only one of many events that have been exploited to help overcome such "reticence." The lesson of Iran is supposed to be that we should develop more destructive strategic weapons, deploy forces prepared for rapid intervention throughout the world, "unleash" the CIA, and otherwise demonstrate our pugnacity.

That such lessons should be drawn from the taking of hostages in Iran is quite revealing. It should be obvious on a moment's thought that a rapid deployment force would have been no more effective than the MX missile system in rescuing the hostages or preventing the takeover of the Embassy, and that it was precisely the policies of military intervention and subversion that led to the Iranian debacle, while subjecting Iranians to a quarter-century of torture, murder and suffering-or "progressive measures of development," as U.S. ideologists describe what was taking place when the U.S.-trained secret police were gouging out eyes of children and much of the rural population was being driven to miserable urban slums while the agricultural system collapsed and Iran practically sank into the sea under the weight of American armaments. It is clear that the hostage crisis served merely as a useful opportunity to advance policies that derive from other interests.

In the past months, NATO, under U.S. pressure, has deployed new advanced missiles, the USSR has invaded Afghanistan, and the Carter Doctrine has been proclaimed, calling for a substantial increase in the military budget including not only intervention forces but also preparations for a peacetime draft and the MX missile system, vast in scale and cost and a major contribution to an escalating arms race. War clouds are gathering. We have entered the period of "the New Cold War."

According to the doctrines of the New Cold Warriors, the search for military bases in the Middle East and the general program of militarization of American society are "defensive measures" taken to protect potential victims of Russian aggression. Senator Church is more honest when he speaks of protecting "our interests"—though the term "our" requires some qualification—a fact that is well understood by those we are preparing to "protect." The general impression here is that the recent meeting of Islamic states in Pakistan was called to condemn the Russian invasion of Afghanistan; true, but only part of the truth. A business-oriented review of economic and political news from the Middle East notes that the meeting "adopted a Saudi-inspired resolution to protect Iran from the effects of an American boycott," and reports that the Gulf countries "are more worried about the potential reaction of the U.S. to the crisis than they are about Soviet intervention itself." The Middle East is heading toward war, one official stated, "but towards a war which would mean the sharing by the superpowers of its oil and mineral wealth" (*An-Nahar Arab Report & Memo*, 4 Feb. 1980).

## A deadly dance of death

In much of the world, the interpretation of the Cold War is somewhat different from the prevailing version offered by the superpower antagonists themselves. The Cold War is perceived, with much reason, as a deadly dance of death in which the superpowers mobilize their own populations to support harsh and brutal measures directed against regions that they take to be within their respective domains, where they are "protecting their legitimate interests." Appeal to the alleged threat of the powerful global enemy has proven to be a useful device for this purpose. In this respect, the Cold War has been highly functional for the superpowers, which is one reason why it persists despite the danger of total destruction if the system misbehaves. When the U.S. moves to overthrow the government of Iran or Guatemala or Chile, or to invade Cuba or Indochina or the Dominican Republic, or to bolster murderous military dictatorships in Latin America or Asia, it does so in a noble effort to defend free peoples from the imminent Russian (or earlier, Chinese) threat. Similarly, when the Soviet Union sends its tanks to East Berlin, Hungary, Czechoslovakia or Afghanistan, it is acting from the purest of motives, in defense of socialism and freedom against the machinations of U.S. imperialism and its cohorts. The rhetoric employed on both sides is similar, and is generally parroted by the intelligentsia in each camp. It has proven effective in organizing support, as even a totalitarian state must do, for brutal measures, which often carry a significant cost for the population of the imperial power as well. The New Cold War promises to be no different.

The greatest threat to world peace, we are told, now lies in Western Pakistan, where the Russians are preparing to march towards the Persian Gulf in order to take control of the Middle East oil that belongs to us as a natural right. We must therefore dispatch military forces to the region and arm General Zia, perhaps the most unpopular ruler that Pakistan has ever had. A Russian spy in Carter's cabinet, at least one who happened to have the strange desire to be incinerated along with the rest of us, could offer no better advice. General Zia's arms will not deter a Russian army any more than 1800 marines in the Gulf, nor is there any indication that the Soviet Union would be insane enough to invade Pakistan; the invasion of Afghanistan, reprehensible though it was, was characteristic of Soviet military actions in that it aimed to maintain a position of power already attained, now under internal attack.

But arms for General Zia, like the rapid deployment force, will be used for internal repression, a fact of which many Pakistanis are gloomily aware as we learn (as if we had to learn it) from the reporting from Pakistan in the foreign press. Like the Arab states that we are about to "defend," the Baluchi who are allegedly threatened by Russian aggression in Western Pakistan seem rather ambivalent about the invasion of Afghanistan. One reason is that they are aware of recent history, even if most Americans are not. They recall that in the mid-1970s, U.S. military helicopters supplied via the Shah were used by the Pakistani army to murder them and destroy their villages. They do not exactly welcome the American "aid" now being offered. The *Manchester Guardian* observes: "More American helicopter gunships blasting Baluchis; the finest Russian propaganda in the world... The West will be in an appalling dilemma, reviled in Baluchistan, the Frontier and Sind as the succourer of the oppressor" (weekly edition, 20 Jan. 1980), and reviled as well by other Pakistanis who may turn to the Russians for support against their tormentor, "defending" them with U.S. aid.

## The likely dynamics of interventionist policies

American planners are presumably not unaware of the likely dynamics: arms for General Zia, internal repression, expansion of Russian influence as the victims turn to the USSR for support, a new Afghanistan, nuclear holocaust. But the dangers are regarded as insignificant in comparison with the importance of overcoming "post-Vietnam reticence" and eliminating the annoying domestic barriers to military intervention and other harsh measures to protect "our interests"—that is, the interests of those whose economic power gives them a dominant influence over policy formation, and who believe that they stand to gain (though "we" may not) by maintaining a world system in which they are free to exploit human and material resources. A serious inquiry into U.S. foreign policy will show that these are the dominant factors that govern it, however they may be obscured by ideological obfuscation.

The United States suffered a defeat in Vietnam, but only a partial defeat. The basic institutions of American society were not affected, and it is therefore only rational to suppose that the interventionist policies of the recent past, which are rooted in these institutional structures, will persist. But an obedient public is a prerequisite for the use of harsh measures to "protect our interests." The awakening of much of the American public from apathy and blind obedience was regarded as a serious threat by dominant groups in the United States, and the West generally. This development of the sixties constituted what the Trilateral Commission analysts call "the crisis of democracy," as popular groups organized to take an active part in democratic politics, rejecting the domination of their natural rulers. A major effort has been undertaken in the "post-Vietnam era" to overcome this crisis and to reestablish what Hans Morgenthau once called "our conformist subservience to those in power." How well this campaign has succeeded is an open question. The recent upsurge of demonstrations, teach-ins, draft resistance and other forms of protest indicates that "post-Vietnam reticence"—that is, the willingness to abide by minimally decent principles of international behaviour—has not been overcome among much of the public, as has been obvious in any event from the quite substantial activism of the 1970s throughout the country.

Other factors too lie behind the drive towards further militarization of our society. The utility of chauvinistic appeals in an election campaign is a minor factor, but a more significant one is the temptation to resort to measures of militarized state capitalism to deal with social and economic crises that appear unmanageable. In the short term, this might be effective, but the damage to American society and its economy will be severe, not to speak of the threat posed to others.

## Waste production and international dominance

But the world is not what it was a generation ago. It is doubtful that the United States, no longer in a position of overwhelming dominance, can devote its resources to the production of waste while maintaining its position in the international system. Efforts to pressure U.S. allies to "bear their share of the burden" are not likely to prove successful. Europe has shown no enthusiasm for the new crusade, and Secretary of Defense Harold Brown met with little success in his recent effort to persuade Japan to undertake a major increase in military spending. American allies may choose to take their own independent initiatives, not only towards the USSR but also towards the Middle East and other resource-rich areas, realizing the long-term fears of American planners. It is worth recalling Henry Kissinger's warning, in explaining the thinking behind the "Year of Europe" in 1973, about "The prospect of a closed trading system embracing the European Community and a growing number of other nations in Europe, the Mediterranean, and Africa" from which the U.S. might be excluded. The proper organization of the world system, in his view, must be based on the recognition that "The United States has global interests and responsibilities" while our allies have "regional interests;" the United States must be "concerned more with the over-all framework of order than with the management of every regional enterprise," these being accorded to our allies, as he explained elsewhere.

Europe and Japan pose a greater potential threat to U.S. world power than the Soviet Union, if they move towards a more independent role. And a U.S.-sponsored New Cold War may press them in that direction, raising the possibility of new and unanticipated crises in the future. In the shorter term, one may perhaps expect the superpowers to create new and more awesome forces of destruction and to try to subjugate those who stand in the way of their global ambitions, marching towards nuclear catastrophe.

## Commitment or disaster

These are not laws of nature, and we need not merely watch as events unfold in their inexorable progression. Human decisions are made within human institutions; alternatives exist and can be pursued. In an era of growing demand for limited resources, the potential for catastrophe is great. The problems that must now be faced are far more severe and deep-seated than those that animated the popular movements of recent years. We can be fairly sure that a refusal to confront them with commitment and courage will prepare the way for disaster.

# Part II:

## U.S.A.: Myth, Reality, Acracy

**Editor's Notes to Chapter 12**

Written in June 1977 for the Japanese journal *Chuo Koron*. The original version (with some additions and the elimination of some redundancies) appears in HR. That is the version reprinted here (with section titles).

This essay is an integrated expanded version of two articles published in *Seven Days* 14 Feb. and 23 May 1977 under the heading "Demystified Zone." See also **IS** and **PE**, in particular the Frontispiece of Vol. 1. (Edward Bernays, born in 1891, was both on his father's side and his mother's side a nephew of Freud's.)

VISTA (Volunteers in Service of America), initiated in 1964 and virtually destroyed by Nixon and Ford, was a sort of Peace Corps for the metropolis.

See now *Trilateralism: The Trilateral Commission and Elite Planning for World Management*, ed. by Holly Sklar. Boston: South End Press, 1980. See *Win*, June 15, 1981, p. 29.

# 12. The Carter Administration: Myth And Reality

In attempting to assess a new Administration in the United States, it is important to bear in mind the extraordinarily narrow spectrum of political discourse and the limited base of political power, a fact that distinguishes the United States from many other industrial democracies. The United States is unique in that there is no organized force committed to even mild and reformist varieties of socialism, The two political parties, which some refer to, not inaccurately as the two factions of the single 'Property Party,' are united in their commitment to capitalist ideology and institutions. For most of the period since the Second World War, they have adhered to a 'bipartisan foreign policy,' which is to say, a one-party state as far as foreign affairs are concerned. The parties differ on occasion with regard to the role of the State, the Democrats generally tending to favor slight increases in state intervention in social and economic affairs, the Republicans tending to favor greater emphasis on private corporate power. Thus under a Democratic Administration, there are likely to be some moves towards 'welfare state' policies along with a more aggressive foreign policy, as the State pursues a more interventionist program at home and abroad. But these distinctions between 'liberals' and 'conservatives' are only marginal in their significance and are at most slight tendencies rather than serious alternatives.

The domestic sources of power remain basically unchanged, whatever the electoral outcome. The major decision-making positions in the executive branch of the government, which increasingly dominates domestic and foreign policy, remain overwhelmingly in the hands of representatives of major corporations and the few law firms that cater primarily to corporate interests, thus representing generalized interests of corporate capitalism as distinct from parochial interests of one or another sector of the private economy. It is hardly surprising, then, that the basic function of the State remains the regulation of domestic and international affairs in the interest of the masters of the private economy, a fact studiously ignored in the press and academic scholarship, but apparent on investigation of the actual design and execution of policy over many years.

In fact, if some Administration were to depart in a significant way from the interests of highly concentrated private corporate power, its behavior would quickly be modified by a variety of simple techniques. Basic decisions concerning the health and functioning of the economy, hence social life in general, remain in the private sector. Decisions made in this realm set the conditions and define the framework within which the political process unfolds. By modifying the economic factors under their control, business interests can sharply constrain actions within the political sphere, But the issue rarely arises, since, as noted, the government, including those who manage the state sector of the economy, remains basically in the hands of private capital in any event.

Extra-governmental sources of ideas and programs are also, naturally, dominated by those who control the basic institutions of production, finance and commerce. The Council on Foreign Relations and the Trilateral Commission, to which I will return, are obvious examples.

## The ideological institutions

The basic uniformity of policy is clearly reflected in the ideological institutions. The mass media, the major journals of opinion, and the academic professions that are concerned with public affairs rarely tolerate any significant departure from the dominant state capitalist ideology. There is, for example, no socialist voice in the press, quite a remarkable fact in the mid-twentieth century. While the pressures of the student movement of the late 1960s caused the universities to relax doctrinal rigidity slightly, there has been no significant opening to the left in academic scholarship or teaching. Political criteria are no longer applied in such a blatant fashion as they were in the 1950s to eliminate dissenting opinion from the academic world. Nevertheless, there are numerous and effective barriers that guarantee the dominance of state capitalist ideology within those sections of academia that might have some impact on social thought or interpretation of contemporary affairs.

As for the mass media, they are major capitalist institutions and it is therefore not surprising that they rarely challenge official doctrine and are committed to guaranteeing that analysis of contemporary events does not stray beyond rigid limits. The business world, however, is not content to rely on the natural process of ideological control that results from the narrow base of ownership, and has developed elaborate programs to control directly the contents of the mass media. In a democracy, the voice of the people is heard, and it is therefore essential to ensure that the voice expressed conforms to the needs and interests of those who retain effective power, or unpleasant conflicts can develop. Hence the emphasis on what has been called 'the engineering of consent,' a term introduced by Edward Bernays, a leading spokesman for the public relations industry and the recipient of academic honors for his contributions to applied psychology. He characterizes the device as 'the very essence of the democratic process, the freedom to persuade and suggest'.

Of course, this 'freedom' is available to those who have the power to exercise it. It is not unrealistic to regard freedom as analogous to a commodity under capitalist democracy. In principle, it is not in short supply, but one has as much as he can purchase. It is no wonder that the privileged often are numbered among the defenders of civil liberties, of which they are the primary beneficiaries. The right to free expression of ideas and free access to information is a basic human right, and in principle it is available to all, though in practice only to the extent that one has the special privilege, power, training and facilities to exercise these rights in a meaningful way. For the mass of the population, escape from the system of indoctrination is difficult. The same is true in practice with regard to legal rights. Elaborate machinery is available under the law for protection of the individual against the abuse of State or private power. The study of criminal justice reveals, however, that here too, to a very considerable extent, one has the rights that one is in a position to purchase.

It is not surprising that the business community should understand 'democracy' in the terms explained by Bernays. What is perhaps unusual about the United States, and important for an understanding of American politics, is the extent to which such views are dominant among the intelligentsia, and the elaborate system of controls that have been evolved over the years to put these principles into effect.

## Totalitarianism and "democracy"

The mechanisms of indoctrination that have evolved in the United States are entirely different from those that operate in the totalitarian societies of the world. Force is rarely used to ensure obedience, though it is well to remember that resort to direct force is not excluded. Recent revelations of the activities of the FBI in disruption and harassment of groups working for social change or even civil rights, the provocation of arson and bombings, incitement of gang warfare, support and direction for a secret terrorist army, and even in one case direct complicity in political assassination, simply remind us of the long and ugly history of the Bureau, which regularly functions as a national political police, enforcing political conformity and obedience. Nevertheless, the primary mechanism employed is not direct force, but rather 'the engineering of consent,' which is achieved through the domination of the flow of information and the means for expressing opinion or analysis. The system has been effective, and these successes too must be understood if one hopes to comprehend the nature of contemporary American society and its political processes.

The ease with which the ideological system recovered from the damage it suffered during the Vietnam war gives a remarkable indication of the effectiveness of these systems of control. When the war came to an end in Apr. 1975, *Asahi Shimbun* commented editorially that 'The war in Vietnam has been in every way a war of national emancipation.' One heard no such comment in the American mass media. The liberal press was willing to concede that American conduct in Indo-China was 'wrong and misguided—even tragic,' but it insisted with near uniformity that the original motives and policy were 'right and defensible': 'Specifically, it was right to hope that the people of South Vietnam would be able to decide on their own form of government and social order' (*Washington Post*). Somehow, 'good impulses came to be transmuted into bad policy,' the editorial continued in the newspaper that had long been regarded as perhaps the most critical among the national media.

Given the well-known historical facts, the editorial judgment of the *Post is* worthy of note. It is not in doubt that the United States first sought to impose French colonial rule in Indo-China, and when this effort failed, instituted what the American counterinsurgency expert General Lansdale called a "fascistic state,' supported massive terror in an effort to crush the South Vietnamese forces that had resisted the French invasion, and finally intervened in force in South Vietnam in an effort to destroy the only mass-based political forces in South Vietnam, a fact always recognized by government experts and planners. All of this took place long before the first battalion of North Vietnamese regular forces was detected in the South, several months after the initiation of systematic and intensive bombing of South and North Vietnam in February 1965 (the United States had been bombing South Vietnam for over 3 years, by that time). Yet the *Washington Post,* knowing the historical record well, is capable of writing that the United States was defending the right of 'the people of South Vietnam... to decide on their own form of government and social order.' And in so doing, it simply expressed the general consensus of American liberalism.

Similarly, as the war came to an end, the *NY Times* analyzed the debate over the war in the following terms:

> There are those Americans who believe that the war to preserve a non-Communist, independent South Vietnam could have been waged differently. There are other Americans who believe that a viable, non-Communist South Vietnam was always a myth... A decade of fierce polemics has failed to resolve this ongoing quarrel.

In short, the hawks allege that we could have won, while the doves reply that victory was always beyond our grasp. As for the merits of these opposing views, which mark the limits of responsible thinking as the *Times* perceives them, we must await the judgment of history, the editors advise.

There is, to be sure, a third position: namely, that the United States simply had no legal or moral right to intervene in the internal affairs of Vietnam in the first place. It had no right to support French imperialism or to attempt—successfully or not-to establish 'a viable, non-Communist South Vietnam' in violation of the 1954 Geneva Accords, or to use force and violence to 'preserve' the fascistic regime it had imposed or to crush the mass-based political forces of the South. But this point of view, represented by the leading elements in the quite enormous peace movement, is simply not part of the debate. In fact, the *Times* refused even to print a letter challenging its interpretation of the debate, though it was willing to publish quite a range of opinion, including a proposal that we undertake nuclear bombardment in Indo-China.

The fundamental position of the peace movement is beyond the limits of responsible discussion because it challenges the basic fight of the United States to use force and violence to ensure its international aims. The responsible debate must be restricted to a question of tactics: could we have won, with different means? Other questions were certainly raised during this 'decade of fierce polemics:' Should we have won? Did we have the right to try? Were we engaged in criminal aggression? But the view that the United States had neither the authority nor the competence to settle the affairs of Indo-China is simply excluded from discussion, as the *NY Times* sets the ground rules. It need not be refuted, but must rather be removed from consciousness.

These editorial responses were quite typical of the liberal press. The remarkable resilience of the ideological system is well illustrated by its success in the two years that have passed since in restoring a badly shattered consensus with regard to the American right of forceful intervention. The official version of the war is that the United States intervened to defend South Vietnam from aggression, and was right to do so, though the methods employed are subject to criticism as 'good impulses came to be transmuted into bad policy.' The peace movement, according to this official doctrine, supported North Vietnamese aggression, while the government, perhaps unwisely, came to the defense of its victims, That such a version of history can be sustained in the face of absolutely massive evidence to the contrary, virtually without articulate objection, is a remarkable testimonial to the effectiveness of the American system of indoctrination and thought control.

It is important, for an understanding of the American scene, to gain some appreciation of the extent of these ideological successes of the propaganda system. In the course of one of his discourses on human rights, President Carter was asked by a CBS newsman whether the United States 'has a moral obligation to help rebuild' Vietnam. Not at all, he explained: 'the destruction was mutual.' We bombed their villages and they shot down our pilots. Since 'we went to Vietnam without any desire... to impose American will on other people' but only 'to defend the freedom of the South Vietnamese,' there is no reason for us 'to apologize or to castigate ourselves or to assume the status of culpability.' Nor do we 'owe a debt.'

Writers of editorials and political commentators find nothing strange in this interpretation of history and expression of Christian morality. When the President says that 'the destruction was mutual' in Vietnam Khrushchev might have said the same about Hungary—literally not one question was raised, nor was even a qualified objection voiced in the national media in the United States.

It is fair to say, I believe, that the current campaign of falsification of history merits comparison with the more audacious achievements of 20th century totalitarianism, though the mechanisms, as noted earlier, are entirely different. That such a campaign would be undertaken was never in question, and was predicted long ago. It is necessary to restore the faith of the public in American benevolence, and to restore the accompanying passivity and obedience on the part of the population, if new interventions are to succeed. And since the institutional factors that shape American foreign policy have in no way been modified, it is fair to assume that the interventionist policies of the past will persist.

Two years after the end of a war in which the United States devastated Indo-China on a scale that has few historical parallels, press commentary virtually ignores the American role in the Indo-Chinese tragedy. When the *NY Times* or

*Newsweek* feature articles on postwar developments in Indo-China, there is literally no reference to the impact of the American attack. In the *NY Times*, for
example, the only reference is that there are 'substantial tracts of land made fal-
low by the war,' with no agent indicated. Furthermore, the picture they portray
is simply one of unrelieved gloom and oppression.

There is, in fact, extensive eyewitness testimony, including journalists of
international repute, visiting Vietnamese professors from Canada, American missionaries and volunteer workers who speak Vietnamese and have an intimate
knowledge of the country where they worked for many years during and long
after the war. This testimony is sharply at variance with the reports presented in
the American press. It is ignored not out of ignorance or because of lack of faith
in the trustworthiness of the sources, but simply because the account presented
does not accord with the requirements of the propaganda apparatus. When the
distinguished American radical historian Gabriel Kolko visited Vietnam in 1976,
the *NY Times* asked him to submit an account of his trip, which they then
refused to print, after having denied *Asahi* the right to print it, Kolko informs
me. Had he described the tribulations of the Vietnamese under oppressive
Communist rule, the report would surely have been featured and would have
received wide comment, as has happened in other cases. But since he portrayed
the courage and commitment of the Vietnamese in trying to construct an egali-
tarian society out of the ruins left by the American attack, the report simply
could not be permitted to reach the attention of the public. Similarly, when a
Mennonite missionary who worked and lived in Vietnam for many years,
remaining for 13 months after the war, testified before Congress on a recent visit
in which he observed great progress despite the 'vast destruction of soil and facilities inflicted by the past war,' there is no mention in the press, and his testimony, along with much else that corroborates it, is eliminated from the official version of history. The ruler of any totalitarian state would be proud of a comparable ideological victory.

The campaign of falsification is undeniably bearing fruit. In the liberal
weekly *Newsweek*, one reads a letter by a reader urging consideration for Richard
Nixon, on the grounds that "We forgave the British, the Germans and the
Japanese, and are currently in the process of forgiving the Vietnamese.' Since the
state propaganda apparatus had been laboring mightily to shift the moral onus
for American aggression and barbarity to the Vietnamese, it is understandable
that the ordinary citizen should applaud our generosity in forgiving the crimes
they committed against us. An editorial in the *Christian Science Monitor*, a leading national daily, which a few years ago was deliberating the relative advantages
of bombing trucks and bombing dams (the latter so much more satisfying to the
pilots, as 'the water can be seen to pour through the breach and drown out huge
areas of farm land, and villages, in its path') now proclaims that the United States
must 'evaluate Vietnam's potentiality as a responsible world citizen.' After the
record of the past 30 years, the United States is entitled to stand in judgment
over Vietnam.

Any thought of reparations to the victims of American savagery and terror is angrily dismissed as an absurdity. Aid is refused. Even this is not enough. In June 1977 the Senate voted 56 to 32 in favor of legislation sponsored by Republican Vice-Presidential candidate Robert Dole that instructs U.S. representatives in international lending organizations to vote against any aid to Indo-China. If such aid is nevertheless granted over U.S. objections, the U.S. must reduce its contribution to these organizations by a corresponding amount. Proposing this legislation, Dole criticized the countries of Indo-China for their "extremely repressive and inhumanitarian character," as distinct from Brazil, Chile, Indonesia and Iran, for example. That there is an element of 'inhumanity' in the Senate vote would be beyond the comprehension of the mass media. Two months later, the Senate defeated a similar amendment to different legislation, motivated, the debate indicates, by concern over U.S. participation in international institutions rather than the intrinsic content of the legislation.

U.S. representatives in international lending institutions are not generally required to try to block aid to repressive regimes. About one third of the $9 billion that the World Bank expects to lend in the fiscal year 1979 will go to 15 of the most repressive regimes, according to the analysis of a Washington-based private research organization that monitors American aid and human-rights efforts, the *NY Times* reports (June 19, 1977). The same group observes that U.S.-supported aid through international financial institutions has been increased to compensate for reductions in direct American support, allegedly motivated by the newly-expressed concern for human rights, a matter to which I will return. Congress, in fact, is making some efforts to restrict aid to repressive regimes, taking seriously the Administration rhetoric concerning human rights. The *Times* report just cited explains the problems this is causing the Carter administration, which 'has been put in the embarrassing position of trying to check the zeal of some lawmakers who say they want to translate President Carter's words into action.' Administration efforts to block these Congressional initiatives tell us a good deal about the meaning and significance of the current human rights campaign.

In fact, while the press tries to make its readers believe that malnutrition and disease in Indo-China are somehow the result of Communist brutality, the United States not only refuses and blocks aid to Indo-China, but even refuses assistance under the 'Food for Peace programme to any exporter which is engaging in, or in the six months immediately preceding the application for such financing has engaged in, any sales, trade, or commerce with North Vietnam or with any resident thereof...' Furthermore, U.S. agricultural commodities are barred to 'any nation which sells or furnishes or permits ships or aircraft under its registry to transport to or from Cuba and North Vietnam any equipment, materials, or commodities so long as they are governed by a communist regime.' When India sought to provide 100 buffaloes to help replace the herds decimated by American terror, they were compelled to channel even that minimal assistance through the Indian Red Cross, to avoid American retribution (*Far Eastern*

*Economic Review*, 25 Feb. 1977). Evidently, the process of 'forgiving the Vietnamese' for their crimes against the United States still has a distance to go.

It is remarkable, and illuminating, that none of this is ever mentioned, just as the American role in Vietnam is characteristically ignored, when the press pontificates about alleged human rights violations in Vietnam. Again, these facts illustrate the efficacy of the awesome American propaganda system.

There is no space for a detailed review here, but it is worth mention that academic scholarship is making its effective contribution to the requisite myth creation. In the *Pentagon Papers* and other documents, there is substantial evidence concerning the imperial planning that motivated the American intervention in support of France and the later efforts to crush the popular movements for independence and social change. Since the 1940s, there was never any doubt in the minds of top planners about 'the unpleasant fact that Communist Ho Chi Minh is the strongest and perhaps the ablest figure in Indo-China and that any suggested solution which excludes him is an expedient of uncertain outcome,' or that Ho had 'captured control of the nationalist movement,' in the words of a State Department policy statement of 1948. As Secretary of State Dean Acheson accurately explained, French military success 'depends, in the end, on overcoming opposition of indigenous population.' The record reported in the *Pentagon Papers* shows that although American intelligence tried very hard to establish that the Viet Minh was controlled by China or Russia, as required by the propaganda system, they were unable to do so. Yet in the face of this ample record, well-known American Asian scholars such as John King Fairbank and Edwin 0. Reischauer not only ignore totally the documentation of explicit and elaborate imperial planning but even claim that U.S. intervention was based on fear of Chinese (later North Vietnamese) expansionism and a failure to understand that we were combating a nationalist revolution. The refusal to make reference to the planning documents in the *Pentagon Papers* is a particularly striking feature of contemporary scholarship on the American involvement of 30 years in Indo-China.

The 'lessons of the war' are also drawn in terms conforming to basic imperialist doctrine. Thus Edwin Reischauer concludes in *Foreign Policy* (Fall 1975) that 'The real lesson of the Vietnam war is the tremendous cost of attempting to control the destiny of a Southeast Asian country against the cross-currents of nationalism,' currents of which he falsely claims the government was unaware. And Secretary of Defense Harold Brown, a leading advocate of heavy bombing during the war, states in *Time* magazine (May 23 1977) that "A lesson we learned from Vietnam is that we should be very cautious about intervening in any place where there is a poor political base for our presence." This is the typical refrain in scholarship, government, and the media. The United States need not abdicate its role as global judge and executioner, but must be more cautious about the prospects for success, and must carefully consider the costs—to the United States—of forceful intervention in violation of the UN Charter, a valid treaty and thus part of "the supreme law of the land." The violation of law, incidentally, was always explicit in imperial planning, for example, in the repeated insistence in the highest level planning documents of the 1950s that American force should be used (even against China if deemed necessary) in response to "local Communist subversion or rebellion *not constituting armed attack*" (my emphasis: the italicized phrase is repeatedly added to make explicit the direct violation of domestic and international law that is intended). The mythology of resistance to aggression was created for public consumption, and is dutifully repeated by propagandists in the mass media and the scholarly professions.

## The rhetoric of human rights

It is against this background of ideological conformism and institutional rigidity that one must assess a new political Administration in the United States. The Carter Administration has sought to convey a new 'image,' namely, a concern for human rights and morality. In a special section of the liberal *Boston Globe* headed "The Carter Crusade for Human Rights" (March 13, 1977), the well-known historian and former adviser to President Kennedy, Arthur Schlesinger, writes that 'President Carter's promotion of human rights as an international issue must be judged thus far, I think, a considerable and very serious success.' In a facing column, correspondent Don Cook of the *Los Angeles Times* explains that 'Because Europeans have lived with the human rights problem in their midst through centuries of revolution and dictatorship, there is a lot more inflammable human material on this side of the Atlantic than there is in the United States.' The land of slavery and genocidal assaults on the American Indians is uniquely privileged, in this regard.

Schlesinger is certainly correct in judging the human rights campaign to be a success, but some questions remain: specifically, what is the nature and significance of this achievement?

One answer is supplied by Schlesinger himself. He writes: 'in effect, human rights is replacing self determination as the guiding value in American foreign policy.' It is a dogma of the state religion in the United States that American policy has been guided by the 'Wilsonian ideal' of freedom and self-determination. Again, it is a tribute to the effectiveness of the propaganda system that this faith can still be maintained after the record of American intervention to prevent self-determination, independence, and—crucially—social change, in Indo-China, Guatemala, the Dominican Republic, Chile, and elsewhere, with the well-documented ensuing horrors.

It is not, of course, that the facts are entirely ignored. I have already noted how the "realist" scholar Norman Graebner invokes the category of "irony" to account for the deviance of practice from the ideal. Other critics of alleged American moralism in foreign policy also provide interesting insights into the ways in which the state religion is defended, even by those who pride themselves on their hard-headed "realism."

Consider Hans Morgenthau, perhaps the most distinguished representative of this school. In much of his writing he has clearly delineated major elements in

American foreign policy. In the early years of the cold war, he warned of "forces that are attempting to rally a confused and patriotic citizenry… to the defense of what seems to be the security of the United States, but what actually is the security of the status quo" "in embarking upon a holy crusade to extirpate the evil of Bolshevism" in the interwar period, "these forces embarked, as they do now, in actuality upon a campaign to outlaw morally and legally all popular movements favoring social reform and in that fashion to make the status quo impregnable to change." (*In Defense of the National Interest*, 1951). In later years he was to be one of the few serious critics of the American war in Indo-China, within "established" scholarship. Yet he was capable of devoting a book to the central thesis that "the purpose of America is not to be understood, as are the purposes of other nations, as the idealization and rationalization of historic events that preceded its formulation, but that the awareness of its existence and its formulation antedate the existence of the nation itself." (Introduction to the 1963 edition of *The Purpose of American Politics*, 1960). This "transcendent purpose" is "the establishment of equality in freedom." "What makes America unique among the nations is that it has… created a society that is still today radically different from the other societies of the modern world" and "superior" to them in "the establishment of freedom conceived as equality of opportunity and minimization of political control." "America has become the Rome and Athens of the Western world, the foundation of its lawful order and the fountainhead of its culture," though unfortunately "America does not know this." "By pursuing its own purpose and in the measure that it achieves it, America gives meaning to the aspirations of other nations and furthers the awakening and achievement of their purpose."

Morgenthau recognized certain defects: America has not yet achieved "the restoration (sic) of a meaningful economic and social order" or "equality in freedom for the American Negro." And in foreign affairs, there were "expeditions into Central America" (but these were "in the nature of isolated forays, primarily for defensive purposes") and "the annexation of the Philippines" ("a temporary aberration"). Furthermore, he recognizes that the "folly" of the doctrine of "manifest destiny… became a justification for almost any addition of territory which the United States had the will and the power to obtain" (citing J.W. Pratt). Such facts have led even sober observers to doubt "the validity of concepts such as national purpose and national interest" and to conclude "that behind them there is at best nothing more than the interests of particular groups, which are identified with the nation and rationalized and justified as such in ideological terms." (See Selection 1).

But such observers are guilty of a simple error of logic: "to reason thus is to confound the abuse of reality with reality itself. Those who confound 'the abuse of reality" (i.e., the real world) with "reality itself" (i.e., the unachieved "national purpose") have fallen into 'the error of atheism, which denies the validity of religion on similar grounds.' Our task is "to maintain and restore the validity of the idea while avoiding the pitfalls of error and abuse."

It is remarkable that a person who has often been a "sober observer" can offer such an analysis of American "uniqueness" and can seriously argue that mere fact is a distortion and abuse of reality, while rhetorical flights constitute the true reality, which even, antedate the existence of the nation itself. The analogy to religious belief is quite appropriate. In fact, nationalist hysteria and state worship have in many respects served as the religion of the intelligentsia, in the modern period.

Arthur Schlesinger's real concern for the principle of self-determination is revealed in a recently declassified memorandum that he presented to President Kennedy shortly before the Bay of Pigs invasion, the first of many attempts to overthrow the Cuban revolutionary government by force, to assassinate Castro, and to undermine the regime by terror and sabotage, poisoning of crops and spreading of disease among farm animals. In this secret memorandum, Schlesinger condemns the "muddling and moralizing conservatism of the Eisenhower period," which was never sufficiently aggressive in international affairs to please liberal ideologists, despite planned and actual military intervention and CIA subversion in Guatemala, Lebanon, and Iran. Schlesinger recognized that it would be necessary to lie about the Bay of Pigs invasion. Thus he counselled that "When lies must be told, they should be told by subordinate officials." The basic decisions should be made "in (the President's) absence so that someone else's head can later be placed on the block if things go terribly wrong." He then outlines a series of answers that the President might give in a press conference. He should deny any knowledge of the facts and describe the invasion as "a purely Cuban operation" by "patriots in exile," rejecting the idea that the U.S. government has any intention of using force to overthrow the Castro regime or contributing force to that purpose unless compelled to do so in the interests of "self-defense." Even Schlesinger is unable to conjure up an answer to the question whether the U.S. has "resolutely enforced the laws forbidding the use of U.S. territory to prepare revolutionary action against another state." Here, the historian adviser is reduced to the response: '????' (*Washington Star Syndicate*, Apr. 30, 1977; the report was successfully suppressed in the national liberal media with the exception of the *Nation*, August 6, 1977). The President, incidentally, rejected this sage advice.

In his history of the Kennedy Administration (*A Thousand Days*), Schlesinger refers to this and other memoranda he submitted and states that they 'look nice on the record because they register his purely technical objections to the planned attack, on grounds of political cost and likelihood of failure.' The facts just cited nowhere appear.

Returning to Schlesinger's dictum on self-determination and human rights as principles guiding American foreign policy, if we take these remarks seriously we are led to a rather cynical appraisal of the human rights crusade. Exactly to the extent that self-determination was the guiding value in the era of Vietnam and Chile, Guatemala and the Dominican Republic, the Congo and Iran, so human rights will be the guiding value henceforth. In short, the human rights campaign is a device to be manipulated by propagandists to gain popular support for counterrevolutionary intervention.

Some Washington correspondents see the point, though they put it in a misleading way. William Beecher of the *Boston Globe* reports that National Security Adviser Zbigniew Brzezinski and others have urged Carter "to continue to take the ideological high ground on human rights not only out of conscience, but also because it may restore American prestige that was badly bruised in Vietnam and during the Watergate scandal...." (March 31 1977). The part played by 'conscience' is indicated by Carter's observations on Vietnam, cited above, and the press response, Or by the case of Brady Tyson of the U.S. delegation to the UN Rights Commission who expressed "profoundest regrets" for the part he said some American officials and private groups had played in subverting the Allende government in Chile, only to be quickly reprimanded and called home to "make sure he understands the ground rules," in the words of the State Department.

The sincerity of the crusade for human rights, and the role played by 'conscience', can be put to the test in other ways. It is easy enough for the Kremlin to denounce human rights violations in the United States and the American sphere of control, and it is equally easy for President Carter to condemn the Russians for their extensive abuse of elementary human rights. The test of sincerity in both cases is the same: how do they respond to violations of human rights at home, or violations that they have backed and for which they share responsibility? In the case of Russian moralists, the answer is plain enough. It is no less plain in the case of President Carter and his acolytes, as the example of Vietnam and Chile clearly illustrates.

To mention one last issue, consider President Carter's response to clear cases of human rights violations in the United States. Take the case of the assassination of Black Panther leader Fred Hampton in Chicago in December 1969 in a 4 a.m. police raid on the Panther headquarters in which Hampton was killed in bed. sleeping and probably drugged (the hail of police bullets was not response to Panther firing, contrary to police lies that were quickly exposed). The families of the murdered Panther leaders undertook a civil suit in Chicago in an effort to obtain some limited redress. During the case, extensive evidence was produced of FBI complicity in the assassination. It was shown that the chief of Panther security, Hampton's personal bodyguard, was an FBI informer and provocateur who had provided the police, through the FBI office, with a dubious report of illegal possession of arms as a pretext for the raid, and also a plan of the apartment with Hampton's bed indicated. Earlier, the FBI had sought to provoke a criminal gang in the Chicago ghetto to attack the Panthers with a fabricated letter claiming that the Panthers were planning to kill its leader. The Chicago Judge refused to permit the jury to consider any of the extensive evidence concerning FBI involvement in this sordid affair. Surely this merits some comment from a passionate advocate of human rights.

The case is perhaps unfair, since the national press has so effectively concealed this amazing case that Carter and his advisers may not even know about it. So let us take another example, which they surely do know, since it has been well-reported. On June 3, 1977, columnist William Raspberry of the *Washington Post* pointed out that:

> If President Carter is serious about freeing political prisoners—if he is genuinely concerned about the whole range of human-rights issues—he needn't look to Africa or Latin America or the Soviet Union. Let him look to North Carolina and the incredible case of the Wilmington 10.

In fact, the case of the Wilmington 10 has received international attention, with demonstrations and protest in Western Europe, far more than in the United States. In 1971, a Black minister, Ben Chavis, eight black teenagers, and a white VISTA volunteer working in the Black ghetto, were indicted on the charge of conspiracy and arson, following racial disturbances in Wilmington, North Carolina. Chavis received a 34 year prison sentence, and the others too received heavy sentences. Since that time, every significant prosecution witness has recanted his testimony, with allegations that it was given under threat or after bribery by the prosecution. In a recent Court hearing, a White minister and his wife testified that Chavis was with them in their Church parsonage when the arson took place, adding that they were prevented by intimidation from testifying at the trial. The Judge at the hearing refused to grant a new trial. As Raspberry points out,

> President Carter may be as powerless to do anything about the Wilmington 10 as he is in the case of, say, Russian dissidents. But it would be a most useful thing if he could bring himself to speak out on it. Human rights, after all, don't begin at the water's edge.

The opportunity to speak out arose a few days later in a televised June 13 press conference. The President was asked to comment on the case by a reporter who noted that Reverend Chavis and others were 'sentenced to prison terms totaling 282 years for what they contend were human rights activities,' and that civil rights groups and 'several prominent business and political and elected leaders in North Carolina, have implored you for your intervention and comments in their behalf,' The President responded as follows:

> Well, the only comment I am free to make under our own system of Government is that I hope that justice will prevail... I trust the system in its entirety... I'm not trying to evade the question; I think that it would be improper for me to try to impose what I think should be a judgment in a case that I've not heard tried and I don't have any direct familiarity with the evidence. I believe that justice will prevail.

Carter's plea concerning the 'strict prohibition... against the encroachment of the executive branch of Government on the judicial branch' hardly rings true.

It is difficult to perceive any impropriety in a properly qualified statement by the President to the effect that if the information reported without serious challenge in the press is accurate, then there has been a miscarriage of justice. As for his objection that he had not heard the case tried and had no direct familiarity with the evidence, it is again difficult to see how this distinguishes the case in hand from many others, in Russia for example, where evidence is far more sparse. As for the expressed belief that 'justice will prevail,' that reveals considerable innocence, at best, with regard to the treatment of blacks and dissidents in the courts, not infrequently.

What the incident does reveal clearly, however, is that under the New Morality, human rights do begin at the water's edge. Actually, even that is not accurate, as we can see in a column by *NY Times* columnist James Reston, reporting from Bonn, West Germany, on June 15, 1977:

> The closer you get to the borders between Western Europe and Communist Eastern Europe, the more the issue of 'human rights' becomes intensely human and personal. In Washington, and even in London and Paris, it is mainly a philosophical question, but here in the Federal Republic of Germany, it is a question of divided families, parents and children, husbands, wives and lovers.

The remark is apt enough with regard to Eastern Europe; violation of human rights there is in a class by itself, within Europe. But it is hardly true that in the Western capitals—particularly Bonn—it is mainly a philosophical question'. Consider just West Germany. Here, in the past several years, thousands of civil servants (who constitute about 15 percent of the work force) have been subjected to disciplinary actions, including termination of employment, for such crimes against the State as participating in demonstrations against the Vietnam war, signing petitions in support of a legal (Communist) party during an electoral campaign, criticizing 'capitalist development' for ecological damage, and so on. The German 'Berufsverbot' ('Ban on professional employment') involves human rights violations that go beyond the worst moments of American 'McCarthyism,' and that have already had a severe 'chilling' effect on academic freedom and the exercise of democratic rights. Furthermore, they have, not surprisingly, raised considerable apprehension in neighboring countries that have some reason to recall earlier episodes of German history. These events raise more than 'philosophical' questions. True, they have barely been reported in the United States, and may be unfamiliar to the political commentator of the *NY Times*. But if that is so, then the problem revealed by his remarks is far deeper than is indicated by the comments themselves.

The special nature of the human rights crusade is revealed in many other ways. Take the case of Iran, a country which may well hold the current world's record for torture of political prisoners. Iran, however, is by far the major purchaser of American arms, having purchased some $15 billion worth in the past five years. Visiting Iran in May 1977, Secretary of State Cyrus Vance stated that

'No... linkage has been discussed' between arms sales and the issue of human rights, in his conversations with the Shah. Joe Alex Morris of the *Los Angeles Times*, reporting on Vance's press conference in Teheran, reports:

> Nothing Vance told reporters after his meeting with the Shah indicated that he had laid particular stress on the (human rights) issue, however. In fact, the secretary appeared at one point to be defending the Shah's tough policies against alleged subversives in his one-party state. 'Each country has a responsibility to itself to deal with terrorist problems,' he said. 'On the other hand, the question of dissent doesn't necessarily involve terrorist actions. It depends on the individual factual situation whether the question of human rights arises.

Once again, we see that what counts as a violation of human rights depends not so much upon the act as upon the agent.

It would be inaccurate to suggest that the United States is simply responding to Iranian requests for arms, closing its eyes to gross violations of human rights because of overriding economic considerations. In fact, the Carter Administration is pressing the Iranians to purchase sophisticated arms that they do not want and probably are incapable of using. A case in point is the effort by the Administration to sell to Iran sophisticated radar surveillance planes that are designed to monitor and control air battles, at a cost of $850 million. Reports from Washington indicate that the U.S. Air Force would have to provide technical personnel to operate the system. 'One of the principal reasons behind the Pentagon pressure for the offer to Iran,' according to the *NY Times* (Apr. 27, 1977) 'was to keep the Boeing production line open, thus reducing the cost of the plane to the Air Force and to keep open the possibility of future sales to European allies,' who have so far refused to purchase the planes, because of their price and complexity.

Arms sales to the oil producing countries have been a significant factor in improving the U.S. balance of trade, and although there has been talk under the Carter Administration of reducing these sales, there is so far little indication of any action in this regard. But one thing at least is clear: the issue of human rights can easily be dispensed with, when need be.

Even the case of the Russian dissidents raises some serious questions. Again, protests over abuse of human rights in the Soviet Union obviously indicate nothing as regards the sincerity of the crusade. Furthermore, there seems to be evidence that Carter's crusade for civil rights East of the Elbe has perhaps been a factor in intensifying the Russian attack on dissidents, which is now described as the worst in a decade. Responding to such reports, "The Carter Administration issued a pointed warning yesterday that it will not be dissuaded from its public campaign for human rights around the world (sic) by the harassment of individual dissidents in foreign countries' (*Washington Post* 3 June 1977). This is a curious response, which raises questions about the purpose of the crusade. If the purpose is to relieve the situation of people who are oppressed, then the nature of the response must surely be a factor in determining whether or how to press the campaign. If, on the other hand, the purpose is 'to restore American prestige,' then the effect on victims becomes irrelevant.

It is worth noting that while the United States obviously is not in a class with the Russians in violations of the Helsinki agreements, still its record is hardly clean. Under the Carter Administration, Tariq Ali of the Fourth International (Trotskyite) has been barred from entering the United States to speak at several American universities. The Justice Department refused a visa to the Peruvian author and peasant leader Hugo Blanco for two years, and maintains the ban against the Belgian Marxist Ernest Mandel. In the case of Hugo Blanco, the Immigration Service offered the absurd rationalization that no evidence had been submitted to 'establish the preeminence of the beneficiary in a particular field, whether literary, political, sociological or philosophical...' Apart from the fact that the claim is grossly false, just consider how many people would be permitted to visit the United States under these conditions. In another case, a Vietnamese nun, visiting in Canada, is reported to have been denied entry to the United States, while the press protests that American correspondents are not authorized to visit Vietnam.

Other actions of the Administration indicate quite clearly how thin and meaningless is the alleged commitment to human rights. Carter's appointment as Ambassador to Iran, a regime established by a CIA-backed coup, is William H. Sullivan, whose best-known accomplishment is his direction of the 'secret war' in Laos, involving a CIA-run mercenary army and a fearsome bombing campaign launched against the defenseless peasant society of Northern Laos, from 1964 to 1969. This was followed by a tour in the Philippines where he was able to oversee American support for the Marcos dictatorship. Sullivan follows Richard Helms, retired head of the CIA, as Ambassador. All of this may make a certain amount of sense, given the origins of the Iranian regime and its role in American global planning, but it hardly has much relation to a crusade for human rights.

Similarly, the Carter Administration, as already noted, has been bending every effort to prevent Congress from enacting a bill that would require U.S. representatives at the World Bank and other international lending institutions to vote against funds or credits for nations that violate human rights. Carter urged that this bill 'would handicap our efforts to encourage human rights improvement.' The logic is not transparent. A more reasonable interpretation is that the legislation would serve to permit some meaningful pressure against client states that are champion human rights violators. For example, U.S. military aid to Argentina was reduced from $32 million to $15 million on grounds of the human rights violations by the military junta, but at the same time the junta received a $105 million World Bank loan, an Inter-American Development Bank loan of $32 million, and a $100-million stand-by credit from the International Monetary Fund (*Seven Days*, 6 June, 1977), By such means, the United States is easily able to undercut any effect of the direct aid reductions. Recall that in the special case of Indo-China, harsh conditions on direct or even indirect U.S. assistance have been proposed by Congress, as well as constraints to prevent aid from other countries.

The aggressive and interventionist American foreign policy of the postwar period has been quite successful in creating a global economy in which U.S.-based corporations can operate with fair freedom and high profits. But there have been failures, for example, in Cuba and Indo-China. When some country succeeds in extricating itself from the U.S.-dominated global system, the immediate and invariable response is to impose harsh conditions (not excluding terror and sabotage) to prevent what are sometimes called 'ideological successes,' in internal documents. In the case of China, Cuba and Indo-China, the fear of planners has always been that the success of social reform or revolution might influence others elsewhere to pursue the same course. Then 'the rot will spread,' as the planners say, causing further deterioration in the U.S.-dominated system. Such considerations were at the heart of imperial intervention in Vietnam since the 1950s. It was feared that the success of the popular, nationalist, and revolutionary communist forces might provide a model for others. If the rot were to spread in such manner to the rest of South-east Asia and beyond, Japan—always the centerpiece of American planning in Asia—might be affected. With the loss of markets and sources of raw materials, it might be induced to accommodate itself to Asian communism, thus escaping from the American system. In effect, this would mean that the United States would have lost the Pacific war, which was fought, in large measure, to prevent Japan from constructing a closed Asian bloc that would exclude the United States.

These ideas are quite explicit in imperial planning since at least 1949, though one would never know this from the study of the press or most "responsible" scholarship.

The business press, offers an occasional exception to the general rule. When American power was defeated in Indo-China, *Business Week* lamented that the 'stable world order for business operations is falling apart', noting particularly the dangers "if Japan cannot continue to export a third of its products to Southeast Asia" (Apr. 7, 1975). As both the secret and public record confirm, a major goal of American policy in Asia 'was to develop markets for Japan in South-east Asia in order to counteract Communist trade efforts and to promote trade between Japan and South-east Asian countries' (Chitoshi Yanaga, *Big Business in Japanese Politics*, Yale: 1968). Today as well it is important to keep the rot from spreading, by maintaining the harshest possible conditions for the Indo-Chinese revolutionaries. It is hoped that along with economic difficulties, internal repression will mount, and the model will seem less attractive. With utter cynicism, American journals now search assiduously for human rights violations in Indo-China—of which there are undoubtedly many, just as there were, for example, in liberated Europe under American occupation—often fabricating evidence if need be, and ignoring entirely any indications of social progress or popular commitment, while dismissing the American role. For some examples, see

Chomsky and Herman, "Distortions at Fourth Hand," (*The Nation* 25 June 1977).

The human rights crusade in the United States is not only limited with regard to place, but also with regard to the concept of 'human rights' itself. In much of the world, the concept of "human rights" is understood to include the right to a decent job, adequate shelter, medical care, food for one's children, and the like, as well as the right to share in the democratic control of production, in determining the character of labor and the nature and disposal of its products. These rights are never mentioned under the New Morality; no discussion of them appears, for example, in the State Department Human Rights Report. In fact, it would be stoutly denied that some of these rights—particularly, to democratic control of production—even exist. But in most of the world, including the United States, these and related matters should be at the very heart of any honest concern for human rights. By dismissing these concerns, the New Morality reveals that its commitment is not to human rights, but rather at best to such rights as may be secured under capitalism.

In considering how human rights might serve as a 'guiding value' in American foreign policy, one should not dismiss the historical record, which is ample. There is indeed a close relationship between human rights and American foreign policy. There is substantial evidence that American aid and diplomatic support increase as human rights violations increase, at least in the Third World. Extensive violations of human rights (torture, forced reduction of living standards for much of the population, police-sponsored death squads, destruction of representative institutions or of independent unions, etc.) are directly correlated with U.S. government support (for some evidence and discussion, see Chomsky and Herman, "The United States Versus Human Rights," *Monthly Review*, Aug. 1977). The linkage is not accidental; rather it is systematic. The reason is obvious enough. Client fascism often improves the business climate for American corporations, quite generally the guiding factor in foreign policy. It would be naive indeed to think that this will change materially, given the realities of American social structure and the grip of the state ideological system.

A realistic analysis can hardly lead to any faith in the current human rights crusade in the United States. Its primary objective, as noted above, is to reconstruct the passivity and obedience on the part of the population that is required if the interventionist policies of the past are to be continued, in the interests of the private power that dominates the State apparatus and sets the basic conditions within which political power functions.

## The Carter Administration and the Trilateral Commission

Turning from myth and propaganda to reality, what are the special features, if any, of the Carter Administration?

Perhaps the most striking feature of the new Administration is the role played in it by the Trilateral Commission. The mass media had little to say about this matter during the Presidential campaign—in fact, the connection of the

Carter group to the Commission was recently selected as 'the best-censored news story of 1976'—and it has not received the attention that it might since the Administration took office. All of the top positions in the government—the office of President, Vice-President, Secretary of State. Defense and Treasury—are held by members of the Trilateral Commission, and the National Security Adviser was its director. Many lesser officials also came from this group. It is rare for such an easily identified private group to play such a prominent role in an American Administration.

The Trilateral Commission was founded at the initiative of David Rockefeller in 1973. Its members are drawn from the three components of the world of capitalist democracy: the United States, Western Europe, and Japan. Among them are heads of major corporations and banks, partners in corporate law firms, Senators, Professors of international affairs—the familiar mix in extra-governmental groupings. Along with the 1980s project of the Council on Foreign Relations (CFR), directed by a committed 'trilateralist, and with numerous links to the Commission, the project constitutes the first major effort at global planning since the War-Peace Studies programme of the CFR during World War II.

The new "trilateralism" reflects the realization that the international system now requires "a truly common management," as the Commission reports indicate. The trilateral powers must order their internal relations and face both the Russian bloc, now conceded to be beyond the reach of Grand Area planning, and the Third World.

In this collective management, the United States will continue to play the decisive role. As Kissinger has explained, other powers have only "regional interests" while the United States must be "concerned more with the overall framework of order than with the management of every regional enterprise." If a popular movement in the Arabian peninsula is to be crushed, better to dispatch U.S. supplied Iranian forces, as in Dhofar. If passage for American nuclear submarines must be guaranteed in South-east Asian waters, then the task of crushing the independence movement in the former Portuguese colony of East Timor should be entrusted to the Indonesian army rather than an American expeditionary force. The massacre of over 60,000 people in a single year will arouse no irrational passions at home and American resources will not be drained, as in Vietnam. If a Katangese secessionist movement is to be suppressed in Zaire (a movement that may have Angolan support in response to the American-backed intervention in Angola from Zaire, as the former CIA station chief in Angola has recently revealed in his public letter of resignation), then the task should be assigned to Moroccan satellite forces and to the French, with the U.S. discreetly in the background. If there is a danger of socialism in southern Europe, the German proconsulate can exercise its "regional interests." But the Board of Directors will sit in Washington.

The founding of the Trilateral Commission coincided with Kissinger's "Year of Europe," which was intended to restore a proper order and hierarchy to the trilateral world (specifically, the "Atlantic Alliance") after the Vietnam failure. A particularly ominous development was, and remains, "the prospect of a closed trading system embracing the European Community and a growing number of other nations in Europe, the Mediterranean, and Africa, a system from which the U.S. might be excluded" (Kissinger). This is the counterpart of the fear that Japan might strike an independent course in East Asia, in part as a result of Communist success on the mainland. American policies towards the Middle East—in particular, the U.S. support for some rise in oil prices—must be understood in this context, a fact I have discussed elsewhere (see my "Stratégie Pétrolière ou Politique du Paix?," *Le Monde Diplomatique* Apr., 1977). The trilateral arrangements are intended to abort these threatening tendencies and ensure American dominance of the world economy, while laying the basis for a more successful West-East and North-South "dialogue."

The Trilateral Commission has issued one major book-length report, namely, *The Crisis of Democracy* (Michel Crozier, Samuel Huntington, and Joji Watanuki, 1975). Given the intimate connections between the Commission and the Carter Administration, the study is worth careful attention, as an indication of the thinking that may well lie behind its domestic policies, as well as the policies undertaken in other industrial democracies in the coming years.

The Commission's report is concerned with the 'governability of democracie.' Its American author, Samuel Huntington, was former chairman of the Department of Government at Harvard, and a government adviser. He is well-known for his ideas on how to destroy the rural revolution in Vietnam. He wrote in *Foreign Affairs* (1968) that "In an absent-minded way the United States in Vietnam may well have stumbled upon the answer to 'wars of national liberation." The answer is "forced-draft urbanization and modernization." Explaining this concept, he observes that if direct application of military force in the countryside "takes place on such a massive scale as to produce a massive migration from countryside to city," then the "Maoist-inspired rural revolution 'may be' undercut by the American sponsored urban revolution." The Viet Cong, he wrote, is "a powerful force which cannot be dislodged from its constituency so long as the constituency continues to exist." Thus "in the immediate future," peace must "be based on accommodation," particularly, since the U.S. is unwilling to undertake the "expensive, time-consuming and frustrating task" of ensuring that the constituency of the Viet Cong no longer exists (he was wrong about that, as the Nixon-Kissinger programs of rural massacre were to show). "Accommodation," as conceived by Huntington, is a process whereby the Viet Cong "degenerate into the protest of a declining rural minority," while the regime imposed by U.S. force maintains power. A year later, when it appeared that "urbanization" by military force was not succeeding and it seemed that the United States might be compelled to enter into negotiations with the NLF (which he recognized to be "the most powerful purely political national organization"), Huntington, in a paper delivered before the AID supported Council on Vietnamese Studies which he had headed, proposed various measures of political trickery and manipulation that might be used to achieve the domination of the U.S.-imposed government, though the discussants felt rather pessimistic about the prospects. On similar assumptions, he has explained that the American invasion of the Dominican Republic to overthrow the popular democratic Bosch regime was 'a success' (for the United States, though not for the impoverished masses whose income drastically declined, or those murdered by death squads or the forces of order placed in power in this American dependency; see my *At War with Asia*, chapter 1, and "The United States Versus Human Rights," cited above).

In short, Huntington is well-qualified to discourse on the problems of democracy.

The Report argues that what is needed in the industrial democracies "is a greater degree of moderation in democracy" to overcome the "excess of democracy" of the past decade. "The effective operation of a democratic political system usually requires some measure of apathy and noninvolvement on the part of some individuals and groups." This recommendation recalls the analysis of Third World problems put forth by other political thinkers of the same persuasion, for example, Ithiel Pool (then chairman of the Department of Political Science at MIT), who explained some years ago that in Vietnam, the Congo and the Dominican Republic, "order depends on somehow compelling newly mobilized strata to return to a measure of passivity and defeatism... At least temporarily, the maintenance of order requires a lowering of newly acquired aspirations and levels of political activity." The Trilateral recommendations for the capitalist democracies are an application at home of the theories of "order" developed for subject societies of the Third World.

The problems affect all of the trilateral countries, but most significantly, the United States. As Huntington points out, "for a quarter-century the United States was the hegemonic power in a system of world order," the Grand Area of the CFR. "A decline in the governability of democracy at home means a decline in the influence of democracy abroad." He does not elaborate on what this "influence" has been in practice, but ample testimony can be provided by survivors in Asia and Latin America.

As Huntington observes, "Truman had been able to govern the country with the cooperation of a relatively small number of Wall Street lawyers and bankers," a rare acknowledgement of the realities of political power in the United States. But by the mid-1960s this was no longer possible since "the sources of power in society had diversified tremendously," the "most notable new source of national power" being the media. In reality, the national media have been properly subservient to the state propaganda system, a fact on which I have already commented. Huntington's paranoia about the media is, however, widely shared among ideologists who fear a deterioration of American global hegemony and an end to the submissiveness of the domestic population.

A second threat to the governability of democracy is posed by the "previously passive or unorganized groups in the population," such as "blacks, Indians,

Chicanos, white ethnic groups, students and women—all of whom became mobilized and organized in new ways to achieve what they considered to be their appropriate share of the action and of the rewards." The threat derives from the principle, already noted, that 'some measure of apathy and noninvolvement on the part of some individuals and groups' is a prerequisite for democracy. Anyone with the slightest understanding of American society can supply a hidden premise: the "Wall Street lawyers and bankers' (and their cohorts) do not intend to exercise 'more self-restraint." We may conclude that the "greater degree of moderation in democracy" will have to be practiced by the "newly mobilized strata."

Huntington's perception of the "concerned efforts" of these strata "to establish their claims," and the "control over... institutions" that resulted, is no less exaggerated than his fantasies about the media. In fact, the Wall Street lawyers, bankers, etc., are no less in control of the government than in the Truman period, as a look at the new Administration or its predecessors reveals. But one must understand the curious notion of "democratic participation" that animates the Trilateral Commission study. Its vision of "democracy" is reminiscent of the feudal system. On the one hand, we have the King and Princes (the government). On the other, the commoners. The commoners may petition and the nobility must respond to maintain order. There must, however, be a proper "balance between power and liberty, authority and democracy, government and society." "Excessive swings may produce either too much government or too little authority." In the 1960s, Huntington maintains, the balance shifted too far to society and against government. "Democracy will have a longer life if it has a more balanced existence," that is, if the peasants cease their clamour. Real participation of "society" in government is nowhere discussed, nor can there be any question of democratic control of the basic economic institutions that determine the character of social life while dominating the state as well, by virtue of their overwhelming power. Once again, human rights do not exist in this domain.

The report does briefly discuss "proposals for industrial democracy modeled on patterns of political democracy," but only to dismiss them. These ideas are seen as "running against the industrial culture and the constraints of business organization." Such a device as German co-determination would "raise impossible problems in many Western democracies, either because leftist trade unionists would oppose it and utilize it without becoming any more moderate, or because employers would manage to defeat its purposes." In fact, steps towards worker participation in management going well beyond the German system are being discussed and in part implemented in Western Europe, though they fall far short of true industrial democracy and self-management in the sense advocated by the libertarian left. They have evoked much concern in business circles in Europe and particularly in the United States, which has so far been insulated from these currents, since American multinational enterprises will be affected. But these developments are anathema to the trilateralist study.

Still another threat to democracy, in the eyes of the Commission study, is posed by "the intellectuals and related groups who assert their disgust with the

corruption, materialism, and inefficiency of democracy and with the subservience of democratic government to 'monopoly capitalism' " (the latter phrase
is in quotes since it is regarded as improper to use an accurate descriptive term
to refer to the existing social and economic system; this avoidance of the taboo
term is in conformity with the dictates of the state religion, which scorns and
fears any such sacrilege).

Intellectuals come in two varieties, according to the trilateral analysis. The
"technocratic and policy-oriented intellectuals" are to be admired for their
unquestioning obedience to power and their services in social management,
while the "value-oriented intellectuals" must be despised and feared for the serious challenge they pose to democratic government, by "the unmasking and delegitimatization of established institutions."

The authors do not claim that what the value-oriented intellectuals write
and say is false. Such categories as "truth" and "honesty" do not fall within the
province of the apparatchiks. The point is that their work of "unmasking and
delegitimatization" is a threat to democracy when popular participation in politics is causing "a breakdown of traditional means of social control." They "challenge the existing structures of authority" and even the effectiveness of "those
institutions which have played the major role in the indoctrination of the
young." Along with "privatistic youth" who challenge the work ethic in its traditional form, they endanger democracy, whether or not their critique is well-
founded. No student of modern history will fail to recognize this voice.

What must be done to counter the media and the intellectuals, who, by
exposing some ugly facts, contribute to the dangerous "shift in the institutional
balance between government and opposition?" How do we control the "more
politically active citizenry" who convert democratic politics into "more an arena
for the assertion of conflicting interests than a process for the building of common purposes?" How do we return to the good old days, when "Truman,
Acheson, Forrestal, Marshall, Harriman, and Lovett" could unite on a policy of
global intervention and domestic militarism as our "common purpose," with no
interference from the undisciplined rabble?

The crucial task is "to restore the prestige and authority of central government institutions, and to grapple with the immediate economic challenges." The
demands on government must be reduced and we must "restore a more equitable
relationship between governmental authority and popular control." The press
must be reined. If the media do not enforce "standards of professionalism," then
"the alternative could well be regulation by the government"—a distinction
without a difference, since the policy-oriented and technocratic intellectuals, the
commissars themselves, are the ones who will fix these standards and determine
how well they are respected. Higher education should be related "to economic
and political goals," and if it is offered to the masses, "a programme is then necessary to lower the job expectations of those who receive a college education." No
challenge to capitalist institutions can be considered, but measures should be
taken to improve working conditions and work organization so that workers will

not resort to "irresponsible blackmailing tactics." In general, the prerogatives of the nobility must be restored and the peasants reduced to the apathy that becomes them.

This is the ideology of the *liberal* wing of the state capitalist ruling elite, and, it is reasonable to assume, its members who now staff the national executive in the United States.

## Prospects for the coming years

The Carter Administration is unlikely to undertake any significant new initiatives in foreign or domestic policy, though there will be some new rhetoric, largely for propaganda purposes. Any American Administration, coming to power in 1977, must face certain challenges. During the Vietnam war, American hegemony in the Grand Area declined, though by now it has been significantly restored. Trilateralism—that is, collective management of the capitalist international order by the major industrial powers, under Washington's supervision—must replace the Grand Area system with its emphasis on exclusive American hegemony. This is entirely natural in an era of multinational corporations with far-flung global interests involving ruling groups in many countries. Nationalist currents in the Third World must be contained, and insofar as possible, elites that will be responsive to the needs of international capitalism must be imposed or supported. Some version of detente must be pursued; that is, an arrangement with the second major superpower, which insists on ruling its imperial domains without undue interference, and will agree to play a relatively minor role elsewhere; an arrangement in which there must, as Kissinger phrased it, be "a penalty for intransigence" if the junior partner in enforcing world order becomes too obstreperous, but in which the danger of superpower confrontation must be reduced. The major resources, particularly energy, must be accessible to the industrial capitalist powers, and largely controlled by the United States. The crucial American interest in ensuring its substantial control of Middle East oil and its distribution must be maintained. The hopes of rolling back Communism in China, still alive in policy-making circles through the mid-1960s, have been abandoned. The United States will cultivate its relations with China, in part as a barrier to Russian influence but also as a way of imposing constraints on the independent development of Japan. Where independent nationalist forces intent on taking control of their own resources and pursuing their own path towards modernization and development have not been destroyed, as in Cuba and Indo-China, barriers must be imposed so as to maximize the difficulties that they will face and to increase the intrinsic pressures, internal to these societies, towards authoritarian rule and repression. Sooner or later, the United States will come to terms with these societies, if they are able to persist in their present course, as it has, after many years, in the case of China, or earlier, the Soviet Union.

Within the trilateral domains, effective controls must be instituted to contain and restrict the pressures towards the extension of democracy. In particular, encroachments on the system of authoritarian private control of production, commerce, and finance must be resisted, and the ideological system must be restored. Insofar as possible, the population must be reduced to the state of compliance and unquestioning passivity of the period before the turmoil of the 1960s, which created a few breaches in the system. The fundamental dogmas of the state religion must be restored to their position of unchallenged domination: the United States is a global benefactor, committed to self-determination, human rights, and general welfare, trying to do good in an ungrateful world, though occasionally erring in its naivete; the United States is not an active agent in world affairs, pursuing the interests of groups that dominate domestic society, but rather only responds to the challenges of evil forces that seek to upset world order, to international aggressors, as in Indo-China, where China and Russia were successfully depicted in this manner during the period when France and the United States were devastating Indo-China.

There are severe problems facing the industrial societies. The crises of energy, pollution, depleted resources, the massive waste of scarce resources in military production and artificially stimulated consumption, unemployment, inflation, stagnation, and so on, must somehow be faced without institutional modification. It is not obvious that there are answers to these problems, at least within the current social order. It is not unlikely that efforts to resolve them without serious institutional change will lead to further extension of centralized planning on the part of (and in the interests of) ruling groups, using the state as an agency of control and coordination. The system may evolve towards what some have called 'friendly fascism'—that is, social structures reminiscent of the fascist order, but without the brutality, barbarism, and cultural degradation of the fascist states.

There is no indication that the Carter Administration is committed to any different path, and even if it were, persistent tendencies in the private economy would pose serious if not insuperable barriers. These seem to me to be the prospects for the years ahead, unless popular forces that now exist only in a limited and scattered form can be organized and mobilized to introduce really significant changes in the domestic social and economic order.

**Editor's Notes to Chapter 13**

Written on November 13, 1976. A modified version appeared in *In These Times* 29 Nov.–5 Dec. under the title "CIA, FBI Activities Span the Globe." For more on FBI activities, see Chomsky's Introduction to *Cointelpro* (Counterintelligence Program), ed. by Cathy Perkus, New York: Vintage, 1976. [MMR]

See **TCW**, in particular the Introduction, and Edward Herman, *The Real Terror Network: Terrorism in Fact and Propaganda* (Boston: South End Press, 1982). See also "The Intelligence Identities Protection Act: Interview with Noam Chomsky." *CounterSpy* May–June 1982: pp. 27–31, reprinted in the RESIST Newsletter 152 (Nov. 1982), pp. 4–7.

# 13. The Secret Terror Organizations Of The U.S. Government

In January 1976, the Pike Committee of the U.S. House of Representatives filed its report on the CIA and the FBI. Though officially secret, the report was leaked to the press and appeared in the *Village Voice*, Feb. 16 and 23. The final report of the Senate Committee on Intelligence Activities (Church Committee) was released in April. These reports supplemented a flood of information from Court cases and other sources. An analysis of this material gives a revealing insight into the role of the secret agencies at home and abroad and into the domestic and international policies of the American government as they have evolved since World War II.

The documents reveal that the CIA and the FBI have been engaged in subversion, terror, instigation of violence and disruption of democratic processes at home and abroad. Furthermore, these programs are not sporadic or "out of control." Rather, they are systematic, relatively independent of political changes, and in general organized at the highest levels of state.

According to the Pike Committee, "All evidence in hand suggests that the CIA, far from being out of control, has been utterly responsive to the instructions of the President and the Assistant to the President for National Security Affairs." The "great majority" of its "covert action projects were proposed by parties outside CIA," that is, by the civilian agencies that use the CIA, in effect, as a secret army of the Presidency.

What were these CIA activities? One primary function of the CIA, from its origins, has been to disrupt democracy in allied or subject countries. From 1948 to 1968 the CIA and "related organizations" expended over $65 million in Italy alone to subvert Italian democracy, in fear of Communist electoral success. These programs formed a part of the successful U.S. government effort, abetted by the labor bureaucracy, to split and weaken the European labor movement and in general to restore European capitalism and ensure U.S. dominance of most of the industrial world. The Pike Committee gives this quantitative estimate: "From 1965 to date, 32 percent of Forty Committee approved covert action projects were for providing some form of financial election support to foreign parties and individuals." The Forty Committee is "the review and approval mechanism for covert action," directly controlled by the President. These efforts to subvert democracy constitute "the largest covert action category" of the CIA and are directed primarily against the Third World. These calculations of course do not include government or related corporate efforts of other sorts to undermine democratic processes, as in Chile or more recently in Thailand.

Much the same is true of the national political police at home. The Church Committee reports that "Each administration from Franklin D. Roosevelt's to Richard Nixon's permitted and sometimes encouraged Government activities to handle essentially political intelligence." The left was the primary target, but not the only one. The investigation of the NAACP, for example, "lasted for over 25 years, although nothing was found to rebut a report during the first year of the investigation that the NAACP had a 'strong tendency' to 'steer clear of Communist activities'." Investigation and disruption of the Socialist Workers Party persisted for 34 years, and in fact continued well after it had allegedly been terminated. What the Pike Committee calls "FBI racism" reached its peak in the 1960s. with the growth of the civil rights and Black movements. Programs to undermine these movements and discredit their leadership were initiated under the Kennedy Administration and extended under Johnson and Nixon, culminating in direct efforts to instigate violence and murder, and, it appears, FBI participation in political assassination in the case of Blank Panther leaders Fred Hampton and Mark Clark.

The CIA was also active at home. The Church Committee reports, for example, that "Nearly a quarter of a million first class letters were opened and photographed in the United States by the CIA between 1953–1973, producing a CIA computerized index of nearly one and one-half million names."

The subversive activities of the executive secret agencies have been regularly adjusted in scale to conform to the perceived threat to state policy. Violence directed against the peace movement and direct instigation of violence by agents placed within the movement increased through the 1960s. By the mid-1960s, every "free university" was under FBI investigation. By 1970, the Church Committee reports, the FBI ordered investigations of every member of SDS and of "every black student union and similar group." Throughout the country, FBI agents, infiltrators, and clandestine terrorist groups went on a rampage, with bombings, assassination attempts, kidnapping, beatings, disruption, robbery, and so on. The pattern was no different abroad.

The Pike Report sheds light on the serious consequences of the general incompetence of the intelligence agencies. In October 1973, for example, a world-wide nuclear alert followed Russian protests over Israeli violations of the cease-fire in Egypt. U.S. intelligence "almost unquestionably (sic) relied on overly-optimistic Israeli battle reports," according to the Pike Committee. "Thus misled, the U.S. clashed with the better-informed Soviets on the latter's strong reaction to Israeli cease-fire violations. Soviet threats to intervene militarily were met with a worldwide U.S. troop alert. Poor intelligence had brought America to the brink of war."

Reading between the lines, we may surmise that the "overly optimistic" reports indicated that the violations were more successful than Russian intelligence knew them to be. Indirectly, then, the Pike Committee report also leads to some interesting speculations with regard to U.S. government policy at the time.

Some of the CIA activities are remarkable in their cynicism. To cite one case, the CIA supported the rebellion of the Kurds in Iraq while the U.S. acted to prevent a political settlement that might have preserved a degree of Kurdish autonomy. Kissinger, Nixon and the Shah also insisted on a "no win" policy so that the revolt would persist, undermining both Iraq and the Kurdish movement. With a shift in international politics, the Kurds were sold out. The U.S. then refused even humanitarian assistance to its former allies as they were crushed by force. The reason was explained to the Pike Committee staff by a high government official: "covert action should not be confused with missionary work." 200,000 Kurds managed to escape. Iran then returned over 40,000 by force "and the United States government refused to admit even one refugee into the United States by way of political asylum even though they qualified for such admittance."

The Committee Reports do not deal with the most sordid programs of the government terror organizations. Thus, nothing is said about the CIA's secret war in Laos or the Phoenix programme in Vietnam, which, according to the Saigon government, claimed over 40,000 victims, in a programme of indiscriminate massacre. The Church Committee presents evidence concerning FBI attempts to incite gang warfare in black ghettos but gives no adequate account of such atrocities as the campaign to destroy the Black Panther Party. Nor does it explore FBI-directed violence, arming and financing of secret terrorist armies, concealing of criminal activities and the like in San Diego and other cities. Nevertheless, the investigations suffice to give a revealing picture of the activities of the U.S. government to control domestic and international society, by means ranging from subversion to force and violence.

A fuller account would trace the activities of the national political police to the Red Scare after World War I, when J. Edgar Hoover rose to prominence as the government acted to destroy the left and undermine labor with the support of the press and business, under "progressive" Attorney-General Palmer who announced his intention "to tear out the radical seeds that have entangled American ideas in their poisonous theories." In fact, the story begins long before. Such an account would also explore the role of American liberalism, quite consistently, in developing and justifying the mechanisms of ideological control. It would approach the present by quoting the speeches by the mass murderer Henry Kissinger on morality in foreign policy, noting that these appear without comment in the liberal press. And it would conclude that nothing will change until mass popular movements develop, here and abroad, that can struggle effectively against the violence of the state, directed and organized by those who rule the state by virtue of their unchallenged domination of the private economy.

**Editor's Notes to Chapter 14**

Reprinted in *American Report* 13 Aug. 1973: p. 3 from *The Real Paper* Boston, 11 July under the title "Watergate is Small Potatoes."

For many other writings by Chomsky on the topic, see the additional bibliography in Chomsky, *Sintáctica y Semántica en la Gramática Generativa.* México: Siglo XXI, 1979, *Noam Chomsky. Bibliografia 1949–1981*, a Cura di Salvatore Claudio Sgroi, CLESP Editore, Padova: 1983, and *Noam Chomsky: A Personal Bibliography, 1951–1986*, comp. by E. F. Konrad Koerner & Matsuji Tajima with the collaboration of C. P. Otero. Amsterdam/Philadelphia: 1986.

Thomas Watson (IBM), James Reston (*NY Times*) and McGeorge Bundy are closely related to the Council of Foreign Relations (see Selection 12).

# 14. Watergate: Small Potatoes

John Dean's list of enemies has elicited indignation and flippancy. Justifiable responses, no doubt, but inadequate ones.

Suppose there had been no Thomas Watson or James Reston or McGeorge Bundy on the White House hate list. Suppose that the list had been limited to true political dissidents, antiwar activists, radicals. Then, one can be sure, there would have been no front page story in *The NY Times* and little attention on the part of responsible political commentators.

But the gang of petty thieves who had taken temporary control over the state executive violated the rules of the game. They were attacking the political center. Their targets included the rich and respectable, spokesmen for official ideology, men who are expected to share power, to design social policy and mold popular opinion. Such people are not fair game for persecution at the hands of the state.

The reaction to the Watergate affair in general exhibits the same moral flaw. What CREEP was trying to do to the Democrats is insignificant in comparison with the bipartisan attack on the Communist Party in the postwar era.

Judicial and other harassment of dissidents and their organizations is the common practice, whoever happens to be in office. Serious civil rights or antiwar groups have regularly discovered government provocateurs among their most militant members.

Watergate is different only in that some of the familiar bipartisan tactics were applied against one of the two components of what has occasionally been called "the Property Party," one of the two candidate-producing organizations that masquerade as political.

A true hypocrite might argue that the state attack on political dissent has generally been within the bounds of the law—at least, as the courts have interpreted the Constitution—whereas the Watergate antics were plainly illegal. But surely it is clear that those who have the power to impose their interpretation of "legitimacy" will so construct and construe the legal system as to permit them to root out their enemies.

The mistake of the Watergate conspirators was that they failed to heed the lesson of the McCarthy hearings 20 years ago. It is one thing to attack the left, the pitiful remnants of the Communist Party, a collapsing liberal opposition that had capitulated in advance by accepting-in fact, creating-the instruments of postwar repression, or elements in the bureaucracy that might impede the state policy of counterrevolutionary intervention and enforcement of global order; it is something else again to turn the same weapons against the U.S. Army.

Having failed to make this subtle distinction, McCarthy was quickly destroyed. Nixon's cohorts, as recent exposures have amply demonstrated, have fallen into the same error of judgment.

The Watergate caper and the sordid story that has since been revealed are not without significance. They indicate, once again, how frail are the barriers to some form of fascism in a state capitalist system in crisis.

Fortunately for us and for the world, McCarthy was a mere thug and Nixon's mafia overstepped the bounds of acceptable trickery and deceit with such obtuseness and blundering vulgarity that they were quickly called to account by powerful forces.

Nixon's front men now plead that in 1969–70 the country was on the verge of insurrection and that it was therefore necessary to stretch the Constitutional limits.

The turmoil of those years was largely a reaction to U.S. efforts to crush the forces of revolutionary nationalism in Indochina. The basic premises of that policy are largely shared by most of the enemies on the Dean Colson list. And the conditions, domestic and international, that have led successive Administrations to guide "Third World Development" into the particular channels that suit the needs of industrial capitalism have not changed.

There is every reason to suppose that similar considerations will impel their successors to implement the same policies, choosing their domestic enemies more judiciously and preparing the ground more thoroughly.

The reaction to Watergate illustrates the dangers well enough. In the midst of the Watergate exposures, Ambassador Godley testified before Congress that 15,000–20,000 Thai mercenaries had been employed by the U.S. in Laos, in direct and explicit violation of Congressional legislation. This confirmation of Pathet Lao charges that had been largely ignored or ridiculed in the West evoked little editorial comment or public indignation, though it is a far more serious matter than anything revealed at the Ervin Hearings.

Liberal political commentators sigh with relief that Kissinger has barely been tainted—a bit of questionable wiretapping, but no close involvement in the Watergate shenanigans.

Yet by any objective standards the man is one of the great mass murderers of modern times. He presided over the expansion of the war to Cambodia (with consequences that are now well-known) and the vicious escalation of the bombings of Laos, not to speak of the atrocities committed in Vietnam as he sought to achieve a victory of some sort for imperial power in Indochina.

But he wasn't implicated in the burglary at the Watergate or the undermining of Muskie, so his hands are clean.

If we try to keep a sense of balance, the exposures of the past several months are analogous to the discovery that the directors of Murder, Inc. were also cheating on their income tax. Reprehensible, to be sure, but hardly the main point.

**Editor's Notes to Chapter 15**

Published, with the assessments of other authors (which is enlightening to compare with Chomsky's) in the *NYR* 22 (25 June 1975) under the general title "The Meaning of Vietnam." (See Editor's Notes to Selection 2.)

For a more extensive discussion, see the article mentioned in the Editor's Notes to Selection 3 and other articles listed in the bibliography referred to in the Editor's Notes to Selection 14 which were published after **FRS**. For the final quote, see Selection 19, n. 9.

See now **TCW**, chs. 3–5.

# 15. The Vietnam War: A Monstrosity

The U.S. government was defeated in Indochina, but only bruised at home. No outside power will compel us to face the record honestly or to offer reparations. On the contrary, efforts will be devoted to obscuring the history of the war and the domestic resistance to it. There are some simple facts that we should try to save as the custodians of history set to work.

In its essence, the Indochina war was a war waged by the U.S. and such local forces as it could organize against the rural population of South Vietnam. Regarding the Geneva Accords of 1954 as a "disaster," Washington at once undertook a programme of subversion throughout the region to undermine the political arrangements. A murderous repression in South Vietnam led to the renewal of resistance. Kennedy involved U.S. forces in counterinsurgency, bombing, and "population control." By 1964 it was obvious that there was no political base for U.S. intervention. In January 1965, General Khanh was moving toward an alliance with anti-American Buddhists and had entered into negotiations with the NLF. He was removed as the systematic bombardment of South Vietnam began, at triple the level of the more publicized bombing of the North. The full scale U.S. invasion followed, with consequences that are well known. The civilian societies of Laos and then Cambodia were savagely attacked in a war that was at first "secret" thanks to the self-censorship of the press.

In January 1973 Nixon and Kissinger were compelled to accept the peace proposals they had sought to modify after the November 1972 elections. As in 1954, the acceptance was purely formal. The Paris Agreements recognized two equivalent parties in South Vietnam, the PRG and the GVN, and established a basis for political reconciliation. The U.S. was enjoined not to impose any political tendency or personality on South Vietnam. But Nixon and Kissinger announced at once that in defiance of the scrap of paper signed in Paris, they would recognize the GVN as the sole legitimate government, its constitutional structure—which outlawed the other party—intact and unchanged.

In violation of the agreements, Thieu intensified political repression and launched a series of military actions. By mid-1974, U.S. officials were optimistically reporting the success achieved by the Thieu regime, with its vast advantage in firepower, in conquering PRG territory where, they alleged, a North Vietnamese buildup was underway. As before, the whole rotten structure collapsed from within as soon as the "enemy" was so ungracious as to respond, and this time Washington itself had collapsed to the point where it could no longer send in bombers.

The American war was criminal in two major respects. Like the Dominican intervention and the Russian invasion of Czechoslovakia, it was a case of aggression, conscious and premeditated. In 1954, the National Security Council stated that the U.S. reserved the right to use force "to defeat local Communist subversion or rebellion not constituting armed attack," i.e., in violation of "the supreme law of the land." The U.S. acted on this doctrine. Furthermore, the conduct of the war was an indescribable atrocity. The U.S. goal was to eradicate the revolutionary nationalist forces which, U.S. officials estimated, enjoyed the support of half the population. The method, inevitably, was to destroy the rural society. While the war of annihilation partially succeeded in this aim, the U.S. was never able to create a workable system out of the wreckage.

Opposition to the war at home made full-scale mobilization impossible and placed some constraints on the brutality of the war planners. By 1971, two-thirds of the U.S. population opposed the war as immoral and called for the withdrawal of American troops. But the articulate intelligentsia generally opposed the war, if at all, on "pragmatic" i.e., entirely unprincipled grounds. Some objected to its horror; more objected to the failure of American arms and the incredible cost. Few were willing to question the fundamental principle that the U.S. has the right to resort to force to manage international affairs. Throughout this period, there was a negative correlation between educational level and opposition to the war, specifically, principled opposition. (The correlation was obscured by the fact that the more articulate and visible elements in the peace movement were drawn disproportionately from privileged social groups.)

The gulf that opened between much of the population and the nation's ideologists must be closed if U.S. might is to be readily available for global management. Therefore, a propaganda battle is already being waged to ensure that all questions of principle are excluded from debate ("avoid recriminations"). Furthermore, the historical record must be revised, and it will be necessary to pretend that "responsible" political groups acting "within the system" sought to end the war, but were blocked in their efforts by the peace movement. People cannot be permitted to remember that the effective direct action of spontaneous movement—both in the United States and among the conscripted army in the field—that were out of the control of their "natural leaders" in fact played the primary role in constraining the war makers.

The U.S. government was unable to subdue the forces of revolutionary nationalism in Indochina, but the American people are a less resilient enemy. If the apologists for state violence succeed in reversing their ideological defeats of the past years, the stage will be set for a renewal of armed intervention in the case of "local subversion or rebellion" that threatens to extricate some region from the U.S.-dominated global system. A prestigious study group twenty years ago identified the primary threat of "communism" as the economic transformation of the communist powers "in ways which reduce their willingness and ability to complement the industrial economics of the West." The American effort to contain this threat in Indochina was blunted, but the struggle will doubtless continue elsewhere. Its issue will be affected, if not determined, by the outcome of the ideological conflict over "the lessons of Vietnam."

### Editor's Notes to Chapter 16

Introduction, dated June 17 1968, to the Italian version of *The New Left*, ed. by Mitchell Cohen & Dennis Hale Boston: Beacon Press, 1967. (*Gli Studenti e la Nuova Sinistra in America*. Antologia a Cura di Enrico Forni, M. Cohen & D. Hale, Bari: De Donato Editore, 1968, pp. ix–xvi). The asterisks indicate the place where a page of the English original is missing. The gap can be filled by the comments on Randolph Bourne in the Introduction to **APNM** or in ch. 6 of **FRS**. For more on the quote from Johnson, see Selection 18.

Randolph Bourne (1886–1918), in the tradition of Thoreau, opposed the "pragmatic" ideas of the liberal intellectuals of his time.

See Seymour Melman, *The Permanent War Economy: American Capitalism in Decline*. New York: Simon & Schuster, 1985, and, recently, *Profits Without Production*. New York: Knopf, 1983. See Selection 20. (Melman is the author of one of the few truly discerning reviews of **APNM**. See *Catholic World* 2.10 (1969), pp. 80–81.)

# 16. The Student Revolt

Why do students rebel? At the moment, endless pages are being filled with acute and learned analysis of this question, but few seem satisfied with the answers. I would like to say something about the topic too, but first, let me digress.

In November, 1960, the *U.S. Naval Institute Proceedings* contained the following item:

> The Art of War: Computations made on an electronic computer by a former president of the Norwegian Academy of Sciences, aided by historians from England, Egypt, Germany, and India, have produced some astounding figures on the frequency and severity of wars. Included in these findings is the fact that since 3,600 B.C. the world has known only 292 years of peace. During this period there have been 14,531 wars, large and small, in which 3,640,000,000 people were killed. The value of the destruction inflicted would pay for a golden belt around the earth 156 kilometers in width and 10 meters thick. Since 650 B.C. there have been 1,656 arms races, only 16 of which have not ended in war. The remainder have ended in economic collapse.

Electronic computer or not, the figures are hardly to be taken seriously, but the general point made is accurate enough. In our century, the insanity has accelerated in pace, leading to a climax on August 6, 1945. Since that time, it is estimated that the United States, which escaped virtually unscathed from the holocaust—in fact with its power enormously enhanced—has spent something like a trillion dollars in "defense." These expenditures have enabled it to defend itself successfully from the North Koreans, and now, from the peasants of Vietnam, who have been subjected to air and artillery bombardment on a scale that has no parallel in the history of warfare. The United States now spends about 1/3 of a billion dollars a year on research and stockpiling of means for chemical and biological warfare (CBW). An editor of *Science*, the journal of the American Association for the Advancement of Science, points out that we are the only nation "chipping away at the psychological barriers to use of CBW." The budget for defoliation and crop destruction in Vietnam for the fiscal year beginning July 1968 is up more than 50 percent over the preceding year. One estimate is that the materials now requisitioned by the defense department for this year will suffice to destroy virtually all the vegetation on 10 million acres. Writing in *Science*, the Harvard University scientist who made that estimate remarks that we are going beyond genocide to biocide. The hideous character of a policy of crop destruction in Asia needs no comment from me.

## The Pentagon and nuclear war

In 1962, a very liberal American administration staffed with leading academic intellectuals was willing to face a high probability of nuclear war (a probability of 1/3 to 1/2, according to Theodore Sorenson) to establish the principle that we, and we alone, have the right to keep missiles on the borders of a potential enemy. In the *NY Times Magazine*, 9 June 1968, Hanson Baldwin, who generally represents the viewpoint of the Pentagon, suggested that our post-Vietnam policy should involve a credible threat that nuclear weapons will be used, for defensive purposes only, of course—in Asia. The notion "defensive purposes" has achieved a rich content in this terrible century. For example, it has been defined as follows:

> We must recognize that an overt act of war has been committed by an enemy when that enemy builds a military force intended for our eventual destruction, and that the destruction of that force before it can be launched or employed is defensive action and not aggression. As a nation we must understand that an overt act of war has been committed long before the delivery of that first blow.

The quotation is from the American Air Force publication *Air Campaigns of the Pacific War*, in 1947. I emphasize that this is not official American government policy, but it is perhaps too close for comfort.

## A race war

At the same time American society is faced with the possibility of a civil war of a particularly sinister kind—a race war. Among the affluent and near affluent —the majority of the population—there is great fear, fear of the dispossessed at home and the wretched of the earth overseas. The fear is very real. It shows itself on the domestic scene in the crime bill now awaiting the President's signature, a bill which, among other things, seeks to overturn recent Supreme Court decisions that grant protection from the police to those who do not know their legal rights or are too powerless to be able to demand them; or in the Internal Security Act of 1968, now in a Congressional Committee, which establishes a crime of peacetime treason, the crime of giving "aid or comfort" to an "adversary" of the United States, that is, a foreign nation or armed group engaged in hostilities against the United States or its Armed Forces. If it becomes law (which, one fervently hopes, it will not), this bill would apply to those who give "aid or comfort" to the inhabitants of an American ghetto which is under military occupation, for example, a not unlikely prospect in the coming months, and it would presumably stifle dissent when the next "Vietnam war" breaks out, wherever it will be.

This same fear shows itself in the international arena in the basis for support of U. S. armed intervention overseas—what we call "aggression" when it is carried out by any other nation. When President Johnson says, as he has, that:

> There are 3 billion people in the world and we have only 200 million of them. We are outnumbered 15 to 1. If might did make right they would sweep over the United States and take what we have. We have what they want,

—when he insinuates that in Vietnam we are defending ourselves against a superior force, he is voicing fears that are deeply felt by many Americans, difficult as this may be to believe.

All of this gives reason for great apprehension about the use of American power in the years to come, an apprehension that is not lessened by the realization that while billions are spent each year on destruction and trips to the moon, our urban centers are rotting and millions live on the edge of starvation. End of digression.

## Why do students rebel?

Let me now return to the question: why do students rebel? Like many questions that are repeatedly asked but never seem to receive a satisfactory answer, this question is wrongly put. The serious question that we must face is not why students rebel, but rather why students are virtually alone, in the white middle classes, in their rebellion, and why they rebel only now, and not before. There is no need to explain why a movement of protest, radical political action, and resistance has arisen. The real question is why so few join it. The answer, no doubt, is that they do not join because they have a stake in the maintenance of the social order, and they do not want their well-being threatened. In the United States, the normal conservatism of those who have achieved some degree of affluence, or who feel that they might, is enhanced by the fear of "Communism," which now verges on paranoia—the fear that others will "take what they have" that is well expressed by the President himself, and clothed in the rhetoric of anti-Communist ideology by the mass media and, to a large extent, the intellectuals who themselves sense the possibility of obtaining power and affluence to a hitherto unknown degree. Students are less susceptible to these pressures They are often literate, honest, and sincere. They do not like the injustice and ugliness of what they see, and therefore they protest, vigorously, as befits the objective situation that confronts them, and they search for ways to change what is intolerable. No elaborate explanations are necessary.

Why the rise in student activism now, and not before? It is not quite true that this is an entirely new phenomenon in the United States. Half a century ago, the outstanding American social critic Randolph Bourne described how World War I brought to leadership a liberal, technical intelligentsia, "immensely ready for the executive ordering of events, pitifully unprepared for the intellectual interpretation or the idealistic focusing of ends." These pragmatic intellectuals, he said, "have absorbed the secret of scientific method as applied to political administration."

The terms of Bourne's indictment of the university and the social values it represents, of the liberal intelligentsia it produces, of the society they expect to manage, might have been drawn from the essays in this collection, a half-century later, essays that have been produced by the young malcontents who do, indeed, represent the hope for the future.

The confrontation that Bourne correctly saw in the making was aborted by the postwar repression. The 1920s saw a flight of American intellectuals to Europe, and the next decade was one of a struggle for survival and attempts to reform a system that had collapsed. Then came the war, the permanent war economy, and the cold war, with its freezing of thought and fear of free inquiry. By the late 1950s, cracks were beginning to show in the monolith. The essays in this collection trace the subsequent evolution of the student movement as the most idealistic and courageous of American youth gave themselves to the struggle against poverty and human degradation at home, and against a brutal war which is only the most obscene example of global repression. It is not merely the failure of the civil rights movement and the horrors of Vietnam that have sparked this movement, but also, no doubt, the disillusionment that followed a promise of improvement. With the New Frontier came a new wave of barbarism, in which the university faculty were deeply involved, not only in implementing counterinsurgency and pacification, but also in apologetics and ideology. All of this has increased enormously the intensity of student revulsion, and the protest and political action that has grown from it.

## The students and the future

In a sense, it is a tribute to American social institutions that the student movement has become a powerful force. The widespread feeling that certain ideals are being fouled attests to the fact that these ideals are deeply rooted. In a similar vein, there is an important sense in which it is true that the deepest faith in America is the faith expressed by the draft resisters, who are expressing their belief that this is a society worth living in even if prison is a part of that life, who hope that their resistance may lead others to examine and terminate their complicity in a criminal war. Whether this faith is justified is a question that will be answered in the coming years. If the student movement can withstand the crisis that seems imminent, as the criminal violence of the government forces dissent inevitably towards resistance, it will then face the task of reconstructing American social institutions. No one could have predicted, a decade ago, the growth of a student movement capable of the achievements of the past few years. It would be idle to speculate today as to the prospects for still more far-reaching accomplishments. The student movement has revitalized the American university, and has formed the leading edge of the struggle against war and racism. It now bears a heavy responsibility, growing in part from what has already been achieved. If it can move forward, perhaps along the lines sketched in these essays, it can become a factor of major importance in modern history. Personally, I tend to believe that if it fails or is crushed, the outlook for the future, for America and for the world, is stark and dismal.

## Editor's Notes to Chapter 17

Transcription of a talk Chomsky gave in a Forum at Oberlin College on Feb. 6, 1969, slightly edited by the author. It was published in *The Activist* (A *Student Journal of Politics and Opinion*) 24 (1969): pp. 26–33 & 40, under the title "Intellectuals and the War Lords."

An address based upon the notes of the Oberlin talk was given by Chomsky to the New York Society for Ethical Culture on Feb. 16, 1969, under the title "Intellectuals and Social Change," and it was published by the SEC (2 West 46th St., New York 10023). This address was the basis for the article "The Student Movement." *The Humanist* Sept.–Oct. 1970: pp. 19–25, which was reprinted under the title "In Defense of the Student Movement" by the Bertrand Russell Peace Foundation in Feb. 1971 as Spokesman Pamphlet no. 9, and in *American Presence in South East Asia*, ed. Malcolm Caldwell, Singapore: Island Publishers, 1971 pp. 29–51.

Cf. **PKF**, ch. 2, especially pp. 70ff.

For more on Sidney Hook see **FRS**, ch. 1, nn. 137 and 138, and **PKF**, ch. 2, n. 42.

On A. J. Muste, see **APNM**, ch. 2. On Dr. Spock, see *Trials of the Resistance* (Editor's Notes to Selection 2). See Selection 19.

On the MLA meeting, see **CD&E**, Selection 11 and pp. 423–424.

On violence, see Introduction, passage including n. 4. See also Selection 19.

# 17. The Politicization Of The University

At the level of generality at which quite a number of Mr. Hook's remarks were pitched I would not disagree with him. In fact I would be in hearty agreement, though I would disassociate myself from a number of statements about the facts which, in my view, are quite fanciful. However, I think that one general place where I would register disagreement is where he applies these very general ideas about democracy and academic freedom to the real world.

## The American "democracy"

I think the real world is different from the one that he is describing. For example, the real world of American society is one which it is very misleading to call simply a democracy. Of course, it is in a sense a democracy, but it is one in which there are enormous inequities in the distribution of power and force. For example, the entire commercial and industrial system is in principle excluded from the democratic process, including everything that goes on within it. The national security bureaucracy, which has recently been called (accurately) the second largest planned economy in the world, is of course in principle subject to democratic procedures but in fact is not. The mass media reflect the distribution of power: everyone who has twenty million dollars is free to open a newspaper, and one knows what this means. Since they reflect the actual distribution of power, not the ideal one, they actually reflect only a very narrow band in the spectrum of possible opinion. In fact the range of possible opinion that reaches any mass audience in the United States is extremely narrow compared to any advanced industrial society except for the Soviet Union and its satellites. It is certainly far narrower than Western Europe.

Now the university happens to be embedded in the matrix of this distribution of force and power, and one can't simply discuss it overlooking that fact. If one does, I think one arrives at extremely unrealistic conclusions. I agree with Mr. Hook that the university should not be politicized, and I object very strongly to the politicization that has come about in the past twenty years under the general cold war psychosis. I think the university, including its scholarship, its science, and its technology, has been seriously subverted by submission to dominant social forces. The people who have accepted this submission argue that they are simply value free and neutral: they answer to the needs of whoever happens to ask them for assistance. That's the conception of being value free that was used as a defense at Nuremberg. There were those who were willing to give their advice on how to run the German economy to anybody, even if Hitler happened to be in power.

Institutions that are powerful are in a position to articulate their needs and to finance the work that is done in answer to those needs. Communities that barely exist in any organized form are not so situated in the distribution of power in society. Consequently, if the university really were value free in any objective sense, it would not be simply answering to the needs imposed on it from the outside, but it would be trying to articulate the needs of those who are in no position to formulate them—the needs of segments of international society or perhaps even a future society—and it would be trying to answer to those needs both in its research and study and teaching. I don't want to over-generalize, but I think to a very significant extent the university has failed to do this, and consequently under the guise of neutrality and value freedom, it has, in effect, subverted its mission. Here, I merely reiterate what is stated, accurately and forcefully, by such radical critics as Dwight Eisenhower, Admiral Rickover, Senator Fulbright and many others who quite accurately describe this fact.

## Reflections on violence

My own view toward this whole set of questions is one which was formulated by one of the few authentic great men in twentieth century America, namely A.J. Muste. Muste gave the following advice to pacifists. He said their task is "to denounce the violence on which the present system is based, and all the material and spiritual evil it entails for the masses of men throughout the world. So long as we are not dealing honestly and adequately with this 90 percent of our problem, there is something ludicrous and perhaps hypocritical about our concern over the 10 percent of violence employed by the rebels against oppression." I would like to apologize in advance for the fact that I am going to do something ludicrous and perhaps hypocritical, in Muste's accurate words, namely, spend a large part of this talk discussing an infinitesimal part of the problems that face the university in American society today, namely, that caused by certain tendencies in the student movement that strike me as irrational, objectionable, and, I suspect, suicidal. I think that the student movement has an historic mission, a mission which, I might add, it has to some extent already realized: the contribution of the student movement in creating disorder in our society which had the effect of lessening the genocidal attack on Vietnam, this is a contribution of historic importance which one cannot overlook. There are others that can be mentioned. But I think the mission for the future is even greater. I am particularly disturbed by the feeling that the tendencies, to which I will return in a moment, may prove self-destructive, and I shall want to discuss these in some detail.

## The real problems of society

First, however, I want to mention—quite inadequately, since I don't command the rhetoric to describe them adequately—some of the real problems, the 90 percent of the problems of the society and the university. The main one is indicated by the fact that since World War II we've spent over a trillion dollars on what is laughably called defense, and unknown amounts for subversion in other countries. We've intervened repeatedly with military force to overthrow governments which we admit to be popular constitutional governments, to maintain in power oppressive dictatorships which are willing to subordinate themselves to our interests. At least once, and perhaps twice, we've forced modern civilization to the brink of destruction. The remarkable thing is that liberals and conservatives alike those in the mainstream of the opinion that reaches a mass audience through the media—they laud this splendid performance. We have people like Roger Hilsman, the spokesman for the liberal Kennedy administration, who considers the prototype of outstanding foreign policy to have been the intervention in Guatemala and Iran. That is the model he said the Kennedy administration should build on, and so it did, as we know. Or people like Frank Darling, a CIA analyst for Southeast Asia for several years and one of the best political scientists dealing with this area, a Kennedy liberal who wrote an excellent book on Thailand, very informative, in which he concludes that "the vast material and diplomatic support provided to the military leaders of Thailand by the United States helped to prevent the emergence of any competing groups who might check the trend toward absolute political rule and lead the country back to a more modern form of government." I stress the phrase "back to a more modern form of government." He is referring to the more modern form of government which did appear immediately after the second world war and which was destroyed by a *coup* supported by American military force that led to a ruthless authoritarian dictatorship which he describes in detail. His recommendation, from this story, is that we continue our fine work, exactly as the Kennedy administration did. On top of this there is, of course, a degree of distortion in the press which may be due to incompetence or may be due to conspiracy; I will not attempt to say here.

## The "moderate" position

Now I think that the liberal reaction to all this has been, in Muste's words "ludicrous and hypocritical." The reaction is typified, for example, by the document put out by Freedom House Public Affairs Institute about a year ago on American-Asian policy, a document signed by numerous academics in international affairs, political science, and Asian Studies. The members of this group, who identified themselves as the moderate segment of American scholarly opinion, expressed a crucial assumption that I quote now: "We must not encourage those elements in other societies committed to the thesis that violence is the best means of effecting change." Then they went ahead to make it quite obvious that what they were opposed to was not the violence but rather the change. They made this clear by condoning our violence in Vietnam, which as they well know, enormously exceeds that which could be mounted by anyone in Vietnamese society, or was mounted by the National Liberation Front in its response to American military force. I might add that people, like Douglas Pike, who parades as a scholar but is in fact an American propagandist, admit that the National Liberation Front military acts were a response to prior American military involvement—a crucial and important fact when one is talking about Viet Cong terror, whatever one may think about it. The moderate scholars further underscore their commitment to violence but opposition to change when they cite as one of the most dramatic changes in Southeast Asia, one of the great successes of American policy, what happened in Indonesia a few years ago. They delicately refrain from mentioning that the most dramatic change that took place there was the elimination from Indonesian society of five hundred thousand living beings, namely, a huge mass of landless peasants and ethnic Chinese. This event was, of course, not an instance of the kind of social change that we have ruled inappropriate and, therefore, is not to be condemned. It was merely one of the most extreme acts of violence in a short period in the world's history, and, therefore, it is a dramatic success. It doesn't fall under our objection to the encouragement of those elements committed to the thesis that violence is the best means of effecting change.

## The position of the hawks

One could go on and on with this. But the point is that this is a fair, not parodied, but fair characterization of one aspect of the mainstream of American opinion, namely the liberal wing. There is, of course, another voice. Namely, that expressed by people like Melvin Laird, who have come out in favor of a first strike, under appropriate circumstances, and who see us locked in battle with an implacable opponent and so on; or people like Hanson Baldwin, military expert of the *NY Times*, who last summer, again, came out in favor of a first strike, or first use of nuclear weapons, for what he refers to as defensive purposes; these latter he specifies as this: bolstering a weak government against subversion and aggression, where, of course, we decide, unilaterally, when this is taking place— as we decided in Vietnam in 1964, when the President's advisors unanimously proposed to him that he undertake an aggressive war, launch an aggressive attack against North Vietnam, bomb the North, and so on.

## Two types of "conspiracy"

This is quite critical for those who talk about American democracy, particularly when they compare this decision (which we learn of from insiders like James Thompson) with the rhetoric that defined the framework of the democratic election of 1964. Now, this was a conspiracy, a conspiracy to violate the supreme law of the land, in fact. Article VI of the Constitution establishes treaties entered into by the United States Government, such as the U.N. charter, as the supreme law of the land, and it quite explicitly, in so many words, excludes acts like undertaking of the bombing of another country. Recall, incidentally, that at that time, as even the Defense Department admits, there were no regular North Vietnamese units in South Vietnam; they came long after. This conspiracy to violate the supreme law of the land of course has not been tried or prosecuted. The kinds of conspiracies that are prosecuted are those of, say, Doctor Spock and others. As becomes perfectly obvious when you look at the latest government list of co-conspirators, of whom I am one, this is a group of people who did exactly one thing in common: namely, they appeared at a press conference on October 2nd to state independently their views against the war and in support of resistance, and then separated, many of them never to meet again. But this is the government's concept of "conspiracy," and it's quite possible, I don't know if it's likely, that a number of them will face several years in jail for their participation in the conspiracy of which this was the central event and in fact the only event that unites all conspirators. So one kind of conspiracy, the one I've just described. is submitted to prosecution and may indeed lead to years in jail for several people. The other kind of conspiracy, which is the kind that we punished at Nuremberg, is not submitted to any judicial action. This fact again reflects the distribution of force in the society, and must be taken into account by anybody who wants to talk about the character of the society.

## Two types of protest

It is no use just using the vague word "democracy." This is a democratic society in many respects. I think we should be happy for those respects, but if we want to be accurate we should look at facts of the sort I mentioned, facts which are prevalent, significant, and which one avoids only at the peril of losing contact with reality. Now I think that the predominant voice in this society, bracketed on the one hand by the Kennedy liberals and on the other hand by the Melvin Lairds, is a voice which has been defined, I think with very great accuracy, by Barrington Moore, one of America's really great historians, in the proceedings of the Academy of Political Science about a year ago. He defined the predominant voice in American society as follows:

"You may protest in words as loud as you like; there is but one condition attached to the freedom we would like very much to encourage; your protests may be as loud as possible, so long as they remain ineffective. Though we regret your suffering very much and would like very much to do something about them, indeed, we have studied them very carefully and have already spoken to your rulers and immediate superiors about these matters, any attempt by you to remove your oppressors by force is a threat to civilized society and the democratic process. Such threats we cannot and shall not tolerate. As you resort to violence, we will, if need be, wipe you from the face of the earth by the measured response that rains down flames from the skies."

## Ideology and apathy

I think if we ask ourselves honestly what this society is like, we will agree that this is the predominant voice. It's a voice that expresses the needs of the American socio-economic elite; it's an ideology which is propounded with varying degrees of subtlety, by a great many American intellectuals and scholars; it's an ideology, we might as well admit, which is accepted, in fact, probably by a large majority of the population, in particular, those who have some belief that they are in, or likely to enter, the affluent society. This predominant voice is based on an attitude of bland acceptance of just about anything. I can't imagine what we could do in Vietnam today that would lead to more than a few raised eyelids. The fact that three million tons of bombs have been dropped there, as compared with the two million tons dropped by the American Air Force in all theaters throughout World War II, is not regarded as unusual violence by the moderate wing of American society.

This kind of apathy is a very deep-seated feature of American culture. It's not just shown in response to the Vietnam war. To give you just one example, which is very close to home for me, let me quote a paragraph from a textbook that my daughter is using in the fourth grade of Lexington Elementary school; as a word of background, Lexington is a professional upper-middle-class community with large support for McCarthy and a very progressive educational system that it takes pride in. This is a section from a book describing the marvels of colonial New England. The protagonist in the story in question is a young boy named Robert who is being told how wonderful things were back in the days when men were men, and so on and so forth. It says the following: "Captain John Mason made plans to capture the Pequot Fort, where the Rhode Island and the Connecticut Colony met. His little army attacked in the morning, before it was light, and took the Pequots by surprise. The soldiers broke down the stockade with their axes, rushed inside, and set fire to the wigwams. They killed nearly all the braves, squaws, and children, and burned their corn and other food. There were no Pequots left to make more trouble. When the other Indian tribes saw what good fighters the white men were, they kept the peace for many years. 'I wish I were a man and had been there,' thought Robert," which is his last word on the subject, or the textbook writer's. Now I don't have any doubt at all that if Germany had won the second world war, little Hans would be reading very similar stories and would be saying, "I wish I were a man and had been there." My daughter was not exposed to some of the statements on that subject of some of the leading New England intellectuals at the time, for example, people like Cotton Mather, who, of the same incident said, "It was supposed that no less than six hundred Pequot souls were brought down to Hell that day," and, who, on another occasion, speaking of those Indians decimated by disease after the Mayflower landing, said, "The woods were almost cleared of these pernicious creatures to make room for better growth."

Now, the consequence of all of this is an absolutely zombielike attitude to things that we do in the world. I mean the kind of attitude that appears when you read, say, in the *New Yorker*, a report (Jan. 11) by Robert Shapley, an outstanding correspondent in Vietnam, which says that our Vietnamese lack something that the Communists have always possessed, namely, a driving urge to get things done for the good of the country. And he quotes one of the tougher Vietnamese, who points out we remain politically and organizationally weak while they are strong, But still he concludes that the United States should support those who lack mass support, who are weak and who can't stand up in any democratic process, as he has just noted, and those who lack any driving urge to —get things done for the good of the country. Those are the ones we should support, and the readers of the *New Yorker*, the majority of whom, I am sure, think we should withdraw from Vietnam, apparently don't see anything odd about this.

## Domestic repression

The same predominant voice is also heard at home. I'm not going to insult your intelligence by detailing domestic repression. A quick look at the New York Civil Liberties Union files shows what law and order mean to the poor in this country, as in all countries. What it means is permanent harassment by the forces of justice. One need not describe things like the murder of three black students in Orangeburg, South Carolina, by police during a peaceful protest against segregation, shot in the back as they lay down wounded. These were events which led to some sympathetic clucking of tongues, I should say, but they did not lead to the formation of a nationwide committee to defend the rights of students. In fact those who have been involved in the civil rights movement in any manner are quite aware of totally hypocritical roles that the American government has played in situations of this sort. The U.S. code gives explicit power to federal authorities to use force to protect the civil rights of citizens against abuse by state officials. But everyone who is involved (I can tell you stories from my minimal involvement) can give examples of cases in which the federal authorities, far from using this power, stood by and took notes while people were being beaten and, on occasion, murdered. I myself have seen cases where federal marshals threw protestors fleeing from the police into the hands of state policemen who then carried them off to what can only be called concentration camps. Others who are more deeply involved can speak about it in much greater detail.

Let me turn to another aspect of the situation which is part of the reality of the society. A couple of days ago I read a recent article by Ralph Nader in which he pointed out that in Pennsylvania alone, two thousand miners die each year of "black lung." Of course this is not a cost calculated by professional economists who study the state of our economy. But suppose that these miners were to seize the mines and demand that reasonable safety standards be enforced (they are imposed, they're not enforced.) We can be sure that if they were to do so, there would be a national movement to prevent "left fascism" from taking over American society and any impoliteness or even vulgarity that resulted from the actions of the miners would be headlined on the front pages as the troops are called in to preserve order. (This in fact happened under F.D.R.. thirty years ago.) Now there are more subtle but equally pernicious forms of violence—not very much more subtle but slightly more so. Consider San Francisco, the present population of which is, I believe, about 20 percent black. There is a community college in San Francisco, a college whose purpose is to serve the needs of the community. From what I can gather it now has 3 percent black students, as compared with 11 percent seven years ago, and 20 percent black in the community. A bill to provide funds to help disadvantaged students to enter college was vetoed by the governor last year. No national committees were formed to investigate this situation, to my knowledge, let alone to deplore it. I need not mention that a college degree is a certificate of entry to the affluent society. Now all of this, in a sense, takes place within a democratic framework. But it is a sense which one can only describe as democratic in a very misleading and partial fashion.

## Participation in a "democratic" society

But let me turn to a much less important issue. Personally, I agree with Mr. Hook in deploring the acts of those who shout down speakers at open meetings, or who break up public demonstrations. For example, in 1965 and 1966, it was impossible to hold any public meetings in Boston in which speakers could stand up and say that they thought that the bombing of North Vietnam ought to be stopped. The reason it was impossible was that the meetings would be broken up in part by students, in particular by MIT students, I'm sorry to say. Meetings on the Boston Common were impossible. The speakers were shouted down, the people who attended were physically attacked. The Arlington Street Church was defaced from the outside, speakers had to be sneaked in through the back door so they wouldn't be attacked by those who thought it wrong for someone to stand up and say, "Let's stop the bombing of North Vietnam." Of course, you couldn't have such meetings in universities. We who were in the universities did not want to see the university buildings destroyed by these students. These events, incidentally, were given front-page stories in the press. For example, the Boston *Globe* after the first such demonstration had a full front page story, and since an entire front page of the press was covered by this, it is obviously no secret. The story, of course, blamed the peaceful demonstrators for provoking by their remarks the acts which caused the meeting to be broken up and destroyed. Liberal senators like Mike Mansfield joined the chorus of protest—protest, that is, against the irresponsibility of the demonstrators who were speaking, only speaking, in a very mild way against the war in Vietnam. I am indeed opposed to all that kind of thing. There were, as I recall, no national committees formed at that time to protect the right of free assembly or peaceful protest.

Let me mention just one other example. At the recent meetings of the Modern Language Association, after an announcement in a widely read magazine (the *New York Review*), after several public meetings of discussion which were openly attended, and after such publicity as far as could be arranged by our limited resources, a few questions were brought up in the business meeting of the MLA. I don't know how many of you know how a professional organization works. The way it usually works is that a very small coterie of executives and professors, some twenty or thirty people, run the entire organization. A few other people show up at business meetings, they're told that this and that decision has been made, and they say "okay." This time, for the first time, there was real discussion of issues; there was genuine participation. There was ample opportunity for anyone to know that this was going to take place, and, in fact, at the meeting, a group of liberal professors, who in fact had nothing to do with the attempt to organize this format, proposed a number of things, such as that the meetings be moved to Chicago after a very misleading and inaccurate ballot concerning this matter had been sent out by the executive. Votes were taken and a number of other things happened, all perfectly peaceful, under the control of an official parliamentarian and with Pinkerton guards at the door to make sure that nobody unauthorized got in. We didn't have the slightest idea who was going to come, and, in fact, had no way of contacting people to ask them to come. Well, this sounds like something of a move towards at least a minimal amount of democracy in an ossified organization. But if you look at the editorial in the *NY Times* on January first, you will get a different view. They described all this as an example of something on the order of "left fascism" taking over the professional organizations. They had no such reaction when the MLA was run by its executive of three or four people, its few trustees, and the few professors that formed the oligarchy that ordinarily runs the organization.

## Freedom in the university

I could give many more examples, pointing to very serious politicization of the universities. It is a fact that the university is very deeply involved in government repression. No question about that. I'll just illustrate with my own community, Cambridge. Each of the two great universities in Cambridge, Harvard and MIT, has an outstanding political science department. The chairman of one of those two departments is also the chairman of the Vietnam study section of the State Department. The chairman of the other happens, at the moment, to hold three quarter of a million dollars of research per year on pacification and counter-insurgency in his function as an executive, I suppose, or at least a participant, in an outside company. I think these two examples meet the *prima facie* conditions that Professor Hook mentioned of possible violations of scholarly integrity, though I would be the last one to press that, frankly. But, these examples are quite typical. We could mention many cases, and, as I say, I'm not suggesting and have not suggested that these two gentlemen be censured for the fact that they take on this work on the ground that it's a violation of their positions as university professors. I do think it's a different issue altogether. But if we're talking about academic freedom and the politicization of the university, we should ask ourselves the simple question, how many study projects at political science departments are concerned with the questions of, say, how poorly armed guerrillas can withstand a fantastic military force by an outside aggressive power, or how many political science programs are concerned simply with the problems of mass politics or revolutionary development in third-world countries, or, for that matter, in our own society? The answer is obvious in advance.

The point is a significant one. It indicates a degree of politicization of precisely the kind President Eisenhower correctly warned against, and which has been noted, again, by people like Rickover and Fulbright. Now, there are people who speak up in favor, say, of a Vietcong victory. Eugene Genovese was mentioned. Just to complete the story, Genovese is now teaching in Sir George Williams University in Montréal. If you look into the Genovese story, you'll discover that there's a reason why he's teaching in Montréal. True, he was not fired from Rutgers, but, in fact, he was not promoted, given no salary raises, and so on. There are many ways of making life unpleasant for a person in a university. I think we should be thankful for the fact that he wasn't fired, but we should be very unthankful for the fact that Eugene Genovese, whom I believe most American historians, no matter what their politics, would agree is one of the outstanding historians on the subject of slavery and the backgrounds of the Civil War, finds it necessary to teach in Sir George Williams University in Canada. Similarly, Staughton Lynd, who was hired by the History Department of Roosevelt University, was turned down by the trustees who simply overruled the Department's' decision. As far as I know, there has been no national committee to investigate the conditions that led Genovese to go to Canada or that were involved in the firing of Staughton Lynd. In fact, these issues did not seem to arouse the concern of those who are, I think, rightly concerned with academic freedom in the universities.

Let me return to Muste's statement. We must denounce the violence on which the present system is based and all the evil, material and spiritual, that this entails for the masses of men throughout the world. So long as we are not dealing honestly and adequately with this 90 percent of their problem, there is something ludicrous and perhaps hypocritical about our concern with the 10 percent of violence employed by the rebels against oppression. Let me point out, for the logicians among you, that this is not an analogy that applies precisely to the questions of student movement to which I want to turn, because the students are neither the 90 percent of oppressors nor the 10 percent of oppressed, but, rather, a different group, and a very important one.

## Fantasies of the left

George Orwell once remarked that political thought, especially on the left, is a sort of a masturbation fantasy in which the world of fact hardly matters. That's true, unfortunately, and it's part of the reason that our society lacks a genuine, responsible, serious left-wing movement. Let me cite the case of a very good friend of mine, a man who is now a professor at Harvard, and who recently wrote an article in *New Left Notes* in which he stated that he thought the goal of university agitation should be to build anti-imperialist struggles in which the university administration is a clear enemy. Now, this man knows Harvard well, but I find it very difficult to believe that he thinks that Nathan Pusey is the representative of imperialism on the Harvard campus. If you know anything about the situation you'll know why for many reasons. Nevertheless, his view displays an attitude which lies behind much of the agitation of the student movement on the campus. The real problem is, unfortunately, a great deal deeper than the university administration.

It seems to me that, in fact, the universities are relatively free, fairly decentralized institutions in which the major decisions are made by the faculty at departmental levels. The temptations are extremely strong to make certain decisions and not others. For those who choose to put their talents to the service of power as it exists in the society, there are certainly many rewards. There are the rewards of prestige, affluence, the illusion of power, sometimes even the reality of power. Those who choose differently can be quite confident that they will receive a good deal of abuse, recriminations, lies, and denunciations in the press and in the university itself, and, perhaps, destruction of their professional careers as well. So, in one sense, the choice is hardly free. But in a much more important sense, the choice is free. That is, the politicization of the universities and the subversion of scholarship, which I think is quite real, is the result of a relatively free choice by students and faculty who have been unwilling to resist the temptations and to face the real difficulties, the very severe difficulties, of standing outside the mainstream.

## Scholarship and action

Take, for example, the question of developing radical scholarship in the universities. I hasten to add at once that I deny the existence of this category. Personally, I believe that objective scholarship free from the ideological restraints which are imposed by the general political consensus and distribution of force would lead to radical conclusions. Let me admit that the burden of fact is upon someone who believes, as I do, that *objective* scholarship will lead to radical conclusions. But that is exactly my point. The failure to develop radical scholarship in this sense is not, if you check, a result of the decrees of trustees and administration. Rather, it follows from the unwillingness of students and faculty to undertake the very hard and serious work that's required, and to face, calmly, but firmly, the abuse that is quite inevitable. In fact, it results from the fear of the faculty that its guild structure will be threatened, a possibility which is a particularly serious matter in the social and behavioural sciences where the content is, in a sense, rather slight, and where, very often, the pretense of professional expertise is used as a defense against the threat of legitimate criticism and analysis. Now, suppose that these barriers were overcome. Suppose, that is, that students and faculty did dedicate themselves, despite the difficulties, to working on objective scholarship, scholarship which, I believe, would lead to radical conclusions. Then it might be that administration and trustees would impose new barriers against the implementation of the study, research, and teaching that led to radical conclusions, and, more specifically, against the kind of action programs that would flow from honest inquiry. At the moment, this is speculation. We don't know that the university will not tolerate such programs, and we don't know because the effort has barely been made. There are cases—I cited a few— of administrative interference and they are deplorable, but they don't really constitute the heart of the problem at the moment. I think it is as misleading and false to say that they do constitute it as it is misleading and false to identify the university administration as the representative of imperialism on the campus. There's nothing radical about being wrong, and this just seems to me factually false.

I think it's very crucial that the effort to construct this objective scholarship be made. I think the Left very badly needs understanding of contemporary society, of its long-range tendencies, of the possibilities for alternative social forms and of how social change can come about. And I think that objective scholarship can contribute to this understanding. But it is hard work and it has to be conducted in a serious and open-minded fashion. There is another reason for carrying out this scholarship, aside from the insight it may lead to, if I'm correct. And that is that it strikes a blow at repressive institutions, a fact which shouldn't be overlooked. For example, a group of Asian scholars (students, as usual) at Harvard have formed a committee of concerned Asian scholars who are trying to reconstruct Asian scholarship on a more objective and, in consequence, a more humane and sympathetic basis. This is very important, I think, for an objective treatment of developing Asian societies and our relation to them. It might succeed in attracting some of the best students and even some of the faculty. If it does, it will help remove one foundation stone of the national psychosis which plays a major role in promoting the sort of general garrison state with its enormous commitment to waste and destruction, with its permanent and mounting threat of nuclear destruction, with its public subsidies to aero-space and much of the other vileness of contemporary society.

## Scientists of the world, unite!

All this leads to a more important point, something which can be done, I think, and ought to be undertaken. Namely, an attempt to organize scientists to refuse military work. It's remarkable that this has really not been undertaken so far. It's beginning to get off the ground. If you look at the front page of today's *NY Times*, you'll see an example. Consider something like the ABM [Antiballistic Missile System]. Most scientists know perfectly well that the ABM is a catastrophe. But it's fairly predictable that after they finished explaining its irrationality to Senate committees, they will go ahead and build it. Now, this is not a law of nature. They can refuse. They can refuse, not only individually, which would be all right, but they can refuse collectively. The point is that lectures on the ABM are irrelevant if, in fact, the ABM is not motivated by a search for security but rather by a need to provide a subsidy to the electronics business. And, there are very good grounds for believing that that is exactly what it is motivated by. I think that if scientists were to organize to refuse to work on the ABM, they would quickly discover that and that would be very educational. If I'm wrong and they stopped it, so much the better of course.

Just as background to support this, let me cite a recent study of the electronics industry association which concluded, last year, that "arms controls agreements during the next decade are unlikely; the likelihood of nuclear war will increase and, thus, for the electronics firms, the outlook is good in spite of the end of hostilities in Vietnam." This is, again, not a law of nature but a fact of society that the general national psychosis to which the universities contribute their particular share permits a public subsidy to the great corporations just as it permits the continual acceleration of the arms race. There is no necessity to take part in criminal acts, like the ABM or like the general use of scholarship, science, and technology for criminal purposes. I believe scientists can organize to refuse. I'd be willing to make a guess that if they do organize to refuse, they'll find themselves in an illegal conspiracy, but that's a matter which one has to face when it comes, if it does. They can also help to try to organize or take part in the change of consciousness, the mass politics, that ultimately provides the only hope for countering, controlling, and ultimately, eliminating the nightmare that they are helping to create.

## Tasks for students

Now, on the basis of such possibilities as these, I think that a good deal of the energy of the student movement is flowing into irrelevant directions. There are tasks to which student agitation might be directed, such as formally severing relations with the IDA (Institute for Defense Analyses), or restructuring the universities, or putting people on committees, and even ending defense work. Many of these things could be undertaken without leading to any objective change in the character of the society and what it does. That worries me very much. You see, at a place like MIT people like the chairman of the political science department learned long ago that you don't do your really unspeakable work in your capacity as a college professor. You do that work in your capacity as a member of a corporation which has been set up for that purpose. From the point of view of the Vietnamese, or the people in Harlem, it makes no difference. From the point of view of the purity of the campus, well, that has been achieved.

But, I think that something like an organization of scientists who refuse to work might be rather different. For one thing, I think it can get somewhere, and, if it does, I think it will strike at deeply entrenched interests. And, if it does, I think it may lead to confrontation and to attempts at repression. As I said, it may become an illegal conspiracy—I suspect it will if it succeeds—and it may become a form of resistance. In general, I think it's fair to expect that effective politics will lead to confrontation and to attempts to repress it, to the extent that it is effective in confronting deeply entrenched social forces. One has to be prepared to face this repression when it comes, but I think that one who takes his own rhetoric seriously will seek to delay a confrontation until he can hope to emerge successful.

This last point indicates a corollary to the remark that successful politics leads to confrontation, namely, that the search for confrontations indicates intellectual bankruptcy. It indicates the lack of effective politics which would if carried out, lead, very likely, to confrontations. And that is something the consequences of which one must face in the student movement. It seems to me that the search for confrontations, aside from revealing a kind of intellectual bankruptcy, a failure to have found effective politics, may also become a manipulative and coercive tactic. I think it often does. It becomes the kind of tactic which attempts to bring people to a certain degree of commitment, not by having it grow out of their own understanding and experience in the realities of the world, but, as the result of a situation which often does not reflect the realities of society. That is manipulative and coercive, and I think also dangerous. I think it is the proper kind of tactic only for a movement of an elitist and authoritarian cast, whatever the people involved may feel about it. They may not be elitist and authoritarian, but means have a way of affecting consciousness. And I think that's important enough to worry about at least.

### "Radical tactics"

Now, I'm also concerned by discussion within the movement of what is called "radical tactics." I think there is a very serious confusion here, and it's a dangerous confusion. It doesn't make any sense to ask whether tactics are radical or not,—in fact you can't ask about the political content of tactics at all (and I'm not making an analytical philosopher's point). It seems to me very important to recognize that tactics should be judged as to whether they are successful or unsuccessful in reaching certain goals which may themselves be the subject of political judgement. When people start concentrating on the character of the tactics, and regarding them as an index of political character, then they are taking an ultimately self-destructive approach. Without impugning anyone's motives, I think that that is the kind of thing that a well-placed police spy would introduce into the movement if he were intent on destroying it. I'm not implying that anyone is a well-placed police spy. Rather, I think one has to ask oneself objectively what is the character, what is the truth, of certain political hypotheses, certain hypotheses about society, and what the likely effects are of carrying out certain tactics. These are decisions which have nothing to do with the labels "radical," "liberal," etc. They have to do with objective, serious evaluation.

### Tasks for intellectuals

In general, I think that if a movement for social change does develop, it will involve many strata of the population with very different outlooks and interests, very different needs, but, I hope, needs that can be related and made compatible. And I think that the main task for intellectuals, aside from resistance to repression and violence, is to try to articulate goals, to try to assess, to try to understand, to try to persuade, to try to organize.

I think that further tasks for intellectuals are to develop an objective scholarship, and also to act collectively and individually to confront repressive institutions when that is the effective politics of the moment rather than merely an exciting thing to do.

## The primary principle in the struggle

One final remark. I've been talking about tactics, but I don't have any faith in my own judgments about tactics. I've been wrong much more often than I have been right. Therefore, you shouldn't have any special faith in my judgments in this respect. In general, our judgments about tactics are very low probability judgments, but I think that these judgments should nevertheless be guided by certain principles. I think the primary principle, especially for people like us, who are, for the most part, among the privileged in society, should be the principle that we keep clearly in mind who we are responsible to. I suggest we are responsible to the people of Vietnam, to the people of Guatemala, to the people of Harlem. In undertaking some form of action, we must ask ourselves what the consequences will be for the people who are at the wrong end of the guns, for the people who can't escape. That's a consideration of overwhelming importance. Even a very well intentioned act, if it strengthens the forces of repression, is no gift whatsoever to those whose fate we, in some sense, bear in our hands. This is a simple and elementary fact, and I think it should be ever present in one's mind.

### Editor's Notes to Chapter 18

Published in *Link* (India) 11. 1 (1968): pp. 94–96, under the title "Political Prospects for the Seventies." The following sentence was omitted: "The Soviet Government has obligingly reinforced this myth—it remains a myth nonetheless—by its brutal suppression of national independence in Eastern Europe and its refusal to grant elementary rights to Soviet citizens."

On American "aid" to the Third World, see now **PE**, in particular volume 1. On "internal aggression," see the Editor's Notes to Selection 1, and Selection 19.

The quote from Johnson appears also in Selection 16.

# 18. Political Prospects

As the twentieth century opened, a leading spokesman of the young Chinese nationalist movement Liang Ch'i-ch'ao, expressed his concern about the potential dangers posed by rising American power, noting that: "Now that the famous expansionist, McKinley, has been elected President, there is no knowing what big things the United States might not do in the twentieth century." Not long before, the American intellectual, Brooks Adams, had prophetically stated: "Our geographical position, our wealth, and our energy preeminently fit us to enter upon the development of Eastern Asia and to reduce it to part of our own economic system."[1]

As the century has progressed from terror to terror, the American economic system has steadily expanded its power and control, engulfing large parts of Latin America and the fringes of Asia and bringing Western Europe substantially within its dominion. The successful suppression of Philippine independence at the turn of the century bears a remarkable resemblance to the ongoing attempt to subdue the Vietnamese. It differs in that the Vietnamese resistance has shown such amazing strength, while the devastating power of American technology has achieved new heights of destructiveness, to little avail. It also differs in the rhetoric that is being used to provide an ideological justification for this latest attempt to "enter upon the development of Eastern Asia and to reduce it to part of our own economic system." The imperialists of the 1890s did not have available to them the convenient theory of "Communist aggression," or the even more useful concept of "internal aggression," to justify their exploits.

## The Philippines Model

The American war against the Philippines not only provides a relevant precedent for American military actions in Asia seventy years later, it also suggests what the future may hold for those nations that do not resist American dominance. The American occupation provided the surface forms of democracy in the Philippines, but the exercise of democratic rights is effectively limited to a small elite. It is estimated by conservative American authorities[2] that the peasantry—about three-quarters of the population—live under conditions not materially different from those of the Spanish occupation. Furthermore, an incipient development towards more general modernization was aborted by American policy.

Similar processes are underway not only in Vietnam, but also in other Asian countries where the American grip is tightening. In Thailand, for example, where there are now more American troops than were in Vietnam in early 1965, the tentative steps towards democratization that were taken in the early post-war years were blocked and reversed by the American policy of military aid to the successive dictatorships following the Phibun coup in 1948. Liberal American Asian specialists regard it as ironic that Phibun, who had collaborated with Japanese fascism, received American support while the liberal reformer Pridi, who had led the Free Thai resistance in cooperation with the American OSS, found it necessary to flee to Communist China. It is not in the least ironic, but a natural consequence of the American policy of "reducing" Eastern Asia "to part of our own economic system."

## Cultural subjugation

As American power struggles to maintain a position of strength in Asia, it creates vested interests in this enterprise in the societies that are drawn into the American web. For example, South Korea, Japan, and Singapore now have a direct and substantial economic stake in the continuation of the Vietnam war or some subsequent military effort. The exercise of American power modifies the social and economic structure of the countries that become partners in American imperialism and poses threats to their independence that they will find increasingly difficult to counter. Not the least of these threats is that of cultural subjugation, one of the most severe long-term effects of the American occupation of the Philippines, for example. Similarly, an American official in Laos is quoted in *Le Monde* in July 1968 as saying that the traditional culture must be "reduced to zero" if there is to be any progress.

This extreme judgement expresses attitudes that have always been held by colonial civil servants, who have uniformly believed that they are acting in the interests of the backward peoples whose welfare they are to administer as they inculcate them with the culture of the mother country and absorb them into its international system. American power is of course enormous, and its exercise has been accompanied by a curious combination of self-righteousness and cynicism that almost defies description. Today, there can be little doubt that as Liang Ch'i-ch'ao had feared, it does pose an unparalleled threat to the independence of small nations and their right to be free from outside intervention or externally supported subversion.

## Latin America

Nowhere is this more clear than in Latin America, traditionally a preserve of the United States. The 1960s were to be a decade of development under the "Alliance for Progress." The actual record, so far, is described as follows by the conservative editor of Inter-American Economic Affairs: [3]

During that period (1960–65) the rate of economic growth dropped sharply from the average for 1950–55 and 1955–60 and the change in the growth rate per capita was even more adverse. During that period the distribution of income became even more unsatisfactory as the gap between the rich and poor widened appreciably. During most of the period a very heavy proportion of the disbursements went to military regimes which had overthrown constitutional governments, and at the end of the period, with almost half of the population of the area under military rule, a significant portion of the aid was going *not* to assist 'free men and free governments' but rather to hold in power regimes to which the people had lost their freedom.

No doubt many regard this too as "ironic." But the factors that have led to this development persist unchanged: hence further ironies are to be expected. The "Johnson diplomacy" has, in effect, declared invalid the treaty obligation undertaken by the United States not to intervene in the internal affairs of other countries of the Americas and today American military missions are functioning throughout Latin America, bolstering unpopular regimes and improving the techniques of police and military repression.

According to the Vice-President of Guatemala, Marroquin Rojas, American bombers are carrying out bombing raids from their Panamanian bases in areas of Guatemala suspected of harboring rebels *(Le Monde Hebdomadaire, 18* Jan. 1968), to the accompaniment of total silence in the American press, which refuses to publish even the reports by outstanding correspondents, let alone to investigate them. Looking elsewhere, it is no secret that the United States is the main support for the Greek dictatorship, though the details of American machinations in Greece come to light only in occasional statements of Andreas Papandreou and a few enterprising reporters. If American troops are sent to Greece to prevent "Communist aggression" in the coming years, the American public will be unprepared to interpret these events.

The American international role is little understood in the United States. It is widely felt that the United States is a kind of public benefactor, bestowing its riches on an ungrateful world, preserving freedom from the aggressive attacks launched or inspired by "international Communism" with its headquarters in Moscow or perhaps Peking. The Soviet Government has obligingly reinforced this myth—it remains a myth nonetheless—by its brutal suppression of national independence in Eastern Europe and its refusal to grant elementary rights to Soviet citizens. Few Americans recognize that our domination of Latin America is, if anything, even more insidious than Soviet control of Eastern Europe, since it is not even accompanied by economic development.

## Paranoid fantasies

Furthermore, many Americans are haunted by vague, but very real fears that their privilege and affluence will be destroyed by the assault of the wretched of the earth at home and abroad. Hence the great concern for "law and order," for controlling the "looters and rioters" in the cities of America who are becoming daily more militant in their rejection of the role assigned to them in American society, a role that offers no escape from poverty and degradation. On the international level, the same fears were succinctly expressed by President Johnson, when he said on November 1, 1966:

> There are three billion people in the world and we only have 200 million of them. We are outnumbered 15 to 1. If might did make right they would sweep over the United States and take what we have. We have what they want.

The President expresses the deep anxieties of many Americans, who believe that in Vietnam, for example, we are defending ourselves from a superior force, from yellow hordes that threaten to overwhelm us. Modern history gives grim testimony of what may happen when a powerful nation is overcome by paranoid fantasies. One should not treat lightly the remarks just quoted, or the very real and widespread feelings that they express.

## Ideological stranglehold

As already noted, the "Communist threat" has been a magnificent propaganda instrument for justifying a policy of intervention in ever-widening domains, a policy that had taken shape long before this threat could cogently be formulated. It has also served well to narrow and distort the range of social thought in the United States. The spectrum of opinion that reaches any mass audience is extremely narrow, far more so than in any Western European democracy, for example. At the same time, there is almost unlimited freedom of expression for the small minority who have the time, the resources, and the training that enable them to escape the ideological stranglehold of the mass media. The pernicious impact of the media goes beyond the restriction of information and opinion. In an important forthcoming essay, D. W. Smythe and H. H. Wilson observed that "the principal function of the commercially supported mass media in the United States is to market the output of the consumer goods industries and to train the population for loyalty to the American economic-political system." They quote a set of specifications given by major national advertisers to TV and radio writers, which states, in particular:

> In general, the moral code of the characters in our dramas will be more or less synonymous with the moral code of the bulk of the American middle class, as it is commonly understood... There will be no material on any of our programs which could in any way further the concept of business as cold, ruthless and lacking all sentiment or spiritual motivation.

They cite further the observations of the American sociologists, Paul Lazarsfeld and Robert Merton, who pointed out, in 1948, that the mass communication media:

> ...not only continue to affirm the status quo but, in the same measure, they fail to raise essential questions about the structure of

society. Hence by leading toward conformism and by providing little basis for a critical appraisal of society, the commercially sponsored mass media indirectly but effectively restrain the cogent development of a genuinely critical outlook.

Much the same can be said of school and even college education. The effect is that formal freedom of inquiry and expression exists—and for this we must be grateful—but not in such a way as to have a significant effect on politics or the social order.

## American Apartheid

Demographic studies indicate that present tendencies, if they persist, will create a society based on a principle of *Apartheid,* with black poverty-stricken urban centers surrounded by affluent white suburbs that have drawn to themselves the cultural and commercial institutions of the city. It is not unlikely that these urban centers will, furthermore, be ringed with physical force. Projecting international tendencies, it would come as no surprise if in the world of the seventies American power is used in a global scale to repress the strivings of those who seek to overturn a decadent and repressive social order and to introduce the revolutionary changes that seem a necessary prerequisite for modernization and industrialization in many parts of the world.

There are long-term processes at work in the development of the American economy that also must be a source of serious concern. Government-induced production has been expanding continuously, and it is, very largely, production for war or waste. The private sector appears to be undergoing a process of centralization of control, and the growth of multinational corporations, or international institutions dominated by American capital, in some ways runs parallel to the forceful extension of the American empire. UN Ambassador George Ball had the following to say about this matter:

> In its modern form, the multinational corporation, or one with world-wide operations and markets, is a distinctly American development. Through such corporations it has become possible for the first time to use the world's resources with maximum efficiency. But there must be greater unification of the world economy to give full play to the benefits of multinational corporations.[5]

This "unification of the world economy" threatens to take place under conditions that will, to use Brooks Adams' words, "reduce it to part of our own economic system," with political and human consequences that are not pleasant to contemplate.

## National Security Managers

The enormous commitment to military spending and other forms of waste and destruction has served to entrench powerful bureaucratic interests, tightly interlocked with corporate and even educational institutions. The famous military-industrial-academic complex may have become a cliche, but it is real enough nevertheless. To a large extent the Vietnam war was designed and executed by the "national security managers" brought to Washington from the universities and from corporate management, and today this seems the group with the greatest stake in pursuing this grim venture, regardless of the cost to the Vietnamese or even to the United States itself. Similarly, its stake is high in ensuring that there will be an unending, expanding American commitment to the management of an American empire, quite apart from any economic interests that might motivate the establishment of American hegemony in large parts of the world.

A projection of present tendencies into the future yields prospects that are bleak indeed. But there are opposing forces as well. The Vietnam war has led to popular revulsion on an unprecedented scale, and to a new willingness to challenge accepted dogma. The civil rights movement has also touched the conscience of many Americans. There is no doubt that within the mainstream of American thought there is now a receptiveness to critical analysis and an awareness that new directions may be needed, all in striking contrast to the mood of the 1950s.

The student movement has changed the state of mind in many universities, and has not been without effect on popular consciousness outside of the campus as well. The Negro community is undergoing dramatic changes, developing a new sense of solidarity and searching for new patterns of thought and action. Whether these forces can work together or in parallel to reform the worst abuses of our society or even to set the stage for significant social change is unclear. Certainly they do not now have the cohesiveness or the intellectual or moral resources to face tasks of this magnitude.

The scope of these tasks is well-expressed by the distinguished Russian physicist, Academician Andrei D. Sakharov, in his recent essay, "Thoughts on Progress, Peaceful Co-existence and Intellectual Freedom": [6]

> It is necessary to change the psychology of the American citizen so that they will voluntarily and generously support their government and worldwide efforts to change the economy, technology and level of living of billions of people. This of course, would entail a serious decline in the United States rate of economic growth.[7] The Americans should be willing to do this solely for the sake of lofty and distant goals, for the sake of preserving civilization and mankind on our planet. Similar changes in the psychology of people and practical activities of governments must be achieved in the Soviet Union and other developed countries.

There is little objective reason to suppose that this is other than a utopian dream. Scepticism, however, must not be permitted to become resignation. The stakes are far too high.

# Notes

1. Both statements quoted in Akira Iriye, *Across the Pacific, An Inner History of American-East Asian Relations*. New York: Harcourt, Brace and World, 1967.

2. See George Taylor, *The Philippines and the United States*, Praeger, 1964.

3. Simon G. Hanson, *Five Years of the Alliance for Progress*, Washington: The InterAmerican Affairs Press, 1967.

4. "Cold War-mindedness and the Mass Media," in *Struggle Against History*, ed. by Neal D. Houghton, New York: Washington Square Press, in press. (It was published in 1968 with the subtitle *U.S. Foreign Policy in an Age of Revolution.)*

5. *NY Times*, 6 May 1967. Cited by Paul Mattick in a perceptive survey entitled "The American Economy," in *International Socialist Journal*, Feb., 1968.

6. Reprinted in the *NY Times*, 22 July 1968.

7. This judgment, incidentally, is not obvious, if we measure "economic growth" in terms of socially useful production.

**Editor's Notes to Chapter 19**

Published in *Liberation* 14.5–6 (1969): pp. 38–43, this piece is the core of the collection, and one of the outstanding articles written by the author.

On "aggression," in particular "internal aggression," see the references in Editor's Notes to Selection 1.

On the "revisionist" work on the cold war, see **FRS**, I.V.

# 19. Some Tasks For The Left

Dire warnings with regard to the state of American society are hardly confined to the left these days. Senator Fulbright has recently warned that the United States is "already a long way toward becoming an elective dictatorship." If we continue on our present course, "the future can hold nothing for us except endless foreign exertions, chronic warfare, burgeoning expense and the proliferation of an already formidable military-industrial-labor-academic complex—in short, the militarization of American life... If, in short, America is to become an empire, there is very little chance that it can avoid becoming a virtual dictatorship as well."[1]

Senator Fulbright was commenting on an attempt to combat the erosion of the constitutional system, typical of all Western parliamentary democracies as centralization of power in the executive continually increases. The attempt is embodied in a "sense of the Senate" resolution that was proposed by the Senate Committee on Foreign Relations. Its report (Apr. 16, 1969) notes that the chief executive "now exercises something approaching absolute power over the life or death of every living American—to say nothing of millions of other people all over the world." It warns that in consequence the American people are threatened "with tyranny or disaster."

## Possibilities of "internal aggression"

The Committee's report recalls the fears expressed by Abraham Lincoln when President Polk "precipitated the clash which began the Mexican War": "Kings had always been involving and impoverishing their people in wars, pretending generally, if not always, that the good of the people was the object. This our Convention undertook to be the most oppressive of all kingly oppressions; and they resolved to so frame the Constitution that no one man should hold the power of bringing oppression upon us." The report notes further that there are 50,000 American troops in Thailand, many "engaged in military support operations against insurgency." It cites a classified memorandum asserting "that the presence of American Armed Forces in Spain constitutes a more significant security guarantee to Spain than would a written agreement." Since the only attack that threatens Spain is what is nowadays called "internal aggression," it is clear what form of "security" is guaranteed by these secret agreements.

The Senate Committee is surely accurate in remarking that domestic tyranny is a likely concomitant to the effort by the "Kingly oppressor" to protect such delightful regimes as those of Spain and Thailand (and Saigon, and Greece, and Brazil...) from "internal aggression." We can expect, with fair confidence, that any serious domestic challenge to American global management or its ideological underpinnings will call forth the repressive force and ultimately the violence of the state. What we may expect, then, is voluntary submission to the coercive ideology of *Pax Americana* and its repressive practices, or the overt use of force to compel obedience; in either case, a form of domestic tyranny.

The attempt to construct an integrated global economy dominated by American capital is one major theme of post-war history. Though there have been setbacks, the project proceeds apace along many paths, and no one can predict the degree to which it will succeed. Evidently, only certain forms of national development are compatible with this aim, and American foreign policy has endeavored to block all others. In practice this has often meant, in Joan Robinson's words, that "the United States crusade against Communism is a campaign against development. By means of it the American people have been led to acquiesce in the maintenance of a huge war machine and its use by threat or actual force to try to suppress every popular movement that aims to overthrow ancient or modern tyranny and begin to find a way to overcome poverty and establish national self-respect."[2]

### Economy and "national defense"

The maintenance of the huge war machine has deeper social roots than the need to protect the regimes of Greece, Spain, and Brazil from internal aggression. Even if American military support were not needed to preserve these bastions of freedom, the militarization of American society would be unlikely to abate. The particular form of state-subsidized capitalism evolving in the United States demands substantial government support for technologically advanced segments of American industry. Under existing social conditions, with public policy largely determined by private empires, it is naturally preparation for war to which the public subsidy is diverted, With the best of will, it is not easy to devise alternative forms of government intervention in the economy that will not conflict with the interests of these private empires, but will rather enhance them. Furthermore, a public subsidy must be tolerable to the population at large. Even a totalitarian state must win some measure of popular support for its policies and expenditures, and "defense of the home" is invariably the last resort. A challenge to the system of preparation for war is not likely to be tolerated.

Such a challenge has arisen in the United States in the last few years, largely from the student movement and the black liberation movements. The rising wave of repression should therefore come as no surprise. The editors of *Monthly Review* have quite correctly noted the analogy to the post-war repression that helped to impose the narrow conservatism that has dominated American life for the past two decades. It is typical of repressive regimes, throughout the world, that they place their harshest and most reactionary figures in control of the Ministries of War and Interior. The Nixon administration has adopted this familiar practice (Laird and Mitchell). A bill now before Congress proposes the establishment of a crime of peacetime treason, with severe punishments for those who give "aid and comfort" to "any foreign nation or armed group which is engaged in open hostilities" with American armed forces. The implications are clear. But even without such "legal" authorization, there are many early signs of what might ultimately become a police state, perhaps, with extensive popular support: coordinated counterinsurgency operations, as in Berkeley; criminal police violence against Black Panthers; harassment by quasi-judicial means; punitive sentencing for minor violations; Congressional investigation of universities, and so on.

Twenty years ago, the contribution of American liberalism to the repression was not small. One of the first acts of the Americans for Democratic Action was "to use guilt-by-association tactics by printing in major urban newspapers the names of the Progressive Party's principal contributors and then listing the organizations on the Attorney-General's list of subversive groups to which these contributors belong—or had belonged,"[3] this well before McCarthy got into the act. The hysterical reaction, in some quarters, to the revival of politics in the Sixties suggests that history may repeat. In these circumstances, even the defense of civil liberties has a radical content.

## A genuine revolutionary movement

The best way to defend civil liberties is to build a movement for social change with a positive programme that has a broad-based appeal, that encourages free and open discussion and offers a wide range of possibilities for work and action. The potential for such a movement surely exists. Whether it will be realized remains an open question. External repression is one serious threat. Factional bickering, dogmatism, fantasies and manipulative tactics are probably a considerably greater danger.

A movement of the left should distinguish with clarity between its long-range revolutionary aims, and certain more immediate effects it can hope to achieve. Specifically, for us today there is no priority higher than bringing the Vietnam war to a quick end with the withdrawal of all American military force, This may be a feasible goal. It would entail the abandonment of a policy that has been pursued for 20 years as part of a more general strategy for constructing an integrated world empire compatible with the perceived needs of American capital and organized in accordance with the dominant principles of American ideology. Nevertheless this particular venture could no doubt be "liquidated" without too severe a blow to the system—fortunately for the people of Vietnam and Laos, for if this were not true, their future would be dim indeed. I continue to believe that nonviolent resistance provides the best means for achieving this goal.

But in the long run, a movement of the left has no chance of success, and deserves none, unless it develops an understanding of contemporary society and a vision of a future social order that is persuasive to a large majority of the population. Its goals and organizational forms must take shape through their active participation in political struggle and social reconstruction. A genuine radical culture can be created only through the spiritual transformation of great masses of people, the essential feature of any social revolution that is to extend the possibilities for human creativity and freedom. There is no doubt that we can learn from the achievements and the failures of revolutionary struggles in the less-developed countries, and it would be as foolish to fail to do so as it would be criminal not to help where we can. It is evident, however, that their experiences cannot be mechanically transferred to a society such as ours. In an advanced industrial society it is, obviously, far from true that the mass of the population have nothing to lose but their chains. and there is no point in pretending otherwise. On the contrary, they have a considerable stake in preserving the existing social order. Correspondingly, the cultural and intellectual level of any serious radical movement will have to be far higher than in the past, as Andre Gorz, for one, has correctly emphasized. It will not be able to satisfy itself with a litany of forms of oppression and injustice. It will have to provide compelling answers to the question of how these evils can be overcome by revolution or large-scale reform. To accomplish this aim, the left will have to achieve and maintain a position of honesty and commitment to libertarian values. It must not succumb to the illusion that a "vanguard party," self-designated as the repository of all truth and virtue, can take state power and miraculously bring about a revolution that will establish decent values and truly democratic structures as the framework for social life. If its only clearly expressed goals are to smash and destroy, it will succeed only in smashing and destroying itself. Furthermore, if a radical movement hopes to be able to combat imperialism, or the kinds of repression, social management and coercion that will be developed by the evolving international economic institutions, it too will have to be international in its organizational forms as well as in the cultural level it seeks to attain. To construct a movement of this sort will be no mean feat. It may well be true, however, that success in this endeavor is the only alternative to tyranny and disaster.

### Libertarian socialism

The threat of tyranny and disaster, or even their early manifestations, do not themselves provide a sufficient basis for the creation of a significant radical mass movement. In fact, this threat may induce a conservative defensive reaction. For a person to commit himself to a movement for radical social change, with all of the uncertainty and hazard that this entails, he must have a strong reason to believe that there is some likelihood of success in bringing about a new social order. This is not merely a matter of satisfaction of personal, material needs, of narrow self-interest in the sense cultivated by capitalist ideology. There is, to be sure, a justification for radical politics even in terms of self-interest in this narrow sense. The enormous waste of resources that are far from boundless and the race towards mutual annihilation on the part of the great powers provide a sufficient reason for a rational man to seek actively for some far-reaching alternative. Beyond this, it is by now widely realized that the economist's "externalities" can no longer be consigned to footnotes. No one who gives a moment's thought to the problems of contemporary society can fail to be aware of the social costs of consumption and production, the progressive destruction of the environment, the utter irrationality of the utilization of contemporary technology, the inability of a system based on profit or growth-maximization to deal with needs that can only be expressed collectively, and the enormous bias this system imposes towards maximization of commodities for personal use in place of the general improvement of the quality of life. All of these are factors in modern life that should lead to the growth of a vigorous left that seeks to replace contemporary barbarism by some form of libertarian socialism. But there is something insufferably arrogant about the belief that "we" are radical because we are humane, and that "they" will join us when they see that it is in their self-interest to do so. Compassion, solidarity, friendship are also human needs. They are driving needs, no less than the desire to increase one's share of commodities or to improve working conditions. Beyond this, I do not doubt that it is a fundamental human need to take an active part in the democratic control of social institutions. If this is so, then the demand for industrial democracy should become a central goal of any revitalized left with a working-class base. (See selection 22.)

## Technology and self-management

In fact, in France and England there has been a renewed interest in industrial democracy and workers' control after a lapse of quite a few years.[4] This is a most welcome development. It is often argued that the formation of enormous planning units—the centralized state bureaucracy, immense corporations, or both acting in concert—is a technological imperative, a requirement for economic health and proper utilization of resources in a complex advanced industrial society. I have yet to see an argument that advanced technology requires centralized autocratic management. The same technology that can strengthen the authority of a narrow elite of owners, managers, or technocrats, might also be used to extend industrial democracy. In its early stages, the industrial system required the kind of specialized labor which, as Adam Smith pointed out, turned men into imbeciles, mere tools of production. Now this is no longer true. With modern technology, tools can be tools and men can be men. The need for managers is a corollary to the specialization of the labor force. It diminishes as the opportunities increase for each participant in the work-force to obtain relevant information when it is needed for decision-making and to achieve the cultural level that enables him to take part in global decisions. Simulation makes it possible to carry out certain experiments without suffering the cost of failure. Automation may provide the possibility to eliminate mind-destroying drudgery. To develop these possibilities in a concrete and detailed form is the proper task for the left. It is a task that can be carried out only by direct participation of manual and intellectual workers; it should lead to blurring, perhaps to the disappearance, of the distinction between these social categories.

What can be plausibly argued is that planning is a necessity in an advanced industrial society. One must, however, bear in mind an observation that is put very well by Ken Coates, in introducing a recent symposium on workers' control:

> If planning has become a crucial need, then it has also become transparently clear that none of the most basic and elementary liberal values can survive such planning upon such a scale, unless it is arranged along lines which are inherently and profoundly democratic.[5]

The problem of how to combine planning with democracy, and so to preserve and significantly extend and enrich liberal values, will not be solved on paper, but only through a combination of practical experience and intellectual analysis. Almost by definition, this is a task for a revitalized movement of the left, a movement that will combine the highest level of science and technology with serious inquiry into the sources and social conditions for creativity and freedom.

## From autocracy to acracy

Questions of this sort barely exist in the academic social sciences. For example, the leading textbook on modern economics describes the range of possible economic systems as falling on a spectrum with complete *laissez faire* and "totalitarian dictatorship of production" as the polar cases:

> the relevant choice for policy today is not a decision between these extremes, but rather the degree to which public policy should do *less* or *more* in modifying the operation of particular private economic activities.[6]

Evidently, basic questions are begged by describing the spectrum of possible systems in these terms. There is quite another spectrum that can be imagined, with democratic and autocratic control of the system of production as the polar cases. Along this dimension, both of Samuelson's polar opposites fall at the same extreme point; both "ideal" private capitalism and "totalitarian dictatorship of production" are forms of autocratic control, to be contrasted with popular democratic control of the economy through workers' councils, commune assemblies, and other forms of popular organization that can be imagined. Similarly, in a recent symposium of the American Academy of Arts and Sciences devoted to "Perspectives on Business,"[7] there is much discussion of the matter of management-vs.-ownership control (and the effect of technology on this distribution of power), but no mention of the possibility that the economic system might be brought under popular democratic control.

The assumptions that guide the mass of scholarship hardly differ from those expressed in manifestoes of the American ruling elite, for example, the report of the study group on *Political Economy of American Foreign Policy*, which identifies Western civilization with capitalist forms (as contrasted to the collectivist denial of freedom, initiative, and progress) and defines "the aim of economic activity in the West (as) the maximization of money income—in one or another of its forms—by individuals through the investment of capital or of labor on one's own account or for, and under the direction of, others."[8] The document goes on, characteristically, to describe this particular perversion in terms of universal ideals. We cannot be merely an "impartial arbiter... maintaining world order," but must be an active leader in the struggle to save Western civilization and the "universal ideals of human freedom, individual growth, and economic justice" which are expressed ("however imperfectly") in the capitalist institutions of the West.

Surely this concept of economic man is a psychological absurdity which leads to untold suffering for those who try to mold themselves to this pattern, as well as for their victims. "Look out for number one" is a prescription for demoralization, corruption, and ultimately general catastrophe, whatever value it may have had in the early stages of industrialization. Cooperation for the common good and concern for the rights and needs of others must replace the dismal search for maximization of personal power and consumption if the barbarism of capitalist society is to be overcome.

## The advantage of the left

The left has the inestimable advantage that it can hope to speak for humane values in opposition to the barbarous irrationality of a competitive society and to the autocratic rule of private economic empires, state bureaucracies, vanguard parties, technocratic-meritocratic elites, or whatever other monstrosities the future may hold. It will have to exploit this advantage if there is to be any hope for a serious, anti-imperialist, anti-militarist movement with a broad base in the advanced societies. Consider again the manifesto cited above. It defines the primary threat of Communism, perceptively, in the following terms:

> It has meant: (1) A serious reduction of the potential resource base and market opportunities of the West owing to the subtraction of the communist areas from the international economy and their economic transformation in ways which reduce their willingness and ability to complement the industrial economies of the West.[9]

Evidently, this interpretation of the communist threat (which goes a long way towards explaining Joan Robinson's judgment, quoted above, that the American crusade against Communism is a campaign against development) will be quite compelling to the rich, who will easily understand why our goal must be to assist "the millhands of Calcutta, the peasants of Egypt and the Indians of Guatemala (to) become politically more reliable and economically more cooperative members of the free world community," able to exercise "the capacity for self-control, for rational and morally valid choices and for responsible actions." American dominance of the world requires such political reliability, cooperativeness, and moral responsibility. For the wealthy and privileged, it is easy to identify American dominance of the world's resources with "the continued existence of human freedom and humane society everywhere." This dominance is threatened by forms of national independence or international cooperation that appropriate resources for the benefit of those who now "complement the industrial economies of the West." This kind of "threat" should be welcomed and encouraged by the left, as should its domestic analogue. An international movement of the left should aim, of course, to reduce inequity, But this is to say that participants in such a movement, in the advanced countries, must be motivated by compassion and brotherhood rather than mere personal greed. In the long run, there is no reason why an equitable distribution of the earth's resources should lead to a decline of standard of living in the advanced countries, if it is combined with an end to the irrational waste and destruction or resources characteristic of the advanced industrial societies. Once again, however, it is clear that a large-scale "cultural revolution" is a prerequisite—or better, a necessary concomitant—for a movement of the left with solid roots in technologically advanced societies.

## A task for radicals

The same considerations hold when we consider the urgent matter of bringing the arms race to an end. In the near future it will no doubt be exceedingly difficult to organize a campaign against militarism with support among workers, technicians, engineers and scientists, who are heavily dependent on the military budget for their employment. When radical students at MIT succeeded in raising a serious challenge to military research, the first reaction of the labor union in the university laboratories was to enter a suit in the federal courts to prevent MIT from dropping military work. The response was not irrational; the New England economy provides no alternative sources of employment. Similar factors will make it quite difficult for engineers, and many scientists, to dissociate themselves from the commitment to war and waste. If a radical movement hopes to make any progress among skilled workers, engineers and scientists, it will have to persuade them that their short-run interest is outweighed by other factors, among them, the personal interest of every rational man in the conversion of intellectual and material resources to reasonable ends, more specifically, in halting the preparation for war that may well lead to a final catastrophe. The task for radicals in this case, is to develop concrete alternatives and to show how they could be realized under different conditions of social organization. Furthermore, they must combat the psychotic world-view that has been constructed to rationalize the race to destruction. They must try to bring about a fundamental change of values, a commitment to general goals that will, once achieved, spell an end to imperial domination, militarism, and oppression.

A decade ago, only a visionary would have been able even to contemplate these questions. Now they are lively and exciting ones. The revisionist historians have succeeded in shattering the illusions that dominated post-war scholarship. Groups such as the North American Conference on Latin America, the Committee of Concerned Asian Scholars, the Union for Radical Political

Economics, and many others, have the potential to revitalize the professions and to create a radical intellectual culture with a broad base in the universities and colleges, with effects that will extend through the media—perhaps newly created for this purpose—the schools, communities and activist organizations of many sorts. Of course these professional groups have been riding the crest of a wave of political activism. Inquiry that is free from the narrow ideological constraints imposed by dominant social institutions will be severely inhibited, and easy to disregard, unless the general political climate is conducive to challenge and innovation. In the absence of a live and healthy radical political movement, the "softer" disciplines will easily be subverted by social pressures, as has so often been the case. At the same time, a movement of the left condemns itself to failure and irrelevance if it does not create an intellectual culture that becomes dominant by virtue of its excellence and that is meaningful to the masses of people who, in an advanced industrial society, can participate in creating and deepening it,

## The university and the left

The prospects seem to me good that the small groups that now exist can grow and interact with one another and with a political movement of the left that is rooted in many strata of American society. I think that for the present, the universities are a natural, and relatively favorable place for such growth and interaction. There is sure to be opposition to the development of scholarship and teaching that is not constrained by the dominant conservative ideology. There will undoubtedly be an effort to repress the activism that is a natural outgrowth of serious inquiry. The universities have been highly politicized by the influence of the dominant social institutions, the national state and the great corporations to which it is closely linked. The natural conservatism of the faculty will combine with the political conservatism imposed by external pressures to set up barriers to free inquiry. Examples of repression can easily be cited. Nevertheless, they should not be exaggerated. It should be recognized that, in any field, there is resistance to innovation on the part of those who have achieved a certain status and prestige. This natural resistance, easy to document, provides a kind of base line in terms of which one must assess the actual political repression that exists in the universities. My personal feeling is that by this measure, which is the correct one, repression on political grounds is not extensive, at the moment. It may grow, but that is not to say that it will necessarily succeed. For the present, there is no strong reason for pessimism, in this regard.

Of particular significance, I think, are certain efforts undertaken in the past year among scientists and engineers. For example, at MIT a handful of graduate students succeeded, within a few months, in organizing a one-day research strike that spread to some 50 colleges, and that led to the formation of active and continuing organizations of students and faculty. This initiative grew out of a sanctuary for an AWOL soldier, Mike O'Conner, which was held at MIT last fall and dramatically changed the political climate on the campus.

## Radical culture and social change

In some ways, the creation of a radical movement of scientists and engineers is analogous to the organization of GI resistance. American imperial dominance is based as much on technique as on mass military force. As Franz Schurmann has rightly pointed out, "it is not likely that, barring a major emergency, the United States could again foot a massive army," and "aside from a few puppet states such as South Korea, no country has been willing to provide the U.S. militarists with the manpower necessary to fight 'limited wars' distant from America's shores...Thus (the U.S.) must depend on technology to fight its wars."[10] Furthermore, scientists and engineers are well aware of the corruption of intelligence imposed by a system so irrational that the majority of engineers are forced to accept employment with NASA, the AEC [Atomic Energy Commission] (in essence, a weapons producing agency), and the Defense Department. There is, therefore, symbolic significance in the fact that a successful movement of scientists and engineers has developed, in part, from an expression of solidarity with a GI resister. By means of such organization of scientists and engineers, the system of subsidy to technologically advanced segments of industry and achievement of global dominance through a subverted technology can be threatened at its most vulnerable point, its personnel. Scientists and engineers can make the same key contribution to a radical culture—ultimately, a successful movement for significant social change—that they now make to militarism and repression.

As already noted, it is inconceivable that the left can achieve real success in an advanced industrial society unless it develops the intellectual resources to provide plausible, concrete solutions to the problems of our society. Those who believe that these problems can be met only when social institutions are reconstructed along democratic lines have the task of showing that this is so. Potential solutions to these problems are of limited interest when they merely appear in technical monographs (though even this would be a far from negligible accomplishment). They must become ingrained in the consciousness of those who will implement them and live under the conditions that they bring into existence. There are many kinds of interaction among scientists, engineers, technicians and skilled workers, the blue collar work force, professionals and other white collar workers, writers and artists, among all of those who must contribute to a vital movement of the left. Some of these connections I have already mentioned; specifically the application of modern technology to creating the conditions for industrial democracy and the rational and humane use of resources is one major task that lies on the immediate horizon. A serious mass movement of the left should involve all of these segments of American society. Its politics and understanding must grow out of their combined efforts to build a new world.

# Notes

1. *Boston Globe* 20 June 1969.

2. "Contrasts in Economic Development: China and India," in Neal Houghton, ed., *Struggle Against History* New York: 1968.

3. Walter Lafeber, *America, Russia and the Cold War*, p. 73. See Christopher Lasch, *The Agony of the American Left*, for a perceptive discussion of the "cultural cold war" of the 1950s.

4. See, for example, the new French journal *Autogestion* and the publications of the Institute for Workers' Control, 91 Goldsmith St., Nottingham, England.

5. *Can the Workers Run Industry?*, Ken Coates, ed., Sphere Books and the Institute for Workers' Control, 1968.

6. Paul Samuelson, *Economics*, sixth edition, 1964.

7. *Daedalus*, Winter, 1969.

8. Woodrow Wilson Foundation and National Planning Association, Holt, 1955. Our humane values are illustrated further, in this important document, in many ways. Thus "constructive wage and social welfare policies are obviously needed"—why?: "to mitigate industrial unrest." At the same time it is necessary to combat the excessive egalitarianism and social welfare legislation undertaken under leftist and socialist governments. The capitalist elite might agree with Stalin that egalitarianism is "a reactionary petty-bourgeois absurdity worthy of some sect of ascetics" (17th Party Congress). The document goes on to insist that we must preserve the right to intervene in support of "older ruling groups" who see "that their future independence lies in alliance with the West," unless the responsible middle class elements have achieved dominance. We must continue to ensure that Western Europe and Japan refrain from "neutralism and pacifism"—in the case of Japan, by making "possible greater Japanese participation in the development of Southern Asia"—a non-negligible factor in the Vietnam war, incidentally. We must combat irrational communist inspired land redistribution, as in Guatemala where (as in Iran) "nationalistic totalitarian or crypto-communist regimes have nearly succeeded in consolidating their rule" (the reference is to Arbenz and Mossadegh). And so on.

9. There are three other aspects to this threat: "A planned disruption of the free world economies;" the higher growth rate of Soviet heavy industry (N.B., the date is 1955); "the fact that Soviet communism threatens not merely the political and economic institutions of the West but the continued existence of human freedom and humane society everywhere."

10. "The Nixon administration and the Vietnam War," paper submitted to the Stockholm Conference on Vietnam, May, 1969.

## Editor's Notes to Chapter 20

Interview published in *Modern Occasions* 1.3 (1971): pp. 317–327, under the title "The Editor Interviews Noam Chomsky."

For the reference to Mitch Goodman's "compendium," see Editor's Notes to Selection 2.

On the militarization of American life, see Seymour Melman, *Pentagon Capitalism*. New York: McGraw Hill, 1970 (see Editor's Notes to Selection 16). See Selection 11.

Seymour Lipset and Norman Birnbaum are sociologists of opposing tendencies. Birnbaum (a founder of the *New Left Review*) aligns himself with Gorz, Habermas, Lefebvre, Mallet, Mandel and Touraine, and he aligns Lipset with Michel Crozier, one of the authors of the report of the Trilateral Commission mentioned in Selection 12 *The Crisis of Industrial Democracy*. Oxford University Press, 1969. pp. 10–11.

On "possessive individualism," see **RL**, ch. 3, note 57.

On the research stoppage of March 4 1969 organized by students and faculty at M.I.T. to express the concern of scientists with the "misuse of scientific and technical knowledge," see "Responsibility," a speech given by Chomsky at Rindge High School on March 4 1970, published in *March 4: Scientists, Students and Society*, ed. by Jonathan Allen, Cambridge: The M.I.T. Press, 1970. See also Dorothy Nelkin, *The University and Military Research: Moral Politics at M.I.T.*, Ithaca: Cornell University Press, 1972. Nelkin writes (p. 67) that "at first [Howard W.] Johnson [president of M.I.T.] appointed eighteen members to the panel; but in response to pressures from SACC for broader representation [SACC was a Science Action Coordinating Committee formed by students to deal specifically with the issue of defense research and other military-related activities on campus with the purpose of generating research, action, self-education, and greater social consciousness], Noam Chomsky, professor of linguistics, and Jerome Lerman, a graduate student and SACC activist, were added. Though Chomsky was giving a series of lectures at Oxford during this time, his presence on the panel was considered so important that he was flown back to M.I.T. each week to attend the meetings."

On the control of the universities, see David N. Smith, *Who Rules the Universities? An Essay in Class Analysis*. New York: Monthly Review Press, 1974.

On "friendly fascism," see now Bertram Gross's *Friendly Fascism: The New Face of Power in America*. Boston: South End Press, 1998.

# 20. The New Radicalism

*1. Do you believe that the re-radicalization of a good part of the American intellectual community and student body that has occurred in the 1960s will continue into the 70s? Did this re-radicalization surprise you, as it did a great many people, or did you in any way foresee it? What obstacles, if any, do you see to its further development?*

The re-radicalization of the 1960s did surprise me, very much, and for that reason, among others, I have little confidence in my own guesses about the near future. I've consistently underestimated—to take one example—the potential of resistance to the war in Indo-China. Five years ago, I never believed that it would be even remotely possible that a generation of youth would courageously refuse to take part in this miserable war, undermining the hopes of the American executive that it could fight a colonial war with a conscript army and forcing it back to the more traditional imperial pattern that is evolving now (there are other factors in this tactical shift, but that would take us far afield). I also did not foresee at all that the conservative ideological consensus would so significantly erode, in large part as a consequence of student activism.

As to the future, I'm reluctant to guess. The movement, so-called, has developed no self-sustaining organizational forms or clear intellectual vision that expresses the understanding, or even the mood of the vast number of mostly young people who feel themselves to be part of it or at least drawn to its fringes. I thought Mitch Goodman's recent "compendium" captured rather well this curious combination of formlessness and vitality, confusion and hopefulness. It's hard for me to believe that students who have taken part in movement activities will slip back very readily to the docility of the 1950s, though of course there will be continuing efforts to restore the mindless consensus, with a margin of ineffectual dissent, that is such a convenience for the managers of domestic and international society. Many American intellectuals seem to be able to reconcile themselves to the systematic destruction of the peasant societies of Indo-China by American technology, just as many of their predecessors found ways to come to terms with Stalin's purge or Hiroshima and Nagasaki. This is much less true of the youth of the sixties, to their credit, and I suspect that Vietnam—the butchery, the deceit, the timid dissent, the contemptible apologetics—will prove to be a formative experience with long-term consequences. On occasion their revulsion expresses itself as antagonism to technology and science, or even to rationality. But for the most part, in my experience at least, it has led to an appreciation of the depth of sustained commitment that will be necessary if Indo-China is to be saved from obliteration, and an appreciation of the scale of the cultural and institutional changes that must be carried out in the United States if other societies that seek independence are to be spared a similar fate. Faced with the awesome scale of these tasks, many return to private concerns-a move often mistaken for apathy. It is not the apathy of the fifties, and a reservoir of sympathy and potential support remains for those who undertake a more activist role.

I'm personally impressed with the large number of young people who are committing themselves to what they see as a long-term effort to bring about a radical transformation of American society. Their efforts to involve themselves in community organizing, developing radical professional groups, and the like, might have long-range significance. Not much of this makes the headlines (except, occasionally, after police or judicial repression, as in Seattle, Philadelphia or right here in Cambridge in the past few months). But with enough persistence and support, it is possible that these efforts might succeed in creating some of the nuclei for a radical movement that will develop from its own internal resources, instead of merely in response to recurrent atrocities in the larger society.

It's important, I think, that such groups continue to have a close relation to university-based movements. They can exploit some of the intrinsic problems (contradictions, if you like) of modern state capitalism. If the universities are to provide the knowledge and skills, as well as the trained manpower, needed to sustain an advanced industrial society, a substantial part of the youth will pass *through* them and they will have to retain a certain degree of freedom and openness. But if so, a radical consciousness will almost certainly develop as a natural consequence of objective study and thinking that frees itself from mythology and an ideological straitjacket. Dogmatism and achievement are incompatible, in the long run, and though some young people will simply accept what they are told and others may be induced to devote themselves to "making it" as the highest goal in life, it is predictable that there will also be free and compassionate and independent minds to challenge prevailing orthodoxies and search for ways to translate a perception of social injustice to some form of action.

In a modern industrial society there will be a need for relatively free and open centers of study and thinking, which will in turn continually create a challenge to irrationality, autocratic structures, deceit and injustice. A radical or reformist social movement will be able to draw upon these centers for participants as well as ideas, while "radicalizing" them by the opportunities it creates for meaningful social action. No movement for social change can hope to succeed unless it makes the most advanced intellectual and technical achievements its own, and unless it is rooted in those strata, of the population that are productive and creative in every domain. It is, in particular, a very important question whether the intelligentsia will see itself as fulfilling a role in social management, or rather as part of the work force. The promise of past revolutions has been betrayed, in part, because of the willingness of the intelligentsia to join or serve a new ruling class, a process that can be compared to the willing submission to state and private power in Western state capitalist societies. As a larger component of the productive work in an industrial society comes to involve skilled workers, engineers, scientists and other intellectual workers, new possibilities may develop for the emergence of a mass revolutionary movement that will not be betrayed by the separation of a vanguard intelligentsia from the labor army that it helps to control, either directly or through the ideological instruments it fashions. So one might hope, at least. Conceivably, as many have argued, worldwide student radicalism may be an incipient stage of such a development—a premature strike of the work force of the future, as Norman Birnbaum put it somewhere.

Any successes will no doubt evoke a repressive response by the dominant autocratic institutions. But for the intellectual community and student body, relatively privileged and affluent in a modern industrial society, there are other and more immediate obstacles to the radicalization that seems to me a likely consequence of honesty and compassion. For one thing, a continued "conformist subservience to those in power" (Hans Morgenthau's accurate phrase) brings narrow personal advantages. Quite apart from this, it is very tempting to immerse oneself entirely in exciting intellectual work—I know this very well from personal experience—but fortunately this becomes quite difficult when some serious and honorable people devote themselves, with courage and conviction, to a struggle for ideals that one knows to be just and deeply important. If this struggle ever becomes a mass movement of the oppressed and exploited, the impulse to contribute to it may intensify, growing both from moral pressure and the desire for self-fulfillment in a decent and humane society.

Perhaps what I say is misleading, given that I inevitably see these problems from the point of view of a certain type of academic intellectual. So let me try to express this possibly distorting factor quite clearly. As for myself, I would like nothing better than to be able to keep to a range of purely intellectual problems that happen to intrigue me greatly. Although it is impossible to overlook the complaint of many students and others that there is no meaningful work, I can't accept it intuitively. There is a great deal of challenging and meaningful work, though I am sceptical as to whether the fundamental problems of man and society can be studied in any very profound manner, at least in ways resembling scientific inquiry, perhaps because of temporary gaps in our understanding, or perhaps because of deeper limitations of human intelligence. These personal tendencies and beliefs probably lead me to underestimate the potentialities of activism or perhaps even social criticism and analysis, as well as to restrict, no doubt improperly, my own personal involvement. I'm sure it leads me to underestimate the sense of alienation and even despair that seems objectively to be an aspect of what many social critics refer to as the proletarianization of the intellectuals.

Many young radical activists tend to be somewhat contemptuous of "conscience radicalism" that grows out of concern for the suffering of others:

Vietnamese, oppressed minorities, exploited workers, for example. They argue, perhaps with justice, that a serious and sustained commitment to radical social change will in general develop only as a response to "one's own oppression" often, therefore, caste rather than class oppression, as women, students in authoritarian schools, victims of repressive life styles and cultural patterns, and so on. So far as I can see, a good part of this caste oppression could be relieved, in principle, without any modification of the distribution of power in state capitalist industrial society. As a rational system of exploitation, capitalism has no inherent need for racist and sexist practices and should be quite ready to tolerate a leveling of all individuals into interchangeable parts of the production process or equivalent units of individual consumption, without invidious distinctions of race or sex or ethnic origin.

To take another case, the same is probably true of the environmental crisis. No doubt the corporations can be bribed to limit pollution by public subsidy or higher prices, and can even turn ecological concerns to their profit by the manufacture of new commodities. Years ago the Ford Motor Company made an abortive effort to "sell safety." By now, environmental concerns may well have created a potential market for new accessories as well as opportunities for rapid obsolescence as technology is developed for coping with pollution. I am not trying to minimize the importance of issues that do not relate directly to the structure of autocratic institutions or the pattern of social control. On the contrary, there is surely no more urgent task, in the short run, than preventing American terror from demolishing the societies of Indo-China, even though there is little doubt that American capitalism can easily survive the loss (to its own population) of the Southeast Asian neocolonial system. But a radical movement that looks to fundamental institutional change, to socialization and democratization of the central industrial, financial, and commercial institutions of a modern society, will have to concentrate on different issues. Such a movement seems still remote.

*2. Do you think that an organized movement (perhaps taking the form of a political party) armed with a definite theory and strategy adapted to American conditions is likely to emerge from the new radicalism? In your view, is such an organized movement at once necessary and desirable? If your reply in this respect is affirmative, what ideological and practical political model would you suggest for this renewed attempt so to organize the Left as to make it effective on the national scene?*

Five years ago I would have regarded such a development as virtually out of the question. Now I'm not so pessimistic. There are many indications of a significant change of general mood, with regard to the problems of industrial society. It is hard to believe that any American sociologist would now seriously propose that the fundamental problems of the industrial revolution have been solved and that the triumph of democratic social evolution in the West signals the end of domestic politics for intellectuals who must have ideologies or utopias to motivate them to social action (Seymour Martin Lipset, in 1960). No doubt many would find Hans Morgenthau's analysis somewhat extreme, when he argues that there is no possibility for a rational solution to the basic problems of contemporary American society within the present framework of distribution of power—virtually a call for revolution, if not an expression of hopeless despair. But this point of view is, in any event, no longer as remote from the mainstream of thinking as it was in the period of celebration of the achievements and promise of the capitalist welfare state, only a few years ago. The change is not limited to intellectuals. I've noticed a very obvious shift in the same direction among many other parts of the population, just from personal experience in talks and meetings. For example, in an industrial suburb of Boston in 1965 I was regarded as a dangerous extremist for suggesting that the United States had no right to bomb North Vietnam. In 1969, in the same town, I spoke to an audience of perhaps ten times the size on problems of modern American society, with an ensuing discussion, quite lively, on fundamental problems of capitalism and the possibilities for workers and community control of industry—unthinkable ideas just a few years earlier. There was discussion, but not assent (except, very substantially, with regard to the Indo-China war). Soon there may be assent. To mention another case, the involvement of students in the efforts of Miners for Democracy and other similar examples throughout the country again, not widely publicized—are encouraging signs. Or consider the recently formed Labor-University Alliance. Though one would not know it from reading the tiny news item buried on the radio-TV page of the *NY Times*, the founding group includes important labor leaders (Leonard Woodcock of the UAW, for one) as well as the president of the National Student Association and other student and faculty participants from various parts of the country who have been active for years in the peace movement and other domestic causes. George Wald deserves great credit for having given the initiative to this development, which is potentially quite important, I think. Working-class opposition to the war has been poorly reported, for the most part. For example, the UAW executive has made strong official statements, which received virtually no mention in the press, and referenda and polls over the years (e.g., Dearborn in 1966, Detroit in 1970) suggest significant, largely unarticulated antiwar sentiment. Whatever criticisms one may make of the unions, they still are the most democratic institutions in the United States, and might recover their position as a leading force for decency and social change. An alliance with left-wing university-based groups, student and faculty, might be significant in the long run. Conceivably, a labor party, or something of the sort, might develop at some stage, particularly, if the crisis of inflation-with-recession proves unresoluble.

A reformist mass party could be very important in the United States in impeding the drift towards what Bertram Gross recently called "friendly fascism" and in defending both democratic rights and the most elementary needs of the poor and the exploited. It might also help provide a framework for badly needed discussion of the mythology of American state capitalism, rarely challenged in the last decades. The recent and forceful challenge to the myth of American international benevolence, carefully fostered by apologists for state power in the cold-war years, should be accompanied by a serious challenge, on a broad scale, to the claims to legitimacy of the private empires that dominate the domestic and international economy, and the state executive that largely serves their interest. Many radicals fear that the growth of a mass reformist party of working people and the "underclass" would divert energies from more radical social change, but I'm personally not sympathetic to these objections. On the contrary, it seems to me that it might very well offer new scope to educational and organizational efforts of a more radical character, which would be all to the good. All of this is speculation, of course, but it seems to me less remote from reality than it might have seemed just a few years ago.

In more direct response to your question, it seems perhaps not unrealistic to look forward to a mass political movement that will be devoted to badly needed reforms, anti-imperialist and anti-militarist, concerned with guaranteeing minimal standards of health, income, education, industrial safety and conditions of work, and overcoming urban decay and rural misery. Within it, or related to it, there might develop a variety of more radical movements that explore the possibility of dismantling the system of private and state power and democratizing basic social and economic institutions through cooperatives and community and workers' control, and that organize and experiment to these ends. I would hate to see the Left too well organized at this stage (not much fear of this in any event), though one would hope that destructive factional squabbling could be overcome in favor of sympathetic and fraternal disagreement and, where possible, cooperation among those who have rather different ideas about what are, after all, rather obscure and poorly understood matters.

3. *Both here and abroad the New Left (as it is somewhat loosely termed) has frequently exhibited tendencies closely relating it to the classic anarchist tradition. Are you in sympathy with such tendencies? If you are in sympathy, in what concrete ways can anarchist aspirations be realized in modern centralized economies such as we live in at present in the West?*

In my personal opinion, anarcho-syndicalist and, in general, libertarian socialist ideals are quite appropriate for an advanced industrial society. There is no longer any material necessity for human beings to be used as tools of production. As syndicalists have been pointing out since the turn of the century, even if one grants that managerial skills are "specialized" and beyond the direct competence of the work force (the extent to which this must be true under the material and cultural conditions that a rational use of modem technology could provide is another question), there is no reason why managers should be answerable to private capital rather than the work force and the community. Back in 1912, an important document of a Welsh miners movement pointed out that "The men who work in the mine are surely as competent to elect [managers] as shareholders who may never have seen a colliery. To have a vote in determining who shall be your foreman, manager, inspector, etc., is to have a vote in determining the conditions which shall rule your working life." Its often argued that centralization of planning and control is a technological imperative. I have yet to see a coherent argument for this. In fact, it is difficult to see why the same technology that permits centralized decision-making might not also be adapted to free workers from stupefying labor and provide them directly with the information needed to make rational decisions democratically. In any institution—factory, university, health center, or whatever—there are a variety of interests that ought to be represented in decision-making: the work force itself, the community in which it is located, users of its products or services, institutions that compete for the same resources. These interests should be directly represented in democratic structures that displace and eliminate private ownership of the means of production or resources, an anachronism with no legitimacy. A centralized bureaucratic state offers little if any improvement, so far as I can see, over rule by a corporate oligarchy weakly constrained by parliamentary institutions, but possessing the centers of production, finance, and information. The New Left has reawakened interest in industrial democracy, workers' control, possibilities of free association of producers, and has also contributed to a renewed concern for human needs that are socially and collectively expressed in place of the ugly and now destructive "possessive individualism" of an anachronistic social system, and in general, concern for freedom from domination by state or private power. I think it has made a real contribution, in these respects. I'm not suggesting that the New Left has made some new theoretical contribution in these areas. On the contrary, we've barely recovered the level of understanding achieved at the time of the great decline of Western radicalism after the first world war. But it has definitely reawakened interest in these questions, more by its general mood and spirit than by any analytic work. Capitalism (as well as the state capitalist or state socialist varieties of autocracy that have developed in industrial societies) requires, for its efficient functioning in the interest of its rulers, a docile and acquiescent population, much as an imperialist state demands passivity and ignorance from its population. By challenging authoritarian patterns of thinking and behaviour and stressing the fundamental human need for free creative work and democratic popular participation in the management of affairs, in every area of life, the New Left threatens to undermine these autocratic structures. If this has taken place in an indefinite and often chaotic manner, with little organization or ideology, nevertheless the changes of mentality and conception, as well as behaviour, are visible enough, and in many ways very hopeful, I think. I recognize, incidentally, that my picture of the New Left is quite different from that of many other commentators; I can only say that much of this commentary appears to me distorted and inaccurate. This reminds me of something I ought to have said in connection with the struggles against "caste oppression." Though in principle they are not, it seems to me, anticapitalist, nevertheless the impulse for liberation may not be easily contained, and might lead on directly to a significant challenge to authoritarian institutions, to centralized control, and to coercive industrial as well as cultural patterns.

*4. What, in your view, are likely to be the cultural effects of the new radicalism? In posing this question, I have in mind the university system in this country as well as literature, art, and such humanistic disciplines as history, sociology and psychology.*

As far as the universities are concerned, I think that the effects of the new radicalism have been in general very positive. The universities have been opened, as never before in my lifetime, to new ideas and independent thinking outside of the natural sciences. During the years of the hegemony of cold-war ideology and glorification of liberal state capitalism, the universities became willing servants of state and private power, not only at an ideological level, but in their direct contributions to social management, so-called counterinsurgency (i.e., techniques for the repression of popular movements), militarization of American society (vastly extended under the Kennedy administration, as Seymour Melman, for one, has pointed out), and the like. Student radicalism has raised a belated and very healthy challenge to this subservience. The politicization of the universities in these years was so profound that it was virtually unnoticed, just as a fish does not notice that he swims in the sea—what else could there be? Such inability to perceive one's own ideological commitments is the extreme limit of subordination to prevailing ideology. But this is a thing of the past, and I doubt that the efforts to reinstitute the conformism of the past generation will be successful in the universities, unless there is a resort to outright force. While noting this, I think one must be aware of the danger of a new politicization of the universities by militant factions within. The danger is slight, and is being enormously exaggerated for political reasons, but that should not lead one to overlook it. We should try to keep the universities as free and as open as possible, recognizing that the primary forces threatening freedom and openness are the powerful institutions, state and private, that dominate the outside society, and their representatives and spokesmen within the university itself.

It seems to me that the humanistic disciplines have been revitalized by the recent challenges to orthodoxy in history and the social sciences, and that the opportunity exists for real progress in these areas. But it will take hard and sustained work. The power of he propaganda apparatus of the state and private institutions is immense. Consider, as an example, the Vietnam war. Though the state executive has, point by point, lost all the arguments, it has nevertheless succeeded in imposing the framework of official fantasy on the general debate. Most critics within the mainstream of opinion tacitly accept the claim that the war pits North Vietnam against South Vietnam, Laos and Cambodia, backed (perhaps mistakenly or in an unacceptable manner) by the United States. The media are virtually unanimous in adopting this framework of discussion, even those segments of the press that oppose the war. The documentation to refute these assumptions is overwhelming, and has been presented (with no refutation or even serious discussion) over and over again. Not with sufficient intensity or scope, however, to overcome the hegemony of the state propaganda apparatus.

In psychology, the narrow concern for control of behaviour and the general strictures of behaviorism, absurd on intellectual grounds, are no longer dominant among serious scientists, though a culture lag, in part ideologically determined, grants them unjustified prestige elsewhere. To what extent this development is related to the new radicalism might be debated. Probably there is some relation, though I think it is actually not great. In literature and the arts I am incompetent to judge.

5. *Do you think that the political awareness of American scientists has changed in the past few years in any significant fashion? What are the prospects of the scientific community (or at least a good part of it) acquiring sufficient radical consciousness enabling it to resist the demands and numerous exactions and impositions of the Pentagon as well as of private corporations intent on profit-making regardless of the damage to the human and natural environment?*

This question is an extremely important one, in my opinion. Take the specific matter of counterinsurgency. There can be little doubt that the power to control or destroy popular movements is increasing, through technology. Popular movements depend on human will and courage, which has limits. The technology of surveillance and destruction can "progress" without significant limits. Furthermore, pseudo-scientific patterns of discourse, much cultivated by the social and behavioural sciences, provide a new and useful ideological device for those who hope to mask force and coercion in technical terminology of problem-solving that may delude people who have no idea what science is about. That most of this is drivel does not, unfortunately, limit its effectiveness. A serious attack on the development of the technology of control and destruction, as well as exposure of the coercive ideologies that try to capitalize on the prestige of science and technology, will surely have to engage scientists in a very determined effort.

More generally, as I mentioned earlier, a Movement for social change in an advanced industrial society will get nowhere unless it offers the widest scope for freedom and cultural progress and draws to itself the intellectual workers, including scientists, who will find in this movement their natural home. Of course, over the past three or four years, there have been notable changes in the attitudes of scientists and others towards the problems you mention. In place of the general unquestioned submission to external demands, there is now some concern over the uses to which one's work will be put and the social effects to which it may contribute. Concrete changes reflecting these concerns are very slight, to my knowledge. There have been some administrative changes. For example, at my own university, after extensive student educational and organizational efforts, and some very effective protest and agitation, a $60 million a year laboratory that is devoted largely to advanced guidance systems for missiles and the related technology of space exploration has been technically "divested," though as far as I know, this has led to little if any substantive change in its actual relations to the university or the work undertaken in the laboratory. A second laboratory, of roughly the same size, where work continues (so far as I know) on counterinsurgency and military problems remains, as before, within the university structure. Efforts at conversion to some socially useful purpose have, not surprisingly, been ineffective, for reasons that have little to do with the university. It is far from obvious that the enormous government subsidy to advanced technology and the industries that rely upon it can be directed away from destruction and waste (military and space, for example), for reasons that have been discussed at length. In this respect, science and technology are in a real bind. They can go out of business, or submit to the demands of external powers. I don't want to exaggerate— for example, a great deal of government-financed research in the universities (including much of the research financed by the DOD [Department of Defense]) is pure science in the best sense. The point is that scientists, even as an organized group, could probably have little effect on a pattern of state investment and subsidy that is intimately related to problems of management of the economy and global power. Radical organization of scientists and engineers is a possibility, perhaps, but its importance will be directly contingent on the emergence of a mass popular movement to which it can contribute, and in which it can be absorbed as an important constituent element.

## Editor's Notes to Chapter 21

Edited transcript of *The Jay Interview*, broadcast by London Weekend TV on July 25, 1976. It was published in *The New Review* 3.29 (1976): pp. 25–32, under the title "How to be an Anarchist: Noam Chomsky talks to Peter Jay."

On the Israeli Kibbutzim, see Martin Buber's book *Paths in Utopia* ("Introduction to Chomsky's Social Theory," n. 65; see also nn. 47ff.) (See now FT.)

On the Spanish revolution, see "Objectivity and Liberal Scholarship" in **APNM** and now Burnett Bolloten's *The Spanish Revolution: The Left and the Struggle for Power During the Civil War*. Chapel Hill: The University of North Carolina Press, 1979 (the Spanish translation, *La Revolución Española: Sus Orígenes, la Izquierda y la Lucha por el Poder Durante la Guerra Civil 1936–1939*. Barcelona/Buenos Aires/México: Ediciones Grijalbo, 1980, includes some later additions and corrections, and also an interesting preface by Gabriel Jackson). In Chomsky's opinion, "Burnett Bolloten's *Grand Camouflage* was a major work, invaluable for students of the Spanish Civil War. His new work, *The Spanish Revolution*, is a work of still greater importance. With its wealth of documentation and insights, it stands as a fine contribution to our understanding of some of the most intriguing events of modern history." See also Frank Mintz, *L'autogestion dans l'Espagne Révolutionnaire*. Paris: Maspéro, and preferably the original version, *La Autogestión en la España Revolucionaria*. Madrid: Ediciones La Piqueta, 1977, in particular the extensive bibliography (divided in periods). A very valuable anthology in English is *The Anarchist Collectives: Worker's Management in the Spanish Revolution (1936–39)*, ed. by Sam Dolgoff, Montréal: Black Rose Books, 1974.

On Whilhelm von Humboldt, see "Introduction...," in particular notes 51, 60 and 61. For an English version of his classic "critique of the State" (written in 1792 but not published in full until 1852), see *The Limits of State Action*. Cambridge: Cambridge University Press, 1969, edited, with an Introduction and Notes, by J.W. Burrow.

On Chomsky's view of "left-wing Marxism," see Introduction, n. 44; on Chomsky as a "derivative fellow traveller" of anarchism, see Introduction, especially text between n. 25 and n. 28.

The quote on page 253 is taken (not quite literally) from **FRS**, VII.v, pp. 351–352.

# 21. The Relevance Of Anarcho-Syndicalism

*Professor Chomsky, perhaps we should start by trying to define what is not meant by anarchism—the word anarchy is derived, after all, from the Greek, literally meaning 'no government'. Now presumably people who talk about anarchy or anarchism as a system of political philosophy don't just mean that, as it were, as of January 1st next year, government as we now understand it will suddenly cease; there would be no police, no rule of the road, no laws, no tax collectors, no Post Office, and so forth. Presumably it means something more complicated than that.*

Well, yes to some of those questions, no to others. They may very well mean no policemen, but I don't think they would mean no rules of the road. In fact, I should say to begin with that the term anarchism is used to cover quite a range of political ideas, but I would prefer to think of it as the libertarian left, and from that point of view anarchism can be conceived as a kind of voluntary socialism, that is, as libertarian socialist or anarcho-syndicalist or communist anarchist, in the tradition of say Bakunin and Kropotkin and others. They had in mind a highly organized form of society, but a society that was organized on the basis of organic units, organic communities. And generally they meant by that the workplace and the neighborhood, and from those two basic units there could derive through federal arrangements a highly integrated kind of social organization, which might be national or even international in scope. And the decisions could be made over a substantial range, but by delegates who are always part of the organic community from which they come, to which they return and in which, in fact, they live.

*So it doesn't mean a society in which there is literally speaking no government so much as a society in which the primary source of authority comes as it were from the bottom up, and not from the top down. Whereas representative democracy, as we have it in the United States and in Britain, would be regarded as a form of from-the-top down authority, even though ultimately the voters decide.*

Representative democracy, as in, say, the United States or Great Britain, would be criticized by an anarchist of this school on two grounds. First of all because there is a monopoly of power centralized in the State, and secondly— and critically—because representative democracy is limited to the political sphere and in no serious way encroaches on the economic sphere. Anarchists of this tradition have always held that democratic control of one's productive life is at the core of any serious human liberation, or, for that matter, of any significant democratic practice. That is, as long as individuals are compelled to rent themselves on the market to those who are willing to hire them, as long as their role in production is simply that of ancillary tools, then there are striking elements of coercion and oppression that make talk of democracy very limited, if even meaningful.

*Historically speaking, have there been any sustained examples on any substantial scale of societies which approximated to the anarchist ideal?*

There are small societies, small in number, that I think have done so quite well, and there are a few examples of large-scale libertarian revolutions which were largely anarchist in their structure. As to the first, small societies extending over a long period, I myself think the most dramatic example is perhaps the Israeli Kibbutzim, which for a long period really were constructed on anarchist principles: that is, self-management, direct worker control, integration of agriculture, industry, service, personal participation in self-management. And they were, I should think, extraordinarily successful by almost any measure that one can impose.

*But they were presumably, and still are, in the frame work of a conventional State which guarantees certain basic stabilities.*

Well, they weren't always. Actually their history is rather interesting. Since 1948 they've been in the framework of the conventional State. Prior to that they were within the framework of the colonial enclave and in fact there was a subterranean, largely cooperative society which was not really part of the system of the British mandate, but was functioning outside of it. And to some extent that's survived the establishment of the State, though of course it became integrated into the State and in my view lost a fair amount of its libertarian socialist character through this process, and through other processes which are unique to the history of that region, which we need not go into.

However, as functioning libertarian socialist institutions, I think they are an interesting model that is highly relevant to advanced industrial societies in a way in which some of the other examples that have existed in the past are not. A good example of a really large-scale anarchist revolution—in fact the best example to my knowledge—is the Spanish revolution in 1936, in which over most of Republican Spain there was a quite inspiring anarchist revolution that involved both industry and agriculture over substantial areas, developed in a way which to the outside looks spontaneous. Though in fact if you look at the roots of it, you discover that it was based on some three generations of experiment and thought and work which extended anarchist ideas to very large parts of the population in this largely pre-industrial—though not totally pre-industrial—society. And that again was, by both human measures and indeed anyone's economic measures, quite successful. That is, production continued effectively; workers in farms and factories proved quite capable of managing their affairs without coercion from above, contrary to what lots of socialists, communists, liberals and others wanted to believe, and in fact you can't tell what would have happened. That anarchist revolution was simply destroyed by force, but during the period in which it was alive I think it was a highly successful and, as I say, in many ways a very inspiring testimony to the ability of poor working people to organize and manage their own affairs, extremely successfully, without coercion and control. How relevant the Spanish experience is to an advanced industrial society, one might question in detail.

*It's clear that the fundamental idea of anarchism is the primacy of the individual—not necessarily in isolation, but with other individuals—and the fulfillment of his freedom. This in a sense looks awfully like the founding ideas of the United States of America. What is it about the American experience which has made freedom as used in that tradition become a suspect and indeed a tainted phrase in the minds of anarchists and libertarian socialist thinkers like yourself?*

Let me just say I don't really regard myself as an anarchist thinker. I'm a derivative fellow traveler, let's say. Anarchist thinkers have constantly referred to the American experience and to the ideal of Jeffersonian democracy very very favorably. You know, Jefferson's concept that the best government is the government which governs least or Thoreau's addition to that, that the best government is the one that doesn't govern at all, is one that's often repeated by anarchist thinkers through modern times.

However, the ideal of Jeffersonian democracy, putting aside the fact that it was a slave society, developed in an essentially pre-capitalist system, that is in a society in which there was no monopolistic control, there were no significant centers of private power. In fact it's striking to go back and read today some of the classic libertarian texts. If one reads, say, Wilhelm von Humboldt's critique of the State of 1792, a significant classic libertarian text that certainly inspired Mill, one finds that he doesn't speak at all of the need to resist private concentration of power: rather he speaks of the need to resist the encroachment of coercive State power. And that is what one finds also in the early American tradition. But the reason is that that was the only kind of power there was. I mean, Humboldt takes for granted that individuals are roughly equivalent in their private power, and that the only real imbalance of power lies in the centralized authoritarian state, and individual freedom must be sustained against its intrusion—the State or the Church. That's what he feels one must resist.

Now when he speaks, for example, of the need for control of one's creative life, when he decries the alienation of labor that arises from coercion or even instruction or guidance in one's work, rather than self-management in one's work, he's giving an anti-statist or anti-theocratic ideology. But the same principles apply very well to the capitalist industrial society that emerged later. And I would think that Humboldt, had he been consistent, would have ended up being a libertarian socialist.

*Don't these precedents suggest that there is something inherently pre-industrial about the applicability of libertarian ideas—that they necessarily presuppose a rather rural society in which technology and production are fairly simple, and in which the economic organization tends to be small-scale and localized?*

Well, let me separate that into two questions: one, how anarchists have felt about it, and two, what I think is the case. As far as anarchist reactions are concerned, there are two. There has been one anarchist tradition—and one might think, say, of Kropotkin as a representative—which had much of the character you describe. On the other hand there's another anarchist tradition that develops into anarcho-syndicalism which simply regarded anarchist ideas as the proper mode of organization for a highly complex advanced industrial society. And that tendency in anarchism merges, or at least inter-relates very closely with a variety of left-wing Marxism, the kind that one finds in, say, the Council Communists that grew up in the Luxemburgian tradition, and that is later represented by Marxist theorists like Anton Pannakoek, who developed a whole theory of workers' councils in industry and who is himself a scientist and astronomer, very much part of the industrial world.

So which of these two views is correct? I mean, is it necessary that anarchist concepts belong to the pre-industrial phase of human society, or is anarchism the rational mode of organization for a highly advanced industrial society? Well, I myself believe the latter, that is, I think that industrialization and the advance of technology raise possibilities for self-management over a broad scale that simply didn't exist in an earlier period. And that in fact this is precisely the rational mode for an advanced and complex industrial society, one in which workers can very well become masters of their own immediate affairs, that is, in direction and control of the shop, but also can be in a position to make the major substantive decisions concerning the structure of the economy, concerning social institutions, concerning planning regionally and beyond. At present, institutions do not permit them to have control over the requisite information, and the relevant training to understand these matters. A good deal could be automated. Much of the necessary work that is required to keep a decent level of social life going can be consigned to machines—at least in principle—which means humans can be free to undertake the kind of creative work which may not have been possible, objectively, in the early stages of the industrial revolution.

*I'd like to pursue in a moment the question of the economics of an anarchist society, but could you sketch in a little more detail the political constitution of an anarchist society, as you would see it, in modern conditions? Would there be political parties, for example? What residual forms of government would in fact remain?*

Let me sketch what I think would be perhaps a rough consensus, and one that I think is essentially correct. Beginning with the two modes of immediate organization and control, namely organization and control in the workplace and in the community, one can imagine a network of workers' councils, and at a higher level, representation across the factories, or across branches of industry, or across crafts, and on to general assemblies of workers' councils that can be regional and national and international in character. And from another point of view one can project a system of governance that involves local assemblies—again federated regionally, dealing with regional issues, crossing crafts, industries, trades and so on, and again at the level of the nation or beyond, through federation and so on.

Now exactly how these would develop and how they would inter-relate and whether you need both of them or only one, well these are matters over which anarchist theoreticians have debated and many proposals exist, and I don't feel confident to take a stand. These are questions which will have to be worked out.

*But there would not, for example, be direct national elections and political parties organized from coast to coast, as it were. Because if there were that would presumably create a kind of central authority which would be inimical to the idea of anarchism.*

No, the idea of anarchism is that delegation of authority is rather minimal and that its participants at any one of these levels of government should be directly responsive to the organic community in which they live. In fact the optimal situation would be that participation in one of these levels of government should be temporary, and even during the period when it's taking place should be only partial; that is, the members of a workers' council who are for some period actually functioning to make decisions that other people don't have the time to make, should also continue to do their work as part of the workplace or neighborhood community in which they belong.

As for political parties, my feeling is that an anarchist society would not forcefully prevent political parties from arising. In fact, anarchism has always been based on the idea that any sort of Procrustean bed, any system of norms that is imposed on social life will constrain and very much underestimate its energy and vitality and that all sorts of new possibilities of voluntary organization may develop at that higher level of material and intellectual culture. But I think it is fair to say that insofar as political parties are felt to be necessary, anarchist organization of society will have failed. That is, it should be the case, I would think, that where there is direct participation in self-management, in economic and social affairs, then factions, conflicts, differences of interest and ideas and opinion, which should be welcomed and cultivated, will be expressed at every one of these levels. Why they should fall into two, three or political parties, I don't quite see. I think that the complexity of human interest and life does not fall in that fashion. Parties represent basically class interests, and classes would have been eliminated or transcended in such a society.

*One last question on the political organization: is there not a danger with this sort of hierarchical tier of assemblies and quasi-governmental structure, without direct elections, that the central body, or the body that is in some sense at the top of this pyramid, would get very remote from the people on the ground; and since it will have to have some powers if it's going to deal with international affairs, for example, and may even have to have control over armed forces and things like that, that it would be less democratically responsive than the existing regime?*

It's a very important property of any libertarian society, to prevent an evolution in the direction that you've described, which is a possible evolution, and one that institutions should be designed to prevent. And I think that that's entirely possible. I myself am totally unpersuaded that participation in governance is a full-time job. It may be in an irrational society, where all sorts of prob-

lems arise because of the irrational nature of institutions. But in a properly functioning advanced industrial society organized along libertarian lines, I would
think that executing decisions taken by representative bodies is a part-time job
which should be rotated throughout the community and, furthermore, should
be undertaken by people who at all times continue to be participants in their
own direct activity.

It may be that governance is itself a function on a par with, say, steel production. If that turns out to be true—and I think that is a question of empirical
fact that has to be determined, it can't be projected out of the mind—but if it
turns out to be true then it seems to me the natural suggestion is that governance
should be organized industrially, as simply one of the branches of industry, with
their own workers' councils and their own self-governance and their own participation in broader assemblies.

I might say that in the workers' councils that have spontaneously developed
here and there—for example, in the Hungarian revolution of 1956—that's pretty much what happened. There was, as I recall, a workers' council of State
employees who were simply organized along industrial lines as another branch of
industry. That's perfectly possible, and it should be or could be a barrier against
the creation of the kind of remote coercive bureaucracy that anarchists of course
fear.

*If you suppose that there would continue to be a need for self-defense, on quite
a sophisticated level, I don't see from your description how you would achieve effective control of this system of part-time representative councils at various levels from
the bottom up, over an organization as powerful and as necessarily technically sophisticated as, for example, the Pentagon.*

Well, first we should be a little clearer about terminology. You refer to the
Pentagon, as is usually done, as a defense organization. In 1947, when the
National Defense Act was passed, the former War Department—the American
department concerned with war which up to that time was called honestly the
War Department—had its name changed to the Defense Department. I was a
student then and didn't think I was very sophisticated, but I knew and everyone
knew that this meant that to whatever extent the American military had been
involved in defense in the past—and partially it had been so—this was now over:
since it was being called the Defense Department, that meant it was going to be
a department of aggression, nothing else.

*On the principle of never believe anything until it's officially denied.*

Right. Sort of on the assumption that Orwell essentially had captured the
nature of the modern state. And that's exactly the case. I mean the Pentagon is
in no sense a defense department. It has never defended the United States from
anyone: it has only served to conduct aggression, and I think that the American
people would be much better off without a Pentagon. They certainly don't need
it for defense. Its intervention in international affairs has never been—well, you
know, never is a strong word, but I think you would be hard put to find a case
—certainly it has not been its characteristic pose to support freedom or liberty

or to defend people and so on. That's not the role of the massive military organization that is controlled by the Defense Department. Rather its tasks are two—both quite antisocial.

The first is to preserve an international system in which what are called American interests, which primarily means business interests, can flourish. And secondly, it has an internal economic task. I mean the Pentagon has been the primary Keynesian mechanism whereby the government intervenes to maintain what is ludicrously called the health of the economy by inducing production — that means production of waste.

Now both these functions serve certain interests, in fact dominant interests, dominant class interests in American society. But I don't think in any sense they serve the public interest, and I think that this system of production of waste and of destruction would essentially be dismantled in a libertarian society. Now one shouldn't be too glib about this. If one can imagine, let's say, a social revolution in the United States—that's rather distant, I would assume—but if that took place, it's hard to imagine that there would be any credible enemy from the outside that could threaten that social revolution—we wouldn't be attacked by Mexico or Cuba, let's say. An American revolution would not require, I think, defense against aggression. On the other hand, if a libertarian social revolution were to take place, say, in Western Europe, then I think the problem of defense would be very critical.

*I was going to say, it can't surely be inherent in the anarchist idea that there should be no self-defense, because such anarchist experiments as there have been have, on the record, actually been destroyed from without.*

Ah, but I think that these questions cannot be given a general answer, they have to be answered specifically, relative to specific historical and objective conditions.

*It's just that I found a little difficulty in following your description of the proper democratic control of this kind of organization, because I find it a little hard to see the generals controlling themselves in the manner you would approve of.*

That's why I do want to point out the complexity of the issue. It depends on the country and the society that you're talking about. In the United States one kind of problem arises. If there were a libertarian social revolution in Europe, then I think the problems you raise would be very serious, because there would be a serious problem of defense. That is, I would assume that if libertarian socialism were achieved at some level in Western Europe, there would be a direct military threat both from the Soviet Union and from the United States. And the problem would be how that should be countered. That's the problem that was faced by the Spanish revolution. There was direct military intervention by Fascists, by Communists and by liberal democracies in the background, and the question how one can defend oneself against attack at this level is a very serious one.

However, I think we have to raise the question whether centralized standing armies, with high technology deterrents, are the most effective way to do that. And that's by no means obvious. For example, I don't think that a Western European centralized army would itself deter a Russian or American attack to prevent libertarian socialism—the kind of attack that I would quite frankly expect at some level: maybe not military, at least economic.

*But nor on the other hand would a lot of peasants with pitchforks and spades...*

We're not talking about peasants; we're talking about a highly sophisticated, highly urban industrial society. And it seems to me its best method of defense would be its political appeal to the working class in the countries that were part of the attack. But again, I don't want to be glib; it might need tanks, it might need armies. And if it did, I think we can be fairly sure that that would contribute to the possible failure or at least decline of the revolutionary force—for exactly the reasons that you mentioned. That is, I think it's extremely hard to imagine how an effective centralized army, deploying tanks, planes, strategic weapons and so on, could function. If that's what's required to preserve the revolutionary structures, then I think they may well not be preserved.

*If the basic defense is the political appeal, or the appeal of the political and economic organization, perhaps we could look in a little more detail at that.*

*You wrote, in one of your essays, that "in a decent society, everyone would have the opportunity to find interesting work, and each person would be permitted the fullest possible scope for his talents." And then you went on to ask: "What more would be required in particular, extrinsic reward in the form of wealth and power? Only if we assume that applying one's talents in interesting and socially useful work is not rewarding in itself." I think that that line of reasoning is certainly one of the things that appeals to a lot of people. But it still needs to be explained, I think, why the kind of work which people would find interesting and appealing and fulfilling to do would coincide at all closely with the kind which actually needs to be done, if we're to sustain anything like the standard of living which people demand and are used to.*

Well, there's a certain amount of work that just has to be done if we're to maintain that standard of living. It's an open question how onerous that work has to be. Let's recall that science and technology and intellect have not been devoted to examining that question or to overcoming the onerous and self-destructive character of the necessary work of society, The reason is that it has always been assumed that there is a substantial body of wage-slaves who will do it simply because otherwise they'll starve. However, if human intelligence is turned to the question of how to make the necessary work of society itself meaningful, we don't know what the answer will be. My guess is that a fair amount of it can be made entirely tolerable. It's a mistake to think that even back-breaking physical labor is necessarily onerous. Many people—myself included—do it for relaxation. Well recently, for example, I got it into my head to plant thirty-four trees in a meadow behind the house, on the State Conservation Commission, which means I had to dig thirty-four holes in the sand. You know, for me, and what I do with my time mostly, that's pretty hard work, but I have to admit I enjoyed it. I wouldn't have enjoyed it if I'd had work norms, if I'd had an overseer, and if I'd been ordered to do it at a certain moment, and so on. On the other hand, if it's a task taken on just out of interest, fine, that can be done. And that's without any technology, without any thought given to how to design the work, and so on.

*I put it to you that there may be a danger that this view of things is a rather romantic delusion, entertained only by a small elite of people who happen, like professors, perhaps journalists and so on, to be in the very privileged situation of being paid to do what anyway they like to do.*

That's why I began with a big 'If.' I said we first have to ask to what extent the necessary work of society—namely, that work which is required to maintain the standard of living that we want—needs to be onerous and undesirable. I think the answer is, much less than it is today; but let's assume there is some extent to which it remains onerous. Well, in that case, the answer's quite simple: that work has to be equally shared among people capable of doing it.

*And everyone spends a certain number of months a year working on an automobile production line and a certain number of months collecting the garbage and...*

If it turns out that these are really tasks which people will find no self-fulfillment in. Incidentally I don't quite believe that. As I watch people work, craftsmen, let's say, automobile mechanics for example, I think one often finds a good deal of pride in work. I think that that kind of pride in work well done, in complicated work well done, because it takes thought and intelligence to do it, especially when one is also involved in management of the enterprise, determination of how the work will be organized, what it is for, what the purposes of the work are, what'll happen to it and so on—I think all of this can be satisfying and rewarding activity which in fact requires skills, the kind of skills people will enjoy exercising. However, I'm thinking hypothetically now. Suppose it turns out that there is some residue of work which really no one wants to do, whatever that may be—okay, then I say that the residue of work must be equally shared, and beyond that people will be free to exercise their talents as they see fit.

*I put it to you, Professor, that if that residue were very large, as some people would say it was, if it accounted for the work involved in producing ninety per cent of what we all want to consume—then the organization of sharing this, on the basis that everybody did a little bit of all the nasty jobs, would become wildly inefficient. Because after all, you have to be trained and equipped to do even the nasty jobs, and the efficiency of the whole economy would suffer and therefore the standard of living which it sustained would be reduced.*

Well, for one thing, this is really quite hypothetical, because I don't believe that the figures are anything like that. As I say, it seems to me that if human intelligence were devoted to asking how technology can be designed to fit the needs of the human producer, instead of conversely—that is, now we ask how the human being with his special properties can be fitted into a technological system designed for other ends, namely production for profit—my feeling is that if that were done, we would find that the really unwanted work is far smaller than you suggest. But whatever it is, notice that we have two alternatives. One alternative is to have it equally shared, the other is to design social institutions so that some group of people will be simply compelled to do the work, on pain of starvation. Those are the two alternatives.

*Not compelled to do it, but they might agree to do it voluntarily because they were paid an amount which they felt made it worthwhile.*

Well, but you see I'm assuming that everyone essentially gets equal remuneration. Don't forget that we're not talking about a society now where the people who do the onerous work are paid substantially more than the people who do the work that they do on choice—quite the opposite. The way our society works, the way any class society works, the people who do the unwanted work are the ones who are paid least. That work is done and we sort of put it out of our minds, because it's assumed that there will be a massive class of people who control only one factor of production, namely their labor, and have to sell it, and they'll have to do that work because they have nothing else to do, and they'll be paid very little for it. I accept the correction. Let's imagine three kinds of society: one, the current one, in which the undesired work is given to wage-slaves. Let's imagine a second system in which the undesired work, after the best efforts to make it meaningful, is shared; and let's imagine a third system where the undesired work receives high extra pay, so that individuals voluntarily choose to do it. Well, it seems to me that either of the two latter systems is consistent with —vaguely speaking—anarchist principles. I would argue myself for the second rather than the third, but either of the two is quite remote from any present social organization or any tendency in contemporary social organization.

*Let me put that to you in another way. It seems to me that there is a fundamental choice, however one disguises it, between whether you organize work for the satisfaction it gives to the people who do it, or whether you organize it on the basis of the value of what is produced for the people who are going to use or consume what is produced. And that a society which is organized on the basis of giving everybody the maximum opportunity to fulfill their hobbies, which is essentially the work for work's sake view, finds its logical culmination in a monastery, where the kind of work which is done, namely prayer, is work, for the self-enrichment of the worker and where nothing is produced which is of any use to anybody and you live either at a low standard of living, or you actually starve.*

Well, there are some factual assumptions here, and I disagree with you about the factual assumptions. My feeling is that part of what makes work meaningful is that it does have use, that its products do have use. The work of the craftsman is in part meaningful to that craftsman because of the intelligence and skill that he puts into it, but also in part because the work is useful, and I might say the same is true of scientists. I mean, the fact that the kind of work you do may lead to something else—that's what it means in science, you know—may contribute to something else, that's very important, quite apart from the elegance and beauty of what you may achieve. And I think that covers every field of human endeavor. Furthermore, I think that if we look at a good part of human history, we'll find that people to a substantial extent did get some degree of satisfaction—often a lot of satisfaction—from the productive and creative work that they were doing. And I think that the chances for that are enormously enhanced by industrialization. Why? Precisely because much of the most meaningless drudgery can be taken over by machines, which means that the scope for really creative human work is substantially enlarged.

Now, you speak of work freely undertaken as a hobby. But I don't believe that. I think work freely undertaken can be useful, meaningful work done well. Also you pose a dilemma which many people pose, between desire for satisfaction in work and a desire to create things of value to the community. But it's not so obvious that there is any dilemma, any contradiction. So it's by no means clear —in fact I think it's false—that contributing to the enhancement of pleasure and satisfaction in work is inversely proportional to contributing to the value of the output.

*Not inversely proportional, but it might be unrelated. I mean, take some very simple thing, like selling ice-creams on the beach on a public holiday. Its a service to society; undoubtedly people want ice-creams, they feel hot. On the other hand, it's hard to see in what sense there is either a craftsman's joy or a great sense of social virtue or nobility, in performing that task. Why would anyone preform that task if they were not rewarded for it?*

I must say I've seen some very cheery-looking ice-cream vendors…

*Sure, they're making a lot of money.*

…who happen to like the idea that they're giving children ice-creams, which seems to me a perfectly reasonable way to spend one's time, as compared with thousands of other occupations that I can imagine.

Recall that a person has an occupation, and it seems to me that most of the occupations that exist—especially the ones that involve what are called services, that is, relations to human beings—have an intrinsic satisfaction and rewards associated with them, namely in the dealings with the human beings that are involved. That's true of teaching, and it's true of ice-cream vending. I agree that ice-cream vending doesn't require the commitment or intelligence that teaching does, and maybe for that reason it will be a less desired occupation. But if so, it will have to be shared.

However, what I'm saying is that our characteristic assumption that pleasure in work, pride in work, is either unrelated to or negatively related to the value of the output is related to a particular stage of social history, namely capitalism, in which human beings are tools of production. It is by no means necessarily true. For example, if you look at the many interviews with workers on assembly lines, for example, that have been done by industrial psychologists, you find that one of the things they complain about over and over again is the fact that their work simply can't be well done, the fact that the assembly line goes through so fast that they can't do their work properly. I just happened to look recently at a study of longevity in some journal of gerontology which tried to trace the factors that you could use to predict longevity—you know, cigarette-smoking and drinking, genetic factors—everything was looked at. It turned out in fact that the highest predictor, the most successful predictor, was job satisfaction.

*People who have nice jobs live longer.*

People who are *satisfied* with their jobs. And I think that makes a good deal of sense, you know, because that's where you spend your life, that's where your creative activities are. Now what leads to job satisfaction? Well, I think many things lead to it, and the knowledge that you are doing something useful for the community is an important part of it. Many people who are satisfied with their work are people who feel that what they're doing is important to do. They can be teachers, they can be doctors; they can be scientists, they can be craftsmen, they can be farmers. I mean, I think the feeling that what one is doing is important, is worth doing, contributes to those with whom one has social bonds, is a very significant factor in one's personal satisfaction.

And over and above that there is the pride and the self-fulfillment that comes from a job well done—from simply taking your skills and putting them to use. Now I don't see why that should in any way harm, in fact I should think it would enhance, the value of what's produced.

But let's imagine still that at some level it does harm. Well okay, at that point the society, the community, has to decide how to make compromises. Each individual is both a producer and a consumer, after all, and that means that each individual has to join in those socially determined compromises—if in fact there are compromises. And again I feel the nature of the compromise is much exaggerated because of the distorting prism of the really coercive and personally destructive system in which we live.

*All right, you say the community has to make decisions about compromises, and of course Communist theory provides for this in its whole thinking about national planning, decisions about investment, direction of investment, and so forth. In an anarchist society it would seem that you're not willing to provide for that amount of governmental superstructure that would be necessary to make the plans, make the investment decisions, to decide whether you give priority to what people want to consume, or whether you give priority to the work people want to do.*

I don't agree with that. It seems to me that anarchist, or, for that matter, left-Marxist structures, based on systems of workers' councils and federations, provide exactly the set of levels of decision-making at which decisions can be made about a national plan. Similarly, State socialist societies also provide a level of decision making—let's say the nation—in which national plans can be produced. There's no difference in that respect. The difference has to do with participation in those decisions and control over those decisions. In the view of anarchists and left-Marxists—like the workers' councils or the Council Communists, who were left-Marxists—those decisions are made by the informed working class through their assemblies and their direct representatives, who live among them and work among them. In the State socialist systems, the national plan is made by a national bureaucracy, which accumulates to itself all relevant information, makes decisions, offers them to the public, and occasionally every few years comes before the public and says, 'You can pick me or you can pick him, but we're all part of this remote bureaucracy.' These are the poles, these are the polar opposites within the socialist tradition.

*So in fact there's a very considerable role for the State and possibly, even for civil servants, for bureaucracy, but it's the control over it that is different.*

Well, you see, I don't really believe that we need a separate bureaucracy to carry out governmental decisions.

*You need various forms of expertise.*

Oh yes, but let's take expertise with regard to economic planning, because certainly in any complex industrial society there should be a group of technicians whose task is to produce plans, and to lay out the consequences of decisions, to explain to the people who have to make the decisions that if you decide this, you're going to likely get this consequence, because that's what your programming model shows, and so on. But the point is that those planning systems are themselves industries, and they will have their workers' councils and they will be part of the whole council system, and the distinction is that these planning systems do not make decisions. They produce plans in exactly the same way that automakers produce autos. The plans are then available for the workers' councils and council assemblies, in the same way that autos are available to ride in. Now of course what this does require is an informed and educated working class. But that's precisely what we are capable of achieving in advanced industrial societies.

*How far does the success of libertarian socialism or anarchism really depend on a fundamental change in the nature of man, both in his motivation, his altruism, and also in his knowledge and sophistication?*

I think it not only depends on it but in fact the whole purpose of libertarian socialism is that it will contribute to it. It will contribute to a spiritual transformation—precisely that kind of great transformation in the way humans conceive of themselves and their ability to act, to decide, to create, to produce, to enquire—precisely that spiritual transformation that social thinkers from the left-Marxist traditions, from Luxembourg say, through anarcho-syndicalists, have always emphasized. So on the one hand it requires that spiritual transformation. On the other hand, its purpose is to create institutions which will contribute to that transformation in the nature of work, the nature of creative activity, simply in social bonds among people, and through this interaction of creating institutions which permit new aspects of human nature to flourish. And then the building of still further libertarian institutions to which these liberated human beings can contribute: this is the evolution of socialism as I understand it.

*And finally, Professor Chomsky, what do you think of the chances of societies along these lines coming into being in the major industrial countries in the West in the next quarter of a century or so?*

I don't think I'm wise enough, or informed enough, to make predictions and I think predictions about such poorly-understood matters probably generally reflect personality more than judgment. But I think this much at least we can say: there are obvious tendencies in industrial capitalism towards concentration of power in narrow economic empires and in what is increasingly becoming a totalitarian state. These are tendencies that have been going on for a long time, and I don't see anything stopping them really. I think those tendencies will continue; they're part of the stagnation and decline of capitalist institutions.

Now it seems to me that the development towards state totalitarianism and towards economic concentration—and of course they are linked—will continually lead to revulsion, to efforts of personal liberation and to organizational efforts at social liberation. And that'll take all sorts of forms. Throughout all Europe, in one form or another, there is a call for what is sometimes called worker participation or co-determination, or even sometimes worker control. Now most of these efforts are minimal. I think that they're misleading, in fact may even undermine efforts for the working class to liberate itself. But in part they're responsive to a strong intuition and understanding that coercion and oppression, whether by private economic power or by the State bureaucracy, is by no means a necessary feature of human life. And the more those concentrations of power and authority continue, the more we will see revulsion against them and efforts to organize and overthrow them. Sooner or later they'll succeed, I hope.

## Editor's Notes to Chapter 22

Written on May 15, 1977, with the title "Industrial Democracy," it was published in *Seven Days*, 20 June 1977: pp. 19–20, under the title "Worker's councils: not just a slice of the pie, but a hand in making it," as part of the series "Demystified Zone" (see Editor's Notes to Selection 12).

See **FRS**, ch. 8, especially n. 17 and 28, and "Equality," cited above (Introduction, n. 30). See now *Self-governing Socialism: A Reader,* ed. by Branko Horvat, Mihailo Markovic & Rudi Supek, White Plains: International Arts and Sciences Press, 1975 (two volumes).

# 22. Industrial Self-Management

In Holland under Nazi occupation, the Dutch Marxist Anton Pannekoek produced his classic study *Workers' Councils,* a distillation of many years of experience and thought in the workers movement. The workers, he wrote, "must be masters of the factories, masters of their own labor, to conduct it at their own will." Such "common ownership must not be confounded with public ownership," a system in which workers are commanded by state officials who direct production. Rather, they must themselves take over complete control of the means of production and all planning and distribution. Capitalism is a "transitional form," combining modern industrial technique with the archaic social principle of private ownership. Advanced industrial technology combined with common ownership "means a free collaborating humanity," the proper goal of the workers movement. He also wrote that "the idea of their common ownership of the means of production is beginning to take hold of the minds of the workers."

Pannekoek's observation with regard to the industrial societies has proven accurate, apart from the United States, though Russian tyranny has repeatedly crushed these aspirations in Eastern Europe. Of course, nothing remotely approaching true industrial democracy exists, but the ideas are alive and the struggle to achieve them continues, a matter of no small concern to international capitalism. Under the heading "To Swedish Labor, Equality is Being Boss," Leonard Silk wrote in the *NY Times* (Apr. 7, 1976) of the fears of Swedish capitalists who "are trying to moderate the drive for equality and control" by maintaining the "strong management prerogatives" of the mixed economy, which is "still regarded with repugnance by many American employers." He warns that American multinationals in Europe "may also come to regard 'co-determination' as a honeymoon compared to the deeper worker control that may lie ahead."

Similarly, the London *Economist* (Feb. 19, 1977), discussing union initiatives in Holland (which are "nothing like the fierce projects pushed by the Danish and Swedish unions"), notes that "the unions are not just after (and have got) a bigger slice of a growing cake, but a hand in choosing the recipe, mixing and baking it as well." Correspondingly, multinational corporations "are casting a sceptical eye on any proposal to invest in Holland." In fact, capital flight is a major device to preserve the old order under attack.

One need not take too seriously the nightmares of those who own and direct the international capitalist economy and its local branches. The extension of democracy to the workplace has so far been limited and the forces aligned in support of the traditional autocratic structures of the "transitional" order as well as those backing state management remain powerful. Still, the pressures towards industrial democracy cannot be discounted.

Great Britain is an interesting case in point. This past January, a government commission headed by Oxford historian Alan Bullock submitted a report proposing worker participation in management of larger firms. The report states that "the coming of the age of democracy in our society is a process that inevitably affects the whole of people's lives, it cannot be excluded from the workplace." Bitterly opposed by industry members on the commission, the report suggests a "2x + y" formula for managerial control: an equal number of worker and shareholder representatives (2x) and a balancing middle group (y). Backing the proposal, Jack Jones of the Transport Workers Union writes that "it took nearly a hundred years to extend the suffrage to every adult man and woman. We cannot afford the luxury of a 100-year wait for the industrial franchise."

Even if the Bullock recommendations were to be implemented, which seems most unlikely, they would fall far short of an "industrial franchise" or the common ownership advocated by libertarian socialism, but would rather constitute a form of modest participation in management. Nevertheless, these proposals go beyond the achievements of continental European labor. Hence the impassioned opposition of representatives of the highly centralized British industrial corporations. The director general of the Confederation of British Industry warned that "unless this report is challenged and discredited the corporate face of Britain will be changed irrevocably..." One hundred subsidiaries of multinational corporations, primarily American, would also be affected. Even if the proposals are shelved, they might be applied in some manner in the nationalized industries, and they have already stirred an intense debate in England and aroused much concern in business circles elsewhere.

The workers' revolution, Pannekoek wrote, "is not a single event of limited duration" but rather "a process of organization, of self-education, in which the workers gradually... develop the force to... build up their new system of collective production." The standard comparison to the extension of suffrage in the 19th century is not without merit. Pressures from the workforce for extending participation, while still limited, may lead to a realization that there is no justification, either technical or moral, for the hierarchic and authoritarian systems of capitalism or its statist varieties.

Bernard Nossiter observes in the *Washington Post* (Jan. 26, 1977) that although issues raised by the Bullock Report seem remote in the United States, where "social legislation... typically lags behind Europe," nevertheless they "someday could reach the United States as well." In fact, the United States has not been entirely insulated from the efforts to extend democratic principles to the central institutions of industrial society. To cite one example, *Business Week* (Mar. 28, 1977) carries a report on a programme of worker participation in a

General Foods Corporation plant, quoting the executive in charge who says that "from the standpoint of humanistic working life and economic results you can consider it a success." Problems remain, however, chief among them "that some management and staff personnel saw their own positions threatened because the workers performed almost too well" in "manag(ing) their own affairs. "

Since early stages of the industrial revolution, this has been the constant objection to democratic procedures. Economically, they have been proven successful, but as a British journal complained a century ago, "they did not leave a clear place for the masters." What is more, experience with workers control may convince those who do the world's work that they need not march to the beat of a drum but can indeed take direct control over the system of production, thus giving real meaning to the concept of democracy.

The left has often been wary about proposals such as the Bullock Report, and with justice. As critics have warned, they may "provide a democratic face for capitalist hierarchy" (Neil Kinnock) and "create a frustrating system which could cast discredit on the very idea of industrial democracy" (Ken Coates and Tony Topham).

The Commission chairman himself speaks of a new relationship between unions and industry "on the basis of which the private sector can continue and be strengthened," and there is no doubt that concern over wages and productivity has been a major factor motivating many supporters of such programs, who hope that they will substitute for other demands. John Dunlop, Harvard Economist and former Labor Secretary, has discussed the importance of European experience with "workers councils" in the context of the concern for "ways of eliciting improved effort and performance," "new ways of training and supervising a work force," and "new procedures to develop discipline and to settle complaints or dissipate protest." Not exactly what Pannekoek, for example, had in mind. No doubt this represents the attitude that will be adopted by defenders of the prevailing autocratic system of industrial control as they seek to divert or control democratic forces.

But the left should nevertheless welcome these developments, while criticizing their limitations and emphasizing the immense gap between participation and true common ownership and management. The experience gained from limited participation, the understanding of one's own powers and of the absurdity of the claims of authority can be a liberating experience that will ultimately bring forth a movement to reshape industrial society, eliminating capitalist domination and state autocracy.

# Part III:

## A Pressing Agenda

## Editor's Notes to Chapter 23

"The Danger of Nuclear War and What We Can Do About It" (editor's title) is the author's commencement address at Fordham University in New York City on May 30, 1982, a week before the Israeli invasion of Lebanon, seen as "imminent." Part of the address (from "If we hope to avert nuclear war…" to the end) appeared as a lead article ("Mirror of Public Opinion") on the editorial page of the *Post-Dispatch* [St. Louis, MO]on June 27, 1982, under the title "The Cold War is a Pretext: Superpowers Use it to Maintain Dominion Over the Third World." An earlier treatment of the topic is his November 11, 1982 talk at Boston University, "Strategic Weapons, the Cold War and the Third World," a greatly expanded version of which is included in *Exterminism and the Cold War*, ed. by *The New Left Review*, London: Verso, 1982, pp. 223–236. See also the following Selection.

Shortly after the Fordham address, Chomsky wrote a major paper, "What Directions for the Disarmament Movement?," completed on July 15, 1982, which was later included in *Beyond Survival: New Directions for the Disarmament Movement*, ed. by Michael Albert and Dave Dellinger, Boston: South End Press, 1983, pp. 249–309. A shortened version had appeared in the *Michigan Quarterly Review* 21 (1982): pp. 601–603. "The Present Danger," *Worldview* 26.2 (1983), pp. 8–11, is essentially the beginning of this shortened version minus the paragraph on the Israeli invasion of Lebanon and two other minor omissions, but with the following coda:

"What, then, are the proper directions for the disarmament movement? It should, certainly, be concerned with controlling and reversing the strategic arms race. It should also be concerned with the proliferation of nuclear weapons; with the vast arms sales of the major (and some minor) powers, which are placing enormous means of destruction in the hands of states that will use them for internal repression or aggression; and with the fact that so-called 'conventional arms' are reaching a point of destructiveness not far below that of nuclear weapons, so that 'small' or 'limited' wars will be extremely costly in human lives.

But there are other issues that cannot be dissociated from this complex and that are in many respects even more crucial: the domestic factors that drive the arms race, the dynamics of the Cold War and its impact on many millions of people, the extraordinary dangers (and horrors) of superpower intervention, the policies that contribute to maintaining or inflaming conflicts and tensions throughout the world, which, apart from the cost to the victims, are the most likely cause of a potential final holocaust. The drift toward this final solution has a seemingly inexorable quality. The factors and powers involved appear to be out of control, beyond our ability to influence or constrain them. We can only hope that this perception is false."

The differences between this viewpoint and the viewpoint associated with E.P. Thompson are even more clear in Chomsky's answer to a question posed to him by David Finkel, the editor of *Changes*, in an interview published in the

July–Aug. issue, pp. 5–6 & 28, under the title "Priorities for the Peace Movement":

"We have differences in emphasis, probably because we have different audiences in mind. From the European point of view, the issues of intervention, while important, are not central in quite the same way they are for Americans. The exception to this would be the French interventions in Africa, which are continuing under the French Socialist Party government, but the French are mostly outside of the peace movement. (I don't think there is a French peace movement. They protest what the United States does, but you can't find any protest in the French press when South Africa attacks Namibia with French planes, or over France selling arms to Indonesia.)But leaving this aside, in terms of the European movement, E.P. Thompson is talking to people who on the whole are less directly involved in intervention. That movement is part of a longterm trend to separate Europe from the superpower Cold War system of confrontation, and this accounts for Thompson's emphasis."

The mini-interview added as a Postscript, due to Robert O'Brian, appeared in *Rockbill* 2.9 (1983): p. 33, "a magazine read by two million people (mostly young adults)."

# 23. The Danger Of Nuclear War And What We Can Do About It

I would like to direct these remarks to a problem that should be of prime concern to any reasonable person, namely, the growing danger of nuclear war and the question of what we can do about it. The growth of concern over this matter in recent months has been dramatic and impressive. It is also eminently realistic. Any sane and rational person who considers the scale and character of contemporary military power, the current vast expansion of the military arsenals of the superpowers, and the proliferation of armaments throughout the world, would surely have to conclude that the likelihood of a global catastrophe is not small.

One might argue, in fact, that it is a miracle that the catastrophe has not yet occurred. From November 1946 to October 1973 there were 19 incidents in which U.S. strategic nuclear forces were involved. (We do not have the record since, nor the record for the USSR and other powers.) That means, to put it plainly, that every U.S. President has regarded the use of nuclear weapons as a live policy option. The examples are instructive. Here are a few.

In February 1947, bombers of the Strategic Air Command armed with nuclear weapons were sent to Uruguay in a show of force at the time of the inauguration of the President of Uruguay. In May 1954, nuclear-armed SAC bombers were flown to Nicaragua as part of the background for the successful CIA group in Guatemala. In 1958, U.S. strategic nuclear forces were involved in the U.S. invasion of Lebanon, and the use of nuclear weapons was apparently threatened if the Lebanese army attempted to resist. In 1962, the Kennedy administration estimated the probability of nuclear war at 1/3 to 1/2 at the peak of the Cuban missile crisis, but was unwilling to accept a settlement that involved complete withdrawal of Russian missiles from Cuba, with simultaneous withdrawal of U.S. missiles from Turkey—the latter, obsolescent missiles for which a withdrawal order had already been issued since they were being replaced by Polaris submarines.

We can learn a great deal by studying these 19 cases in detail, and they are not the only ones when the use of nuclear weapons was threatened or seriously considered. Other powers have also issued nuclear threats. Those who speak of a likelihood of nuclear war are hardly alarmist. To reduce this likelihood is imperative. The question is: What direction should these efforts take? Where should energies be focused, if they are to be maximally effective in averting this catastrophe?

The primary question that should concern us is this: How is nuclear war likely to break out? We can realistically assume that any military conflict between the superpowers will quickly become a nuclear conflict, and an unlimited one. The central question, then, is this: What are the likely sources of superpower conflict?

It is unlikely that such a conflict will break out in Europe. It is hard to imagine that either superpower will launch a military attack there. But war may break out elsewhere, engaging the superpowers. Possible examples are all too numerous. Thus, Secretary of the Navy John Lehman observed recently that a U.S. naval blockade of Cuba and Nicaragua might trigger a global conflict. Current U.S. war games in the Caribbean are only one indication that such an eventuality is not remote. The Chinese invasion of Vietnam in 1979 might well have evoked a Russian response, leading to a U.S. reaction and a nuclear conflict. An Israeli invasion of Southern Lebanon is imminent. It is likely to involve Syria, and to evoke Soviet actions in support of Syria with a U.S. response that may trigger a nuclear war. NATO General Thomas Kelley recently stated that "If we have a world war III, it will probably start here in the Mediterranean when a local conflict burns out of control"—a realistic forecast. There are many similar examples.

The conclusion is that if we hope to avert nuclear war, the size and character of nuclear arsenals is a secondary consideration. Even if nuclear arsenals were vastly reduced, a nuclear interchange would be a devastating catastrophe. Most important is an effort to lessen tensions and conflicts at the points where war is likely to erupt. If we are willing to face this issue, we will find that there is a great deal that we can do, since not infrequently U.S. policy has been instrumental in maintaining and inflaming tensions and conflicts. In this connection, we should note that the distinction between nuclear and "conventional" armaments is too crude. In the latter category, there is an important difference between anti-tank weapons designed for deterrence in Europe and Attack Carriers or the Rapid Deployment Force. Intervention capacity constitutes the bulk of the military budget, and it may increase the danger of nuclear war even more than a new generation of nuclear monsters. More crucial still are policies that contribute to tensions that may lead to war, engaging the superpowers. This is a category of questions that deserves far more attention than it has received from those who hope to forestall a nuclear war.

When I say that the size and character of nuclear arsenals is secondary, I do not mean to suggest that it is unimportant. Quite the contrary. President Reagan's sabre-rattling has evoked mass popular movements of protest, which in turn have impelled his administration to at least a rhetorical commitment to curbing the arms race. In his latest proposal (Eureka, Illinois, May 9), the crucial phrase was that "many years of concentrated effort" will be required to implement his proposals—perhaps 10–15 years, to judge by comment from various spokesmen. During these "many years," weapons development will continue, including the MX missile program, which, as Air Force Chief of Staff Lewis Allen has stated, will have a first-strike capability, and Pershing II missiles, which will have a five-minute flight time from German bases to Moscow. A recent review in *Science* (May 7) points out that these developments may lead the USSR to adopt a "Launch on warning strategy," which means that tensions short of actual military conflict may lead to nuclear war. It is the development of such new advanced systems as these that Archbishop Raymond Hunthausen of Seattle had in mind when he warned of the possibility of a U.S. "nuclear war of aggression," comparing this weapons development program to Auschwitz because of "the enormous sinful complicity that is necessary for the eventual incineration of millions of our brother and sister human beings." Proposals for a nuclear freeze and for implementation of the SALT II agreements are very significant, though nevertheless secondary, for the reasons I have mentioned.

If we hope to do something serious to avert nuclear catastrophe, we must be willing to face certain additional questions. We must inquire into the domestic factors that drive the Pentagon system. Repeatedly, U.S. planners have turned to military Keynesianism as a device of economic management. The Pentagon system has come to serve as the state sector of the economy, offering a guaranteed market for high technology production, subsidizing industrial research, and in general, serving as a system of industrial policy planning. In fact, every advanced industrial economy has a substantial component of state coordination and planning, and as a number of commentators have observed, the Pentagon system in the U.S. is rather similar in its functioning to such agencies as the Ministry of International Trade and Industry (MITI) in Japan. There is, however, a crucial difference, since MITI is oriented towards commercial sales whereas our system of state planning is oriented towards military production, in effect, the production of high technology waste. It is hardly surprising that Japanese industry outdoes ours in world trade. This problem did not arise when the U.S. was in a world-dominant position some years ago, but it most definitely does arise today. There will probably be a major conflict within business circles over this matter in coming years, since the U.S. economy cannot remain competitive apart from arms sales if it is devoted to waste production while our rivals engage resources for commercial ends. This is a complex story, but again, one that must be faced if we hope to end the arms race and avert the nuclear catastrophe that may result from it.

This leads finally to what may well be the main question, namely, the dynamics of the Cold War. Why do the superpowers amass these arsenals of destruction? Each has an answer, and it is the same answer. Each superpower describes its system as "defensive." Each is concerned only to deter its violent opponent, bent on global conquest. There is an element of truth in each of these parallel stories, but they are largely myth. If we hope to do more than protest impending destruction, if we hope to control and reverse the race towards mutual annihilation, if we hope to protect the actual as well as the potential victims, then we must come to understand the reality that lies behind the elaborate mythology of the Cold War. This is not very difficult, if we attend to the facts.

The basic fact is that the Cold War system is highly functional for the super-powers, which is why it persists, despite the likelihood of mutual annihilation if the system breaks down by accident, as sooner or later it will. The Cold War provides a framework within which each of the superpowers can use force and violence to control its own domains, appealing to the threat of the superpower enemy to mobilize its own population and recalcitrant allies, as even a totalitarian state must do.

In the case of Guatemala, for example, it would have been difficult—In fact, ludicrous—for the U.S. government to claim that the United States was threatened with destruction when a moderate reformist government, with policies resembling those of the New Deal, attempted to take over unused lands of the United Fruit Company to turn them over to miserable peasants. Matters appeared different when the government claimed that Guatemala was merely the outpost of international Communism, an advance base for a superpower aiming at global conquest, armed with nuclear weapons, with an ample record of brutality and atrocities. With the cooperation of the media, this ridiculous claim was advanced, and believed, justifying U.S. intervention to save the Free World from destruction by an enemy of Hitlerian proportions—and, incidentally, turning Guatemala into a literal hell on earth, as it remains today, with periodic infusions of U.S. military assistance.

When the USSR invaded Hungary two years later, it resorted to essentially the same rhetoric. This too was a "defensive" intervention, undertaken to ward off the superpower enemy. The same record has been replayed, on both sides, for 35 years. The crucial point is that the propaganda works, or at least it has worked until very recently. To a significant extent, the Cold War has been a system of tacit cooperation, a massive propaganda system that has effectively disguised the actions taken by the superpowers to maintain control over their own domains. For us, the Cold War has in effect been a war against much of the Third World, and for our tacit partners in global repression, a war against their own subject populations and in some cases Third World peoples as well.

Strategic nuclear weapons also play their role in this system, a fact that is easy enough to discern from the unfolding events and sometimes even from the pronouncements of planners. Consider, for example, the final presentation to Congress by President Carter's Secretary of Defense, Harold Brown, in which he pointed out that given our strategic nuclear capabilities, "our other forces become meaningful instruments of military and political power." Very true, and the real point. For each of the superpowers, strategic nuclear weapons make it possible to conduct subversion, intervention, and sometimes outright aggression, without fear of deterrence. As for "limited yield," tactical nuclear weapons, they are primarily designed for use against an enemy too weak to strike back. General Nathan Twining, Chairman of the Joint Chiefs of Staff during the Eisenhower Administration, once explained that "These weapons, if employed once or twice on the right targets, at the right time, would... stop future subversion and limited wars before they start." They can be used even for a preemptive strike against "future subversion," as in the Congo, Cuba and Vietnam (his examples), a device that might be cheaper for us than counterinsurgency.

The Cold War has carried with it enormous costs, primarily, of course, for the victims, but also for the superpowers themselves. They have been forced, in the first place, to bear the material costs of a militarized society, which are not small. And beyond that, there are moral costs, which should not be lightly dismissed. It is not very nice to think about the reality of Guatemala, where tens of thousands of children die of starvation every year while agricultural land is converted to export crops, most of the population labors under conditions of semi-slavery, and peasants, teachers, union leaders, priests, centrist political figures and others are gunned down by death squads directed from the Presidential Palace—conditions that result directly from repeated U.S. intervention. It is nicer to believe that we are defending someone from the Russians. The same is true throughout much of the world. The Cold War has enabled us to maintain this pretense, as it has for our partner in global repression. It has enabled us to avert our eyes from many terrible scenes throughout the world, and also to contribute to perpetuating them.

This is the real meaning of the Cold War, and we should not forget it when we turn our attention to the fact that this system of oppression and massacre may, in the end, engulf us as well.

## POSTSCRIPT: What can young people do?

*Dr. Chomsky, you have taken quite an interest in politics lately. Could you tell us what a linguist's interest is in effecting political change?*

My interest in politics, in the broad sense, is not really recent, It goes back to childhood, though I was never what might be called a political activist until about 20 years ago, with the rise of the civil rights and antiwar movements. My interest in political change is not as a linguist, but as a person. As a linguist, I'm interested in discovering the nature of human language and, more generally, the nature of the human capacity for thought and self-expression. As a person, I would like to see a world fit for human beings. This one, in many ways, is not, and there is a good deal that we can do about the matter.

*What initiatives can young people take for the service of humankind?*

The possibilities are rich, and are, in fact, bounded only by one's willingness to commit time, energy and thought. The world is facing a serious danger of nuclear war—an event that will be terminal for our civilization. U.S. government policies are significantly increasing the threat of war. New weapons systems now being introduced pose a serious threat to Americans, and to everyone else, because they lower the threshold for war, and may even compel the Russians to adopt a computerized response strategy (so-called "launch-on-warning" strategy) that makes war virtually inevitable. Furthermore, U.S. policies in such regions as the Middle East and Central America are increasing tension and conflict and raising the probability that the superpowers will come into conflict, with a strong likelihood of nuclear war, perhaps by accident or misperception. Quite apart from this there is vast suffering in the world to which our policies in the past and present have contributed. For example, in Latin America, in large part under our influence, there is a plague of state terror and torture, vast numbers of children die of malnutrition and millions of others starve while croplands are devoted to exports, and millions more live under conditions of semi-slavery. To a considerable extent these conditions result from U.S. government policies that we have supported or at least tolerated. In our society, which has unparalleled resources and advantages, there is a scandalous failure to meet elementary human needs. Beyond that, we tolerate modes of hierarchy and oppression, based on race, sex, the wage system that compels people to rent themselves to the owners of the economy to survive, and other conditions that should be intolerable to a free and humane person.

What can young people do about this? Everything. None of these things result from immutable physical laws. They are all results of human decisions in human institutions. The decisions and the institutions can be modified, perhaps extensively, if enough people commit themselves with courage and honesty to the search for justice and freedom.

## Editor's Notes to Chapter 24

This article, which complements the preceding Selection, appeared in the London *Guardian* on July 12, 1982. It was excerpted from "The U.S. and Israel: A Case Study for the Disarmament Movement," completed on June 20, 1982 and published in *Our Generation* 15.3 (Fall 1982): pp. 37–47, and also in END papers, special, Spokesman Pamphlet 81, 1982, pp. 3–17. A modified version had appeared earlier in MERIP Reports 108–109 (Sept.–Oct. 1982): pp. 36–41 & 54, under the title "Israel's Invasion and the Disarmament Movement."

Chomsky's first article on the invasion of Lebanon, "Thoughts on the Israeli Invasion of Lebanon, " was written on June 14, 1982 and published in *Middle East International* 179 (1982): pp. 9, 10 & 16, under the title "Reflections on Israel in Lebanon." It also appeared, without footnotes, as an editorial ("Israel's Onslaught") in *Inquiry* Aug. 1982: pp. 3–4, which was reprinted in the RESIST Newsletter 150 (Aug.–Sept. 1982): pp. 1–2 & 7. Two other articles, "Lebanon: September 1982" (written on Sept. 8) and "U.S. Interests and the Arab-Israel Conflict" (written on Oct. 3), appeared together in *Colombia Report* (*U.S.-Latin America & International Analysis*), 12.4, n. 3 (Nov. 1982): pp. 2–7. See now **FT** (see editor's note to Selection 7).

On the issue of Israel's role in Central America, see Israel Shahak's *Israel's Global Role: Weapons for Repression* Belmont: Association of Arab-American University Graduates, 1982, with an introduction by Chomsky (written in August 1981). See also Chomsky's "Human Rights and Central America" (excerpted from a talk he gave at a conference on U.S.-Israeli involvement in Central America held in Chicago on the first anniversary of the invasion of Lebanon) and Arnaldo Ramos' "Israel and Central America" (presented at the same conference) in *Palestine Human Rights Newsletter* 3.5 (Aug. 1983).

# 24. Priorities For Averting The Holocaust

On June 12, 1982, over half a million people demonstrated in New York, calling for a halt to the nuclear arms race. The demonstration was unusual in its size, and even more so in the favorable media coverage it received. At about the same time, in scattered cities throughout the country, a few thousand people demonstrated in protest over the Israeli invasion of Lebanon and the barely-disguised U.S. Government support for it. A strong case can be made that the latter actions constituted the more direct and appropriate response to the very real danger of nuclear war, though this was not their specific intent. It is not difficult to see why.

We may begin with the highly plausible assumption that any military conflict between the superpowers will quickly escalate to nuclear conflict. Furthermore, even if the nuclear arsenals were much reduced, a nuclear strike would be devastating in its consequences. It follows that the primary concern of those who hope to reduce the likelihood of a nuclear holocaust will be to settle, or at least limit, the conflicts and tensions that threaten to involve the superpowers.

The likelihood of such conflict in Europe today is very slight. In many parts of the Third World, however, regional conflicts or outside intervention may easily lead to engagement of the superpowers. Possible examples are all too numerous, but none are so threatening as those of the Middle East.

The Israeli invasion of Lebanon provides an illuminating case study. It falls only a few steps short of engaging the superpowers, with the highly probable consequence of nuclear war. The Israeli attack might well have proceeded to Syria proper, leading to some Russian moves in support of their ally. Even the hint of such moves would bring in the United States in force—recall the strategic nuclear alert in October 1973 when it appeared that the USSR might undertake some action to enforce the ceasefire in Egypt. The rest can be left to the imagination.

This is not to say that one should not be concerned with the superpower arms race or the proliferation of nuclear weapons. In fact, the relation between the level of nuclear arms and the likelihood of their use is not an entirely simple one; recall that on the one occasion when nuclear weapons were used, there were two in existence—and if two more had been in existence, in enemy hands, the U.S. would have hesitated to bomb Hiroshima and Nagasaki for fear of retaliation. Nevertheless, it is clear enough that existing arsenals pose an enormous hazard, and that the new weapons systems now being planned or deployed will bring the world closer to nuclear war. Efforts to reverse the escalation in the capacity for nuclear destruction are imperative, though secondary.

The broader context of Israeli planning (based on the assumption that U.S. support will always be forthcoming) highlights further the continuing danger of nuclear war. Since 1973, Israel and the United States have been committed to removing Egypt from the Arab-Israeli conflict; only after the October war were they willing to accept President Sadat's offer, quite explicit in February 1971, of a full peace treaty that would turn Egypt into an American client state. The shock of the 1973 war and its aftermath led to a reassessment. Sadat's earlier proposals were accepted, though only in part. Kissinger's "shuttle diplomacy" and "interim agreement" were designed to exclude Egypt from the conflict while leaving Israel in a position to control the bulk of the occupied territories in accordance with the Israeli (Labor) Government's "Allon Plan."

At the same time, it was necessary to fend off annoying Arab efforts to settle the conflict peaceably on essentially the terms proposed by Sadat in 1971, but now with a Palestinian state in the West Bank and Gaza Strip. The U.S. was compelled to veto a UN Security Council resolution to this effect in January 1976. (The resolution, which was introduced and backed by the Arab "confrontation states" and supported by the PLO, called for a two-state settlement with recognized borders and guarantees for the security and territorial integrity of both states.)

The Camp David agreements carried the arrangements further, leading finally to Israeli withdrawal from the Sinai after a "national trauma" that appears to have been largely staged for a domestic and American audience. The completion of this withdrawal was one crucial event of spring 1982. A second significant event of this period was the annexation (in effect) of the Golan Heights. A third was the implementation of the Sharon-Milson plan for suppressing any form of independent political expression in the occupied territories. These policies led to the harsh and brutal repression in these areas (including the Golan) that received some limited and inadequate attention in the U.S. press when Arabs were killed outright. The regular daily oppression and humiliation under the "benign occupation" generally passes without notice.

The next step was the invasion of Lebanon. Its primary aims were to destroy the social and political structures of the PLO, while eliminating the possibility of any response as Israel proceeds towards more efficient repression in the occupied territories leading to ultimate annexation; and to establish, at least in the southern part of Lebanon, an Israeli client regime that will sooner or later provide Israel with access to the waters of the Litani river, a long-standing aim of Israeli government policy.

Since early 1982, Israel has been seeking a pretext for the invasion of Lebanon, the obvious next step in the unfolding design. Since none was provided, a pretext was manufactured, the plausible assumption being that any story, however fanciful, would be defensible in the United States given the influence of "supporters of Israel" in the propaganda system and their past successes in constructing an acceptable history. (The United States, of course, is the only country that really counts, in this connection.) The attempt to assassinate Israeli Ambassador Argov led to Israeli bombings with many casualties, though Israel had not the slightest reason to suppose that the PLO was involved in this savage act—and, as at once became clear, it was not.

A PLO rocket attack, in retaliation for the bombing of heavily-populated areas in Lebanon, then served as the long-awaited pretext for the invasion, on the grounds that Israel was acting in "self-defense" and could not tolerate regular shelling of its northern settlements. There had been no PLO shelling of Israel from the July 1981 cease-fire until May 1982 (in response to Israeli bombing), while Israel had carried out thousands of intrusions into Lebanese territory, air space and territorial waters, apart from numerous other provocations.

The timing of the Israeli invasion may have been influenced by the fact that elections were scheduled for August in Lebanon. There might have been some slight hope for an internal resolution of Lebanon's travail. The Israeli invasion is designed to ensure that Israel will be in a position to determine the form of any possible settlement, as would otherwise not have been the case.

Though the final outcome is not yet fully determined, it is likely that Israel will achieve its primary objectives. The next steps are easy to imagine. Israel will continue to move towards annexation of the occupied territories, employing whatever measures will be necessary, in accordance with the assumption of General Sharon that "quiet on the West Bank requires the destruction of the PLO in Lebanon" and the advice of *New Republic* editor Martin Peretz that Israel should administer to the PLO "a lasting military defeat which will clarify to the Palestinians in the West Bank that their struggle for an independent state has suffered a setback of many years."

Wasting no time, Israel dissolved the elected city councils of Dura and Nablus in the West Bank, replacing the city council of Dura by "five Arab moderates" ("moderate" is the technical term for "Arab collaborator" in the American press). An official in the Israeli civil administration told the *NY Times* correspondent that "the moderates were now less vulnerable to intimidation by the Palestinian Liberation Organization because of the success of the Israeli invasion of Lebanon."

Longer-term planning is also fairly predictable. Syria is ruled, with quite extraordinary brutality, by a minority sect. Israel will work to destabilize it, so that Syria and Lebanon will be restored to a system rather like that of the Ottoman Empire, with local dependencies of an ethnic-religious character dominated by Israel, a powerful militarized state serving as an American "strategic asset." Similar plans are being contemplated for Iraq, where Israel's interest lies in an eventual partition into Sunni, Shiite and Kurdish states. This is one motive for Israel's support for Iran in the Iran-Iraq conflict. Another motive is that Israel perceives the possibility of a military coup (perhaps post-Khomeini) that will restore the kinds of Irano-Israeli relations that existed under the Shah.

The long-term objective may be an alliance of Iran (now restored to the West), Turkey and Israel, ruling the region in alliance with the United States—the ultimate source of their power. Some Israeli commentators go further still. In the official ideological journal of the World Zionist Organization, Oded Yinon suggests that "the political goal of Israel in the 1980s on its Western front" is to dismember Egypt, after reconquest of the Sinai, overturning the "mistaken peace agreement" with Sadat—no major problem, he suggests, since Egypt is "a corpse". He outlines with specific detail a plan such as that just reviewed for the restoration of an Ottoman-style arrangement for the region, including also the Arabian peninsula.

(On a still broader scale, this alliance may be extended to include South Africa, which has been the recipient of direct Israeli assistance in its own rather comparable efforts to maintain instability and disorder along its borders. Israel has also increasingly come to serve U.S. interests in Central America. The new military regime in Guatemala alleges that "we succeeded because our soldiers were trained by the Israelis.")

Within Israel itself, opposition to these tendencies exists, but it's increasingly becoming marginalized. David Shipler of the *NY Times* quotes an Israeli sociologist who says: "This country is in two camps—the people who want to talk to the Palestinians and the people who want to hit them. And the people who want to hit them have won." In fact, they had won long ago, despite much illusion fostered in the United States concerning the Labor party.

The Israeli invasion of Lebanon, and the policy context in which it took place, provides only one illustration of how a nuclear war is likely to erupt, a particularly significant one for the United States because of the primary U.S. role in support of Israel's "civilized terrorism" over many years.

There are many other examples. Sometimes, the operative factors are largely or completely out of control; in such cases, we can deplore ominous developments and their human consequences but can do little about them. Sometimes, as in the case discussed here, the U.S. bears a heavy share of the responsibility for existing tensions and conflicts; and correspondingly, there is a great deal that we might do to relieve them. It is well to remember that for much of the human race, concern over a possible nuclear war may seem rather abstract and remote, a luxury granted those who do not have to face such conditions of daily existence as starvation, state terrorism, virtual slavery, military attack and subversion, harsh deprivation of minimal human rights. These same issues must also be the primary ones for people who hope to resist World War III in a meaningful way.

A narrow focus on strategic weapons tends to reinforce the basic principle of the ideological system, mirrored in the propaganda of our tacit partner in global oppression: that the superpower conflict is the central element of world affairs, to which all else is subordinated.

In fact, the history of the cold war demonstrates with great clarity that the threat of the superpower enemy has consistently been manipulated by each of the superpowers to mobilize its domestic population and recalcitrant allies in support of aggression, intervention and subversion in its own domains, allegedly in "defense" against a powerful enemy bent on its destruction.

It is a matter of little moment that superpower rhetoric may come to be believed by leadership groups and the mainstream intelligentsia. In the USSR, for example, these elements may really be able to persuade themselves that they are acting in self-defense when they attack Czechoslovakia or Afghanistan; and in the U.S. they may truly come to believe that the U.S. was acting in self-defense when it overthrew the government in Guatemala, or invaded Vietnam, or bombed a defenseless peasant society in northern Laos. And in Israel, Indonesia and elsewhere, naked aggression may also be seen as an exercise in self-defense.

The superpower conflict is real enough, but the true history of the modern period is seriously distorted in the interests of the superpowers, by the simplistic interpretations of the cold war system that suppresses its functional role in providing the framework for intervention and subversion, employing the rhetoric of "self-defense" and "containment." The potential of the mass disarmament movement is enormous and it faces a task of historic significance, but it may fade away as quickly as it arose—with little impact on the drift towards catastrophe that brought it into being—unless it is able to break away from the assumptions of the prevailing doctrinal system, and to devote its energies to the more demanding and more uncomfortable questions that this system is designed to mask.

## Editor's Notes to Chapter 25

This article was written on May 15, 1983. An edited version (with unaccepted and perhaps unacceptable modifications—they seem to miss the point) was published in *New Statesman* on July 29, pp. 16–17, under the title "The Shadow of the Great Satan: Noam Chomsky on U.S. Imperialism, A foreign policy designed to serve the domestic interests of those who own and manage the U.S. economy," "the first article in an occasional series about the way American society is developing under President Reagan."

An aspect of the topic is treated more extensively in "Patterns of Intervention," in *The Deadly Connection: Nuclear War and U.S. Intervention* (transcripts from a conference held at MIT Decemebr 4 & 5, 1982), American Friends Service Committee, Cambridge, MA, 1983, pp. 33–40.

The brief article added as a Postscript was written on November 21, 1983 for *Rivista Anarchica* (Milan), which published an Italian translation in its 14.1 (1984): issue, pp. 5–6, under the title "La Nuova Frontiera di Reagan." An earlier article entitled "The Foreign Policy of the Reagan Administration," written for the Italian newspaper *Il Messaggero* on July 13, 1981, appeared as "The Age of Reagan: Everything Old is New Again" in *LINK*, Nov. 2.15, pp. 4,5.

In an interview conducted by Joel Goodfader, senior editor of the *Harvard International Review*, and published in its issue 5.5 (1983) under the title "Cycles in U.S. policy: Of Cold War and Constraints," Chomsky points out that the policies of the Reagan Administration, which are quite similar to the policies of the Kennedy Administration, are "quite different in their outcome. Kennedy's policies basically worked, whereas Reagan's reapplication basically fails, and that's just the difference in the objective status of the United States as a world power in 1960 versus 1980." Also, "Reagan has failed completely to stir up the chauvinistic passions that Kennedy, for example, succeeded very well in stirring up. Compare Reagan's efforts to move to a more interventionist stance, particularly in Central America, with Kennedy's efforts. Kennedy actually invaded South Vietnam in 1962. That's an event that doesn't appear in official party history in the United States, but it took place nevertheless. In 1962, the American Air Force began the systematic bombardment of South Vietnam. That's what we call aggression when somebody else does it."

In the same interview, he is asked what initiatives he would take if he were to wake up the following morning and find himself as the Secretary of State. His answer deserves to be pondered (see also Selection 1):

"First of all, I'd move towards a genuine disarmament, because I think the current technical problems that the United States is pursuing are probably going to drive the Russians to some kind of launch-on-warning strategy which almost guarantees the destruction of the United States sooner or later. The first thing I'd do is abort these programs and move toward some genuine disarmament. Then I would move at once to put an end to the American policy of supporting various neo-Nazi monsters all over the world, particularly in Central America, which is the most striking case. I'd move toward the international consensus and so on. However, though I could add a whole range of other policies, I should add this qualification: I couldn't do any of these things. The fact is that the constraints of parameters within which any policy-maker operates are rather narrow, and they're set from the outside, they're set by real interests. The real interests in society are those of the people that own it. Objective power lies elsewhere. Decision-making power does not lie in the political sphere."

For a broader discussion of the aid-torture correlation, see **PE**, in addition to Herman's study (see p. 168 above).

# 25. U.S. Foreign Policy

In history and the social sciences it is difficult to discover principles of any generality and force, but there are a few. One is that every action of every state is undertaken solely for defensive purposes and with awesome nobility of intent, though the leadership may fall into error because of ignorance, the complexities of history, or the machinations of whoever happens to be the current "Great Satan," to borrow Khomeni's useful contribution to contemporary political discourse. To establish this Truth, it is only necessary to turn to the published record. In the case of the U.S., we learn from it that under Carter "human rights is replacing self-determination as the guiding value in American foreign policy" (Arthur Schlesinger), that we fall "into foreign disasters like Vietnam mainly through an excess of righteousness and disinterested benevolence" (John K. Fairbank), that "unlike the Soviet Union, the U.S. does not want to convert anyone to a specific political, social, or economic system" (Walter Laqueur), that "our policy is not rooted in any national material interest of the United States, as most foreign policies of other countries in the past have been" (Charles E. Bohlen), and so on, with much consistency. An investigation of the USSR (or other lesser powers) would reveal that the scope of this law of history is quite broad.

Other evidence suggests a somewhat different picture. We find that planning is generally rational in the short term and that its goals relate directly to the interests of those who own and manage the domestic economy and who employ state power to realize their interests (called "the national interest") to the extent—generally large—that they can. In the early years of World War II, top State Department planners along with the Council on Foreign Relations developed the concept of a "Grand Area" that would be subordinated to the needs of the American economy as part of "an integrated policy to achieve military and economic supremacy for the United States within the non-German world" (later beyond). The domain "strategically necessary for world control" was to include the Western hemisphere, the Far East and the former British Empire, to be dismantled in an exercise called "anti-colonialism" in American scholarship, but perceived as an effort "to elbow us out" by British officials. Plans were outlined for particular areas and for a global economic order in which American interests would be paramount. These programs met with considerable success, though by 1970 the U.S. was no longer so clearly "the hegemonic power in a system of world order," as a Trilateral Commission study observes.

One component of this system of world power was a regular pattern of intervention, taking various forms, to counter threats to U.S. hegemony, as in Greece, Iran, Guatemala, Indochina, Cuba, the Congo, Brazil, the Dominican Republic, Chile, El Salvador, among others. By the 1970s, it was recognized that the U.S. would have to delegate responsibility to regional powers: the U.S. must be "concerned more with the overall framework of order than with the management of every regional enterprise" (Henry Kissinger). In the crucial Middle East area, where it was necessary to hold what the State Department described as "the greatest material prize of world history," the role of the local gendarme was assigned to Iran and Israel, finally just Israel after the fall of the Shah. In Africa, French forces "keep West Africa safe for French, American, and other foreign oilmen" (and others) as *Business Week* explained. In Central America, when the congressional human rights program blocked direct intervention, the task was assigned to Argentine neo-Nazis and to Israel, a willing and efficient ally that is able to perform such tasks as supplying a computerized system to monitor water and electricity use so that death squads can be sent if too many people seem to be using some apartment. And so on. Laqueur is right in holding that the U.S. cares little about the political systems in its dependencies—specifically, about democracy—but the social and economic systems were always a prime concern. In particular, these had to be "open societies," meaning open to U.S. economic penetration and political control. Where a society fails this test, it is subject to a range of penalties of a familiar sort.

Intervention often succeeded, including, to a degree that is often underestimated, in Indochina, where the perceived threat of successful social and economic development under a radical nationalist leadership was averted, probably for a long time. A crucial decision of 1961 converted the mission of the Latin American military from "hemispheric defense" (perhaps against Martians) to "internal security," that is, war against their own populations. The result was a plague of repression without precedent in the bloody history of the continent as National Security States were established with American support, directed by military officers "indistinguishable from the war criminals hanged at Nuremberg after World War II" who "passed through the Inter-American Defense College in Washington" and used "the methods of Heinrich Himmler's extermination squads" (Charles Maechling, who led counterinsurgency and internal-defense planning for Kennedy and Johnson from 1961–66).

This was the most lasting contribution of the Kennedy liberals to Latin America. Their contribution to Indochina need not be discussed. They were impressed by its success in providing a "shield" behind which Indonesia could re-enter the Free World, earning its credentials with the slaughter of hundreds of thousands of landless peasants and the creation of a "paradise for investors" who were impeded only by the rapacity of the Indonesian military"a gleam of light in Asia," as James Reston wrote in the *NY Times*, after the massacres. Maxwell Taylor and others attributed these successes to U.S. accomplishments in South Vietnam, while Secretary of Defense McNamara described them as a "dividend" for the "well-justified" U.S. military aid in the Sukarno years, a story reenacted in Chile with some new twists. The Human Rights Administration subsequently played its part by providing crucial diplomatic and military support for the near-genocidal Indonesian invasion of East Timor, still in progress. Many other examples may be cited.

The commitment of the U.S. to human rights has occasionally been studied, for example by Latin Americanist Lars Schoultz who found that "aid has tended to flow disproportionately to Latin American governments which torture their citizens," to "the hemisphere's relatively egregious violators of fundamental human rights." In contrast, aid is uncorrelated with need. The correlation between aid and human rights violations, though clear, is understated in Schoultz's study: he does not consider what might be called "the right to live" (namely, to food, work, medical care, etc.), which does not figure in U.S. human rights legislation; and he omits various other forms of intervention such as "making the economy scream" under Allende, directing aid from international lending institutions to one's favorite torturers, etc. In some cases, as in Argentina, the U.S. worked hand-in-hand with the USSR.

It is, of course, impossible to deduce a causal connection from a correlation; thus it would be unfair to conclude that U.S. planners positively enjoy torture and murder. Some insight into the meaning of the correlation is given by a study of broader scope conducted by economist Edward S. Herman. He found the same aid-torture correlation, but also found that U.S. aid was closely correlated to improvement in the investment climate. The explanation for the initial correlation now becomes clear. Given the nature of state power, aid naturally goes to those who show due concern for the climate for business operations, which tends to benefit from torture of dissidents, murder of union and peasant organizers or priests working with the poor, etc. Hence U.S. support correlates with torture, death squads and degradation, as a consequence of the primary commitment of U.S. foreign policy, human rights being as relevant a concern as democracy and self-determination, apart from the ideological institutions.

How does the Reagan administrations' policy fit into this long-term picture? The domestic program of the Reagan administration is designed to transfer resources from the poor to the wealthy and to revitalize the economy by state intervention. In the U.S., this means expanding the state-guaranteed market for high technology waste (armaments) along with state subsidies for research and development. The new "supercomputers," for example, will be subsidized by the Pentagon (DARPA), the Department of Energy (heavily engaged in nuclear weapons research) and NASA, which has a large responsibility for aircraft design, and they will be the primary users, as in the case of the earlier history of the computer industry.

To convince the electorate to support a program of this sort is hopeless unless they are properly frightened. It comes as no surprise, then, that the Reagan administration from its first moment has been seeking an international confrontation. Early efforts to construct a Soviet threat in El Salvador ran afoul of an unexpected popular reaction, a residue of the "Vietnam syndrome," a dread disease that afflicted much of the American population with such terrifying symptoms as insight into the nature of U.S. foreign policy and distaste for oppression and massacre. Imaginative stories were devised about Libyan hit-men roaming Washington to ambush our Leader, then a Libyan attack on the Sudan which offered the opportunity for the U.S. to flex its muscles and put Quaddafi "back in his box" (George Shultz). One aim of the remarkably well-publicized invasion of Nicaragua is presumably to induce the Sandinistas to call for Soviet or Cuban aid, so that the U.S. can impose a blockade and, if lucky, achieve something like the Cuban missile crisis, when the "best and the brightest" courageously faced a probability of 1/2 to 1/3 of nuclear war to establish the principle that the U.S. has the right to place missiles on the borders of the Soviet Union (obsolete missiles, for which a withdrawal order had already been given), though they do not have the equivalent right. It is worth bearing in mind that this is generally regarded as "perhaps the finest hour of John F. Kennedy's Presidency" (Graham Allison).

Similar remarks hold for the administration's latest success in Lebanon. Shultz's negotiations pointedly excluded Syria, presenting it with a *fait accompli* that it would be sure to reject, so that Caspar Weinberger could issue a stern warning to the Great Satan and its "proxies" who were blocking peace. No one would have expected Israel to withdraw unconditionally if presented with a comparable Lebanese-Syrian agreement under the Russian aegis—putting aside here other questions, such as the ratification of the right of aggression and massacre implicit in the terms of the Israel-Lebanon accords. It would have been possible to bring Syria into the "peace process," with an eye to realizing the Syrian withdrawal scheduled for summer 1982 and aborted by the Israeli invasion, even to include the USSR in accordance with the wishes of the Lebanese government. But the political capital would have been much reduced.

Meanwhile, vastly expanded war spending was motivated by a window of vulnerability that has now gone the way of Kennedy's missile gap, concocted for similar purposes. There is every reason to expect continued sabre-rattling, heightened intervention, and threats of war.

These are not novelties in post-war U.S. history. The situation was similar in 1950, when NSC 68 called for a huge military expansion and a "rollback" strategy against the USSR just prior to the Korean war; or 1961, when Kennedy initiated a program of massive rearmament, counterinsurgency and confrontation that resembles Reagan's in many respects. Military buildups have been unrelated to any new security threat, but closely correlated with domestic issues, including the perceived need for a stimulus for production and for intervention in the third world to maintain "open societies." The Great Satan is always available in times of need, and its own violence and brutality have regularly been exploited to justify programs adopted for other ends. Again, there is considerable symmetry in this regard in world affairs.

This system is a highly dangerous and unstable one. There is a serious threat of superpower confrontation in the Middle East and possibly Central America, not to speak of the consequences for the local populations. Advances in military technology vastly increase the likelihood that confrontation or even tension will explode into nuclear war. It is not easy to view the future with much optimism.

## POSTSCRIPT: The Foreign Policy of the Reagan Administration

To understand the foreign policy of the Reagan administration, one must begin by considering its domestic program, which has two basic components: first, transfer of resources from the poor to the rich by reducing welfare, fiscal measures, etc.; and second, a vast increase in the state sector of the economy. Given the particular institutional structures of the U.S., the state does not intervene in the economy by direct coordination and industrial policy planning, but primarily by creating a state-guaranteed market for production, a device that interferes minimally with the prerogatives of private capital. For familiar reasons, this program is conducted through the military system, whereby the state finances research, development and production of advanced technology, the leading sectors of American industry. In the later stages of the Carter administration, proposals were advanced for cutting back social programs and increasing military spending. The Russian invasion of Afghanistan and the Iran hostage crisis were exploited to gain public support. Reagan inherited and considerably extended these plans.

This is a classic pattern. There have been three major postwar periods of increased militarization of the economy: 1950, 1961, 1981. In no case was there any relevant change in the international climate. In each case there was a problem of "getting the country moving again" as the Kennedy ideologues expressed it, and international crises were manufactured or exploited to justify the process. In fact, the Reagan domestic and foreign programs are strongly reminiscent of the Kennedy period.

Since the public must pay the costs of "reindustrialization" in this style, they must be properly frightened. A natural concomitant of these domestic programs is the search for confrontation with the superpower enemy. Thus associated with domestic militarization is a more militant foreign policy: increased counterinsurgency, subversion, confrontation, and so on. All of this is classic, not only in the U.S.

Reagan's first "foreign policy crisis" was in El Salvador. Carter had regarded the problem there as a local one: to enable the gangsters installed and backed by the U.S. to terrorize the population into submission, under the guise of "reform." Reagan pursued the same program while escalating the rhetoric: massacre of peasants in El Salvador was now defense of the U.S. against the "evil empire" that was seeking to take over the world. While Carter had made some effort to support business groups in the Nicaraguan coalition, Reagan moved at once to a war against Nicaragua using U.S.-organized mercenaries, mainly from the Somozist National Guard. The intent surely is to compel the Sandinistas to move towards more authoritarian measures and to call for Soviet or Cuban aid, in which case the U.S. will be able to impose a blockade or invade directly, perhaps even achieving a confrontation similar to the Cuban missile crisis. Meanwhile Reagan sought confrontation with other "Russian proxies." Absurd stories were circulated about Libyan "hit men" roaming Washington to assassinate our Leader, about a projected Libyan invasion of the Sudan, and so on. Only forthright and courageous U.S. military measures averted these catastrophes. Carter had sought to undermine the Bishop regime in Grenada by economic pressures. Reagan moved at once, in 1981, to preparations for direct invasion, with large-scale military exercises in the Caribbean clearly aimed at Grenada.

In the Middle East, Reagan backed the Israeli invasion of Lebanon throughout, including the invasion of West Beirut. The U.S. then arranged a "peace settlement" between Israel and Lebanon, accepted under duress by the Lebanese government that had been installed under Israeli guns, which left southern Lebanon under effective Israeli control. The negotiations pointedly excluded Syria, and in fact were designed to ensure Syrian rejection so that there could be another confrontation with the "Great Satan," to adopt Khomeini's useful term. Had the U.S. been interested in peace in Lebanon, it would have called upon Israel to withdraw unconditionally as demanded by the UN Security Council (with hypocritical U.S. assent), and it would have requested that Syria withdraw as had been scheduled in the summer of 1982, a possibility that was aborted by the Israeli invasion and that may have been a factor in the timing of the invasion. The U.S. would also have brought the USSR into the negotiations as requested by the pro-American Gemayel government. Conceivably, this might have succeeded, but the U.S. much preferred the advantages of confrontation with the Russians and their "proxies," meanwhile setting the stage for partition of most of Lebanon between Israel and Syria with the likelihood of further conflict.

The coup and massacre in Grenada afforded the pretext for the long-planned invasion there, again in defense against the Great Satan. It is a remarkable tribute to the power of contemporary state propaganda systems that the "threat" to the U.S. posed by the emerging superpower of Grenada was seriously discussed and widely believed. In fact, the "liberation" was generally approved with enthusiasm in the U.S.; it will be recalled that Hitler was the most popular leader in Germany's history as long as he was winning cheap victories.

A major problem faced by any U.S. leadership is to overcome what is called "the Vietnam syndrome," a dangerous disease that afflicted much of the American population in the latter stages of the Vietnam war with such threatening symptoms as distaste for massacre and aggression and a degree of sympathy for suffering and brutalized people. A variety of cures have been pursued with varying success. The return to Kennedy-style domestic militarization and foreign subversion and aggression is an indication of the success of the state in reducing popular impediments to the pursuit of its essential functions.

Nevertheless, the battle is far from won. There is far more domestic opposition to these policies than there was 20 years ago, and furthermore, while the superpowers have of course increased in absolute strength, both have suffered a loss in their ability to coerce and control. Other factors, such as the advances in the technology of destruction, narrow the range in which confrontation may fall short of total disaster, however. It requires a good deal of optimism to suppose that the pathology of modern civilization can be arrested before termination of the human experiment.

## Editor's Notes to Chapter 26

This enlightening piece was written on February 6, 1984, at the request of *Cambio 16* (a Spanish counterpart to *Newsweek* or *Time* published in Madrid). A Spanish translation appeared in *Cambio 16*.46 (1984): pp. 52–55, under the title "Chomsky y el Candor de Orwell," which was reprinted "1984: el de Orwell" in *Unomasuno* 23 & 24 May 1984: pp. 1, 12 and 1, 14). It was also translated into French as "1984: Celui d'Orwell et le Notre," *Magazine Libertaire* (1984): pp. 6–11.

The English original ("a complete transcription of a remarkable and extended discussion between Chomsky and the journalists" *[New York Review,* May 31 1984, p. 48] attending a convention of the Northwest Broadcast News Association held in Minneapolis in Mach 1984) first appeared in *The Thoreau Quarterly* 16. 1–2 (1984): pp. 13–50. It was reprinted in *Update* 11.3 (1984): pp. 10–11, and included in *1984 and After,* ed. by M. Hewitt and D. Roussopoulos. Montréal: Black Rose Books, 1984, pp. 66–73.

On Stanley Karnow's *Vietnam: A History* (which was the basis for the recent TV series), see Chomsky's "The Vietnam War in the Age of Orwell, *Race & Class* 25 (1984): pp. 41–60, completed on November 15, 1983, or the shortened version "The best-selling of Vietnam," *Boston Review* 9.1 (1984): pp. 8–12.

A way of characterizing Chomsky's work is to say that it is essentially concerned with two major questions: His writings on cognitive psychology and philosophy are concerned with what he calls "Plato's problem," that is, the question of how we know so much even though we have so little evidence; his writings on the analysis of ideology are essentially concerned with what he calls, "Orwell's problem, "that is, the question of how we know so little about the social and political world when we have so much relevant evidence. The basic answer to the second question lies in the nature of the propaganda system. (See **KL**, ch. 5.) As he puts it in a recently published interview ("The Manufacture of Consent." *Open Road,* Spring 1984: pp. 16–17), "there are a vast number of people who are uninformed and heavily propagandized, but fundamentally decent. The propaganda that inundates them is effective when unchallenged, but much of it goes only skin deep. If they can be brought to raise questions and apply their decent instincts and basic intelligence, many people quickly escape the confines of the doctrinal system and are willing to do something to help others who are really suffering and oppressed. This is naturally less true of the better-educated and 'more sophisticated' (that is, more effectively indoctrinated) groups who are both the agents and often the most deluded victims of the propaganda system."

In the same interview (conducted in August 1983) he sees "little reason to believe that the future will be very long, since "a cold look at the facts suggests that we are moving inexorably towards nuclear war." There is still hope, however, as he said in answer to a question after a talk on Lebanon he delivered at the Harvard School of Public Health on December 15, 1983. The first step would be to bring about "a very significant change in the way the population perceives what's happening in the world. "The second step ("which won't come unless the first one comes") would be the willingness of the people "to do something to prevent things from going on the way they are." The domain in which practically anyone can make a contribution is therefore fairly well defined.

For more on "brain-washing under freedom," see **PE** and **TCW** (see. pp. 12–13 above).

# 26. 1984: Orwell's And Ours

Last May, a remarkable event took place in Moscow. A courageous news-caster, Vladimir Danchev, denounced the Russian war in Afghanistan over Moscow radio in five broadcasts extending over a week, calling on the rebels "not to lay down their arms" and to fight against the Soviet "invasion" of their coun-try. The Western press was overwhelmed with admiration for his startling depar-ture from "the official Soviet propaganda line." In the *NY Times*, one commen-tator wrote that Danchev had "revolted against the standards of double-think and newspeak. "In Paris, a prize was established in his honor to be given to "a journalist who fights for the right to be informed." In December, Danchev returned to work after psychiatric treatment. A Russian official was quoted as saying: "He was not punished, because a sick man cannot be punished."

The event was considered to have afforded a glimpse into the world of 1984, and Danchev's act was justly regarded as a triumph of the human spirit, a refusal to be cowed by totalitarian violence.

What was remarkable about Danchev's action was not merely the protest, but the fact that he referred to the Russian invasion of Afghanistan as "an inva-sion." In Soviet theology, there is no such event as "the Russian invasion of Afghanistan." Rather, there is a "Soviet defense of Afghanistan" against bandits supported from abroad. As in the case of most propaganda systems, here too there is a kernel of truth concealed in a massive lie. The Mujahidin do operate from "sanctuaries" in Pakistan, where CIA and Chinese agents oversee the flow of arms, and the guerrillas take credit for having destroyed 50 percent of all schools and hospitals along with many other acts regarded as "atrocities" by the invaders, who have stated that they will withdraw if Afghanistan is secured from attack from Pakistan. This stance is dismissed by the West on the proper grounds that aggressors should withdraw "unconditionally," as the UN Security Council insisted, with U.S. support that was quickly withdrawn, in the case of Israel's invasion of Lebanon. The West has also been justly indignant when the Russians cynically denounce the "terrorism" of the resistance, or when they claim, absurd-ly, to be defending Afghanistan from these "bandits" who murder innocents.

The USSR protests that it was invited in, but as the London *Economist* grandly proclaimed, "an invader is an invader unless invited in by a government with some claim to legitimacy." Only in Orwellian Newspeak can such aggres-sion be characterized as "defense against externally supported terrorism."

Orwell's *1984* was largely drawn from the practice of *existing* Soviet society, which had been portrayed with great accuracy by Maximov, Souvarine, Beck and many others. It was only in cultural backwaters such as Paris that the facts were long denied, so that Khrushchev's revelations and later Solzhenitsyn's reiteration of the familiar story came as such a revelation at a time when the intelligentsia were prepared to march in a different parade. What was striking about Orwell's vision was not his portrayal of existing totalitarianism, but his warning that it could happen here.

So far, at least, that has not come to pass. Industrial capitalist societies bear little resemblance to Orwell's Oceania—though the terror-and-torture regimes they have imposed and maintained elsewhere achieve levels of violence that Orwell never depicted, Central America being only the most obvious current case.

Implicit in the press coverage of the Danchev affair was a note of self-congratulation: it couldn't happen here. Here, it requires little courage to defy the government on a point of doctrine. Certainly no Danchev has been sent to a psychiatric hospital for calling an invasion an "invasion." But let us inquire further into just why this is the case. One possibility is that the question does not arise because, statistical error aside, there are simply no Danchevs here: journalists and other intellectuals are so subservient to the doctrinal system that they cannot even perceive that "an invader is an invader unless invited in by a government with a claim to legitimacy," when it is the U.S. that is the invader. This would be a stage beyond what Orwell imagined, a stage beyond what Soviet totalitarianism has achieved. Is this merely an abstract possibility, or is it an uncomfortably close assessment of our own world?

Consider the following facts. In 1962, the U.S. Air Force began its direct attacks against the rural population of South Vietnam, with heavy bombing and defoliation, as part of a program intended to drive millions of people into camps where, surrounded by barbed wire and armed guards, they would be "protected" from the guerrillas they were supporting, the "Vietcong," the southern branch of the former anti-French resistance (the Vietminh). This is what we call "aggression," "an invasion," when conducted by some official enemy. The GVN had no legitimacy and little popular support, and in fact its leadership was regularly overthrown in U.S.-backed coups when it was feared that they might arrange a settlement with the South Vietnamese enemy. Some 70,000 "Vietcong" had already been killed in a U.S.-directed terror campaign before the outright U.S. invasion in 1962. The U.S. invaders continued to block all attempts at political settlement, and in 1964 began preparations for a vast escalation of the war against the south combined with an attack against North Vietnam, Laos and later also Cambodia.

For the past 22 years, I have searched in vain for even a single reference in mainstream journalism or scholarship to an "American invasion of South Vietnam," or American "aggression" in South Vietnam. In the American doctrinal system, there is no such event. There is no Danchev, though in this case it took no courage to tell the truth, merely honesty. Even at the peak of opposition to the U.S. war, only a minuscule portion of the articulate intelligentsia opposed the war on grounds of principle—on the grounds that aggression is wrong—while most came to oppose it, well after leading business circles did, on the "pragmatic" grounds that the costs were too high. Popular attitudes, incidentally, were rather different. As late as 1982, over 70 percent of the population (but far fewer "opinion leaders") regarded the war not just as a mistake, but as "fundamentally and morally wrong," a problem known as "the Vietnam syndrome" in American political discourse.

These facts should give us pause. How was such astonishing subservience to the doctrinal system achieved? We can begin to understand by looking more closely at the debate in mainstream circles between the "hawks" and the "doves." The hawks were those, like journalist Joseph Alsop, who felt that with sufficient dedication the war could be won. The doves agreed with liberal historian Arthur Schlesinger that it probably could not, though like him, they took for granted that "we all pray that Mr. Alsop will be right." It was a "hopeless cause," as critic Anthony Lake recently observed. All agree that it was "a failed crusade" undertaken for motives that were "noble" though "illusory" and with "the loftiest intentions," in the words of Stanley Karnow in his recent best-selling history, highly regarded for its critical candor.

Strikingly omitted from the debate is the view that the U.S. could have won, but that it would have been wrong to allow aggression and massacre to succeed. This was the position of the authentic peace movement (if the war was a "hopeless cause," why bother to protest and disrupt it, why suffer the consequences of that protest, which were often severe?).

This quite typical commentary illustrates the genius of "brainwashing under freedom." In a totalitarian system, it is required only that official doctrine be obeyed. In the democratic systems of thought control, it is deemed necessary to take over the entire spectrum of discussion: nothing must remain thinkable apart from the Party Line. State propaganda is often not expressed, merely presupposed as the framework for discussion among right-minded people. The debate, therefore, must be between the "doves" and "hawks," the Schlesingers and the Alsops. The position that the U.S. is engaged in aggression, and that such aggression is wrong, must remain unthinkable and unexpressed, with reference to the Holy State. The "responsible critics" make an estimable contribution to this cause, which is why they are tolerated, indeed honored.

The nature of Western systems of indoctrination was not perceived by Orwell and is typically not understood by dictators, who fail to comprehend the utility for propaganda of a critical stance that incorporates the basic assumptions of official doctrine and thereby marginalizes authentic and rational critical discussion, which must be blocked. There is rarely any departure from this pattern. Perhaps the sharpest critic of the American war in mainstream journalism was Anthony Lewis, who argued that the U.S. involvement began with "blundering efforts to do good" but by 1969, it was clear that it was "a disastrous mistake."

Few academic scholars were more critical of U.S. policy than John K. Fairbank, who informed the American Historical Society in his December 1968 presidential address, a year after the Tet offensive had convinced much of the corporate elite to abandon the effort to subjugate South Vietnam, that we entered the war in an "excess of righteousness and disinterested benevolence," but it was a mistake to do so, as events showed. Few dictators can boast such total conformity to Higher Truths.

The devices that are used to ensure such obedience are effective though not overly subtle. Consider, for example, what is universally called the "peace process" in the Middle East: the Camp David accords of 1978–9. Few ask why the inhabitants of the territories under Israeli occupation reject the "peace process" with virtual unanimity. A moment's thought suffices to provide the reason. As was obvious at once, the "peace process" served to remove Egypt from the conflict so that Israel would then be free, with U.S. support, to extend its settlement and repression in the occupied territories and attack Lebanon, exactly as it has been doing since. But such elementary observations are excluded from "responsible" discussion; the U.S. is committed to the creation of a powerful and expansionist Israel as a "strategic asset." Anything that contributes to this end is, by definition, the "peace process." The term itself eliminates any further discussion: who can be against peace?

There are thousands of similar examples. The U.S. Marines in Lebanon are the "peace-keeping force," and actions taken against them are "terrorism." For much of the population, they are simply consummating the Israeli invasion with its "new order:" the rule of right-wing Christians and privileged Muslim sectors over the poor and disadvantaged whose "terrorism" in their own eyes is resistance, a point of view excluded from discussion here. When Israel bombs villages near Baalbek with 500 casualties, mostly civilians, including 150 schoolchildren, that is not "terrorism" but "retaliation," and it receives no comment or censure here: as an American ally, Israel inherits the right of aggression and massacre. Often, unwanted facts are simply suppressed. The "secret bombings" of Laos and Cambodia were "secret" because the media refused to report the ample evidence available. The U.S.-backed Indonesian aggression in Timor, leading to the death of perhaps 200,000 people and a Biafra-style famine, was effectively suppressed for over four years. Renewed attacks on the population are in progress now, and are also being suppressed.

I doubt that any story has ever received the coverage of the downing of KAL Flight 007 last fall, sure proof that the Russians are the most barbaric devils since Attila the Hun so that we must place Pershing missiles in Germany and step up the war against Nicaragua. The densely printed *NY Times* index devotes seven full pages to the atrocity in September 1982 alone. In the midst of the furor, UNITA, the "freedom fighters" supported by the U.S. and South Africa, took credit for downing an Angolan jet with 126 killed. There was no ambiguity, the plane was not off course flying over sensitive installations, there was no RC 135 U.S. reconnaissance jet nearby confusing the issue (possibly jamming radar). It was simple premeditated murder. The incident received 100 words in the *NY Times* and no comment anywhere in the media.

This is not the only such case. In Oct. 1976, a Cuban airliner was bombed by CIA-backed terrorists, killing 75 civilians. In 1973 Israel downed a civilian plane lost in a sandstorm over the Suez canal with 110 killed. There was no protest, only editorial comments about how "No useful purpose is served by an acrimonious debate over the assignment of blame" (*NY Times*). Four days later, Prime Minister Golda Meir visited the U.S. where she was troubled with no embarrassing questions and returned with new gifts of military aircraft. Contrary to recent falsehoods, Israel refused to pay compensation or to accept any responsibility; it offered only ex gratia payments, funded by the usual generous donor from abroad. In 1955, an Air India plane carrying the Chinese delegation to the Bandung conference was blown up in the air in what the Hong Kong police called a "carefully planned mass murder." An American defector later claimed that it was he who planted the bomb in the service of the CIA. None of these incidents demonstrates "barbarism;" all have been quickly forgotten.

One can offer thousands of such examples. In such ways, history is shaped in the interests of those in power.

All of this falls under the rubric of what Walter Lippmann, in 1921, called "the manufacture of consent," an art which is "capable of great refinements" and will lead to a " revolution" in "the practice of democracy." This art has been much admired in the social sciences. The well-known American political scientist Harold Lasswell wrote in 1933 that we must avoid "democratic dogmatisms," such as the belief that people are "the best judges of their own interests." Democracy permits the voice of the people to be heard, and it is the task of the intellectual to ensure that this voice endorses what farsighted leaders know to be the right course. Propaganda is to democracy what violence is to totalitarianism. The techniques have been honed to a high art, far beyond anything that Orwell dreamt of. The device of feigned dissent, incorporating the doctrines of the state religion and eliminating rational critical discussion is one of the more subtle means, though simple lying and suppression of fact and other crude techniques are also highly effective.

It should be noted that ideological control (Agitprop) is far more important in the democracies than in states that rule by violence, and is therefore more refined, and more effective. There are no Danchevs here, except at the remote margins of political debate.

For those who stubbornly seek freedom, there can be no more urgent task than to come to understand the mechanisms and practices of indoctrination. These are easy to perceive in the totalitarian societies, much less so in the system of "brainwashing under freedom" to which we are subjected and which all too often we serve as willing or unwitting instruments.

## Editor's Notes to Chapter 27

Selection 27, "An Inquiry into Global Capitalism," is an edited transcription of Chomsky's keynote address (archived and made available by Alternative Radio: *www.alternativeradio.org*, we gratefully acknowledge) at the Oct. 3, 1997, conference celebrating the life and work of Professor Eqbal Ahmad, the noted Pakistani scholar, teacher and activist, at Hampshire College, Amherst, Massachusetts, where he was a member of the faculty. Chomsky has written again on his old friend's work in his review of Ahmad's *Confronting Empire* Cambridge: South End Press, 2000. Interviews with David Barsamian (*Dawn Books & Authors*, June 19, 2001).

A major theme of this address is the contours of the evolving world scene (see **WOON**, 2.6), a theme further developed in the next three selections.

The expression "really existing market capitalism" is meant to recall, not without irony, "really existing socialism," commonly used, half a century ago, by some apologists of Stalinism to counter those that argued that from early on the Soviet Union had nothing in common with genuine socialism. Chomsky is perhaps the author who has most forcefully argued that in fact it was the very opposite; see, in particular, his article "The Soviet Union Versus Socialism" (written on September 2, 1985, at the request of the Canadian journal *New Internationalist*, which understandably neglected to publish it), which first appeared in *Our Generation* 17.2 (1986): pp. 47–52, and was later included in D. I. Roussopoulos, ed., *The Radical Papers,* Montréal: Black Rose Books, 1987, pp. 47–52. See also the Introduction to this book, n. 13.

For an insightful account of David Ricardo's new "science," which "allegedly showed that the poor majority could only be harmed by efforts to help them" (Chomsky) with the certainty of the "principle of gravitation," see Rajani Kanth, *Political Economy and Laissez-Faire*, New York: Rowman and Littlefield, 1986, and, for further discussion, **WOON**, esp. 2.6. (Chomsky takes Ricardo to be much more the godfather of contemporary "neoliberal" economics than Adam Smith, who in his view was more thoroughly pre-capitalist than Ricardo was.)

For more on the unorthodox views on economics of Nobel Laureate Joseph Stiglitz, former chair of Clinton's Council of Economic Advisors and former chief economist at the World Bank, who for Chomsky is "one of the most important and influential, and [he thinks] intelligent" analysts, see "Whose World Order: Conflicting Visions," *Monetary Reform Magazine*, 10 (2000): pp. 15–29, a talk Chomsky gave at Massey Hall, Toronto, Canada, on March 22, 1998, and again at the University of Calgary on September 22, 1998; on the work of Nobel laureate Amartya Sen, see **DD** 7.7 (a relevant recent book by Sen is *Development as Freedom*. New York: Anchor Books, 1999).

For more on the U.S. as "the mother country and bastion of modern protectionism,"see **P&P**, ch. 5, and references there, in particular Paul Bairoch, *Economics and World History,* Chicago:University of Chicago Press, 1993, where the quote is taken from; for more detail on the U.S. case, see Alfred Eckes,

*Opening America's Market: U.S. Foreign Trade Policy Since 1776,* Chapel Hill & London: University of North Carolina Press, 1995; on then Secretary of the Treasury James Baker's boast, **P&P**, ch. 5, and **WOON**, ch. 2.1; on a whole range of related topics, see **POP**. The 1989 "highly regarded study of the U.S. takeover of Brazil" by Gerald Haines, senior historian of the CIA, is also discussed in **Y501**, ch. 7, **WOON**, 2.3–4, and **P&P**, ch. 7.

There is a more extended discussion on the MAI and the "ultimate weapon" in selection 28, where the Internet is discussed again. (See also the Editor's Notes to 28.)

# 27. An Inquiry Into Global Capitalism

There was an interesting front-page article in the *NY Times*. The headline read: "Making Sure War Crimes Aren't Forgotten." It was about the Clinton Administration's new ambassador-at-large on war crimes issues. The task of the new position is to see that atrocities do not fade into history and that war crimes and other crimes against humanity gain a higher priority in American foreign policy. "The new position is the brain child of Secretary of State Madeleine Albright, long an advocate of international justice."

There are a few oversights in the article. One of them is that it failed to give credit where credit is due. The suggestion was actually made in 1971 in a prestigious international affairs journal, the *Journal of International Affairs*, hard to miss. Nevertheless, despite the lack of recognition and the slight delay, Eqbal Ahmad should be gratified that his suggestion is finally being taken up by the Clinton Administration as the brain child of its distinguished long-time advocate of international justice. Unfortunately, gratification is tempered by a closer look.

## The war crimes issue: Two very different proposals

Eqbal's proposal differs from the Clinton-Albright version in fundamental, related respects. The first one is that his suggestion was bitterly condemned. In fact, it elicited outrage and tantrums, while the Clinton-Albright version is highly praised. A related fact is that Eqbal's proposal was that criminals be brought to justice, and he gave specific examples of people clearly guilty of terrible crimes and easily within the reach of the stern advocates of international justice. The Clinton-Albright proposal, in contrast, is restricted to a carefully selected category of crimes, namely, those that can be charged to someone else's account. The underlying moral principles are not particularly attractive. They could have readily been embraced by a host of figures who perhaps it would be more polite to leave unnamed.

There's a related difference. Eqbal's proposal would have had important consequences in relieving pain and misery. The reasons are obvious to anyone who takes an honest look at the scale of atrocities and the factors that lead to them and who recognizes a few truisms. One, that people are responsible for the foreseeable consequences of their own acts, and two, that it is their own acts that they can effectively control. Things follow from that, too obvious to mention. The purposes of the Clinton-Albright version are plainly different. If there are beneficial human consequences, it will be incidental to different ends.

The admiration for the Clinton-Albright initiative comes as no surprise. Quite generally, unchallenged power elicits triumphalism and adulation. In fact, that's been a good part of the role of intellectuals throughout history. These practices have significant consequences. They help mobilize support for new exercises of power which are rarely benign, as the historical record demonstrates with considerable clarity. In the present case, adulation of power has reached fairly remarkable levels.

## Dangerous concomitants of unchallenged power

It's long been conventional to describe U.S. policies as guided by what's called Wilsonian idealism while those who are called realists object that we lack the means to conduct our crusades of global ameliorism and should not neglect our own interests in the service of others. Actually, I'm quoting a distinguished historian. It may be polite, again, to leave the name unmentioned.

We've passed beyond those conventions. Today we can read distinguished commentators explaining that U.S. foreign policy has entered a "noble" phase, even acquiring a "saintly glow." (I'm quoting a review of the topic in the *NY Times*, unusual only in the quality of the rhetoric, which would not be easy to match, apart from some cases that it would, again, be impolite to mention.) These are very natural and extremely dangerous concomitants of unchallenged power. That power has many strands. Another truism is that modern states are closely integrated with financial and manufacturing institutions that, on the one hand, largely dominate the state and, on the other, rely very heavily on it for subsidy and protection. In today's world all of this is embedded in an array of international institutions that the international business press describes as a "de facto world government," referring to G-7, the seven richest countries, the international financial institutions, the World Trade Organization [WTO], and other structures that are constructed and designed to serve the interests of the transnational corporations that intend to control the global economy. The U.S. stands at the center of that nexus, though of course not without challenge, and the triumphalism goes well beyond the saintly glow of foreign policy.

Another aspect is also articulated in the business press, which records "Capital's Clear Subjugation of Labor for Fifteen Years," and the radical shift in the economic balance of power between management and workers. I'm quoting *Barron's* and the *Financial Times* of London. It's these developments that made Federal Reserve Board chairman Alan Greenspan so optimistic about sustainable economic expansion in recent Congressional testimony that he gave. His optimistic forecast, he explained, is based on the atypical restraint on compensation increases resulting mainly from greater worker insecurity, which is an obvious desideratum for a decent society.

The same point was made in the 1997 economic report of the President, taking pride in the Administration's achievements, which they attributed in part to changes in labor market institutions and practices that underlie the significant wage restraint that bolsters the health of the economy. That's "health" in a sense of the term that's natural and welcome to the increasingly narrow sectors of power and privilege.

The war crimes issue is a specific case of this complex. It raises themes that are definitely worth exploring in depth and detail. One could easily write a richly detailed and important volume about them, many such volumes, in fact, including the story that primarily concerned Eqbal twenty-five years ago and is still unthinkable in the general intellectual culture. But I want to put all that aside and turn to a different aspect of the same array of issues, one that is less dramatic than the trail of tortured and mutilated corpses that litters a good part of the world, namely the radical shift in the economic balance of power described by the business press which has been deepening the divide between the rich and the poor internationally for many years and is also bringing the Third World home to the rich societies in the sense that it's instituting within them some of the structural features of Third World societies. Of course, there are great differences in scale between very rich and very poor societies, and there are also differences in method. But the structural features are remarkably similar.

Any Third World society that you visit, you discover a sector of enormous wealth and privilege, often obscene wealth and privilege, and a large mass of people who range from modest survival to real misery, and then a superfluous population who have to be controlled or removed. In the course of the radical shift in the economic balance of power, something similar has happened in the rich societies as well, most notably the U.S. and the U.K., but others are being dragged along. As I mentioned, the scale is different, of course, and the methods are different, so in more civilized societies like ours the superfluous population is not removed by social cleansing and state terror, as often in our dependencies, but by more civilized means, notably the enormous expansion of the crime control industry. That's another phenomenon that merits a prominent place in an inquiry into what's going on in the world.

When we condemn official enemies, we assign to their account not only those who are murdered outright, but also the far greater numbers of victims of policies for which they bear responsibility, victims of hunger, disease, and so on. And that's quite right. The same considerations should apply to crimes in which we have a hand. An honest inquiry, if this were imaginable, would compile a horrendous record if those standards were applied. The institutional and ideological factors that help to create and sustain this record remain in place. In this case, too, willingness to consider the questions would not only keep crimes from fading into history, but, more importantly, go a long way toward preventing their renewal and the renewal of others like them.

## Human development: a shocking record

An honest inquiry might begin by looking at the fact that while I'm speaking, roughly a thousand children will die from easily preventable disease and almost twice that many women will die or suffer serious disability in pregnancy or childbirth for lack of simple remedies and care. Those figures come from recent publications of UNICEF [United Nations International Children's Emergency Fund], which estimates the cost of overcoming such tragedies at a quarter of the annual military expenditures of the so-called developing societies, many of them developing downwards, in fact. That's about 10 percent of U.S. military spending. It's all too easy to go on.

An accurate inquiry into these questions is no easy task, but it's one that an honest person ought to want to undertake, the more so to the extent that they have a share in privilege in power. As we often discover, that means a share in responsibility as well. Let me now turn to some of the factors that such an inquiry would, I think, unearth.

One crucial question has to do with the sources of economic growth and development. Before proceeding with that, economic growth and development are very different things, often uncorrelated, in fact. In India, for example, one of the poorest states is Kerala, which far surpasses the rest of the country and actually approaches First World standards in quality of life indices, like mortality, literacy, fertility, and so on. That's a consequence of specific social policies, particularly policies that address women's rights, as Harvard economist Amartya Sen and others have pointed out. Human development there happens to be very high, economic growth very low, for one reason because investors are not ecstatic about the social policies that lead to those ends.

There are many similar cases around the world, in India and elsewhere, but let me turn to the Western hemisphere, where our influence and hence responsibility is overwhelming. I don't have to review the record, which is shocking, particularly in regions where U.S. influence has been the greatest. But even the cold statistics are pretty shocking. The most recent UNICEF report on basic indicators reveals that the richest country in the world has the worst record among the industrial societies. By such standards as child mortality and others, it ranks right alongside of Cuba, a poor Third World country that has been under unremitting attack by the hemispheric superpower for almost forty years. We also hold the record for hunger, child poverty and similarly through a whole range of basic social indicators. This is a country so rich that the level it had reached in the eighteenth century was not achieved by the upper classes in England until early in this century, let alone anybody else in the world.

There are many similar examples, and they are well worth examining. There's even a technical term for countries that have a high rate of economic growth and a low ranking in human development. They're called "economic miracles." There's a long list of them. Some of them are pretty revealing. One of the most revealing cases is Brazil. It's long been considered the potential colossus of the South. It's been called that for seventy years, which ought to rival the colossus of the North. It was under mostly British influence, but the U.S. took control of it in 1945, turning Brazil into a testing area for modern scientific methods of industrial development based solidly on capitalism. I'm quoting a highly regarded academic study by a well-known diplomatic historian, Gerald Haines. On the side, he is also the senior historian of the CIA. He concludes that the experiment was carried out with the best of intentions. He mentions that foreign investors benefited. He said that planners sincerely believed that the people of Brazil would benefit as well. I won't insult your intelligence by describing how they benefited, as Brazil became the Latin American darling of the international business community under military rule, quoting again the business press, while the World Bank at the same time reported that two-thirds of the population did not have enough food for normal physical activity. Haines is writing in 1989, and at that time he describes America's Brazilian policies as enormously successful, a real American success story, an economic miracle which in fact far surpassed Chile in growth rates, as well as others.

1989, when he was writing, was what was called the Golden Year by the business world, with profits tripling over 1988, while industrial wages, which were already among the lowest in the world, declined another 20 percent. The U.N. report on human development at that time ranked Brazil next to Albania. When the disaster began to hit the wealthy as well, as it did shortly after, then the modern scientific methods of development based solidly on capitalism, as Haines called them, instantly became transformed into proofs of the evils of socialism and statism. That's another quick transition that takes place regularly when needed. Those of you who are looking for careers in the intellectual world should take notes. That's the sort of thing you have to be able to do reflexively.

To appreciate the achievement, it's well to remember that Brazil is one of the richest countries in the world. It has enormous advantages, including half a century of dominance and tutelage by the U.S., with benign intent, which just happened to serve self-interest while leaving the majority of the population in misery. And of course it's off the screen when we solemnly address the issues of moral responsibility, censure and, more important, prevention. Because it goes on, since the roots are unchanged, they remain.

## Economic growth: two obvious questions

Let's turn to the narrower question of economic growth, recall, very different from development by any sensible measure. Here not a great deal is understood. A good example is the U.S., the best-studied society. In the U.S. approximately two-thirds of U.S. per capita economic growth is unexplained. It's attributed to what economists call the "residual," which is described as the measure of our ignorance by Robert Solow, who won a Nobel Prize for studying it. And that's the best-studied case. If you look at estimates for the rest of the world, they range from 5 percent to 95 percent unexplained. So it's not a very well understood topic. But there are some fairly solid generalizations. They come out pretty clearly when you ask some simple questions. It's not in question that two centuries ago, today's First World and Third World, North and South—all these are euphemisms, of course—were much more similar. That raises two questions, obviously. The first question is, Who developed and who didn't? The second question is, Can we find the causes of the differences?

The first question is very easily answered. We know who developed and who didn't. Europe developed, and those who escaped European control. Period. The U.S., which escaped European control, and Japan, which was able to hold off the West. They developed. Japan in fact brought its colonies along in tow. Japan was a brutal colonizer and ruler, but it differed from the West in the way it treated its colonies. And that difference shows today. Japan developed its colonies. It didn't rob them. Korea and Formosa, now Taiwan, during the period of Japanese rule, developed at approximately the same rate as Japan itself. By the late 1930s, when the Second World War came, they were more or less at the level of Japan, which is not to underplay Japanese brutality and violence, which were extreme, but these are just different techniques of rule and domination. And they in fact are developed societies, and that's it. The U.S., Japan, its colonies and the growth region around the Japan overseas Chinese capital area. That's it.

Let's turn to the second question. What caused the differences? Noticing who developed and who didn't already begins to give you the answers. There are two aspects to this question. One aspect is what prevented development in the South. The second is what facilitated it in the North. Here there is a fair degree of understanding. It's actually a staple of economic history, standard, mainstream economic history, that compulsory liberalization was a major factor in developing and delaying development in the South and de-industrializing relatively advanced economies. That continues to the recent period, and it's acknowledged in power centers. For example, the recently released U.S. documents that come out after thirty years or so, they have recently released documents from the early 1960s, including the report of John F. Kennedy's Latin America mission, which issued a secret report as he came into office assessing the situation in Latin America. It criticized what it called the "baleful influence" of the International Monetary Fund, which was pursuing the 1950s version of what's today called the Washington consensus, or structural adjustment, or neoliberalism. In fact, the recognition of that was part of the argument for the Alliance for Progress, which ended up having the familiar range of successes and failures, successes for the rich and failures for the poor. By accident.

In contrast, every developed country, bar none, from England to today's so-called tigers, radically violated neoliberal principles. Contrary to what the term "neoliberal" suggests, the principles are neither novel nor consistent with the ideals of classical liberalism. The operative ideology of the global economy for hundreds of years has been what we might call really existing free-market capitalism, which means, market discipline is great for you, but I need the protection of a nanny state, except for a temporary advantage when the playing field is tilted in my favor, typically as a result of earlier violence and state intervention. There's no time, of course, to run through the history, which is remarkably consistent, but let me just mention a few milestones.

Compare India and England. It sounds like a ridiculous comparison, but it isn't. In the eighteenth century, India was the commercial and manufacturing center of the world. India produced more iron than all of Europe. As late as the

1820s, British engineers were going to India to learn advanced steelmaking techniques. India was subjected to compulsory liberalization, by force, while England resorted to very high protection to allow its own industry to develop. The most striking case is textiles, which is invariably the vanguard of industrial development. The process of liberalization for you and protection for me began very early in the eighteenth century. Later in the century, Indian manufacturers had to face tariffs of about 75 percent in England.

In 1813, a British Parliamentary inquiry determined that Indian textiles could be sold so much more cheaply than domestic production that they simply barred Indian textiles from the British market entirely. Meanwhile, English textiles flooded India under forced liberalization and subsidy. The same was done for a whole range of other industries, including even shipbuilding, a particularly striking case because India had an advanced shipbuilding industry and the British admiralty actually very much wanted Indian-built ships for their own wars. But that was barred explicitly by Parliament on the grounds that it was necessary to de-industrialize India and develop British industry. The consequences are quite visible.

A famous fact is that Britain finally did turn to liberal internationalism, namely in 1846, that's after 150 years of protectionism, violence and creation of the world's strongest and most efficient state had enabled it to gain more than twice the per capita industrialization of any competitor so that a level playing field looked reasonably safe. There were plenty of reservations. India and the other colonies were kept as controlled markets during the period of so-called liberalization. Coincidentally, 1846 was the first year in which India exported no cotton goods at all and had to import cloth from England, which by then was pre-eminent in textile production, not as a result of the miracles of the market. Textiles are just the most striking example of a very general pattern which has perpetuated throughout the history of economic development until today.

Exactly the same is true of the U.S. It freed itself from British control and was able to undertake the same policies as the mother country. The U.S. has been a leader in protectionism since its origins. In the 1820s it was able to bar cheaper British textiles by very high tariffs, just as Britain had done. Without such measures, it's estimated that almost half of the emerging textile industry in New England would have been destroyed, with large-scale effects on industrial growth generally. We'd still be pursuing our comparative advantage in exporting fur if it had not been for such measurers.

The same was true of steel later in the century—and energy, in fact virtually all of the bases of modern industry right up till today, and I stress today. The Reaganites are a particularly striking example. They were masters in the art of really existing market doctrine. They extolled the glories of the market to the poor at home and the service areas abroad while they were boasting to the business world that Reagan had granted more import relief to U.S. industry than any of his predecessors in more than half a century. That's James Baker, at the time Secretary of the Treasury. He was overly modest. In reality it was more protection than all predecessors combined. As they presided over the greatest swing toward protectionism since the nineteenth century, shifting the U.S. from being the world's rhetorical champion of multilateral free trade to one of its leading challengers. I'm quoting *Foreign Affairs* in its review of the decade of the 1980s.

The Reaganites led the sustained assault on the free trade principle by the rich and the powerful from the early 1970s that's deplored in the major scholarly review of this topic by a GATT [General Agreement on Tariffs and Trade] economist, the trade organization that preceded the WTO. He estimates the restrictive effects of Reaganite measures at about three times those of other leading industrial countries, and those were very high. The high protection during these period is a large part of the reason for the increasing gap between the industrial world and the poorer countries, which has been growing since the 1960s.

Notice that there's nothing hidden about this. I'm quoting perfectly standard sources. One had to really admire the audacity of those who proclaim neoliberal principles as the path to development throughout modern history and even applaud the traditional U.S. devotion to free trade. The actual record is so radically different, from the origins until today, that one has to wonder what goes on the minds of the people who produce this stuff. In fact, the studies by economic historians very much understate the point. The reason is that they concentrate on a narrow issue, namely protectionism. The way the academic world is divvied up, protectionism falls in the economics department and other things fall in some other department. So nobody studies what's going on. There are other issues that belong here.

### Huge taxpayer subsidies to the corporations

The clearest and most obvious example which springs to mind at once, as soon as you look at the topic, although oddly you don't find it discussed, is cotton. How did the Industrial Revolution get started? Because there was cheap and available cotton. How was cotton kept cheap and available? Not exactly by market principles. It was kept cheap and available by extermination or expulsion of the native population in the southeastern U.S. and by slavery. Those are rather serious interferences with the market. But that doesn't figure in economic history when you talk about the measures of economic growth, because that's something you rarely study, if at all, in the history department.

There are contemporary analogs to that. The obvious contemporary analog is energy, the energy on which the industrial economies now rely. It's the counterpart to cotton 250 years ago. The so-called Golden Age of postwar economic development relied on cheap and abundant oil. It's kept that way largely by force, and so matters continue. A substantial part of the Pentagon budget today is devoted to keeping Middle East oil prices within a certain range, the range that the U.S. and its energy companies consider appropriate: not too high, because that would harm profits generally, but also not too low, because the energy corporations, which are mostly American, want the profits. That feeds back into the U.S. economy in all sorts of ways.

As far as I know, there's only one technical study of this topic by a Department of Energy consultant. He concludes that Pentagon expenditures amount of a subsidy of 30 percent of the market price of oil, demonstrating "that the current view that fossil fuels are inexpensive is a complete fiction." Estimates of the alleged efficiencies of trade and conclusions about economic growth are of very limited validity if we ignore hidden costs of this kind, which are numerous. The Pentagon budget is a huge subsidy to the oil price and distorts radically all calculations if you take it into account, but it overlooks a lot of other things. For example, there's a huge flow of U.S. dollars to Arab oil producers, actually to the monarchies that run the states in our interest. That's done largely through various tax manipulations. It's been going on since 1950. It amounts to a huge gift from the taxpayer to the U.S. oil companies, another factor that would enter into the calculation if you were trying to make a realistic analysis of the costs and efficiencies of trade.

Much the same is true of this swing toward protectionism since the 1970s that the GATT economists deplore. Only the swing toward protectionism was only part of the sustained assault on free trade principles that was accelerated under Reaganite "rugged individualism." Another chapter of the story includes the huge transfer of public funds to private power, often done under the traditional guise of security, that raised military research and development spending in constant dollars even past the record levels of the 1960s. Without such extreme measures of market interference, it's very doubtful that the U.S. automotive, steel, machine tool, semiconductors industries and others would have survived Japanese competition or would have been able to forge ahead in emerging technologies with very broad effects through the economy. And that continues.

Just a couple of days ago there was an honest headline in the *Wall Street Journal*. It said, in effect, that the International Trade Commission's steep tariffs on Japan protect U.S. makers of supercomputers. That was correct. The purpose of the International Trade Commission's decision was to protect U.S. supercomputer manufacturers, primarily Cray. Cray is called "private enterprise," which I suppose is some kind of bad joke. Its technology relies very heavily on public subsidy, and its market has been the Pentagon and the Department of Energy (pure private enterprise). Japanese firms have yet to sell a single supercomputer to agencies funded by the U.S. government in any way (that includes universities), though they're certainly competitive. Meanwhile, Japan is regularly bashed, quite accurately, for the measures it takes to protect its own industry and services. The entire farce is completely natural under the rules of really existing free market capitalism.

England and the U.S. have been followed by others, all developed societies. I'll omit discussion of other cases, but it's about the same. There's a lot more to say about this, and there is indeed plenty of variation and complexity to consider. But the generalizations I mentioned are pretty hard to miss. They really stand out if you look at the historical record.

There is a domestic analog. The same is true internally, increasingly now. That basic story is familiar too, and I'm not going to review it. But there has been increasingly a combination of protection and subsidy for the rich and stern market discipline for everyone else which has had far-reaching effects during this period of capital subjugation of labor in the past two decades, most notably in the U.S. and the U.K. The effects are very sharp. There's no better symbol of the process than Newt Gingrich, who happens to be the country's leading welfare freak. For years, he has held the prize in bringing federal subsidies to his rich constituents in Cobb Country, Georgia. That's a region where the whole economy is based very heavily on government subsidy, including the new ventures in biotechnology. Newt just sneaked yet another half billion dollars into the expanding military budget for his favorite local charity, Lockheed Martin, so as to maintain the cycle of dependency for the folks who really matter.

It's interesting to see that the basic facts are in some fashion acknowledged, even by the strongest advocates of neoliberal doctrine, notably the World Bank. The Bank imposes those programs with one voice, while another voice warns that their likely consequences will be very harmful, if not disastrous. Whatever one thinks of the neoliberal program, structural adjustment and so on, there are some facts that are not in dispute. Among them is the fact that these programs tend to reduce expenditures for education and health, to increase inequality, and to reduce labor's share in income. That is, they undermine just those factors that underlie sustained economic growth, as the Bank agrees, in fact insists with its other voice. The chief economist of the World Bank, formerly chief of Clinton's Council of Economic Advisors, not long ago wrote an article in the World Bank research journal on lessons of the East Asian miracle. He attributed the miracle in large part to the fact that government took major responsibility for the promotion of economic growth, abandoning what he calls the "religion that markets know best and intervening to enhance technology transfer, relative equality, education and health." To fill out the story, also industrial planning and coordination. That's all true, and exactly the opposite of what the World Bank prescribes.

The World Bank just released its annual world development report. It's a useful volume to read. This one was produced at a cost of $3 million and with a vast publicity apparatus. These volumes are supposed to represent mainstream economic thought. It's been quite interesting over the years to watch the oscillations in policy and theory, which are pretty radical. The new report is another departure, and an interesting one, although it's not a departure in all respects. So, for example, the role of the Bank is ignored, as usual, and although 3,600 businesses in 69 countries were surveyed for information, another part of the world's population remains in oblivion. They had no input into the report. This report, however, does depart from earlier ones in attempting to bring in lessons of economic history and also in stressing the important role of the state, notably on the miracle economies of East Asia. It also provides data on the growth of the state in recent years almost everywhere, but particularly in the rich countries, the OECD [Organization for Economic Cooperation and Development] countries, the rich man's club. In these countries, government expenditures are going up, and they're almost twice those of the poor countries as a percentage of Gross Domestic Product [GDP], and they're increasing, while they're dropping for the poor countries. You can draw some conclusions from that.

The report points out that for human welfare to be advanced, the state's ability to undertake and promote collective actions efficiently must be increased. Despite some departures from the religion, the Bank's version of history remains seriously flawed in interesting and important respects. This revised version holds that the state must be powerful and intrusive, but in restricted ways, basically through improving market conditions so that private power can serve as the engine of growth and development, which is not at all what history reveals, or the modern period, or its own studies. The new report still avoids the crucial matter of state initiative and coordination in the rich countries. Take its own chosen example of what it calls private-public interaction, namely the Internet, which in fact was planned, designed, developed and funded by the state, that means, the public, since the 1960s and has just now been handed over to private corporate power, which is happily announcing plans to cut out large parts of it for internal business operations and for the rest to control access and impose a kind of commercial TV model. That's not exactly interaction, but it's quite typical.

### A very sharp attack on democracy

A central part of neoliberal doctrine is what's called "minimizing the state." That's long-standing World Bank doctrine. It runs exactly counter to its analysis and technical studies, and now even its proposals, which is maybe something worth thinking about. But putting that aside, minimizing the state means maximizing something else. That is, decision-making continues. It doesn't disappear, but it continues elsewhere. Where does it continue? The doctrine tells you that it shifts to the people, but again, that hardly rises to the level of a bad joke. The decisions are shifted into the hands of unaccountable private power, actually totalitarian institutions that are unaccountable, and it shifts away from the public arena, where at least in principle there can be some measure of public participation and influence and control. That amounts to a very sharp attack on democracy. It's intended that way and obviously has that character. And it's not at all surprising that private power appreciates it, and it's only reasonable to suppose that it will continue. At least they'll try.

One very important current example is what's called the Multilateral Agreement on Investment [MAI]. That's an extraordinary investor rights treaty which is now working its way through the OECD and the WTO. In the WTO it's being blocked by Third World countries, primarily India and Malaysia, who are not interested in becoming wholly-owned subsidiaries of foreign-based transnationals. But in the OECD, the rich countries, there are no such barriers, and it will probably go through, perhaps by its target date of May 1998. The treaty provisions are worth a close look.

I'll skip the details, but they are worth looking at. In brief, it ends up being great news for investors, and pretty bad for everyone else. However, there's a problem: the public, which remains annoying. You can reduce democracy, but it's hard to eliminate it totally. Almost everywhere in the world, the public opposes such measures, which is kind of intriguing, because there is massive propaganda in favor of them and almost nothing in the public arena against them. But people continue to oppose them, by large majorities. The *Wall Street Journal* had an interesting article about that. They once again denounced the labor movement for opposing so-called "fast track" legislation that allows trade agreements to be implemented without interference by Congress. The MAI is never mentioned in this connection (have a look) but probably it's a major concern, maybe the major concern. The *Wall Street Journal* warned that labor has what it called an "ultimate weapon," the fact that a majority of the population opposes the fast track proposal. That's labor's ultimate weapon: people foolishly believe that they ought to know what's happening to them and have a voice in determining it.

There's a way to counter the ultimate weapon. The MAI negotiations are conducted in virtual secrecy. It doesn't matter what people think. You can't fail to be impressed by the silence of the media and the intellectual community, which must know about all of this and they must understand its implications. It is not a secret. In the U.S. the silence, to my knowledge, is total, apart from the fringes, although the basic facts are readily available on the Internet, for example, which has not yet been restricted to more profitable purposes. The official reason for fast track, which is repeated in the press, is that "the basic principle of negotiations is that only one person, namely the President, can negotiate for the U.S." That's the official position that you read. That's not quite accurate. That's the basic principle of negotiations over trade, but not of negotiations. Compare, for example, human rights treaties. Here the basic principle is quite different. The U.S. has one of the world's worst records, literally, maybe the worst record in the world, maybe the Cook Islands is still ahead of us. Very few human rights conventions are ever even signed. Those that are signed are held up for years in Congress. When they are finally accepted, which is very rare, they're accepted with explicit conditions that make them inapplicable in the U.S. So in a precise sense, we've endorsed no human rights treaties. It's a little different for trade. Trade is one thing, torture and rights of women and children are something else.

These seem to me some of the contours of the evolving world scene. It's pretty easy to look at them and be disheartened. But that is a very serious error. It's first of all an error of analysis and secondly an error of will. It's an error of analysis because we've been through all this before, repeatedly, and despite many ups and downs, the cycle is basically upwards. Subordination to power may seem high today, but it was much worse in the 1950s, and it was much worse than that in the 1920s, and so on back to earlier days. Today it's an important task to protect the very limited health care system. Forty years ago that wasn't a problem because the system didn't exist. There are many similar examples.

Furthermore, this has become a much more civilized society since the 1960s and indeed as a result of the ferment of the 1960s. The concern for the rights of oppressed peoples, for human rights generally, for the environment and many other matters have reached levels that could never have been anticipated in the 1960s. The same is true to public opposition to terror and aggression. There was no public opposition to impede John F. Kennedy and Robert McNamara when they sent the U.S. Air Force to bomb South Vietnamese peasants in 1961 and initiated programs of crop destruction and other measures to control the population of South Vietnam, which was always the main target of the U.S. assault, contrary to mythology. The Reaganites tried to duplicate those policies much closer to home. It must have been their model. They did it almost point by point as soon as they came into office, but they couldn't. They tried, and it aroused enormous public opposition. They had to resort to a pretty impressive international terror network. The results were awful, but direct attack, as in Indochina, would have been far worse.

There are many other cases, including the Gulf War if you look at it realistically. Furthermore, the resistance to the cynical onslaught of the Washington consensus is worldwide and substantial. There are major protests in Brazil, supported even by the conservative National Bishops Conference, throughout Central America, peasant organizations in Haiti, in South Africa, many other places. There's also a reviving labor movement here. Most of this isn't front-page news. One isn't very likely to read here the important declaration of the Association of Central American Campesino Organizations that was released a few months ago in San José, Costa Rica, and similarly many others. But things are happening, as in the past, when they have often had very positive effects, and there's no reason to doubt that they might today. In fact, today's struggles are similar to those of the past. But they start on a higher plane, with greater hopes for success. There are no known limits to how great that success might be in advancing the cause of freedom and justice, the cause for which Eqbal has been such an eloquent advocate in his words and actions for so many inspiring years.

### Editor's Notes to Chapter 28

Selection 28,"The Multilateral Agreement on Investment [MAI]," is the edited transcription of a talk (archived and made available by Alternative Radio, *www.alternativeradio.org*, we gratefully acknowledge) given on March 6, 1998, in Cambridge, MA, as part of the Harvard Trade Union Program. The "ultimate weapon" (see also Selections 27 and 30) is discussed further in **POP**, chs. 6 and 7. Information about recent developments is usually available from Public Citizen: *www.citizen.org* .

The resistance to "fast-track" legislation was also a victim of the atrocious crime of September 11th. As the Associated Press reported on July 26, 2002, "Urged on by President Bush, House and Senate negotiators agreed late last night on a bill that would give the president broad powers to negotiate new trade agreements... that Congress can approve or reject but cannot change...the compromise also contains 85 percent to 90 percent of the language in the Senate bill that provides extensive new benefits, costing up to $12 billion over 10 years, to workers who are dislocated as a result of foreign competition...The House passed its bill in December by a 215–214 vote. Most Democrats opposed it, saying it did not adequately protect worker and environmental rights."

On the Internet, see also selection 28. In his *Rich Media, Poor Democracy: Communication Politics in Dubious Times* (revised edition), New York: New Press, 1999, Robert McChesney documents the way previous alliances in the media were being extended to the Internet (and how the growth of media chains led to a contraction of range of opinions). One of the more innovative views of regulation in the Internet era by a legal expert is due to Lawrence Lessig, an antitrust scholar specializing in computer law. In his view, the headlong commercialization of the Internet threatens its decentralization and openness, and he argues that wide-open innovation, competition and free expression are essential features of the Internet as a network with open access and public software standards so that anyone can communicate over it. See Lessig, *The Future of Ideas: The Fate of the Commons in a Connected World,* New York: Random House, 2001.

On Ricardo's new "science," see the Editor's Notes to selection 27. On the thesis that the current global system (in which "trade" consists in substantial measure of centrally-managed intrafirm transactions and interactions among huge institutions, totalitarian in essence, designed to undermine democratic decision-making and to safeguard the masters from market discipline) is nothing like classical free-market capitalism, the term "corporate mercantilism" being a closer fit, see **WOON**, 2.6, and the discussion in reference 165 (Peter Phillips, *Challenge*, Jan.–Feb. 1992).

The neo-Hegelian ascendancy of the present corporate system of "collectivist legal entities" (Horwitz) is further discussed in **P&P**, ch. 4. References there and elsewhere to a good scholarly literature on the subject include Robert Brady, *Business as a System of Power.* Somerset: Transaction Pub, 2001; Martin Sklar, *The Corporate Reconstruction of American Capitalism, 1890–1916,*

Cambridge: Cambridge University Press, 1988; Charles Sellers, *The Market Revolution* Oxford: Oxford University Press, 1994; and particularly Morton Horwitz, *The Transformation of American Law*, vol. II Oxford: Oxford University Press, 1994, esp. ch. 3. See also C. P. Otero, Introduction to **CD&E**, p. 13ff.

# 28. The Multilateral Agreement On Investment [MAI]

Let's start with questions about investment and trade, since that's on the agenda. To take something concrete, let's take the recent and soon to be reiterated debate about "fast track." It was an interesting debate, or rather, non-debate, which took place about it. The fast track legislation had, I would guess, close to a 100 percent enthusiastic support in the press. If you could find a criticism of it, I'd like to see it. The issue was called a "no-brainer," so obvious they had to pass it. There was a huge amount of business propaganda in favor of it.

### "The ultimate weapon"

Interestingly, the public never budged. It started by being opposed. It ended by being opposed. So much opposed that Congress had to vote it down. The *Wall Street Journal* had an interesting article when the handwriting was on the wall just before the vote, saying that despite the fact that the advantages of fast track were so obvious and it was such a no-brainer, not worth discussing, nevertheless the opponents of fast track, they said, had an "ultimate weapon," namely the population was against it. That's part of the problem with having a formal democracy. Sometimes it's difficult to get rid of the ultimate weapon. Usually you can pretty well marginalize it, but it's kind of around. When the state does not have the power to coerce by force, as it loses that power, which it had here, any of you who know labor history know that. The U.S. has a long and very violent labor history, much more so than other developed countries, in large part because state force was invoked simply to destroy independent unionism, until, by the 1920s they had practically wiped it out. But that's now eroded. It's not gone, of course, but it's much less, and therefore this ultimate weapon is harder to deal with. You have to do it in other ways, propaganda, marginalization, all sorts of things. But in this case the ultimate weapon prevailed and fast track didn't pass.

The discussion about fast track, or really non-discussion, was interesting in a number of respects. For one thing, the argument for fast track was that the government can't work out complex trade negotiations which would be very beneficial for us unless it has the fast track authorization. Without that its hands are tied. Right while that argument was being presented day after day in the headlines, a group of twenty-five Representatives in the House sent a letter to President Clinton, saying that they were puzzled. They wanted to know how it was possible, given the fact that the opponents' hands were tied by the lack of fast track which they hadn't had for a couple of years, how had they been able to spend three years in detailed negotiations, in secret, about the Multilateral Agreement on Investment, which is a long, complex treaty that they've been meeting at the OECD [Organization for Economic Cooperation and Development] one week a month ever since May 1995 and they've somehow been able to do that even though they're unable to carry out negotiations. So they asked for an explanation of that. They also asked for an explanation of something else: Since we have this thing called the Constitution, according to which international commerce is the responsibility of Congress, how come the administration was able to carry out these complex, detailed negotiations that are impossible without ever informing Congress? Congress has never been informed about the Multilateral Agreement on Investment. In fact, the only reason it was ever discovered was because activists managed to leak some of the details. It was well known in the business community, of course. Chambers of Commerce were full of it.

The MAI, which if you don't know about you ought to, was initiated in May 1995 at the World Trade Organization. It's basically a huge investor rights agreement which gives investors the right to do anything they feel like. It was initiated at the World Trade Organization [WTO]. The U.S. wanted to ram it through there. But it was stopped. In the WTO, again, you have this ultimate weapon: there are a lot of countries around, like India, Malaysia and others, that aren't particularly eager to become wholly-owned subsidiaries of big transnationals. So they objected to the proposals that were coming through in the MAI. The rich countries had to withdraw it, because they obviously weren't going to get it easily through the WTO which, whatever you think about it, is vaguely democratic in the sense that the UN is kind of minimally democratic. A lot of highly non-democratic states are participants, whereas in the OECD it's the rich men's club. So they dropped the World Trade Organization path and shifted over to the OECD. That's the twenty-nine richest countries. What happens there is mainly determined by the few big, rich, powerful ones, the U.S., Germany and Japan.

In the OECD it's not certain, but it's likely that some such agreement would make it through the OECD. Once it's passed through the OECD, the rest of the world is forced to accept it; they don't have any choices. Once it becomes the condition on investment, then the rest of the world is told, "Take it or leave it". Either we close off our markets to you and you go down the tube, or you do things our way. So that's the way to get rid of the ultimate weapon in that case.

There's another problem, and that is domestic opinion in the OECD countries. That's also an ultimate weapon. The way that was taken care of is the same way that Congress was taken care of, and the Constitution, namely, by secrecy. So not only was Congress not informed, but the public was not informed. Remember, this has been going on since May 1995. It's all very well known to the business community. The Chambers of Commerce already had a publication on it in January, 1996. All the transnationals are up to their ears in it. But as far as I'm aware, the first break in silence in the U.S. was in December 1997, when the *Chicago Tribune* had a pretty good article on it. Actually there was one earlier case that I discovered, and that was in the *Journal of Commerce*, which is sort of a business-trade publication. They had some discussion of it. But in any kind of press that might reach the "ultimate weapons," it was completely concealed up until the 1997 article in *Chicago Tribune* in the ideological centers around here, where it really matters what people think, so they're a lot tighter. Boston and so on pride themselves on their liberalism, like this building does, but what that means is rigid, doctrinaire controls to ensure that nothing gets out because in places like this it's really important what people think. So in the East Coast the first break that I found was on February 13, when the *NY Times* agreed to allow an ad to appear by Public Citizen and a couple of other groups. It was well done and accurate. It had a detailed description of MAI. After that there have been a few small breaks here and there.

In Australia (I have friends there who monitor the press for me) apparently the first break was in January of this year [1998]. It broke into the Australian *Financial Review*, which had an article about it. Then a couple of critical articles came. Discussions have been going on for the last couple of months. In England there's been one or two stories leaking through over the years. In Canada, where there's been pressure, there have been a few articles in the press, and a certain amount of discussion, mainly from labor. In the U.S. there was nothing. It's not that they don't know about it (the editors of the *NY Times* obviously know about it; it's a big issue), but you've got to make sure that the ultimate weapon isn't used too early. Remember, this was aimed at May 1997; the target date for signing this was supposed to be May 1997. In that case it would have passed before anyone noticed. But now it's May 1998, so you get a couple of months, if you get organized, to think about it.

### A euphemism: "defense industrial base"

Coming back to the Congressional letter, they wanted to know first, how come it was possible to carry out these negotiations for three years when it's impossible in the absence of fast track, so we're told, and secondly, how it could be done without notifying Congress, given that Congress under the Constitution has the responsibility for international commerce? I haven't yet been able to find out what kind of an answer, if any, they got to the letter. You certainly won't find it out from reading the newspapers. But, in fact, most of Congress didn't even know about it until around then. And they found out about it only by advocacy of grassroots organizations. The treaty, or a draft of the treaty, leaked in January 1997 from France. It was then circulated through informal networks: the Internet, a couple of small foundations in Washington interested in trade issues. Things got around. There was a big meeting about it here in Boston last May. There's a Boston-based group that's working on it. I was out of the country at the time. But my recollection is that it never even got reported. Maybe it made it to some small radio station. But the ideological centers made certain that nobody would find out about it.

It shouldn't amaze you. If you want to get a job in the press and work your way up, you have to follow rules, just as if you want to become a professor at a university in one of the ideological fields. The rules may not be written on paper, but you internalize them. If you don't learn those rules, you don't make it through to a position where you have enough authority to do things. That's true of the press and the universities. So that shouldn't be amazing. I agree, it is kind of amazing, but in a way it's quite natural. In fact, what is to me the most intriguing aspect of all of this is that it's now close to three years, and it's been possible in free countries (where you don't have security forces running around smashing people's heads) to do this in secrecy, although everyone with any power and authority knows about it. When it's finally beginning to break through, there's very great pressure to try to keep it down.

Defenders of the MAI have one good argument. I think we should recognize that. It's the argument that the critics don't know what they're talking about. That's true. You really don't know what you're talking about. For example, every country in the OECD has submitted lots of reservations to the MAI. Nobody knows what they are. You could guess, and occasionally something leaks out about them, but basically you don't know. Even the draft treaty, a January 1997 draft, maybe it's been changed. Some of the wording is vague. You don't know exactly what it means. So defenders of it can rightly say that the critics are really speaking from ignorance, thanks to the success of the media, the educated classes and the journals of opinion in ensuring that the public will stay ignorant and the weapon won't be wielded, they hope.

That was one interesting aspect of fast track (these questions that were raised by Congress). But there were other interesting aspects. Fast track was supposed to be about free trade. There are a couple of reasons why that can't possibly be true. For one thing, the agreements that they are talking about are not free trade agreements. There's nobody who believes in free trade, except maybe for somebody else. It's always for other people, like welfare mothers, who should recognize the discipline of the market. But not Newt Gingrich's rich constituents. They've got to get government subsidies.

That's the way the international system works, too. In Sub-Saharan Africa they have to understand the marvels of free trade. But the whole history of the U.S. has been radically protectionist. Sometimes it's extreme, like the Reagan Administration. We would barely have an economy now if the Reagan Administration hadn't in effect closed off the U.S. market to cheaper Japanese and other East Asian production in automobiles, steel, semiconductors, and so on, as well as pouring in massive subsidies. They usually cover them by national security. There's a thing called the "defense industrial base" in the U.S. which has to be supported by taxpayers through the Pentagon. Defense industrial base is a euphemism. It means high-tech industry. (That's how my salary gets paid, for example, at MIT.) MIT is one of the funnels by which the public unwittingly pays the cost of high-tech industry and accepts the risks.

That's true of just about every dynamic sector of the economy. If that does-n't work, then, as in the 1980s, the U.S. just uses basically force to compel other countries to accept what are called "voluntary export restrictions." When the U.S. says, "Do something voluntarily," that means, "Do it or else." So other countries, like Japan, "voluntarily" agreed to restrict their exports while the U.S. poured massive taxpayers subsidies to enable industry to recapitalize. American management, who had been so busy playing financial games that they'd fallen way behind the rest of the world through the 1970s (which was recognized), so the military system took on its usual function, going back to the early 19th century, to make sure that American industry is functioning properly through tax-payer subsidies, and organized through the Air Force a program called Mantech (flexible manufacturing technology), which was to try to overcome the management gap in the U.S., the inability of American executives and managers to comprehend the new flexible, lean production techniques that were being used so effectively in Japan. At taxpayer expense, these systems were devised and developed, robotization, automatization, getting rid of workers. Through these various devices American industry, meaning the wealth of American industry, was saved. But the incomes and wages of most of the population, in fact a majority of the population, actually declined since the late 1970s. The average family income still, despite the so-called boom, was below what it was in 1989. Meanwhile, corporate profits are still off the map. But those are systems that are designed. They don't come by economic laws or laws of nature. They're policy decisions. They're designed, and they have nothing to do with free trade.

Just a couple of weeks ago the Clinton Administration announced that it was barring Japanese supercomputers from the U.S., setting tariffs so high that you couldn't bring in Japanese supercomputers. The purpose was stated straight in the *Wall Street Journal*. It was to save Cray Research, which has now been bought out by somebody else. That used to be the big producer of supercomputers. It's called a private corporation, which means its profits are private, but it costs are 100 percent paid by the public. Its markets are government procurement, research and development is mostly done through public subsidy, through military and other devices, but then Cray Research puts it together. Now they make the profit. So it's a private corporation. But one of the reasons it was able to have a market was that the U.S. had barred better Japanese supercomputers from any government institution, even from universities. It's called free trade.

I'm just talking about the last few years, not the nineteenth century, when the U.S. was the leader in protectionism. And that continues right up till today. If you look at the so-called free trade agreements, they're kind of a mixture of liberalization and protectionism. They're very carefully crafted to serve particular interests, namely the interests of those who design the agreements, not surprisingly. But they have highly protectionist elements (like intellectual property rights, for example) designed to prevent technological development and scientific progress and even industrial progress, and to ensure that the big corporations, like the big pharmaceutical corporations, can monopolize the technology of the future.

They don't do that because they're so smart. Over half of R&D [Research and Development] in pharmaceuticals comes straight out of your pocket through public funds, and high tech is even higher. But once they get the drugs or the medicines that they can then market, they want to make sure that, say, India, which has a pharmaceutical industry, doesn't figure out cheaper and smarter ways to make these things. The new intellectual property rights regime of the World Trade Organization [WTO] bars that for the first time in history by imposing far heavier restrictions and protection on patents than ever existed, and certainly restrictions that none of the developing countries ever dreamed of accepting during the period of their growth, like the U.S. and Germany. But now you can use it to clamp down on others. And that's just a piece of it. There's a whole mixture of protectionism and liberalization.

## People with sentiments and feelings

Strikingly, free trade theory, if you really go back to what it's supposed to have meant, say, Smith and Ricardo, it was based on free movement of labor, which was not totally false back in the early nineteenth century. As you by violence wiped out the indigenous population in this country and Australia, you could get free movement of all the excess labor (like convicts in England) and send them over here, and then a huge flow of immigration in the middle of the century. I think the peak of immigration per capita in the U.S. was around 1850. So it was true in a sense that there was free movement of labor, not exactly by free market principles. Nothing like that is the case. There's supposed to be free movement of labor, free movement of knowledge, which is increasingly important today, but that's exactly what's blocked by the new protectionist regime of the WTO, intellectual property rights. So free movement of labor is blocked, free movement of knowledge is blocked.

What they want is free movement of capital, which is itself kind of interesting. Ricardo didn't believe in it. Ricardo, the great icon of free trade, understood very well that the theory of comparative advantage wouldn't work if you had free movement of capital. If all capital could make more money by textiles in England than by wine in Portugal, to take the famous example, it would all move to England and you'd have no wine. You had to assume relative immobility of capital in order for the theory to get off the ground. He understood that. He didn't think that was a big problem. In part, it wasn't so big a problem, because in those days capital meant land, mostly, and you couldn't move that. Ricardo also held, interestingly, that if investors in England realized that they could make more profit somewhere else, say, Portugal, they wouldn't invest there anyway, because they would have so much feeling of solidarity and community spirit and loyalty to the people of England that they would never do such things and they'd be willing to take a loss to do it.

You have to remember that even as late as Ricardo, this was pre-capitalist. People still had the idea that human beings had sentiments and feelings and cared about one another and all this old-fashioned stuff, and that they weren't just driven solely by the need to maximize consumption and profit, like atoms of greed. This is all pre-capitalist mentality, like Smith, and even in Ricardo you still find it. Free movement of capital is a very recent idea. In fact, even the post-Second World War system didn't have it. The time it probably peaked was around 1900, when Britain was pretty much running the world and it was on the gold standard. At that point they did have relatively free trade and a lot of movement of capital. In fact, the level of globalization today relative to the economy is approximately back to what it was around 1900 in most respects. It's not a historically novel thing.

After the Second World War, when Britain and the U.S. constructed a kind of new world order, it's commonly called a system of liberalization. But that's only half true. They did intend to liberalize trade. They wanted to increase trade, but they wanted to restrict capital movements (the Bretton Woods system, as it was called). That was the original role of the IMF (it's now reversed) to regulate capital flows and make sure that countries had the capacity to control capital import and export, but to try to free up trade. They did this for two reasons, which both the British and American economists recognized. The British with [John Maynard] Keynes, who headed the group; in the U.S. it was Harry Dexter White, Roosevelt's representative. They both recognized (what is probably true) that liberalization of finance and liberalization of trade are inconsistent. If you liberalize finance you're probably going to restrict trade. The record of the last thirty years supports that. It's been a period of trade restriction, but also of capital liberalization.

## Mobility of capital and the social contract

That was one reason. The other reason, very important, is that they also recognized that if capital flows are free, it's going to be an extremely powerful weapon against the welfare state, which was very popular at that time and still is to an extent. But at that time it had enormous support, and they couldn't tear it apart. If capital was free to flow out of any country that tried to introduce measures to improve education or health or equalization of wages or anything for human welfare, if capital is free to flow out, it's going to terminate these programs. It's a weapon which will put an end to those programs. So what was developed is what was called a system of "embedded liberalism," meaning efforts to liberalize trade but to control capital flow, both for the purpose of liberalizing trade and for the purpose of allowing governments (meaning people through governments) to implement some kind of social contract.

This was broken down around 1970, dismantled by the Nixon Administration, Thatcher, and so on. By now the system is pretty well eroded so we do have a very free flow of capital, and the MAI [Multilateral Agreement on Investment] wants to make it even more free. This has also, as I said, been a peri-

od of increased protectionism (that's well understood by international economists). It's also a period in which capital, financial capital in particular, has
become what is called by a lot of economists a "virtual Senate," meaning it can
make the decisions, particularly in the less rich countries, over what social policy will be. If they try to do anything for their own populations, zip, you go somewhere else. Even for the rich countries that's true.

The period of liberalization of capital has also, as you know, been a period
of very strong attack against the social contract that had been slowly developed
through centuries of struggle, which is being dismantled, primarily in the U.S.
and England, the Anglo-American countries in general, but also to an extent in
Europe and elsewhere, because it is an integrated economy and it's hard to keep
away from the "virtual Senate." So wages in the U.S., for example, by around
1990, were already lower than in Europe and Japan, far lower than in Europe.
Working hours are longer. Other countries just have to go along.

So mobility of capital has its points. But none of this is free trade, in fact,
quite the opposite. So one further problem about the fast track being involved
with free trade is that these aren't free trade agreements. They're talking about
something else. They're talking about investor and financial rights agreements.
It's whatever you like, but it's not free trade. It's some other thing.

## A question solely about democracy

Another problem about the argument for fast track and free trade is that fast
track has nothing to do with free trade. Even the most firm believer in free trade,
and there are a few scattered around (ideologists who believe in free trade, maybe
they're right, maybe they're wrong, who knows), they're so scattered they have
almost no impact on policy, but they exist. Those people might be very strongly
opposed to fast track, because fast track is not about free trade. Fast track is about
democracy. That's obvious on the face of it. The fast track issue is: Should the
public have the right to know what's being done to them? That's the fast track
question. Should there be deliberation and discussion of international agreements, or should it be done in secret by the executive with Congress given a couple of hours to say yes? The question is solely about democracy, and the most passionate advocate of free trade could also be strongly opposed to fast track if they
also happen to believe in democracy, because that's the only issue that arises. You
take a look at the whole non-debate over the question, and you'll see that wasn't
raised.

The final point about fast track that was not discussed is what it was really
about. Since it's in secret, we really don't know, but you can make a good guess.
It's a pretty good guess that it was not about bringing Chile into NAFTA. Maybe
they want to do that and maybe they don't, but that's pretty small potatoes. What
it was about, I presume, was MAI. Fast track, if it did get through, would allow
the MAI treaty to go through without any discussion (that's a big story already;
it's not like improving trade with Chile by some percentage). And that was never
mentioned. At least I couldn't find a mention in the press that this was the issue

behind fast track. This is the collection of fast track considerations, which are coming back. The MAI is right on the agenda and has very important implications. It will be interesting to see whether "the ultimate weapon" can manage to make it break through into public discussion or whether it will just be rammed down people's throats as another fraudulent free trade agreement.

[Question from the floor]

How would I refine the patent system? First of all, let's look at what it is. Up until recently, patents were fairly loose. In fact, part of the reason for the growth of the electronics industry in the U.S. in the 1970s is that the patent regime was pretty loose so there was a lot of interaction and leakage, which sort of made sense because it was mostly paid for by the public anyway. It was mostly coming through the Pentagon and NASA, the whole cover-up for high-tech industry through which you guys pay for my salary, for example: GE [General Electric] profits. As I mentioned, in pharmaceuticals, about 50 percent of R&D [Research and Development] was governmental, up until about 1990: In electronics, it's run about 50 percent to two-thirds since the Second World War; in computers, it was a 100 percent funded by the public in the 1950s because they were unmarketable; containerization was a 100 percent funded by the public; automation, almost entirely funded by the public because they were unprofitable. So the public would take the risks, and finally, when they get somewhere, you hand it over to private industry and they get the gains. Of course, they do it the way they want. Automation was not designed to, say, put more power into the hands of skilled mechanics, as it could have been, but rather to de-skill them and put more control into the hands of managers. That's what happens when you work it through a state system, which is basically linked up to private power.

Or take, say, the big new excitement, the Internet. The World Bank just came out with a development report in which they reversed course. They say it's important to have powerful states. They give one example of really good state-corporate fruitful interaction, which they recommend as a model for the future. The example they give is the Internet, which is a beautiful example. For thirty years the Internet was a 100 percent funded by the public, meaning through the state. All the ideas, the technology, the innovations, all came from the public sector. Now, right now, in the mid-1990s, it's being handed over to private capital. Bill Gates would love to run the Internet. As late as 1994 he didn't have enough interest in it even to go to conferences about it. It's fine for the public to have all the ideas and all the initiative and do everything, and then when it's all done he's delighted to take it over. He's a fine parasite. In fact, the way he puts it, in his own words, "Microsoft has achieved its position by embracing and extending ideas" (ideas that come from the public sector). But that's the World Bank's model of public-private cooperation.

That's the way R&D works. In the U.S. it's mostly hidden in the Pentagon system or the NIH [National Institute of Health]. But other countries have similar systems. There's no way that corporations are going to cut into their profits if they don't have to. If they have to, they will, but if the public is going to pay for it, why should they pay for it? And given the kinds of socio-political systems that the U.S. and Australia and so on have, which are basically corporate run, although there is a government which is to some extent under popular control, that's what you have. So how would you refine it? It's a little bit like asking: "Suppose we were living under a king. How would you make it better?" You could go to the king and plead with him to be a little bit more benevolent (like instead of whipping and torturing people, maybe he should give them a little money at Christmas; that would make things better). If you want to refine an autocracy, you can try to get it to be a somewhat more benevolent autocracy. Of course, there's another possibility. That is get rid of the king.

I have one bone to pick with the critics of the MAI. That is, though I think what they're saying is correct, they are pointing out that this thing gives corporations extraordinary rights, way more than they ought to have. But I think there's something more to be said: They shouldn't have any rights at all. They're totally illegitimate. They're just forms of totalitarian structure. They're unaccountable private tyrannies. What's more, they're an innovation. They're not part of American history. Until early in this century, a corporation was like a bunch of people who decided to get together and build a bridge over the Charles River here in Boston and got a charter from the state to do it. If they did it, performing a public service, the corporation's finished. They're partnerships.

The change did not take place by legislation. It took place by courts. Out of the legislative system, they were given extraordinary powers. There were old-fashioned conservatives in those days; there aren't any anymore. They call themselves conservatives, but they're not. But in those days conservatives condemned corporations as a form of communism. It's the term we would now call totalitarianism. Because in fact they were completely autocratic structures. Internally they're as close to totalitarian as you can imagine. They're unaccountable. They were given the rights of immortal persons, which means they have freedom of speech, so they're allowed to advertise. Why should a collectivist legal institution have the right to free speech? That's totally inconsistent with everything that the founding fathers were for, classical liberalism. Rights are supposed to inhere in persons, not in collective institutions. They're given the right of freedom from search and seizure, which means you can't find out what they're doing. So just as you have a right to keep the police out of your home, these objects have the right to keep the public from knowing what they're up to. All of these rights are actually completely illegitimate and indeed were regarded that way not very long ago, about a hundred years ago. The corporatization of America took place in the early part of the [20th] century.

With all the talk about globalization, let me say again, it's approximately at the level of pre-1913. Furthermore, it's almost entirely within what's called the triad. About 75 percent of world trade is within the U.S., Europe and Japan. You take a look at what goes to the so-called developing countries, most of it goes to about ten of them. These regions in the triad have parliamentary democracies. They're not going to be afraid of military coups. There isn't going to be a military coup in the U.S. These are countries where the mechanisms already exist without any change to control all of this. You don't need any revolutionary change. The only revolutionary change you would need is to start taking the Constitution seriously. That would be the change.

In fact, you can go back to the position of mainstream American thought a century ago. Just think what the U.S. was a century ago. Take the AFL-CIO [American Federation of Labor and Congress of Industrial Organizations], not a super-radical outfit. At the end of the nineteenth century, they were having passionate speeches in their conventions saying that the mission of labor is to ensure democracy in the workplace, meaning working people ought to own the places that they work and control what happens there and decide what happens on the shop floor and decide about investment. That's the basis for democracy. The slogan of the Republican Party in the mid-nineteenth century was that wage labor is approximately like chattel slavery. Workers out here in Lynn were condemning the Boston abolitionists and deriding them because they were opposed to chattel slavery but they were in favor of wage slavery. The *NY Times* was having editorials right after the Civil War saying, We got rid of slavery, but we still have wage slavery, which isn't that much different. In the whole working-class movement throughout the nineteenth century this was standard thought. This is as American as apple pie. There's nothing radical about it.

The major countries of the world are in a position to introduce very substantial changes in the system if the "ultimate weapon" ever get themselves organized.

### Systems of protection of private power

However, I don't want to end without saying something about patents, because that's an interesting case.

The patent regimes up until fairly recently were pretty flexible. During the periods of their development, the U.S. barely observed patents. Germany and Italy and the rest of them, up into the 1960s and 1970s, had very limited patent restrictions. The richer countries always wanted to enforce them, of course, because they already had the technology and development. But nobody else paid any attention (and remember that the U.S. is kind of a latecomer; it moved into it along the way). When patent regimes were finally established internationally, as they finally were, they had to do with processes. That meant you could patent a process. So if Merck Pharmaceutical has some new drug, they could patent the process by which they designed it. But you couldn't patent the product up until the current Uruguay Round. That means that if the Indian or Brazilian pharmaceutical industry found a smarter way to produce that drug, they could do it. That's very important: for one thing because it allows knowledge to spread and for another because it increases technological and scientific progress. It increases human progress, economic progress, because you can do things better.

The new regimes, started in the Uruguay Round, was process and product. So there's a process patent which runs twenty years and then a product patent which runs something like another twenty years. This locks things in so that nobody can get into it. The idea is to raise prices of drugs, raise profits of pharmaceuticals, cut out innovation and ensure that the few conglomerates that are going to run the industry will do it. Also, this is highly uneconomical. There's a good study by Dean Baker, an economist at the Economic Policy Institute, who just did some of the calculations and pointed out that if the R&D that is funded almost half by the public in pharmaceuticals was just a 100 percent, so all the R&D was public, and you eliminated patents, there'd be an enormous economic benefit. There would be less profit, but pharmaceuticals would be much cheaper, the same innovation would take place because you're funding all the R&D, and the differences are enormous. I don't remember the exact numbers, but they're huge differences.

So these are just systems of protection of private power. When you ask, in a small country like Australia, I agree, alone there's nothing much you can do. You've just got to try to survive. But why be alone? The labor movement is supposed to be an international movement. International solidarity makes all the difference. For example, if there was enough international solidarity to close down overseas Caterpillar plants, Caterpillar workers here would have won the strike. Caterpillar used its enormous profits and flexibility of capital to create excess productive capacities elsewhere. Pretty consciously, they didn't hide it. They wanted excess productive capacities as a weapon against American workers. First of all, they have no right to do anything because they're totally illegitimate. But the decision that handed them over the huge profits while keeping wages down enabled them to do that. Over and above that, if there had been enough international solidarity, workers wouldn't be going to work in the Caterpillar plants. That's the only kind of thing that can save Australia or Haiti or most countries.

Can the labor movement fight back against it, against the policies that are going on? Sure. The policies of liberalization of capital flow, which are a big factor in what's going on in the world, are quite recent. They are government decisions, since the 1970s, primarily. They can be reversed. The countries that have been able to protect themselves from this. Take, say, Chile, in Latin America. Chile is the one country that has had some kind of economic development. But not through the free market, incidentally, contrary to what's claimed. They did have a free market experiment when Pinochet came in in 1973, run by the Chicago boys. It was a complete disaster. It led to a total collapse of the Chilean economy in 1982. The state in 1982 owned more of the economy than it had under Allende, the so-called bad guy. Then they moved to a sort of mixed economy. One of the elements in it was control of capital flow. So Chile is the only Latin American country that has controls that are a barrier against short-term investment. That means when you invest in Chile you have to put 30 percent of it in some long-term investment. There are other devices like that for countries to try to save themselves from this short-term, speculative flow (the "virtual Senate") that wipes them out.

Incidentally, the MAI is designed to stop those options. But other countries can use them. The U.S. always used them. The U.S. had capital controls up until the 1970s. Germany and Japan up until the 1980s. South Korea up until the late 1980s. In fact, that's probably the reason for the South Korean achievement. They were able to control capital as well as labor. They were forced to liberalize capital flow, and I think that's a good part of what's happening now. They were forced to liberalize capital flow before they had a regulatory system in place. Then you get free market failures like they got.

Korean economic development has been absolutely spectacular, and not in a very pretty way. Korean labor was brutally repressed. It was under a dictatorship. But since the 1960s, since the Park dictatorship, growth rates have been phenomenal. It's been eight or 10 percent a year for about thirty years. In 1970, Korean wages were about a third of Mexican wages. By 1990 they were three times Mexican wages. And Mexico was the one having the economic miracle. The same is true is you compare Korea with the Philippines. Around 1970 they were about the same. Now South Korea is probably twenty times as rich. It was a huge achievement, done in a miserable way. But you can't deny what happened.

By the late 1980s, the state role was declining and the big Korean conglomerates (the *chaebols*) were becoming much more powerful and more free of state control. As a condition on entry into the OECD, Korea was forced to liberalize its financial markets. The debt was not all that high: it was about as high in 1982 relative to GNP. So it's not like something new. In fact, the whole Third World debt problem that everybody's talking about, relative to the economies, is about the same as the debt of American railroads about a century ago, when they couldn't pay their debt. Take a look at the quantities, that was about at the scale relative to the economy of the Third World debt today. These things are not unmanageable. In growing economies, the U.S. happens to have a growing economy, highly protectionist, a big market, they were able to overcome it. In South Korea, the basis of economic development is pretty solid: industry, educated workforce, by comparative standards reasonable health standards. For a small country this is a pretty good achievement. Whether it can survive the current financial assaults, I don't know. Undoubtedly there was a lot of cronyism and chicanery and cheating, most of which grew during the period of privatization. As the *chaebols*, the conglomerates, got more powerful, they also got more corrupt. These are largely market failures. But they happen, and it's got to be overcome. It's got to be more transparent, more democratic. The basis of a solid economy is certainly there. It is now under tremendous attack by sharp speculative capital flows, and again, it's kind of like the Australia story. Alone, I don't think Korea can do much about this. With international cooperation, it could. I suppose that U.S. and other corporations are just waiting to pick up pieces of the economy cheap and then they can turn it into Mexico.

## Editor's Notes to Chapter 29

Selection 29, "Terror and Just Response" is Chomsky's Znet commentary of July 2, 2002, with footnotes. (We are grateful to Z Communications: *www.zmag.org*.) It is the only one of the new additional selections that was originally written as a scholarly paper, not delivered first as a talk. In a sense it is the written counterpart of two talks on terrorism he gave after September 11, 2001. The first, "The New War Against Terror" (Oct. 18, 2001) was sponsored by The Technology & Culture Forum at MIT, which for many years has fostered discussion of the critical issues of the day, paying special attention to the ethical implications of scientific discovery and technological change (people everywhere were able to join those listening in many rooms at MIT via the World Wide Web). The second, "The World After September 11," he gave at the Conference of the American Friends Service Committee (AFSC), and Tufts University's Peace and Justice Studies Program and Peace Coalition on "After September 11th: Paths to Peace, Justice and Security," Tufts University, Dec. 8, 2001, a written version of which is included in the new (2002) edition of **P&E** (a book that covers the terror of the 1980s in some detail) as ch. 6. See also **TT**, **CT**, **NMH**, **NGDL**, and **RS**.

A collection of edited and updated interviews by a variety of interviewers from all over the world on the terror of September 11, 2001, with the lean title *9-11*, New York: Seven Stories Press, 2001, became Chomsky's first bestseller (rightly described on the bestseller list as "an alternative view of the U.S.-led war on terrorism") shortly after the book was published at the end of the year.

In "Terror and Just Response" Chomsky, understandably, does not go beyond saying that he had a chance to see first-hand some of the consequences of Turkish repression of Kurds "when visiting the unofficial Kurdish capital of Diyarbakir several months after 9-11." There is more in the remark than meets the eye, and it is of some interest. The reason he had a chance is that "Scarcely two months after the European Union praised Turkey for passing new laws protecting freedom of expression, the authorities in Ankara [were] using anti-terrorism legislation to prosecute Mr. Chomsky's Turkish publisher," Fatih Tas. (Robert Fisk, "Turkey Prosecutes Chomsky Publisher for Essay on Kurds." *The Independent*, Jan. 24, 2002.) Tas's alleged crime was "propaganda against the indivisible unity of the nation" for having published *American Interventionism* (as the collection of essays in Turkish translation was titled), presumably because it includes statements such as the following:

"The Kurds have been miserably oppressed throughout the whole history of the modern Turkish state... In 1984, the Turkish government launched a major war in the south-east against the Kurdish population... The end result was pretty awesome: tens of thousands of people killed, two to three million refugees, massive ethnic cleansing with some 3,500 villages destroyed."

Since Chomsky saw this prosecution as "a very severe attack on the most elementary human and civil rights," he wrote to the offices of the United Nations high commissioner for human rights pointing out that amendments to Turkish law were supposed to have provided greater freedom of expression, not less. He then flew to Turkey for the publisher's first court appearance on February 13th, planning to meet with Kurdish activists, as a direct test of Turkey's freedoms. (See Chomsky's Diyarbakir speech, posted on ZNet's Foreign Policy Watch, March 25, 2002.)

There were a number of reports on the trial. (Thanks to David Peterson for making several of them available to me). The following quote is from the report by The Associated Press (*NY Times*, Feb. 13, 2002):

"Tas said he believed that Chomsky's presence at the hearing had helped him escape a jail sentence.

"If Chomsky hadn't been here… we wouldn't have expected such a verdict," he said.

No charges were filed against Chomsky himself. Lawyers for the defense had requested that he be included in the case as a co-defendant, but the prosecution declined to charge him.

Chomsky said before the hearing that Americans had a responsibility to monitor and protest human rights abuses in Turkey, a close U.S. ally."

# 29. Terror And Just Response

September 11th will surely go down in the annals of terrorism as a defining moment. Throughout the world, the atrocities were condemned as grave crimes against humanity, with near-universal agreement that all states must act to "rid the world of evildoers," that "the evil scourge of terrorism"—particularly state-backed international terrorism—is a plague spread by "depraved opponents of civilization itself" in a "return to barbarism" that cannot be tolerated. But beyond the strong support for the words of the U.S. political leadership—respectively, George W. Bush, Ronald Reagan, and his Secretary of State George Shultz —interpretations varied: on the narrow question of the proper response to terrorist crimes, and on the broader problem of determining their nature.

## The official U.S. definition of "terrorism"

On the latter, an official U.S. definition takes "terrorism" to be "the calculated use of violence or threat of violence to attain goals that are political, religious, or ideological in nature... through intimidation, coercion, or instilling fear."[2] That formulation leaves many questions open, among them, the legitimacy of actions to realize "the right to self-determination, freedom, and independence, as derived from the Charter of the United Nations, of people forcibly deprived of that right..., particularly peoples under colonial and racist regimes and foreign occupation..." In its most forceful denunciation of the crime of terrorism, the UN General Assembly endorsed such actions, 153–2.[3]

Explaining their negative votes, the U.S. and Israel referred to the wording just cited. It was understood to justify resistance against the South African regime, a U.S. ally that was responsible for over 1.5 million dead and $60 billion in damage in neighboring countries in 1980–88 alone, putting aside its practices within. And the resistance was led by Nelson Mandela's African National Congress, one of the "more notorious terrorist groups" according to a 1988 Pentagon report, in contrast to pro-South African RENAMO, which the same report describes as merely an "indigenous insurgent group" while observing that it might have killed 100,000 civilians in Mozambique in the preceding two years.[4] The same wording was taken to justify resistance to Israel's military occupation, then in its 20th year, continuing its integration of the occupied territories and harsh practices with decisive U.S. aid and diplomatic support, the latter to block the longstanding international consensus on a peaceful settlement.[5]

Despite such fundamental disagreements, the official U.S. definition seems to me adequate for the purposes at hand,[6] though the disagreements shed some light on the nature of terrorism, as perceived from various perspectives.

Let us turn to the question of proper response. Some argue that the evil of terrorism is "absolute" and merits a "reciprocally absolute doctrine" in response.[7] That would appear to mean ferocious military assault in accord with the Bush doctrine, cited with apparent approval in the same academic collection on the "age of terror:" "If you harbor terrorists, you're a terrorist; if you aid and abet terrorists, you're a terrorist—and you will be treated like one." The volume reflects articulate opinion in the West in taking the U.S.-U.K. response to be appropriate and properly "calibrated," but the scope of that consensus appears to be limited, judging by the evidence available, to which we return.

More generally, it would be hard to find anyone who accepts the doctrine that massive bombing is the appropriate response to terrorist crimes—whether those of September 11th, or even worse ones, which are, unfortunately, not hard to find. That follows if we adopt the principle of universality: if an action is right (or wrong) for others, it is right (or wrong) for us. Those who do not rise to the minimal moral level of applying to themselves the standards they apply to others—more stringent ones, in fact—plainly cannot be taken seriously when they speak of appropriateness of response; or of right and wrong, good and evil.

## An uncontroversial case as illustration

To illustrate what is at stake, consider a case that is far from the most extreme but is uncontroversial; at least, among those with some respect for international law and treaty obligations. No one would have supported Nicaraguan bombings in Washington when the U.S. rejected the order of the World Court to terminate its "unlawful use of force" and pay substantial reparations, choosing instead to escalate the international terrorist crimes and to extend them, officially, to attacks on undefended civilian targets, also vetoing a Security Council resolution calling on all states to observe international law and voting alone at the General Assembly (with one or two client states) against similar resolutions. The U.S. dismissed the ICJ on the grounds that other nations do not agree with us, so we must "reserve to ourselves the power to determine whether the Court has jurisdiction over us in a particular case" and what lies "essentially within the domestic jurisdiction of the United States"—in this case, terrorist attacks against Nicaragua.[8]

Meanwhile, Washington continued to undermine regional efforts to reach a political settlement, following the doctrine formulated by the Administration moderate, George Shultz: the U.S. must "cut [the Nicaraguan cancer] out," by force. Shultz dismissed with contempt those who advocate "utopian, legalistic means like outside mediation, the United Nations, and the World Court, while ignoring the power element of the equation;" "Negotiations are a euphemism for capitulation if the shadow of power is not cast across the bargaining table," he declared. Washington continued to adhere to the Shultz doctrine when the

Central American Presidents agreed on a peace plan in 1987 over strong U.S. objections: the Esquipulas Accords, which required that all countries of the region move towards democracy and human rights under international supervision, stressing that the "indispensable element" was the termination of the U.S. attack against Nicaragua. Washington responded by sharply expanding the attack, tripling CIA supply flights for the terrorist forces.

Having exempted itself from the Accords, thus effectively undermining them, Washington proceeded to do the same for its client regimes, using the substance—not the shadow—of power to dismantle the International Verification Commission (CIVS) because its conclusions were unacceptable, and demanding, successfully, that the Accords be revised to free U.S. client states to continue their terrorist atrocities. These far surpassed even the devastating U.S. war against Nicaragua that left tens of thousands dead and the country ruined perhaps beyond recovery. Still upholding the Shultz doctrine, the U.S. compelled the government of Nicaragua, under severe threat, to drop the claim for reparations established by the ICJ.[9]

There could hardly be a clearer example of international terrorism as defined officially, or in scholarship: operations aimed at "demonstrating through apparently indiscriminate violence that the existing regime cannot protect the people nominally under its authority," thus causing not only "anxiety, but withdrawal from the relationships making up the established order of society."[10] State terror elsewhere in Central America in those years also counts as international terrorism, in the light of the decisive U.S. role, and the goals, sometimes frankly articulated; for example, by the Army's School of the Americas, which trains Latin American military officers and takes pride in the fact that "Liberation Theology... was defeated with the assistance of the U.S. Army."[11]

It would seem to follow, clearly enough, that only those who support bombing of Washington in response to these international terrorist crimes—that is, no one—can accept the "reciprocally absolute doctrine" on response to terrorist atrocities or consider massive bombardment to be an appropriate and properly "calibrated" response to them.

## A new phase of the "war on terror"

Consider some of the legal arguments that have been presented to justify the U.S.-U.K. bombing of Afghanistan; I am not concerned here with their soundness, but their implications, if the principle of uniform standards is maintained. Christopher Greenwood argues that the U.S. has the right of "self-defense" against "those who caused or threatened... death and destruction," appealing to the ICJ ruling in the Nicaragua case. The paragraph he cites applies far more clearly to the U.S. war against Nicaragua than to the Taliban or al-Qaeda, so if it is taken to justify intensive U.S. bombardment and ground attack in Afghanistan, then Nicaragua should have been entitled to carry out much more severe attacks against the U.S. Another distinguished professor of international law, Thomas Franck, supports the U.S.-U.K. war on grounds that "a state is responsible for the consequences of permitting its territory to be used to injure another state"; fair enough, and surely applicable to the U.S. in the case of Nicaragua, Cuba, and many other examples, including some of extreme severity.[12]

Needless to say, in none of these cases would violence in "self-defense" against continuing acts of "death and destruction" be considered remotely tolerable; acts, not merely "threats."

The same holds of more nuanced proposals about an appropriate response to terrorist atrocities. Military historian Michael Howard proposes "a police operation conducted under the auspices of the United Nations... against a criminal conspiracy whose members should be hunted down and brought before an international court, where they would receive a fair trial and, if found guilty, be awarded an appropriate sentence." Reasonable enough, though the idea that the proposal should be applied universally is unthinkable. The director of the Center for the Politics of Human Rights at Harvard argues that "The only responsible response to acts of terror is honest police work and judicial prosecution in courts of law, linked to determinate, focused and unrelenting use of military power against those who cannot or will not be brought to justice."[13] That too seems sensible, if we add Howard's qualification about international supervision, and if the resort to force is undertaken after legal means have been exhausted. The recommendation therefore does not apply to 9-11 (the U.S. refused to provide evidence and rebuffed tentative proposals about transfer of the suspects), but it does apply very clearly to Nicaragua.

It applies to other cases as well. Take Haiti, which has provided ample evidence in its repeated calls for extradition of Emmanuel Constant, who directed the forces responsible for thousands of deaths under the military junta that the U.S. was tacitly supporting (not to speak of earlier history); these requests the U.S. ignores, presumably because of concerns about what Constant would reveal if tried. The most recent request was on September 30, 2001, while the U.S. was demanding that the Taliban hand over Bin Laden.[14] The coincidence was also ignored, in accord with the convention that minimal moral standards must be vigorously rejected.

Turning to the "responsible response," a call for implementation of it where it is clearly applicable would elicit only fury and contempt.

Some have formulated more general principles to justify the U.S. war in Afghanistan. Two Oxford scholars propose a principle of "proportionality:" "The magnitude of response will be determined by the magnitude with which the aggression interfered with key values in the society attacked;" in the U.S. case, "freedom to pursue self-betterment in a plural society through market economics," viciously attacked on 9-11 by "aggressors... with a moral orthodoxy divergent from the West." Since "Afghanistan constitutes a state that sided with the aggressor," and refused U.S. demands to turn over suspects, "the United States and its allies, according to the principle of magnitude of interference, could justifiably and morally resort to force against the Taliban government."[15]

On the assumption of universality, it follows that Haiti and Nicaragua can "justifiably and morally resort to" far greater force against the U.S. government. The conclusion extends far beyond these two cases, including much more serious ones and even such minor escapades of Western state terror as Clinton's bombing of the al-Shifa pharmaceutical plant in Sudan in 1998, leading to "several tens of thousands" of deaths according to the German Ambassador and other reputable sources, whose conclusions are consistent with the immediate assessments of knowledgeable observers.[16] The principle of proportionality therefore entails that Sudan had every right to carry out massive terror in retaliation, a conclusion that is strengthened if we go on to adopt the view that this act of "the empire" had "appalling consequences for the economy and society" of Sudan so that the atrocity was much worse than the crimes of 9-11, which were appalling enough, but did not have such consequences.[17]

Most commentary on the Sudan bombing keeps to the question of whether the plant was believed to produce chemical weapons; true or false, that has no bearing on "the magnitude with which the aggression interfered with key values in the society attacked," such as survival. Others point out that the killings were unintended, as are many of the atrocities we rightly denounce. In this case, we can hardly doubt that the likely human consequences were understood by U.S. planners. The acts can be excused, then, only on the Hegelian assumption that Africans are "mere things," whose lives have "no value," an attitude that accords with practice in ways that are not overlooked among the victims, who may draw their own conclusions about the "moral orthodoxy of the West."

One participant in the Yale volume (Charles Hill) recognized that 11 September opened the *second* "war on terror." The first was declared by the Reagan administration as it came to office 20 years earlier, with the rhetorical accompaniment already illustrated; and "we won," Hill reports triumphantly, though the terrorist monster was only wounded, not slain.[18] The first "age of terror" proved to be a major issue in international affairs through the decade, particularly in Central America, but also in the Middle East, where terrorism was selected by editors as the lead story of the year in 1985 and ranked high in other years.

### The first phase: serious war crimes

We can learn a good deal about the current war on terror by inquiring into the first phase, and how it is now portrayed. One leading academic specialist describes the 1980s as the decade of "state terrorism," of "persistent state involvement, or 'sponsorship,' of terrorism, especially by Libya and Iran." The U.S. merely responded, by adopting "a 'proactive' stance toward terrorism." Others recommend the methods by which "we won:" the operations for which the U.S. was condemned by the World Court and Security Council (absent the veto) are a model for "Nicaragua-like support for the Taliban's adversaries (especially the Northern Alliance)." A prominent historian of the subject finds deep roots for the terrorism of Osama Bin Laden: in South Vietnam, where "the effectiveness of Vietcong terror against the American Goliath armed with modern technology kindled hopes that the Western heartland was vulnerable too."[19]

Keeping to convention, these analyses portray the U.S. as a benign victim, defending itself from the terror of others: the Vietnamese (in South Vietnam), the Nicaraguans (in Nicaragua), Libyans and Iranians (if they had ever suffered a slight at U.S. hands, it passes unnoticed), and other anti-American forces worldwide.

Not everyone sees the world quite that way. The most obvious place to look is Latin America, which has had considerable experience with international terrorism. The crimes of 9-11 were harshly condemned, but commonly with recollection of their own experiences. One might describe the 9-11 atrocities as "Armageddon," the research journal of the Jesuit university in Managua observed, but Nicaragua has "lived its own Armageddon in excruciating slow motion" under U.S. assault "and is now submerged in its dismal aftermath," and others fared far worse under the vast plague of state terror that swept through the continent from the early 1960s, much of it traceable to Washington. A Panamanian journalist joined in the general condemnation of the 9-11 crimes, but recalled the death of perhaps thousands of poor people (Western crimes, therefore unexamined) when the President's father bombed the barrio Chorillo in December 1989 in Operation Just Cause, undertaken to kidnap a disobedient thug who was sentenced to life imprisonment in Florida for crimes mostly committed while he was on the CIA payroll. Uruguayan writer Eduardo Galeano observed that the U.S. claims to oppose terrorism, but actually supports it worldwide, including "in Indonesia, in Cambodia, in Iran, in South Africa,… and in the Latin American countries that lived through the dirty war of the Condor Plan," instituted by South American military dictators who conducted a reign of terror with U.S. backing.[20]

The observations carry over to the second focus of the first "war on terror": West Asia. The worst single atrocity was the Israeli invasion of Lebanon in 1982, which left some 20,000 people dead and much of the country in ruins, including Beirut. Like the murderous and destructive Rabin-Peres invasions of 1993 and 1996, the 1982 attack had little pretense of self-defense. Chief of Staff Rafael ("Raful") Eitan merely articulated common understanding when he announced that the goal was to "destroy the PLO as a candidate for negotiations with us about the Land of Israel,"[21] a textbook illustration of terror as officially defined. The goal "was to install a friendly regime and destroy Mr. Arafat's Palestinian Liberation Organization," Middle East correspondent James Bennet writes: "That, the theory went, would help persuade Palestinians to accept Israeli rule in the West Bank and Gaza Strip."[22] This may be the first recognition in the mainstream of facts widely reported in Israel at once, previously accessible only in dissident literature in the U.S.

These operations were carried out with the crucial military and diplomatic support of the Reagan and Clinton administrations, and therefore constitute international terrorism. The U.S. was also directly involved in other acts of terror in the region in the 1980s, including the most extreme terrorist atrocities of the peak year of 1985: the CIA car-bombing in Beirut that killed 80 people and wounded 250; Shimon Peres's bombing of Tunis that killed 75 people, expedited by the U.S. and praised by Secretary of State Shultz, unanimously condemned by the UN Security Council as an "act of armed aggression" (U.S. abstaining); and Peres's "Iron Fist" operations directed against "terrorist villagers" in Lebanon, reaching new depths of "calculated brutality and arbitrary murder," in the words of a Western diplomat familiar with the area, amply supported by direct coverage.[23] Again, all international terrorism, if not the more severe war crime of aggression.

In journalism and scholarship on terrorism, 1985 is recognized to be the peak year of Middle East terrorism, but not because of these events: rather, because of two terrorist atrocities in which a single person was murdered, in each case an American.[24] But the victims do not so easily forget.

This very recent history takes on added significance because leading figures in the re-declared "war on terror" played a prominent part in its precursor. The diplomatic component of the current phase is led by John Negroponte, who was Reagan's Ambassador to Honduras, the base for the terrorist atrocities for which his government was condemned by the World Court and for U.S.-backed state terror elsewhere in Central America, activities that "made the Reagan years the worse decade for Central America since the Spanish conquest," mostly on Negroponte's watch.[25] The military component of the new phase is led by Donald Rumsfeld, Reagan's special envoy to the Middle East during the years of the worst terrorist atrocities there, initiated or supported by his government.

No less instructive is the fact that such atrocities did not abate in subsequent years. Specifically, Washington's contribution to "enhancing terror" in the Israel-Arab confrontation continues. The term is President Bush's, intended, according to convention, to apply to the terrorism of others. Departing from convention, we find, again, some rather significant examples. One simple way to enhance terror is to participate in it, for example, by sending helicopters to be used to attack civilian complexes and carry out assassinations, as the U.S. regularly does in full awareness of the consequences. Another is to bar the dispatch of international monitors to reduce violence. The U.S. has insisted on this course, once again vetoing a UN Security Council resolution to this effect on December 14th, 2001. Describing Arafat's fall from grace to a position barely above Bin Laden and Saddam Hussein, the press reports that President Bush was "greatly angered [by] a last-minute hardening of a Palestinian position... for international monitors in Palestinian areas under a UN Security Council resolution;" that is, by Arafat's joining the rest of the world in calling for means to reduce terror.[26]

Ten days before the veto of monitors, the U.S. boycotted—thus undermined—an international conference in Geneva that reaffirmed the applicability of the Fourth Geneva Convention to the occupied territories, so that most U.S.-Israeli actions there are war crimes—and when "grave breaches," as many are, serious war crimes. These include U.S.-funded Israeli settlements and the practice of "wilful killing, torture, unlawful deportation, wilful depriving of the rights of fair and regular trial, extensive destruction and appropriation of property...carried out unlawfully and wantonly."[27]

The Convention, instituted to criminalize formally the crimes of the Nazis in occupied Europe, is a core principle of international humanitarian law. Its applicability to the Israeli-occupied territories has repeatedly been affirmed, among other occasions, by UN Ambassador George Bush (September 1971) and by Security Council resolutions: 465 (1980), adopted unanimously, which condemned U.S.-backed Israeli practices as "flagrant violations" of the Convention; 1322 (Oct. 2000), 14–0, U.S. abstaining, which called on Israel "to abide scrupulously by its responsibilities under the Fourth Geneva Convention," which it was again violating flagrantly at that moment. As High Contracting Parties, the U.S. and the European powers are obligated by solemn treaty to apprehend and prosecute those responsible for such crimes, including their own leadership when they are parties to them. By continuing to reject that duty, they are enhancing terror directly and significantly.

Inquiry into the U.S.-Israel-Arab conflicts would carry us too far afield. Let's turn further north, to another region where "state terror" is being practiced on a massive scale; I borrow the term from the Turkish State Minister for Human Rights, referring to the vast atrocities of 1994; and sociologist Ismail Besikci, returned to prison after publishing his book *State Terror in the Near East*, having already served 15 years for recording Turkish repression of Kurds.[28] I had a chance to see some of the consequences first-hand when visiting the unofficial Kurdish capital of Diyarbakir several months after 9-11. As elsewhere, the crimes of September 11th were harshly condemned, but not without memory of the savage assault the population had suffered at the hands of those who appoint themselves to "rid the world of evildoers," and their local agents. By 1994, the Turkish State Minister and others estimated that 2 million had been driven out of the devastated countryside, many more later, often with barbaric torture and terror described in excruciating detail in international human rights reports, but kept from the eyes of those paying the bills. Tens of thousands were killed. The remnants—whose courage is indescribable—live in a dungeon where radio stations are closed and journalists imprisoned for playing Kurdish music, students are arrested and tortured for submitting requests to take elective courses in their own language, there can be severe penalties if children are found wearing Kurdish national colors by the omnipresent security forces, the respected lawyer who heads the human rights organization was indicted shortly after I was there for using the Kurdish rather than the virtually identical Turkish spelling for the New Year's celebration; and on, and on.

These acts fall under the category of state-sponsored international terrorism. The U.S. provided 80 percent of the arms, peaking in 1997, when arms transfers exceeded the entire Cold War period combined before the "counter-terror" campaign began in 1984. Turkey became the leading recipient of U.S. arms worldwide, a position it retained until 1999 when the torch was passed to Colombia, the leading practitioner of state terror in the Western hemisphere.[29]

State terror is also "enhanced" by silence and evasion. The achievement was particularly notable against the background of an unprecedented chorus of self-congratulation as U.S. foreign policy entered a "noble phase" with a "saintly glow," under the guidance of leaders who for the first time in history were dedicated to "principles and values" rather than narrow interests.[30] The proof of the new saintliness was their unwillingness to tolerate crimes near the borders of NATO—only within its borders, where even worse crimes, not in reaction to NATO bombs, were not only tolerable but required enthusiastic participation, without comment.

U.S.-sponsored Turkish state terror does not pass entirely unnoticed. The State Department's annual report on Washington's "efforts to combat terrorism" singled out Turkey for its "positive experiences" in combating terror, along with Algeria and Spain, worthy colleagues. This was reported without comment in a front-page story in the *NY Times* by its specialist on terrorism. In a leading journal of international affairs, Ambassador Robert Pearson reports that the U.S. "could have no better friend and ally than Turkey" in its efforts "to eliminate terrorism" worldwide, thanks to the "capabilities of its armed forces" demonstrated in its "anti-terror campaign" in the Kurdish southeast. It thus "came as no surprise" that Turkey eagerly joined the "war on terror" declared by George Bush, expressing its thanks to the U.S. for being the only country willing to lend the needed support for the atrocities of the Clinton years—still continuing, though on a lesser scale now that "we won." As a reward for its achievements, the U.S. is now funding Turkey to provide the ground forces for fighting "the war on terror" in Kabul, though not beyond.[31]

Atrocious state-sponsored international terrorism is thus not overlooked: it is lauded. That also "comes as no surprise." After all, in 1995 the Clinton administration welcomed Indonesia's General Suharto, one of the worst killers and torturers of the late 20th century, as "our kind of guy." When he came to power 30 years earlier, the "staggering mass slaughter" of hundreds of thousands of people, mostly landless peasants, was reported fairly accurately and acclaimed with unconstrained euphoria. When Nicaraguans finally succumbed to U.S. terror and voted the right way, the U.S. was "United in Joy" at this "Victory for U.S. Fair Play," headlines proclaimed. It is easy enough to multiply examples. The current episode breaks no new ground in the record of international terrorism and the response it elicits among the perpetrators.

## The proper response to acts of terror

Let's return to the question of the proper response to acts of terror, specifically 9-11.

It is commonly alleged that the U.S.-U.K. reaction was undertaken with wide international support. That is tenable, however, only if one keeps to elite opinion. An international Gallup poll found only minority support for military attack rather than diplomatic means.[32] In Europe, figures ranged from 8 percent in Greece to 29 percent in France. In Latin America, support was even lower: from 2 percent in Mexico to 16 percent in Panama. Support for strikes that included civilian targets was very slight. Even in the two countries polled that strongly supported the use of military force, India and Israel (where the reasons were parochial), considerable majorities opposed such attacks. There was, then, overwhelming opposition to the actual policies, which turned major urban concentrations into "ghost towns" from the first moment, the press reported.

Omitted from the poll, as from most commentary, was the anticipated effect of U.S. policy on Afghans, millions of whom were on the brink of starvation even before 9-11. Unasked, for example, is whether a proper response to 9-11 was to demand that Pakistan eliminate "truck convoys that provide much of the food and other supplies to Afghanistan's civilian population," and to cause the withdrawal of aid workers and a severe reduction in food supplies that left "millions of Afghans... at grave risk of starvation," eliciting sharp protests from aid organizations and warnings of severe humanitarian crisis, judgments reiterated at the war's end.[33]

It is, of course, the assumptions of planning that are relevant to evaluating the actions taken; that too should be transparent. The actual outcome, a separate matter, is unlikely to be known, even roughly; crimes of others are carefully investigated, but not one's own. Some indication is perhaps suggested by the occasional reports on numbers needing food aid: 5 million before 9-11, 7.5 million at the end of September under the threat of bombing, 9 million six months later, not because of lack of food, which was readily available throughout, but because of distribution problems as the country reverted to warlordism.[34]

There are no reliable studies of Afghan opinion, but information is not entirely lacking. At the outset, President Bush warned Afghans that they would be bombed until they handed over people the U.S. suspected of terrorism. Three weeks later, war aims shifted to overthrow of the regime: the bombing would continue, Admiral Sir Michael Boyce announced, "until the people of the country themselves recognize that this is going to go on until they get the leadership changed."[35] Note that the question whether overthrow of the miserable Taliban regime justifies the bombing does not arise, because that did not become a war aim until well after the fact. We can, however, ask about the opinions of Afghans within reach of Western observers about these choices—which, in both cases, clearly fall within the official definition of international terrorism.

As war aims shifted to regime replacement in late October, 1000 Afghan leaders gathered in Peshawar, some exiles, some coming from within Afghanistan, all committed to overthrowing the Taliban regime. It was "a rare display of unity among tribal elders, Islamic scholars, fractious politicians, and former guerrilla commanders," the press reported. They unanimously "urged the U.S. to stop the air raids," appealed to the international media to call for an end to the "bombing of innocent people," and "demanded an end to the U.S. bombing of Afghanistan." They urged that other means be adopted to overthrow the hated Taliban regime, a goal they believed could be achieved without death and destruction.[36]

A similar message was conveyed by Afghan opposition leader Abdul Haq, who was highly regarded in Washington. Just before he entered Afghanistan, apparently without U.S. support, and was then captured and killed, he condemned the bombing and criticized the U.S. for refusing to support efforts of his and of others "to create a revolt within the Taliban." The bombing was "a big setback for these efforts," he said. He reported contacts with second-level Taliban commanders and ex-Mujahiddin tribal elders, and discussed how such efforts could proceed, calling on the U.S. to assist them with funding and other support instead of undermining them with bombs. But the U.S., he said, "is trying to show its muscle, score a victory and scare everyone in the world. They don't care about the suffering of the Afghans or how many people we will lose."[37]

The plight of Afghan women elicited some belated concern after 9-11. After the war, there was even some recognition of the courageous women who have been in the forefront of the struggle to defend women's rights for 25 years, RAWA (Revolutionary Association of the Women of Afghanistan). A week after the bombing began, RAWA issued a public statement (Oct. 11) that would have been front-page news wherever concern for Afghan women was real, not a matter of mere expediency. They condemned the resort to "the monster of a vast war and destruction" as the U.S. "launched a vast aggression on our country," that will cause great harm to innocent Afghans. They called instead for "the eradication of the plague of Taliban and Al Qaeda" by "an overall uprising" of the Afghan people themselves, which alone "can prevent the repetition and recurrence of the catastrophe that has befallen our country..."

All of this was ignored. It is, perhaps, less than obvious that those with the guns are entitled to ignore the judgment of Afghans who have been struggling for freedom and women's rights for many years, and to dismiss with apparent contempt their desire to overthrow the fragile and hated Taliban regime from within without the inevitable crimes of war.

In brief, review of global opinion, including what is known about Afghans, lends little support to the consensus among Western intellectuals on the justice of their cause.

## Facts that cannot be ignored without peril

One elite reaction, however, is certainly correct: it is necessary to inquire into the reasons for the crimes of 9-11. That much is beyond question, at least among those who hope to reduce the likelihood of further terrorist atrocities.

A narrow question is the motives of the perpetrators. On this matter, there is little disagreement. Serious analysts are in accord that after the U.S. established permanent bases in Saudi Arabia, "Bin Laden became preoccupied with the need to expel U.S. forces from the sacred soil of Arabia" and to rid the Muslim world of the "liars and hypocrites" who do not accept his extremist version of Islam.[38]

There is also wide, and justified, agreement that "Unless the social, political, and economic conditions that spawned Al Qaeda and other associated groups are addressed, the United States and its allies in Western Europe and elsewhere will continue to be targeted by Islamist terrorists."[39] These conditions are doubtless complex, but some factors have long been recognized. In 1958, a crucial year in postwar history, President Eisenhower advised his staff that in the Arab world, "the problem is that we have a campaign of hatred against us, not by the governments but by the people," who are "on Nasser's side," supporting independent secular nationalism. The reasons for the "campaign of hatred" had been outlined by the National Security Council a few months earlier: "In the eyes of the majority of Arabs the United States appears to be opposed to the realization of the goals of Arab nationalism. They believe that the United States is seeking to protect its interest in Near East oil by supporting the *status quo* and opposing political or economic progress..." Furthermore, the perception is accurate: "our economic and cultural interests in the area have led not unnaturally to close U.S. relations with elements in the Arab world whose primary interest lies in the maintenance of relations with the West and the status quo in their countries..."[40]

The perceptions persist. Immediately after 9-11, the *Wall Street Journal*, later others, began to investigate opinions of "moneyed Muslims": bankers, professionals, managers of multinationals, and so on. They strongly support U.S. policies in general, but are bitter about the U.S. role in the region: about U.S. support for corrupt and repressive regimes that undermine democracy and development, and about specific policies, particularly regarding Palestine and Iraq. Though they are not surveyed, attitudes in the slums and villages are probably similar, but harsher; unlike the "moneyed Muslims," the mass of the population have never agreed that the wealth of the region should be drained to the West and local collaborators, rather than serving domestic needs. The "moneyed Muslims" recognize, ruefully, that Bin Laden's angry rhetoric has considerable resonance, in their own circles as well, even though they hate and fear him, if only because they are among his primary targets.[41]

It is doubtless more comforting to believe that the answer to George Bush's plaintive query, "Why do they hate us?," lies in their resentment of our freedom and love of democracy, or their cultural failings tracing back many centuries, or their inability to take part in the form of "globalization" in which they happily participate. Comforting, perhaps, but not wise.

Though shocking, the atrocities of 9-11 could not have been entirely unexpected. Related organizations planned very serious terrorist acts through the 1990s, and in 1993 came perilously close to blowing up the World Trade Center, with much more ambitious plans. Their thinking was well understood, certainly by the U.S. intelligence agencies that had helped to recruit, train, and arm them from 1980 and continued to work with them even as they were attacking the U.S. The Dutch government inquiry into the Srebrenica massacre revealed that while they were attempting to blow up the World Trade Center, radical Islamists from the CIA-formed networks were being flown by the U.S. from Afghanistan to Bosnia, along with Iranian-backed Hizbollah fighters and a huge flow of arms, through Croatia, which took a substantial cut. They were being brought to support the U.S. side in the Balkan wars, while Israel (along with Ukraine and Greece) was arming the Serbs (possibly with U.S.-supplied arms), which explains why "unexploded mortar bombs landing in Sarajevo sometimes had Hebrew markings," British political scientist Richard Aldrich observes, reviewing the Dutch government report.[42]

More generally, the atrocities of 9-11 serve as a dramatic reminder of what has long been understood: with contemporary technology, the rich and powerful no longer are assured the near monopoly of violence that has largely prevailed throughout history. Though terrorism is rightly feared everywhere, and is indeed an intolerable "return to barbarism," it is not surprising that perceptions about its nature differ rather sharply in the light of sharply differing experiences, facts that will be ignored at their peril by those whom history has accustomed to immunity while they perpetrate terrible crimes.

# Notes

1. Bush cited by Rich Heffern, *National Catholic Reporter*, 11 Jan. 2002. Reagan, *NY Times*, 18 Oct. 1985. Shultz, U.S. Dept. of State, *Current Policy* No. 589, June 24, 1984; No. 629, Oct. 25, 1984.

2. *U.S. Army Operational Concept for Terrorism Counteraction*. TRADOC Pamphlet No. 525–37, 1984.

3. Res. 42/159, 7 Dec. 1987; Honduras abstaining.

4. Joseba Zulaika and William Douglass, *Terror and Taboo* (New York, London: Routledge, 1996), 12. 1980–88 record, see "Inter-Agency Task Force, Africa Recovery Program/Economic Commission, *South African Destabilization: the Economic Cost of Frontline Resistance to Apartheid*, NY, UN, 1989, 13, cited by Merle Bowen, *Fletcher Forum*, Winter 1991. On expansion of U.S. trade with South Africa after Congress authorized sanctions in 1985 (overriding Reagan's veto), see Gay McDougall, Richard Knight, in Robert Edgar, ed., *Sanctioning Apartheid*. Trenton, NJ: Africa World Press, 1990.

5. For review of unilateral U.S. rejectionism for 30 years, see my introduction to Roane Carey, ed., *The New Intifada*. London, New York: Verso, 2000; see sources cited for more detail.

6. It is, however, never used. On the reasons, see Alexander George, ed., *Western State Terrorism*. Cambridge: Polity-Blackwell, 1991.

7. Strobe Talbott and Nayan Chanda, introduction, *The Age of Terror: America and the World after September 11*. New York: Basic Books and the Yale U. Center for the Study of Globalization, 2001.

8. Abram Sofaer, "The United States and the World Court," U.S. Dept. of State, *Current Policy*, No. 769 (Dec. 1985). The vetoed Security Council resolution called for compliance with the ICJ orders, and, mentioning no one, called on all states "to refrain from carrying out, supporting or promoting political, economic or military actions of any kind against any state of the region." Elaine Sciolino, *NYT*, 31 July 1986.

9. Shultz, "Moral Principles and Strategic Interests," Apr. 14, 1986, U.S. Dept. of State, *Current Policy* No. 820. Shultz Congressional testimony, see Jack Spence in Thomas Walker, ed., *Reagan versus the Sandinistas*. Boulder, London: Westview, 1987. For review of the undermining of diplomacy and escalation of international state terror, see my *Culture of Terrorism*. Boston: South End, 1988; *Necessary Illusions*. Boston: South End, 1989; *Deterring Democracy*. London, New York: Verso, 1991. On the aftermath, see Thomas Walker and Ariel Armony, eds., *Repression, Resistance, and Democratic Transition in Central America*. Wilmington: Scholarly Resources, 2000. On reparations, see Howard Meyer, *The World Court in Action*. Lanham, MD, Oxford: Rowman & Littlefield, 2002, ch. 14.

10. Edward Price, "The Strategy and Tactics of Revolutionary Terrorism," *Comparative Studies in Society and History.* 19.1_; cited by Chalmers Johnson, "American Militarism and Blowback," *New Political Science* 24.1, 2002.

11. SOA, 1999, cited by Adam Isacson and Joy Olson, *Just the Facts.* Washington: Latin America Working Group and Center for International Policy, 1999, ix.

12. Greenwood, "International law and the 'war against terrorism'," *International Affairs* 78.2 (2002), appealing to par. 195 of *Nicaragua v. USA*, which the Court did not use to justify its condemnation of U.S. terrorism, but surely is more appropriate to that than to the case that concerns Greenwood. Franck, "Terrorism and the Right of Self-Defense," *American Journal of International Law* 95.4 (2001).

13. Howard, *Foreign Affairs*, Jan/Feb 2002; talk of Oct. 30, 2001 (Tania Branigan, *Guardian*, Oct. 31). Ignatieff, *Index on Censorship* 2, 2002.

14. *NYT*, Oct. 1, 2001.

15. Frank Schuller and Thomas Grant, *Current History*, Apr. 2002.

16. Werner Daum, "Universalism and the West," *Harvard International Review*, Summer 2001. On other assessments, and the warnings of Human Rights Watch, see my *9-11* (New York: Seven Stories, 2001), 45ff.

17. Christopher Hitchens, *Nation*, June 10, 2002.

18. Talbott and Chanda, *op. cit.*

19. Martha Crenshaw, Ivo Daalder and James Lindsay, David Rapoport, *Current History, America at War*, Dec. 2001. On interpretations of the first "war on terror" at the time, see George, *op. cit.*

20. *Envío* (UCA Managua), Oct.; Ricardo Stevens (Panama), NACLA *Report on the Americas*, Nov/Dec; Galeano, *La Jornada* (Mexico City), cited by Alain Frachon, *Le Monde*, Nov. 24, 2001.

21. For many sources, see **FT** Boston: South End, 1983; updated 1999 edition, on South Lebanon in the 1990s; **PE** New York: Claremont, 1986; Pluto, London, 2002; **WOON**.

22. Bennet, *NYT*, Jan. 24, 2002

23. For details, see essay in George, *op. cit.*

24. Crenshaw, *op. cit.*

25. Chalmers Johnson, *Nation*, Oct. 15, 2001.

26. Ian Williams, *Middle East International*, 21 Dec. 2001, 11 Jan. 2002. John Donnelly, *Boston Globe*, Apr. 25, 2002; the specific reference is to an earlier U.S. veto.

27. Conference of High Contracting Parties, *Report on Israeli Settlement*, Jan.–Feb. 2002 (Foundation for Middle East Peace, Washington). On these matters see Francis Boyle, "Law and Disorder in the Middle East," *The Link* 35.1 (2002).

28. For some details, see my *New Military Humanism.* Monroe ME: Common Courage, 1999, ch. 3, and sources cited. On evasion of the facts in the State Department Human Rights Report, see Lawyers Committee for Human Rights, *Middle East and North Africa.* New York, 1995, 255.

29. Tamar Gabelnick, William Hartung, and Jennifer Washburn, *Arming Repression: U.S. Arms Sales to Turkey During the Clinton Administration.* New York and Washington: World Policy Institute and Federation of Atomic Scientists, October 1999. I exclude Israel-Egypt, a separate category. On state terror in Colombia, now largely farmed out to paramilitaries in standard fashion, see particularly Human Rights Watch, *The Sixth Division* (September 2001) and Colombia Human Rights Certification III, Feb. 2002. Also, among others, Médicos Sin Fronteras, *Desterrados* (Bogota' 2001).

30. For a sample, see *New Military Humanism* and my *A New Generation Draws the Line* (London, NY: Verso, 2000).

31. Judith Miller, *NYT*, 30 Apr. 2000. Pearson, *Fletcher Forum* 26.1, (2002).

32. http://www.gallup.international.com/terrorismpoll-figures.htm; data from Sept. 14–17, 2001.

33. John Burns, *NYT*, Sept. 16, 2001; Samina Amin, *International Security* 26.3, Winter 2001–02). For some earlier warnings, see *9-11*. On the postwar evaluation of international agencies, see Imre Karacs, *Independent on Sunday* (London), 9 Dec. 2001, reporting their warnings that over a million people are "beyond their reach and face death from starvation and disease." For some press reports, see my "Peering into the Abyss of the Future," Lakdawala Memorial Lecture, Institute of Social Sciences, New Delhi, Nov. 2001, updated Feb. 2002.

34. *Ibid.*, for early estimates. Barbara Crossette, *NYT*, Mar. 26, and Ahmed Rashid, *WSJ*, 6 June 2002, reporting the assessment of the UN World Food Program and the failure of donors to provide pledged funds. The WFP reports that "wheat stocks are exhausted, and there is no funding" to replenish them (Rashid). The UN had warned of the threat of mass starvation at once because the bombing disrupted planting that provides 80 percent of the country's grain supplies (AFP, Sept. 28; Edith Lederer, AP , Oct.

18, 2001). Also Andrew Revkin, *NYT*, Dec. 16, 2001, citing U.S. Department of Agriculture, with no mention of bombing.

35. Patrick Tyler and Elisabeth Bumiller, *NYT*, 12 Oct. quoting Bush; Michael Gordon, *NYT*, 28 Oct. 2001, quoting Boyce; both p. 1.

36. Barry Bearak, *NYT*, Oct. 25; John Thornhill and Farhan Bokhari, *Financial Times*, Oct. 25, Oct. 26; John Burns, *NYT*, Oct. 26; Indira Laskhmanan, *BG*, 25, 26 Oct. 2001.

37. Interview, Anatol Lieven, *Guardian*, Nov. 2, 2001.

38. Ann Lesch, *Middle East Policy* IX.2, June 2002. Also Michael Doran, *Foreign Affairs*, Jan.–Feb. 2002; and many others, including several contributors to *Current History*, Dec. 2001.

39. Sumit Ganguly, *Ibid.*

40. For sources and background discussion, see my **WOON**, 79, 201f.

41. Peter Waldman et al., *WSJ*, 14 Sept. 2001; also Waldman and Hugh Pope, *WSJ*, 21 Sept. 2001.

42. Aldrich, *Guardian*,22 Apr. 2002.

## Editor's Notes to Chapter 30

This last selection, "A World Without War," a culmination in more than one way, is the written version of Chomsky's featured opening address at the second World Social Forum [WSF] on January 31, 2002, in Porto Alegre (Brazil), posted on Znet on May 29, 2002. (We are grateful to Z Communications: *www.zmag.org*. As this book goes to press, the Znet section of zmag.org has just posted "Confronting the Empire," the talk Chomsky gave to about 15,000 people in a huge stadium, with overflow halls, on January 31, 2003, at the third WSF, an event "quite impressive and exciting—hard to imagine a few years ago." Here is the opening paragraph: "We are meeting at a moment of history that is in many ways unique—a moment that is ominous, but also full of hope.")

The WSF was a five-day gathering of "about 40,000 activists" of diverse grass-roots groups from "about 150 countries," under the theme "Another World Is Possible," "intended as a dramatic counterpoint to the meetings of the World Economic Forum in New York." Though Chomsky was "only one of a parade of radical luminaries due in for the conference," including Nobel peace laureate Rigoberta Menchú of Guatemala, he "was treated like a Hollywood celebrity by the mostly European and Brazilian press corps [there], his entry greeted with a fusillade of camera flashes." (The quotes are from the report by Hector Tobar in the *Los Angeles Times* of Feb. 1, 2002.) A few days later his presence was to trigger a quite different, and differently significant, reaction in the unofficial Kurdish capital of Diyarbakir, still under Turkish rule (see the Editor's Notes to selection 29).

This address may be read as a sort of Chomsky's counterpart both to Rousseau's 1755 "discourse" on inequality, "in many ways a revolutionary tract" (see "Language and Freedom" in **FRS** or in **ChR**) and to the call to international solidarity and action in the most famous of manifestos, itself a sort of sequel to the analysis of the roots of inequality that prepared the ground for the French Revolution of a quarter of a century later. No wonder Chomsky has been seen as "a new Rousseau," that is, the Rousseau of our age. (See the section "Justice vs Power" of "The third emancipatory phase of history," my introduction to Chomsky's *Language and Politics*, revised and enlarged second edition, AK Press.

Interestingly, the 1848 call was made in Europe at the very time in which, not far from Boston, very literate working people, unhappy because their culture was being taken away from them, without the benefit of socialist writings or the help of foreign radicals (as Chomsky likes to emphasize), were doing what they could to resist the degrading "new spirit of the age" ("gain wealth, forgetting all but self") still being drilled into everyone's head today, which "was repugnant to an astonishingly large section of the earlier American community." The story is told in Norman Ware's *The Industrial Worker: 1840–1860*, Chicago: Ivan Dee, 1990,—a reprint of the 1924 edition, the source of the three phrases just quoted, which Chomsky takes to be "the first major study of the mid-19th century labor press (and to [his] knowledge still the only one)," as he writes in **P&P**, p.

85, mostly "fascinating" quotes from the labor press about the labor movement in eastern Massachusetts around 1850–1860.

Though separated by only two centuries and a half, it is a long, long way from Rousseau's 1755 challenge of the legitimacy of virtually every social institution and the individual control of property and wealth ("usurpations... established only on a precarious and abusive right," which, "having been acquired only by force, force could take them away without [the rich] having grounds for complaint," he argued) and Chomsky's "A World Without War." The final sentence of this address is not a bad measure of the distance: "It is hard to overestimate what is at stake" in our day and age.

# 30. A World Without War

I hope you won't mind if I set the stage with a few truisms. It is hardly exciting news that we live in a world of conflict and confrontation. There are lots of dimensions and complexities, but in recent years, lines have been drawn fairly sharply. To oversimplify, but not too much, one of the participants in the conflict is concentrated power centers, state and private, closely interlinked. The other is the general population, worldwide. In old-fashioned terms, it would have been called "class war."

## The ongoing conflict: primary issues

Concentrated power pursues the war relentlessly, and very self-consciously. Government documents and publications of the business world reveal that they are mostly vulgar Marxists, with values reversed, of course. They are also frightened—back to 17th century England in fact. They realize that the system of domination is fragile, that it relies on disciplining the population by one or another means. There is a desperate search for such means: in recent years, Communism, crime, drugs, terrorism, and others. Pretexts change, policies remain rather stable. Sometimes the shift of pretext along with continuity of policy is dramatic and takes real effort to miss: immediately after the collapse of the USSR, for example. They naturally grasp every opportunity to press their agenda forward: 9-11 is a typical case. Crises make it possible to exploit fear and concern to demand that the adversary be submissive, obedient, silent, distracted, while the powerful use the window of opportunity to pursue their own favored programs with even greater intensity. These programs vary, depending on the society: in the more brutal states, escalation of repression and terror; in societies where the population has won more freedom, measures to impose discipline while shifting wealth and power even more to their own hands. It is easy to list examples around the world in the past few months.

Their victims should certainly resist the predictable exploitation of crisis, and should focus their own efforts, no less relentlessly, on the primary issues that remain much as they were before: among them, increasing militarism, destruction of the environment, and a far-reaching assault against democracy and freedom, the core of "neoliberal" programs.

The ongoing conflict is symbolized right now by the World Social Forum [WSF] here and the World Economic Forum [WEF] in New York. The WEF—to quote the national U.S. press—is a gathering of "movers and shakers," the "rich and famous," "wizards from around the world," "government leaders and corporate executives, ministers of state and of God, politicians and pundits" who are going to "think deep thoughts" and address "the big problems confronting humankind." A few examples are given, for example, "how do you inject moral values into what we do?" Or a panel entitled "Tell Me What You Eat," led by the "reigning prince of the New York gastronomic scene," whose elegant restaurants will be "mobbed by forum participants." There is also mention of an "anti-forum" in Brazil where 50,000 people are expected. These are "the freaks who assemble to protest the meetings of the World Trade Organization." One can learn more about the freaks from a photo of a scruffy-looking guy, with face concealed, writing "world killers" on a wall.

At their "carnival," as it is described, the freaks are throwing stones, writing graffiti, dancing and singing about a variety of boring topics that are unmentionable, at least in the U.S.: investment, trade, financial architecture, human rights, democracy, sustainable development, Brazilian-African relations, GATS, and other marginal issues. They are not "thinking deep thoughts" about "big problems;" that is left to the wizards of Davos in New York.

The infantile rhetoric, I presume, is a sign of well-deserved insecurity.

The freaks at the "anti-forum" here are defined as being "opposed to globalization," a propaganda weapon we should reject with scorn. "Globalization" just means international integration. No sane person is "anti-globalization." That should be particularly obvious for the labor movement and the left; the term "international" is not exactly unknown in their history. In fact, the WSF is the most exciting and promising realization of the hopes of the left and popular movements from their modern origins for a true International, which will pursue a program of globalization concerned with the needs and interests of people, rather than of illegitimate concentrations of power. These, of course, want to appropriate the term "globalization," to restrict it to *their* peculiar version of international integration, concerned with their own interests, those of people being incidental. With this ridiculous terminology in place, those who seek a sane and just form of globalization can be labelled "anti-globalization," derided as primitivists who want to return to the stone age, to harm the poor, and other terms of abuse with which we are familiar.

The wizards of Davos modestly call themselves the "international community," but I personally prefer the term used by the world's leading business journal, the *Financial Times*: "the masters of the universe." Since the masters profess to be admirers of Adam Smith, we might expect them to abide by his account of their behavior, though he only called them "the masters of mankind"—that was before the space age.

Smith was referring to the "principal architects of policy" of his day, the merchants and manufacturers of England, who made sure that their own interests are "most peculiarly attended to" however "grievous" the impact on others, including the people of England. At home and abroad, they pursue "the vile maxim of the masters of mankind:" "all for ourselves and nothing for other people." It should hardly surprise us that today's masters honor the same "vile maxim." At least they try, though they are sometimes impeded by the freaks—the "great beast," to borrow a term used by the Founding Fathers of American democracy to refer to the unruly population that did not comprehend that the primary goal of government is "to protect the minority of the opulent from the majority," as the leading Framer of the Constitution explained in the debates of the Constitutional Convention.

## A stark choice: hegemony or survival

I'll return to these matters, but first a few words about the immediate topic of this session, which is closely related: "A World Without War." We cannot say much about human affairs with any confidence, but sometimes it is possible. We can, for example, be fairly confident that either there will be a world without war or there won't be a world—at least, a world inhabited by creatures other than bacteria and beetles, with some scattering of others. The reason is familiar: humans have developed means of destroying themselves, and much else, and have come dangerously close to using them for half a century. Furthermore, the leaders of the civilized world are now dedicated to enhancing these dangers to survival, in full awareness of what they are doing, at least if they read the reports of their own intelligence agencies and respected strategic analysts, including many who strongly favor the race to destruction. Still more ominous, the plans are developed and implemented on grounds that are rational within the dominant framework of ideology and values, which ranks survival well below "hegemony," the goal pursued by advocates of these programs, as they frankly insist.

Wars over water, energy and other resources are not unlikely in the future, with consequences that could be devastating. For the most part, however, wars have had to do with the imposition of the system of nation-states, an unnatural social formation that typically has to be instituted by violence. That's a primary reason why Europe was the most savage and brutal part of the world for many centuries, meanwhile conquering most of the world. European efforts to impose state systems in conquered territories are the source of most conflicts underway right now, after the collapse of the formal colonial system. Europe's own favorite sport of mutual slaughter had to be called off in 1945, when it was realized that the next time the game was played would be the last. Another prediction that we can make with fair confidence is that there won't be a war among great powers; the reason is that if the prediction turns out to be wrong, there will be no one around to care to tell us.

Furthermore, popular activism within the rich and powerful societies has had a civilizing effect. The "movers and shakers" can no longer undertake the kinds of long-term aggression that were options before, as when the U.S. attacked South Vietnam 40 years ago, smashing much of it to pieces before significant popular protest developed. Among the many civilizing effects of the ferment of the 1960s was broad opposition to large-scale aggression and massacre, reframed in the ideological system as unwillingness to accept casualties among the armed forces ("the Vietnam syndrome"). That is why the Reaganites had to resort to international terrorism instead of invading Central America directly, on the Kennedy-Johnson model, in their war to defeat liberation theology, as the School of the Americas describes the achievement with pride. The same changes explain the intelligence review of the incoming Bush-I administration in 1989, warning that in conflicts against "much weaker enemies"—the only kind it makes sense to confront—the U.S. must "defeat them decisively and rapidly," or the campaign will lose "political support," understood to be thin. Wars since have kept to that pattern, and the scale of protest and dissent have steadily increased. So there are changes, of a mixed nature.

When pretexts vanish, new ones have to be concocted to control the great beast while traditional policies are continued, adapted to new circumstances. That was already becoming clear 20 years ago. It was hard not to recognize that the Soviet enemy was facing internal problems and might not be a credible threat much longer. That is part of the reason why the Reagan administration, 20 years ago, declared that the "war on terror" would be the focus of U.S. foreign policy, particularly in Central America and the Middle East, the main source of the plague spread by "depraved opponents of civilization itself" in a "return to barbarism in the modern age," as Administration moderate George Shultz explained, also warning that the solution is violence, avoiding "utopian, legalistic means like outside mediation, the World Court, and the United Nations." We need not tarry on how the war was waged in those two regions, and elsewhere, by the extraordinary network of proxy states and mercenaries—an "axis of evil," to borrow a more up-to-date term.

It is of some interest that in the months since the war was re-declared, with much the same rhetoric, after 9-11, all of this has been entirely effaced, even the fact that the U.S. was condemned for international terrorism by the World Court and Security Council (vetoed) and responded by sharply escalating the terrorist attack it was ordered to terminate; or the fact that the very people who are directing the military and diplomatic components of the re-declared war on terror were leading figures in implementing terrorist atrocities in Central America and the Middle East during the first phase of the war. Silence about these matters is a real tribute to the discipline and obedience of the educated classes in the free and democratic societies.

It's a fair guess that the "war on terror" will again serve as a pretext for intervention and atrocities in coming years, not just by the U.S.; Chechnya is only one of a number of examples. In Latin America, there is no need to linger on what that portends; certainly not in Brazil, the first target of the wave of repression that swept Latin America after the Kennedy administration, in a decision of historic importance, shifted the mission of the Latin American military from "hemispheric defense" to "internal security"—a euphemism for state terror directed against the domestic population. That still continues, on a huge scale, particularly in Colombia, well in the lead for human rights violations in the hemisphere in the 1990s and by far the leading recipient of U.S. arms and military training, in accord with a consistent pattern documented even in mainstream scholarship.

The "war on terror" has, of course, been the focus of a huge literature, during the first phase in the '80s and since it was re-declared in the past few months. One interesting feature of the flood of commentary, then and now, is that we are not told what "terror" is. What we hear, rather, is that this is a vexing and complex question. That is curious: there are straightforward definitions in official U.S. documents. A simple one takes terror to be the "calculated use of violence or threat of violence to attain goals that are political, religious, or ideological in nature..." That seems appropriate enough, but it cannot be used, for two good reasons. One is that it also defines official policy, called "counterinsurgency" or "low-intensity conflict." Another is that it yields all the wrong answers, facts too obvious to review though suppressed with remarkable efficiency.

The problem of finding a definition of "terror" that will exclude the most prominent cases is indeed vexing and complex. But fortunately, there is an easy solution: define "terror" as terror that *they* carry out against *us*. A review of the scholarly literature on terror, the media, and intellectual journals will show that this usage is close to exceptionless, and that any departure from it elicits impressive tantrums. Furthermore, the practice is probably universal: the generals in South America were protecting the population from "terror directed from outside," just as the Japanese were in Manchuria and the Nazis in occupied Europe. If there is an exception, I haven't found it.

## A serious threat to the human species

Let's return to "globalization," and the linkage between it and the threat of war, perhaps terminal war.

The version of "globalization" designed by the masters of the universe has very broad elite support, not surprisingly, as do the so-called "free trade agreements"—what the *Wall Street Journal*, more honestly, has called "free investment agreements." Very little is reported about these issues, and crucial information is simply suppressed; for example, after a decade, the position of the U.S. labor movement on NAFTA, and the conforming conclusions of Congress's own Research Bureau (the Office of Technology Assessment, OTA), have yet to be reported outside of dissident sources. And the issues are off the agenda in electoral politics. There are good reasons. The masters know well that the public will be opposed if information becomes available. They are fairly open when addressing one another, however. Thus a few years ago, under enormous public pressure, Congress rejected the "fast track" legislation that grants the President authority to enact international economic arrangements with Congress permitted to vote "Yes" (or, theoretically, "No) with no discussion, and the public uninformed. Like other sectors of elite opinion, the *WSJ* [*Wall Street Journal*] was distraught over the failure to undermine democracy. But it explained the problem: opponents of these Stalinist-style measures have an "ultimate weapon," the general population, which must therefore be kept in the dark. That is very important, particularly in the more democratic society, where dissidents can't simply be jailed or assassinated, as in the leading recipients of U.S. military aid, such as El Salvador, Turkey, and Colombia, to list the recent and current world champions (Israel-Egypt aside).

One might ask why public opposition to "globalization" has been so high for many years. That seems strange, in an era when it has led to unprecedented prosperity, so we are constantly informed, particularly in the U.S., with its "fairy tale economy." Through the 1990s, the U.S. has enjoyed "the greatest economic boom in America's history—and the world's," Anthony Lewis wrote in the *NY Times* a year ago, repeating the standard refrain from the left end of the admissible spectrum. It is conceded that there are flaws: some have been left behind in the economic miracle, and we good-hearted folk must do something about that. The flaws reflect a profound and troubling dilemma: the rapid growth and prosperity brought by "globalization" has as a concomitant growing inequality, as some lack the skills to enjoy the wondrous gifts and opportunities.

The picture is so conventional that it may be hard to realize how little resemblance it has to reality, facts that have been well-known right through the miracle. Until the brief late '90s boomlet (which scarcely compensated for earlier stagnation or decline for most people), per capita growth in the "roaring '90s" was about the same as the rest of the industrial world, much lower than in the first 25 post-war years before so-called "globalization," and vastly lower than the war years, the greatest economic boom in American history, under a semi-command economy. How then can the conventional picture be so radically different from uncontroversial facts? The answer is simplicity itself. For a small sector of the society, the '90s really were a grand economic boom. That sector happens to include those who tell others the joyous news. And they cannot be accused of dishonesty. They have no reason to doubt what they are saying. They read it all the time in the journals for which they write, and it accords with their personal experience: it is true of the people they meet in editorial offices, faculty clubs, elite conferences like the one the wizards are now attending, and the elegant restaurants where they dine. It's only the world that is different.

Let's have a quick look at the record over a longer stretch. International economic integration—one facet of "globalization," in a neutral sense of the term—increased rapidly before World War I, stagnated or declined during the interwar years, and resumed after World War II, now reaching levels of a century ago by gross measures; the fine structure is more complex. By some measures, globalization was greater before World War I: one illustration is "free circulation of labor," the foundation of free trade for Adam Smith, though not his contemporary admirers. By other measures, globalization is far greater now: one dramatic example—not the only one—is the flow of short-term speculative capital, far beyond any precedent. The distinction reflects some central features of the version of globalization preferred by the masters of the universe: to an extent even beyond the norm, capital has priority, people are incidental.

The Mexican border is an interesting example. It is artificial, the result of conquest, like most borders, and has been porous in both directions for a variety of socioeconomic reasons. It was militarized after NAFTA by Clinton in order to block the "free circulation of labor." That was necessary because of the anticipated effects of NAFTA in Mexico: an "economic miracle," which would be a disaster for much of the population, who would seek to escape. In the same years, the flow of capital, already very free, was expedited further, along with what is called "trade," about 2/3 of which is now centrally-managed within private tyrannies, up from half before NAFTA. That is "trade" only by doctrinal decision. The effects of NAFTA on actual trade have not been examined, to my knowledge.

A more technical measure of globalization is convergence to a global market, with a single price and wage. That plainly has not happened. With respect to incomes at least, the opposite is more likely true. Though much depends on exactly how it is measured, there is good reason to believe that inequality has increased within and across countries. That is expected to continue. U.S. intelligence agencies, with the participation of specialists from the academic professions and the private sector, recently released a report on expectations for 2015. They expect "globalization" to proceed on course: "Its evolution will be rocky, marked by chronic financial volatility and a widening economic divide." That means less convergence, less globalization in the technical sense, but more globalization in the doctrinally preferred sense. Financial volatility implies still slower growth and more crises and poverty.

It is at this point that a clear connection is established between "globalization" in the sense of the masters of the universe and the increasing likelihood of war. Military planners adopt the same projections, and have explained, forthrightly, that these expectations lie behind the vast expansion of military power. Even pre-September 11th, U.S. military expenditures surpassed those of allies and adversaries combined. The terror attacks have been exploited to increase the funding sharply, delighting key elements of the private economy. The most ominous program is militarization of space, also being expanded under the pretext of "fighting terror."

The reasoning behind these programs is explained publicly in Clinton-era documents. A prime reason is the growing gap between the "haves" and the "have-nots," which is expected to continue, contrary to economic theory but consistent with reality. The "have-nots"—the "great beast" of the world—may become disruptive, and must be controlled, in the interests of what is called "stability" in technical jargon, meaning subordination to the dictates of the masters. That requires means of violence, and having "assumed, out of self-interest, responsibility for the welfare of the world capitalist system," the U.S. must be far in the lead; I'm quoting diplomatic historian Gerald Haines, also the senior historian of the CIA, describing U.S. planning in the 1940s in a scholarly study. Overwhelming dominance in conventional forces and weapons of mass destruction is not sufficient. It is necessary to move on to the new frontier: militarization of space, undermining the Outer Space Treaty of 1967, so far observed. Recognizing the intent, the UN General Assembly has reaffirmed the Treaty several times; the U.S. has refused to join, in virtual isolation. And Washington has blocked negotiations at the UN Conference on Disarmament for the past year over this issue—all scarcely reported, for the usual reasons. It is not wise to allow citizens to know of plans that may bring to an end biology's only experiment with "higher intelligence."

As widely observed, these programs benefit military industry, but we should bear in mind that the term is misleading. Throughout modern history, but with a dramatic increase after World War II, the military system has been used as a device to socialize cost and risk while privatizing profit. The "new economy" is to a substantial extent an outgrowth of the dynamic and innovative state sector of the U.S. economy. The main reason why public spending in biological sciences has been rapidly increasing is that intelligent right-wingers understand that the cutting edge of the economy relies on these public initiatives. A huge increase is scheduled under the pretext of "bioterror," just as the public was deluded into paying for the new economy under the pretext that the Russians are coming— or after they collapsed, by the threat of the "technological sophistication" of third world countries as the Party Line shifted in 1990, instantly, without missing a beat and with scarcely a word of comment. That's also a reason why national security exemptions have to be part of international economic agreements: it doesn't help Haiti, but it allows the U.S. economy to grow under the traditional principle of harsh market discipline for the poor and a nanny state for the rich —what's called "neoliberalism," though it is not a very good term: the doctrine is centuries old, and would scandalize classical liberals.

One might argue that these public expenditures were often worthwhile. Perhaps, perhaps not. But it is clear that the masters were afraid to allow democratic choice. All of this is concealed from the general public, though the participants understand it very well.

Plans to cross the last frontier of violence by militarization of space are disguised as "missile defense," but anyone who pays attention to history knows that when we hear the word "defense," we should think "offense." The present case is no exception. The goal is quite frankly stated: to ensure "global dominance," "hegemony." Official documents stress prominently that the goal is "to protect U.S. interests and investments," and control the "have-nots." Today that requires domination of space, just as in earlier times the most powerful states created armies and navies "to protect and enhance their commercial interests." It is recognized that these new initiatives, in which the U.S. is far in the lead, pose a serious threat to survival. And it is also understood that they could be prevented by international treaties. But as I've already mentioned, hegemony is a higher value than survival, a moral calculus that has prevailed among the powerful throughout history. What has changed is that the stakes are much higher, awesomely so.

The relevant point here is that the expected success of "globalization" in the doctrinal sense is a primary reason given for the programs of using space for offensive weapons of instant mass destruction.

## The mirage of the promised land

Let us return to "globalization," and "the greatest economic boom in America's history—and the world's" in the 1990s.

Since World War II, the international economy has passed through two phases: the Bretton Woods phase to the early '70s, and the period since, with the dismantling of the Bretton Woods system of regulated exchange rates and controls on capital movement. It is the second phase that is called "globalization," associated with the neoliberal policies of the "Washington consensus." The two phases are quite different. The first is often called the "golden age" of (state) capitalism. The second phase has been accompanied by marked deterioration in standard macroeconomic measures: rate of growth of the economy, productivity, capital investment, even world trade; much higher interest rates (harming economies); vast accumulation of unproductive reserves to protect currencies; increased financial volatility; and other harmful consequences. There were exceptions, notably the East Asian countries that did not follow the rules: they did not worship the "religion" that "markets know best," as Joseph Stiglitz wrote in a World Bank research publication shortly before he was appointed chief economist, later removed (and winning the Nobel prize). In contrast, the worst results were found where the rules were rigorously applied, as in Latin America, facts widely acknowledged, among others, by Jose' Antonio Ocampo, director of the Economic Commission for Latin America and the Caribbean (ECLAC), in an address before the American Economic Association a year ago. The "promised land is a mirage," he observed; growth in the 1990s was far below that of the three decades of "state-led development" in Phase I. He too noted that the correlation between following the rules and economic outcomes holds worldwide.

Let us return, then, to the profound and troubling dilemma: the rapid growth and great prosperity brought by globalization has brought inequality because some lack skills. There is no dilemma, because the rapid growth and prosperity are a myth.

Many international economists regard liberalization of capital as a substantial factor in the poorer outcomes of Phase II. But the economy is a complex affair, so poorly understood that one has to be cautious about causal connections. But one consequence of liberalization of capital is rather clear: it undercuts democracy. That was understood by the framers of Bretton Woods: one reason why the agreements were founded on regulation of capital was to allow governments to carry out social democratic policies, which had enormous popular support. Free capital movement creates what has been called a "virtual Senate" with "veto power" over government decisions, sharply restricting policy options. Governments face a "dual constituency:" voters, and speculators, who "conduct moment-by-moment referendums" on government policies (quoting technical studies of the financial system). Even in the rich countries, the private constituency prevails.

Other components of investor-rights "globalization" have similar consequences. Socioeconomic decisions are increasingly shifted to unaccountable concentrations of power, an essential feature of neoliberal "reforms" (a term of propaganda, not description). Extension of the attack on democracy is presumably being planned, without public discussion, in the negotiations for a General Agreement on Trade in Services (GATS). The term "services," as you know, refers to just about anything that might fall within the arena of democratic choice: health, education, welfare, postal and other communications, water and other resources, etc. There is no meaningful sense in which transferring such services to private hands is "trade," but the term has been so deprived of meaning that it might as well be extended to this travesty as well.

The huge public protests in Quebec last April at the Summit of the Americas, set in motion by the freaks in Porto Alegre a year ago, were in part directed against the attempt to impose the GATS principles in secret within the planned Free Trade Area of the Americas (FTAA). Those protests brought together a very broad constituency, North and South, all strongly opposed to what is apparently being planned by trade ministers and corporate executives behind closed doors.

The protests did receive coverage, of the usual kind: the freaks are throwing rocks and disrupting the wizards thinking about the big problems. The invisibility of their actual concerns is quite remarkable. For example, *NYT* economics correspondent Anthony DePalma writes that the GATS agreement "has generated none of the public controversy that has swirled about [WTO] attempts to promote merchandise trade," even after Seattle. In fact, it has been a prime concern for years. As in other cases, this is not deceit. DePalma's knowledge about the freaks is surely limited to what passes through the media filter, and it is an iron law of journalism that the serious concerns of activists must be rigidly barred, in favor of someone throwing a rock, perhaps a police provocateur.

The importance of protecting the public from information was revealed dramatically at the April Summit. Every editorial office in the U.S. had on its desk two important studies, timed for release just before the Summit. One was from Human Rights Watch, the second from the Economic Policy Institute in Washington; neither organization is exactly obscure. Both studies investigated in depth the effects of NAFTA, which was hailed at the Summit as a grand triumph and a model for the FTAA, with headlines trumpeting its praises by George Bush and other leaders, all accepted as Gospel Truth. Both studies were suppressed with near-total unanimity. It's easy to see why. HRW analyzed the effects of NAFTA on labor rights, which, it found, were harmed in all three participating countries. The EPI report was more comprehensive: it consisted of detailed analyses of the effects of NAFTA on working people, written by specialists on the three countries. The conclusion is that this is one of the rare agreements that has harmed the majority of the population in all of the participating countries.

The effects on Mexico were particularly severe, and particularly significant for the South. Wages had declined sharply with the imposition of neoliberal programs in the 1980s. That continued after NAFTA, with a 24 percent decline in incomes for salaried workers, and 40 percent for the self-employed, an effect magnified by the rapid increase in unsalaried workers. Though foreign investment grew, total investment declined, as the economy was transferred to the hands of foreign multinationals. The minimum wage lost 50 percent of its purchasing power. Manufacturing declined, and development stagnated or may have reversed. A small sector became extremely wealthy, and foreign investors prospered.

These studies confirm what had been reported in the business press and academic studies. The *WSJ* reported that although the Mexican economy was growing rapidly in the late '90s after a sharp post-NAFTA decline, consumers suffered a 40 percent drop in purchasing power, the number of people living in extreme poverty grew twice as fast as the population, and even those working in foreign-owned assembly plants lost purchasing power. Similar conclusions were drawn in a study of the Latin American section of the Woodrow Wilson Center, which also found that economic power had greatly concentrated as small Mexican companies cannot obtain financing, traditional farming sheds workers, and labor-intensive sectors (agriculture, light industry) cannot compete internationally with what is called "free enterprise" in the doctrinal system. Agriculture suffered for the usual reasons: peasant farmers cannot compete with highly-subsidized U.S. agribusiness, with effects familiar throughout the world.

Most of this was predicted by critics of NAFTA, including the suppressed OTA and labor movement studies. Critics were wrong in one respect, however. Most anticipated a sharp increase in the urban-rural ratio, as hundreds of thousands of peasants were driven off the land. That didn't happen. The reason, it seems, is that conditions deteriorated so badly in the cities that there was a huge flight from them as well to the U.S.. Those who survive the crossing—many do not—work for very low wages, with no benefits, under awful conditions. The effect is to destroy lives and communities in Mexico and to improve the U.S. economy, where "consumption of the urban middle class continues to be subsidized by the impoverishment of farm laborers both in the United States and Mexico," the Woodrow Wilson Center study points out.

These are among the costs of NAFTA, and neoliberal globalization generally, that economists generally choose not to measure. But even by the highly ideological standard measures, the costs have been severe.

None of this was allowed to sully the celebration of NAFTA and the FTAA at the Summit. Unless they are connected to activist organizations, most people know about these matters only from their own lives. And carefully protected from reality by the Free Press, many regard themselves as somehow failures, unable to take part in the celebration of the greatest economic boom in history.

Data from the richest country in the world are enlightening, but I'll skip the details. The picture generalizes, with some variation of course, and exceptions of the kind already noted. The picture is much worse when we depart from standard economic measures. One cost is the threat to survival implicit in the reasoning of military planners, already described. There are many others. To take one, the ILO reported a rising "worldwide epidemic" of serious mental health disorders, often linked to stress in the workplace, with very substantial fiscal costs in the industrial countries. A large factor, they conclude, is "globalization," which brings "evaporation of job security," pressure on workers, and a higher workload, particularly in the U.S. Is this a cost of "globalization?" From one point of view, it is one of its most attractive features. When he lauded U.S. economic performance as "extraordinary," Alan Greenspan stressed particularly the heightened sense of job insecurity, which leads to subdued costs for employers. The World Bank agrees. It recognizes that "labor market flexibility" has acquired "a bad name... as a euphemism for pushing wages down and workers out," but nevertheless, "it is essential in all the regions of the world... The most important reforms involve lifting constraints on labor mobility and wage flexibility, as well as breaking the ties between social services and labor contracts."

In brief, pushing workers out, pushing wages down, undermining benefits are all crucial contributions to economic health, according to prevailing ideology.

## The effects of neoliberal programs

Unregulated trade has further benefits for corporations. Much, probably most, "trade" is centrally-managed through a variety of devices: intrafirm transfers, strategic alliances, outsourcing, and others. Broad trading areas benefit corporations by making them less answerable to local and national communities. This enhances the effects of neoliberal programs, which regularly have reduced labor share of income. In the U.S., the 1990s were the first postwar period when division of income shifted strongly to owners of capital, away from labor.

Trade has a wide range of unmeasured costs: subsidizing energy, resource depletion, and other externalities not counted. It also brings advantages, though here too some caution is necessary. The most widely hailed is that trade increases specialization—which reduces choices, including the choice to modify comparative advantage, otherwise known as "development." Choice and development are values in themselves: undermining them is a substantial cost. If the American colonies had been compelled to accept the WTO regime 200 years ago, New England would be pursuing its comparative advantage in exporting fish, surely not producing textiles, which survived only by exorbitant tariffs to bar British products (mirroring Britain's treatment of India). The same was true of steel and other industries, right to the present, particularly in the highly protectionist Reagan years—even putting aside the state sector of the economy. There is a great deal to say about all of this. Much of the story is masked in selective modes of economic measurement, though it is well known to economic historians and historians of technology.

As everyone here is aware, the rules of the game are likely to enhance deleterious effects for the poor. The rules of the WTO bar the mechanisms used by every rich country to reach its current state of development, while also providing unprecedented levels of protectionism for the rich, including a patent regime that bars innovation and growth in novel ways, and allows corporate entities to amass huge profits by monopolistic pricing of products often developed with substantial public contribution.

Under contemporary versions of traditional mechanisms, half the people in the world are effectively in receivership, their economic policies managed by experts in Washington. But even in the rich countries democracy is under attack by virtue of the shift of decision-making power from governments, which may be partially responsive to the public, to private tyrannies, which have no such defects. Cynical slogans such as "trust the people" or "minimize the state" do not, under current circumstances, call for increasing popular control. They shift decisions from governments to other hands, but not "the people:" rather, the management of collectivist legal entities, largely unaccountable to the public, and effectively totalitarian in internal structure, much as conservatives charged a century ago when opposing "the corporatization of America."

## Increasing disillusionment with what remains of democracy

Latin American specialists and polling organizations have observed for some years that extension of formal democracy in Latin America has been accompanied by increasing disillusionment about democracy, "alarming trends," which continue, analysts have observed, noting the link between "declining economic fortunes" and "lack of faith" in democratic institutions (*Financial Times*). As Atilio Borón pointed out some years ago, the new wave of democratization in Latin America coincided with neoliberal economic "reforms," which undermine effective democracy, a phenomenon that extends worldwide, in various forms.

To the U.S. as well. There has been much public clamor about the "stolen election" of November 2000, and surprise that the public does not seem to care. Likely reasons are suggested by public opinion studies, which reveal that on the eve of the election, 3/4 of the population regarded the process as largely a farce: a game played by financial contributors, party leaders, and the Public Relations industry, which crafted candidates to say "almost anything to get themselves elected" so that one could believe little they said even when it was intelligible. On most issues, citizens could not identify the stands of the candidates, not because they are stupid or not trying, but because of the conscious efforts of the PR industry. A Harvard University project that monitors political attitudes found that the "feeling of powerlessness has reached an alarming high," with more than half saying that people like them have little or no influence on what government does, a sharp rise through the neoliberal period.

Issues on which the public differs from elites (economic, political, intellectual) are pretty much off the agenda, notably questions of economic policy. The business world, not surprisingly, is overwhelmingly in favor of corporate-led "globalization," the "free investment agreements" called "free trade agreements," NAFTA and the FTAA, GATS, and other devices that concentrate wealth and power in hands unaccountable to the public. Also not surprisingly, the great beast is generally opposed, almost instinctively, even without knowing crucial facts from which they are carefully shielded. It follows that such issues are not appropriate for political campaigns, and did not arise in the mainstream for the November 2000 elections. One would have been hard-pressed, for example, to find discussion of the upcoming Summit of the Americas and the FTAA, and other topics that involve issues of prime concern for the public. Voters were directed to what the PR industry calls "personal qualities," not "issues." Among the half the population that votes, heavily skewed towards the wealthy, those who recognize their class interests to be at stake vote for those interests: overwhelmingly, for the more reactionary of the two business parties. But the general public splits its vote in other ways, leading to a statistical tie. Among working people, noneconomic issues such as gun ownership and "religiosity" were primary factors, so that people often voted against their own primary interests—apparently assuming that they had little choice.

What remains of democracy is to be construed as the right to choose among commodities. Business leaders have long explained the need to impose on the population a "philosophy of futility" and "lack of purpose in life," to "concentrate human attention on the more superficial things that comprise much of fashionable consumption." Deluged by such propaganda from infancy, people may then accept their meaningless and subordinate lives and forget ridiculous ideas about managing their own affairs. They may abandon their fate to the wizards, and in the political realm, to the self-described "intelligent minorities" who serve and administer power.

From this perspective, conventional in elite opinion particularly through the last century, the November 2000 elections do not reveal a flaw of U.S. democracy, but rather its triumph. And generalizing, it is fair to hail the triumph of democracy throughout the hemisphere, and elsewhere, even though the populations somehow do not see it that way.

The struggle to impose that regime takes many forms, but never ends, and never will as long as high concentrations of effective decision-making power remain in place. It is only reasonable to expect the masters to exploit any opportunity that comes along—at the moment, the fear and anguish of the population in the face of terrorist attacks, a serious matter for the West now that, with new technologies available, it has lost its virtual monopoly of violence, retaining only a huge preponderance.

But there is no need to accept these rules, and those who are concerned with the fate of the world and its people will surely follow a very different course. The popular struggles against investor-rights "globalization," mostly in the South, have influenced the rhetoric, and to some extent the practices, of the masters of the universe, who are concerned and defensive. These popular movements are unprecedented in scale, in range of constituency, and in international solidarity; the meetings here are a critically important illustration. The future to a large extent lies in their hands. It is hard to overestimate what is at stake.

# Index of Names

# Ordering Information

AK Press
674-A 23rd Street,
Oakland, CA 94612-1163,
USA

Phone: (510) 208-1700
E-mail: akpress@akpress.org
URL: www.akpress.org
Please send all payments (checks, money orders, or cash at your own risk)
in U.S. dollars. Alternatively, we take VISA and MC.

AK Press
PO Box 12766,
Edinburgh, EH8 9YE,
Scotland

Phone: (0131) 555-5165
E-mail: ak@akedin.demon.uk
URL: www.akuk.com
Please send all payments (cheques, money orders, or cash at your own
risk) in U.K. pounds. Alternatively, we take credit cards.

For a dollar, a pound or a few IRC's, the same addresses would be delighted to provide you with the latest complete AK catalog,
featuring several thousand books, pamphlets, zines, audio products and
stylish apparel published & distributed by AK Press. Alternatively, check
out our websites for the complete catalog, latest news and updates, events,
and secure ordering.

# Also available from AK Press

**Language and Politics** by Noam Chomsky, ed. C. P. Otero
$28.00. ISBN 1 902593 82 0
An enormous collection of over fifty interviews conducted with Chomsky from 1968 to the present. The interviews add a personal dimension to the breadth of Chomsky's written canon—equally covering his analysis in linguistics, philosophy and politics.

**Addicted to War** by Joel Andreas
$8.00. ISBN 1 902593 57 X
*Addicted to War* takes on the most active, powerful and destructive military in the world. Hard-hitting, carefully documented, and heavily illustrated, it reveals why the United States has been involved in more wars in recent years than any other country. Read Addicted to War to find out who benefits from these military adventures, who pays—and who dies.
"A witty and devastating portrait of U.S. military policy."—Howard Zinn

**The Politics of Anti-Semitism** ed. by Alexander Cockburn and Jeffrey St. Clair
$11.95. ISBN 1 902593 77 4
How did a term, once used accurately to describe the most virulent evil, become a charge flung at the mildest critic of Israel, particularly concerning its atrocious treatment of Palestinians? Edited by Cockburn and St. Clair of the print and online journal *Counterpunch* and includes contributors Cynthia Mckinney, Robert Fisk, Michael Neumann, Norman Finklestein, Yuri Avneri and Yigal Bronner.

**Workers Councils** by Anton Pannekoek
$15.00. ISBN 1 902593 56 1
"Good, solid, working-class literature."—Noam Chomsky
In this timeless text, Anton Pannekoek provides his analysis of how we can create and sustain this practical model for social equality. Includes introductory interview with Noam Chomsky.

**Facing the Enemy** by Alexandre Skirda
$17.95. ISBN 1 902593 19 7
The finest single volume history of European Anarchism is finally available in English. Drawing on decades of research, Alexandre Skirda traces anarchism as a major political movement and ideology across the 19th and 20th centuries illuminating the Bakuninist secret societies, the clash with Marx, the mass trade unions, illegalists, bombers, assasins and the revolutionary heroism of the Russian and Spanish revolutions.

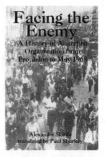

**No Gods No Masters (2 vols.)** by Daniel Guerin
Vol. I $18.95. ISBN 1 873176 64 3
Vol II $16.95. ISBN 1 873176 69 4
This is the first English translation of Guerin's monumental anthology of Anarchism. It details, through a vast array of hitherto unpublished documents, writings, letters and reports, the history, organization and practice of the anarchist movement—its theorists, advocates and activists.
Book I includes the writings of Max Stirner, Pierre-Joseph Proudhon, Mikhail Bakunin, James Guillaume, Max Nettlau, Peter Kropotkin, Emma Goldman and Cesar de Paepe amongst others
Book II includes work from the likes of Malatesta, Emile Henry, Emile Pouget, Augustin Souchy, Gaston Leval, Voline, Nestor Makhno, the Kronstadt sailors, Luigi Fabbri, and Buenaventura Durruti.

**Moving Forward** by Michael Albert
$11.95. ISBN 1 902593 41 3
If not capitalism, then what? In *Moving Forward* Albert argues that we have to change how we conceive of work and wages, rewarding effort and sacrifice rather than output, and moving from heirarchical workplace structures to worker self-management. From here he moves to a proposal for how we might organize the larger functions of the economy in workers' councils and a general discussion of how our society might look with a participatory economy.

**The Spanish Anarchists: The Heroic Years 1868–1936** by Murray Bookchin
$19.95. ISBN 1 873176 04 X
A long-awaited new edition of the seminal history of Spanish Anarchism. Hailed as a masterpiece, it includes a new prefatory essay by the author. Murray Bookchin has written widely on politics, history and ecology. His books *To Remember Spain: The Anarchist And Syndicalist Revolution Of 1936, Anarchism, Marxism and the Future of the Left* and *Social Anarchism Or Lifestyle Anarchism: An Unbridgeable Chasm* are all published by AK Press.

**Quiet Rumors: An Anarcha-Feminist Reader** ed. Dark Star Collective
$15.00. ISBN 1 902593 40 5
From consciousness-raising groups to hair-razing punk rockers, here's a fascinating window into the development of the women's movement, in the words of the women who moved it. These classic essays span the century, providing welcome context for feminism as part of a larger politics of liberation and equality. Includes Emma Goldman, Peggy Kornegger, Voltairine DeCleyre, Alice Nutter and others.

# Noam Chomsky CDs/DVDs available from AK Audio

**Distorted Morality** DVD by Noam Chomsky
$25.00 ISBN 1 905293 76 6
Here Chomsky offers a devastating critique of America's current War on Terror—arguing that it is a logical impossibility for such a war to be taking place. Chomsky presents his reasoning with refreshing clarity, drawing from a wealth of historic knowledge and analysis. The DVD includes a shorter; more recent talk on the danger, cruelty, and stupidity of the U.S. and Israel's policy of Pre-emptive War and a lively Q&A session all in an easily searchable user friendly format.

**The Emerging Framework of World Power: Everlasting War** CD by Noam Chomsky
$14.98. ISBN 1 902593 75 8
Chomsky's state-of-the-world address. America's leading foreign policy critic surveys the role of the U.S. in a post-911 world—and finds nothing has changed.

**The New War on Terrorism: Fact and Fiction** CD by Noam Chomsky
$14.98. ISBN 1 902593 62 6
"We certainly want to reduce the level of terror... There is one easy way to do that... stop partici-pating in it."—Noam Chomsky, from the CD
What is terrorism? And how can we reduce the likelihood of such crimes, whether they are against us, or against someone else? With his vintage flair, penetrating analysis, and ironic wit, Chomsky, in perhaps his most anticipated lecture ever—delivered a month after 9/11, and his first public statement—makes sense of a world apparently gone mad.

**Free Market Fantasies: Capitalism in the Real World** CD by Noam Chomsky
$13.98. ISBN 1 873176 79 1
**An American Addiction: Drugs, Guerillas, Counterinsurgency—U.S. Intervention in Colombia** CD by Noam Chomsky
$13.98. ISBN 1 902593 44 8

**Propaganda and Control of the Public Mind** 2XCD by Noam Chomsky
$20.00. ISBN 1 873176 68 6
"The war against working people should be understood to be a real war. It's not a new war. It's an old war. Furthermore it's a perfectly conscious war everywhere, but specifically in the U.S... which happens to have a highly class-conscious business class... And they have long seen themselves as fighting a bitter class war, except they don't want anybody else to know about it." [Noam Chomsky, from the CD]

**Case Studies In Hypocrisy: U.S. Human Rights Policy** 2XCD by Noam Chomsky
$20.00. ISBN 1 902593 27 8
With the recent celebration of the fiftieth anniversary of the Universal Declaration Of Human Rights, and America's undisputed position as the world's only superpower, the contrast between the rhetoric and the reality of U.S. foreign policy has never been more stark. With his inimitable penetrating analysis and dry wit, Chomsky leads us through the murky blood-soaked reality of America's New World Order.

**For A Free Humanity: For Anarchy** 2XCD by Noam Chomsky/Chumbawamba
$18.00 ISBN 1 873176 74 0
**Prospects For Democracy** CD by Noam Chomsky
$14.98 ISBN 1 873176 38 4

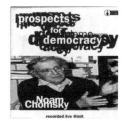

# Also available from AK Audio

**Come September** CD by Arundhati Roy
$14.98. ISBN 1 92593 80 4
In this acclaimed Lannan Foundation lecture, Arundhati Roy speaks poetically to power on the U.S. government's "War on Terror", globalization, and the misuses of nationalism. With lyricism and passion, Roy combines her literary talents and encyclopedic knowledge to expose injustice and provide hope for a future world. Includes question and answer with Howard Zinn.

**Arists in a Time of War** CD by Howard Zinn
$14.98. ISBN 1 902593 65 0
In this brand new lecture, recorded a month after 9/11, America's finest social historian examines the role, and response, of artists in society, and particularly, during wartime and crisis.

**Life in Occupied America** CD by Ward Churchill
$14.98. ISBN 1 902593 72 3
The systematic elimination of the American Indians didn't end with Columbus, smallpox laden blankets or the scalp bounty. Here, pre-eminent Native activist/scholar Ward Churchill passionately unveils the 500-year conquest and demonstrates its continuation today.

**Mob Action Against the State** 2XCD Various
$20.00 ISBN 1 902593 51 0
The Bay Area is rich in local radicals, and most of them have taken a turn at the microphone of the Bay Area Anarchist Bookfair. Here's an all-star collection from the speakers' corner of the bookfair: Jello Biafra, Lawrence Ferlinghetti, Roxanne Dunbar-Ortiz, Christian Parenti, Craig O'Hara, Ruth Wilson Gilmore, Cindy Milstein, Lorenzo Komboa Ervin, and Barry Pateman.

**Pacifism and Pathology in the American Left** CD by Ward Churchill
$14.98 ISBN 1 902593 58 8

**Taking Liberties: Policing, Prisons and Surveliance in an Age of Crisis** CD by Christian Parenti
$14.98 ISBN 1 902593 63 4

**Stories Hollywood Never Tells** CD by Howard Zinn
$13.98. ISBN 1 902593 36 7

**In a Pig's Eye** 2XCD by Ward Churchill
$20.00 ISBN 1 902593 50 2

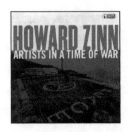

**Beating the Devil** CD by Alexander Cockburn
$14.98 ISBN 1 902593 49 9
In this collection of recent talks, maverick commentator Alexander Cockburn defiles subjects ranging from Colombia to the American presidency to the Missile Defense System. Whether he's skewering the fallacies of the war on drugs or illuminating the dark crevices of secret government, his erudite and extemporaneous style warms the hearts of even the stodgiest cynics of the left.

**A People's History of the United States: A Lecture at Reed College** 2XCD by Howard Zinn
$20.00 ISBN 1 873176 95 3
Here Zinn explains with great humor and passion how his teaching, his history and his activism are parts of the same project. The stories of social movements—labor, civil rights, feminists, antiwar—are usually left out or grossly distorted in mainstream history writing. The efforts of Zinn and others to recover and pass on those stories offers to their students, to their readers and to us, models, ideas, inspirations for how and why we might go about challenging and changing the structures of power.

**Prisons on Fire: George Jackson, Attica & Black Liberation** CD produced by the Freedom Archives
$14.98 ISBN 1 902593 52 9

**Monkeywrenching The New World Order** 2XCD Various
$20.00 ISBN 1 902593 35 9

**175 Progress Drive** CD by Mumia Abu-Jamal
$14.98 ISBN 1 902593 45 6

**The Prison Industrial Complex** CD by Angela Davis
$14.98 ISBN 1 902593 22 7

**Heroes and Martyrs: Emma Goldman, Sacco & Vanzetti and the Revolutionary Struggle** 2XCD by Howard Zinn
$20.00 ISBN 1 902593 26 X

**All Things Censored** CD by Mumia Abu-Jamal
$14.98 ISBN 1 902593 06 5